THE ZODIAC ALMANAC

THE ZODIAC ALMANAC

STERLING ETHOS
New York

STERLING ETHOS
New York

STERLING ETHOS and the distinctive Sterling Ethos logo are registered trademarks of Sterling Publishing Co., Inc.

Compilation © 2024 Union Square & Co., LLC

Portions of this book were excerpted and condensed from:
Zodiac Signs: Aries by Jeff Hinshaw, Text © 2020 Jeff Hinshaw
Zodiac Signs: Taurus by Courtney O'Reilly, Text © 2020 Courtney O'Reilly
Zodiac Signs: Gemini by Colin Bedell, Text © 2020 Colin Bedell
Zodiac Signs: Cancer by Alice Sparkly Kat, Text © 2020 Alice Sparkly Kat
Zodiac Signs: Leo by Bess Matassa, Text © 2020 Bess Matassa
Zodiac Signs: Virgo by Bess Matassa, Text © 2020 Bess Matassa
Zodiac Signs: Libra by Gabrielle Moritz, Text © 2020 Gabrielle Moritz
Zodiac Signs: Scorpio by Danny Larkin, Text © 2020 Danny Larkin
Zodiac Signs: Sagittarius by Nathaniel Craddock, Text © 2020 Nathaniel Craddock
Zodiac Signs: Capricorn by Kelsey Branca, Text © 2020 Kelsey Branca
Zodiac Signs: Aquarius by Taylor Moon, Text © 2020 Taylor Moon
Zodiac Signs: Pisces by Shakirah Tabourn, Text © 2020 Shakirah Tabourn

All rights reserved. No part of this publication may be reproduced, stored in a retrieval system, or transmitted in any form or by any means (including electronic, mechanical, photocopying, recording, or otherwise) without prior written permission from the publisher.

ISBN 978-1-4549-5748-5
ISBN 978-1-4549-5749-2 (e-book)

Library of Congress Control Number: 2024935092

For information about custom editions, special sales, and premium purchases, please contact specialsales@unionsquareandco.com.

Printed in Malaysia

2 4 6 8 10 9 7 5 3 1

unionsquareandco.com

Cover and interior design by Stacy Wakefield Forte
Cover art and chapter openers by Cai & Jo Limited
Additional image credits appear on page 320.

PREFACE viii

ARIES 1

TAURUS 31

GEMINI 55

CANCER 79

LEO 107

VIRGO 135

LIBRA 165

PISCES 269

AQUARIUS 239

CAPRICORN 213

SAGITTARIUS 187

SCORPIO 161

IMAGE CREDITS 320

ABOUT THE AUTHORS 321

PREFACE

INTERPRETING THE MOVEMENTS of celestial bodies can produce as many stories as there are stars in the sky. How can the hour and physical location of your birth have dictated so many aspects of your personality? How can it be used to tell you more about yourself and how you interact with the people around you? This comprehensive guide starts there, traveling with you around the astrological calendar, from fiery Aries to steady Taurus; from dazzling Leo to intense Scorpio, whose movements are guided by the waters of the underworld.

This book is for everyone: if you aren't sure of where to start, just look up your birthday and find your sun sign. Or maybe you're well aware of your sun sign—you might even have a Capricorn shirt or two. This book is also for the more serious adepts: you've looked up your birth chart or have had it analyzed, and you know your sun, moon, and rising signs. You would never go on a third date without looking up your potential partner's. In that case, keep this guide on hand for easy reference when you want a nuanced look at the twelve archetypes of the zodiac from some of the most exciting voices in astrology today.

The authors in this guide present a range of views on the ancient science of astrology. Although the major features of each sign are consistent across practices, each of the eleven contributors bring their own philosophies, voices, and lived experiences to the way they interpret each one. Many of the contributors to this book are also writing about their own signs, which means they can confront head on the feeling that more reductive guides can be alienating. It's so easy to feel like "Aquarius: aloof, detached, emotional" doesn't explain you. That's why it's so important to have a more nuanced understanding of the ways in which the motivations of each sign can push and pull each other, creating the individualized pieces of art that are your friends, family, and coworkers.

Each of the twelve zodiac signs detailed in this book are divided into several sections: the sign as child, adult, in love, and at work. Through this progression, we can learn more about how the traits of the sign manifest at various ages, ultimately compelling us to meet our soulmates and follow our dreams to a fully embodied existence. You will learn about your sign (and others') as it achieves consciousness and grows into maturity, seeks partnership and friendship, and finds fulfillment in a chosen profession—encompassing both traditional careers and more holistic life goals, like travel and spiritual experience. Following the strengths and challenges of your sign—whether sun, moon, and rising (each of which you can bookmark with the ribbons in this book)—can be a path to understanding more about how to live an aligned existence. In this way, astrology can bring you personal satisfaction, helping you stay more open to truly connected and communicative relationships.

As you read, you will also experience hints of greater knowledge, should you wish to continue your study of astrology: the influence of your sign across the twelve houses; the influence of dominant planets on your sign; modalities, symbols, and elements. Although these are by no means necessary to understand this book, they are presented in clear and accessible language so that you can get a glimpse of all of the fascinating complexity of astrology, as well as how deep you can go if you jump in to learning more. Each author also adds their own spin on each overreaching topic, from a sign's signature MO ("Sagittarius: when God closes a door, throw a chair through the window") to specific concerns for your sign ("Cancer and the Freelance Economy"). You may know Gemini as the Twins, but a more detailed examination of the myth of Castor and Pollux can provide insight into just how important the ethic of union is to this sign: it animates everything a Gemini is or will be.

Please enjoy *The Zodiac Almanac*, and best wishes for all those who are curious about this world and desire a greater understanding of the gravity that moves the stars and our hearts in equal measure.

—*Editors of Sterling Ethos*

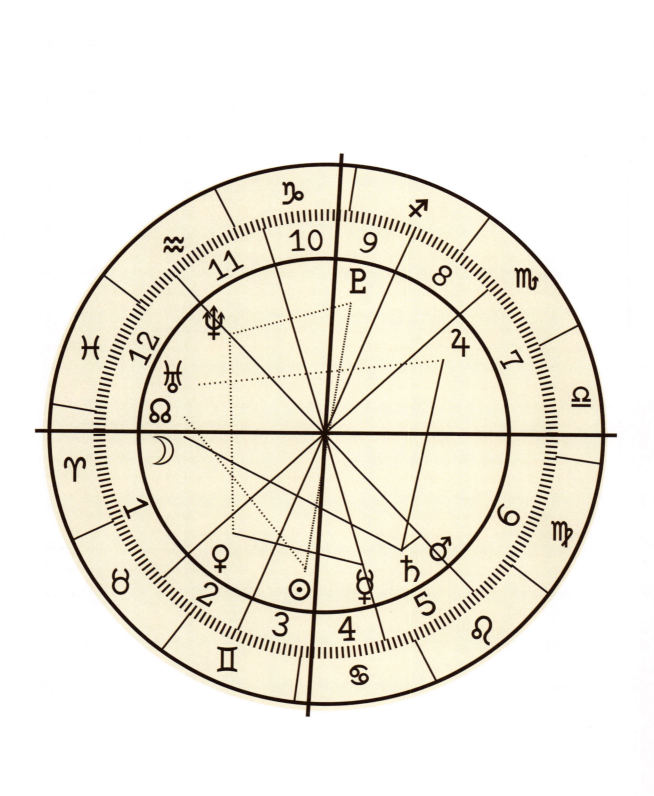

how to read
A BIRTH CHART

FIRST, IF YOU'D like to start reading this book based on your sun sign only, that is completely fine. Your sun sign is said to be central to who you are. It's what motivates you, your ego, your core personality. As Kirah Tabourn writes in the Pisces chapter: "The sun represents your essential self, your central personality, your vitality, who you came here to be, how you shine, your self-expression, and the energy you need to recharge with." The sun sign is also the sign you'd generally use when reading your own horoscope. To find it, all you need to do is find the zodiac sign with the range of dates that contains your birthday.

But that's not the whole story. Eventually, you may also want to determine your moon and rising sign (also called your ascendent), which can dictate your emotional self and the persona you present to the world, respectively. Many of the individual chapters in this book contain deeper dives into zodiac archetypes in their function as moon or rising signs, which can add new dimension to your understanding of your own personality (or your parents', or your friends', or your partner's).

If you'd like to learn more about your astrological self, the next step is the birth chart (also called a natal chart). Maybe you've looked at your chart before, or maybe you've had a reading from a trained professional. Either way, you should come in armed with the date, physical location, and time of your birth. Originally, this information was used to construct a birth chart with physical tools, but these days it's more common to use software. One popular app is TimePassages, and there are also several birth chart generators available online.

It's common to be a little overwhelmed when seeing a birth chart for the first time. The amount of information it contains can be daunting. But just know that this chart is essentially a map of the heavens as they appeared at the moment of your birth. The twelve sections of the circular chart divide the locations of planets into separate "houses." Further analysis can reveal the angles between planets (aspects)—and more. You'll find some investigation into these subtleties within the pages of this book, which can help you understand astrology in new and different ways.

ARIES

MAR. 21–APR. 19

text by Jeff Hinshaw

element — FIRE

symbol — THE RAM

modality — CARDINAL

house — FIRST

ruler — MARS

ARTLIFE

INTRODUCTION

When the sun moves through the zodiacal archetype Aries, we are on the precipice of Mother Nature's most epic of rituals—the blooming of spring. Any human who chose to incarnate on this planet during this very ripe-with-potential time of year aligned themselves with the vibration of a sprouting seed. Connecting with nature in this way is so important when establishing an astrology practice. All too often we rely on traditional interpretations of astrological archetypes, but by first simply bringing our awareness to nature, we can connect on a much more intimate level with this ancient practice. What is taking place in the world around you during Aries season? What is nature inviting you into?

Aries season is a precious time of year (March 21–April 19). Marking the spring equinox in the Northern Hemisphere, this is the time of year when day and night are in equal measure. As a tipping point of the year, the days grow longer and warmer. We see little buds sprouting out from the soil. Trees start to show little bits of green. Baby ducklings hatch, wobbling behind their mothers, greeting this New World with innocence and hope. Already there's a softening shift this creates from the often-typecast Aries archetype of the "Angry Warrior" charging full speed ahead. Pause for just a moment and simply witness the world this time of year. Behold the gentle thawing from the long, frigid winter. Everything and everyone, great and small, is waking up from a deep slumber. This is the soul-centered invitation for Aries: to be like the beginning of Spring.

When the sun enters Aries, everyone feels this shift and becomes an honorary Aries. An intuitive awareness of the individual's path arises. Over these thirty days, the collective is gifted the opportunity to realign with their innate birthrights as individual members of the human race. We reaffirm who we are, why we are here, and where we are going. At the beginning of spring, there's an expansion forward into a whole new cycle. We take ownership of life. We learn the art of lovingly taking up space. We are reinvigorated with a sense of hope. We open up our minds and hearts to receiving new solutions for approaching the world. We are more prepared than ever.

For some this may mean bravely going back out in the world after winter. For others, we declare creative goals, start new projects, take control of our lives, and reestablish our sense of individuality. From an energetic perspective, Aries individuals experience the world through this lens of reality all year long. This will manifest in many different ways for the Aries, of course, because the soul lesson here is about individuation. However, amongst the many differences, what we can be certain of with Aries is this one uniting truth—the desire to grow, expand, and create new life.

FIRE

Each astrological sign is paired with one of the four elements: Fire-Earth-Air-Water. The elements appear in this order, and the pattern continues in this sequence throughout the astrological journey. When observing this pattern, notice how the element of fire initiates.

Aries, as the first sign of the astrological journey, is then, of course, not only a Fire sign but also the first Fire sign. Fire signs include: Aries, Leo, and Sagittarius. These three vibrant signs all exude a warmth, spark for life, and independence. Like fire itself, Fire signs tend to be uplifting and remind us that this human experience is sacred and worth living. Imagine a slow-steady warm fire in a chimney. Perhaps one in a cozy living room that you would curl up next to with a book. Connect to the times when candles are lit. This might be when setting the mood at dinner or in the bedroom. This reflects the deep desires of Aries (and other Fire signs) to experience passion and romance. Candles are often lit during holidays and birthdays to celebrate and commemorate an initiation into a new phase of life. Aries (and other Fire signs) evoke the spirit of gratitude and celebration. We also light candles during ceremonies or vigils to memorialize someone's life. Thus, there's also a deeper, reverent side to the faithful flame.

However, fire can also be fickle, reckless, and even temperamental. A single spark can set off an entire forest fire, and if we aren't paying attention we might get burned. If you've ever tried to start a fire you might recall it takes focus and patience to get the flame to light. And once lit, the need for fuel is imperative in order to keep the fire burning. It is so important for Aries, and other Fire signs, to be fed emotionally, mentally, socially, and spirituality. Oftentimes we will look to fire to lead the way, like a torch in a nighttime forest, but their lives need substance and fuel in order to sustain. Fire signs need to be nurtured and managed carefully, although they may not admit it. It's important to feed Aries with loving encouragement and praise and to offer them new opportunities for adventure and expression. Since Fire signs hold such capacity to charge others with new life and vitality, they need to be reminded to slow down.

If Aries takes on too much, which they do all too often, Aries, just like fire, is subject to burning out. Fire signs, although invigorating and full of life, may also swing into bouts of low energy, hopelessness, and depression. What's important for fire is to not fight the tendency to rest and recover. Just think about the times when you do make a fire. For instance, during summer vacation nights for bonfires and s'mores. We enjoy each other's company, share stories and songs. This reflects Fire's social, extroverted, and creative side. But of course the fire does not last all night long. Before too long we put the fire out. This represents Fire's deep need to withdraw. Fire, as outward and energetic as it appears, is the one element that we interact with in spurts and moments in time. Fire cannot be sustained by always burning. It is so important to rest and to have time off. For even when the fire burns out completely, it harnesses the unique ability to regenerate its power from the ashes and start anew, all within a matter of seconds.

PERSONAL FIRE

The astrological wheel can be divided into four quadrants. Respectfully, the four quadrants represent the four seasons (Spring-Summer-Autumn-Winter). The signs in each quadrant join together to form the four levels of relational awareness. These levels include:

1. Personal (Aries-Taurus-Gemini)
2. Intrapersonal (Cancer-Leo-Virgo)
3. Interpersonal (Libra-Scorpio-Sagittarius)
4. Collective (Capricorn-Aquarius-Pisces)

Aries as the first sign of the entire journey is the initiator to the first level of relational awareness, also known as personal. The personal quadrant of our astrological journey includes the first three signs: Aries-Taurus-Gemini. There is one personal sign for each of the three modalities. Cardinal signs will always initiate a new quadrant of relational awareness. Aries initiates personal. Cancer initiates intrapersonal. Libra initiates interpersonal. Capricorn initiates collective. This reflects the importance of relationship the cardinal modality encourages throughout the astrological journey. These three signs (Aries-Taurus-Gemini) deeply embody their elements through personal possession and singularity. Often telling their individual story through the lens of their element, the personal signs connect us with a particular intimacy. Like a singular flame, Aries the Ram offers us the purest essence of fire. The lone lantern, Aries is on a personal quest for freedom, expansion, and adventure, and they will inspire you to do the same.

CONSCIOUS FIRE

When grouping each of the three Fire-Earth-Air-Water sequences together, they form the three levels of consciousness of the astrological journey. These levels include:

Conscious (Aries-Taurus-Gemini-Cancer)

Subconscious (Leo-Virgo-Libra-Scorpio)

Superconscious (Sagittarius-Capricorn-Aquarius-Pisces)

Aries as the first sign of the entire journey is the initiator to the first level of consciousness, also known as conscious. The conscious tier of our astrological journey includes the first four signs: Aries-Taurus-Gemini-Cancer. There is one conscious sign for each of the four elements. Fire will always initiate a new tier of consciousness. Aries initiates conscious. Leo initiates subconscious. Sagittarius initiates superconscious. This reflects the inspiration the element of fire sparks throughout the astrological journey.

In order to gain a true understanding of Aries, it is important to observe Aries in context with the other conscious signs. These four signs hold a deep awareness of the here and now. Their subjective point of view allows for an authenticity. Their understanding of the present moment allows them to navigate conscious reality in an attentive and mindful way. Conscious signs intuitively comprehend the laws of nature and culture. This often gifts them the ability to responsively connect with their immediate surroundings in a tangible way. Aries does this through the lens of fire, with confidence, passion, and ambition.

CARDINAL FIRE

Each astrological sign is paired with one of three modalities: cardinal-fixed-mutable. The modalities appear in this order, and the pattern continues in this sequence throughout the astrological journey. When observing this pattern, notice how the modality of cardinal initiates.

Cardinal signs initiate a season and represent the beginning. Cardinal signs are proactive, pioneering, and forward-moving. Aries as cardinal fire gives its particular expression of fire a double elementation. Cardinal signs hold a

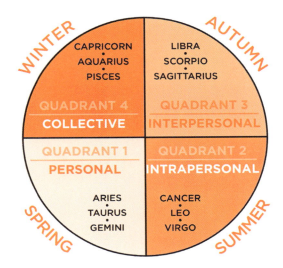

similar quality to that of fire. This makes Aries proactive with optimism, pioneering with creation, and forward-moving with warmth and compassion. Cardinal fire reflects the ability to perceive what one would like to accomplish, while harnessing the confidence to set out on the path toward achievement.

CARDINAL CROSS

The four cardinal signs join together to create what is known as the cardinal cross. These four signs represent the four sacred points of the year in the Northern Hemisphere: the Spring Equinox (Aries), Summer Solstice (Cancer), Autumn Equinox (Libra), and Winter Solstice (Capricorn).

The four cardinal signs join together to form a soul pact. There is a deep-felt shared mission between the four cardinal signs. They join together through relationship. Aries is the individual. Libra is the other/relationship. Cancer represents the mother/matriarchy. Capricorn represents the father/patriarchy. Through the power of activism, cardinal signs honor our ancestors and the past to move us forward. Their joint mission is to bring about intergenerational healing.

Because these signs share the same modality, they are each expressed through the lens of different elements: *cardinal fire* (Aries), *cardinal water* (Cancer), *cardinal air* (Libra), *cardinal earth* (Capricorn). Their shared modality and differences in elementation join together to expand one another's potential. Aries initiates with Fire, bringing forth the empowerment of individual birthrights. Cancer initiates with water, reflecting the importance of home and lineage. Libra initiates with air, communicating the importance of equality and collaboration. Capricorn initiates with earth, instituting the importance of tradition, commitment, and public appearance. In order for Aries to become the fullest, highest expression of itself, Aries must learn lessons from these other three cardinal signs.

Aries forms a square with cardinal signs Cancer and Capricorn. Aries as a Fire sign contrasts both water (Cancer) and earth (Capricorn). Forming a square with these two signs indicates karmic resistance with enormous potential for breakthrough. This foreshadows Aries's challenges in relationship to family, mother, and home (Cancer), and authority, father, and rules (Capricorn). This will be a continual theme for us to explore throughout the entire chapter.

Aries forms an opposition with Libra. In soul-centered astrology, all signs evolve through their polar sign, the sign on the opposite side of the wheel. Polar signs help to bring each other back into loving balance at the center of the wheel. Throughout the Aries journey this opposition to Libra will forever present opportunities for Aries to evolve and expand. We will refer back to the polarity of Libra in every section in this chapter, as it forms the basis of evolution for the Aries archetype.

RULING PLANETS

Each astrological sign forms a resonant connection with a planetary body. This is often referred to as a ruling planet. Traditional astrologers assign Mars as the ruling planet for Aries, while esoteric astrologers assign Mercury. Both of these planets are important to consider when forming an intimate relationship with Aries.

Aries is a masculine sign and greatly expresses itself through the planetary body Mars. As the fourth planet from the sun, Mars is the planet of action, activity, outward ambition, physical inertia, and primal desires. When observing the glyph for Mars, also the same gender symbol for

helps guide Aries toward the aspiration of conscious communication. Mercury is the planet of intellectual transmission. In its lowest expression or manifestation, this breezy planet speaks of themes such as a scattered mentality, anxiety, and recklessness with words. In its highest manifestation, Mercury is the planet of cosmic communication, channeling messages from divine. Consciously attuning oneself with the planet Mercury allows Aries to rule from the intuitive mental planes. Ruling over the head, this upgrades Aries from the head-banging aggression of the Ram to the connection with cognitive brain function.

When we consider both these planets, we realize that Mars will often relate to Aries in their younger years, whereas Mercury will indicate where Aries is heading in their later years. Mars will be felt in the Aries's personality and ambition, whereas Mercury will offer us a window into the soul purpose for Aries. The astrological sign both ruling planets reside in at the time of the Aries's birth greatly informs the individual Aries's expression, bringing shades of diversity to our fierce, pioneering Ram. Throughout this chapter, we will touch base with both Mars and Mercury to see how their pulls come into play.

SELF-DISCOVERY

All twelve astrological signs live within. Whether you are an Aries or not, you will benefit from reading this chapter and deepening your connection to the Aries archetype. Before courageously galloping off, let's discover what this exploration of Aries may mean to you. Pull up your birth chart and look to see where the Aries zodiac lives. Even if no planets reside in this assertive sign, Aries will still dwell somewhere in your birth chart. The symbol for Aries is ♈. Look to the circumference of the wheel and locate this sign. Which house does Aries line up with?

male energy, an erect arrow points northeast-skyward, toward the rising sun. Often considered to represent a shield and spear, the symbol appears to represent an upright male phallus. In its lowest state, this fiery planet connects us to anger, aggression, violence, competition, and even war. In its highest, most aligned state, Mars is the planet of cosmic action guiding us forward toward the principles of divine masculinity.

As Aries evolves through its polar sign Libra, Aries upgrades from the physical inertia of Mars to the activation of the intuitive mental plane with Mercury. Now Aries harnesses the ability to consider with intellectualization. As the smallest and closest planet to the sun, Mercury

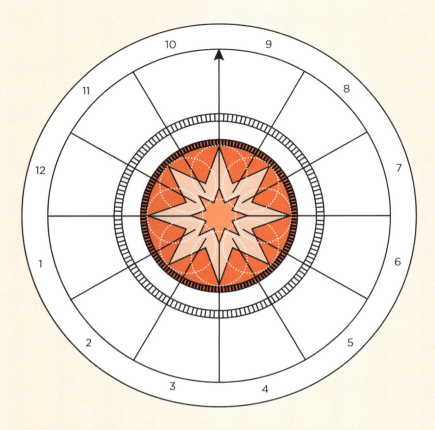

The twelve houses of an astrological birth chart. You will notice House 1 starts on the left-hand sign and moves counterclockwise.

THE 12 HOUSES

See above for a visual guide to the twelve houses. How do the themes of this particular house resonate with your intention for picking up this book? Below I will offer you deeper guidance.

FIRST HOUSE—THE HOUSE OF SELF. The Aries zodiac was on the eastern horizon rising at the time of your birth. In other words, you're an Aries Rising! This chapter offers you an opportunity for self-discovery and the awakening of your rising potential.

SECOND HOUSE—THE HOUSE OF MATERIAL. A pioneer with finances, this chapter holds the potential to awaken within you a deeper connection with self-worth and personal value. How might you more ambitiously own your right to take up space?

THIRD HOUSE—THE HOUSE OF COMMUNICATION. A straight shooter with your words, use this chapter to inspire deeper thought and intellectualism. Perhaps write, journal, and create dialogue based off of your findings. How might you be inspired to more earnestly communicate your truth?

FOURTH HOUSE—IMUM COELI (BELOW THE SKY). Midnight of the Soul. The House of Home. The Aries zodiac was directly below you at the time of your birth. This chapter may come to represent an opportunity for deeper healing around mother, home, and ancestors. How might Aries encourage you to make self-care more of a pursuit or priority?

FIFTH HOUSE—THE HOUSE OF SELF-EXPRESSION. A fiery whippersnapper indeed, this chapter holds the potential to spark passion and play in your life. Open yourself up to dialogue with your inner child. How might your new discoveries of Aries inspire you to express your creativity in the world?

SIXTH HOUSE—THE HOUSE OF SERVICE. An independent worker, you likely take control of your life through systems of improvement. How does the energy of Aries inspire confidence in organizing your own individual offerings to the world? How might you better take control of your life and health through holistic services?

SEVENTH HOUSE—DESCENDANT. THE HOUSE OF RELATIONSHIP. The Aries zodiac was setting at the time of your birth. This chapter may come to represent an opportunity to rediscover the art of collaboration and compassionate communication. How does Aries offer you greater balance? How might Aries activate partnership in your life?

EIGHTH HOUSE—THE HOUSE OF TRANSFORMATION. Fierce and intense, you likely dive headfirst into esoteric shadow realms. Notice what the information in this chapter brings up for you. If a line resonates, hold on to it, close your eyes, and drop even deeper. How does Aries's energy awaken within you the desire for rebirth and renewal?

NINTH HOUSE—THE HOUSE OF HIGHER LEARNING. An original thinker and lone scholar, you likely benefit from ambitiously pursuing activities that expand the horizons of your mind and your world. How might your new discoveries of Aries spark a deeper commitment to your astrological studies?

TENTH HOUSE—MIDHEAVEN. The House of Vocation. The Aries zodiac was directly above you in the sky at the time of your birth. This chapter may call upon the most moral and public version of yourself. How does the Aries archetype act as a resource for stepping up to the podium of your own personal empowerment?

ELEVENTH HOUSE—THE HOUSE OF COMMUNITY. Idealistic and innovative, you likely benefit from surrounding yourself with ambitious and forward-thinking communities. How does Aries stimulate inspiration in your life? How might this chapter guide you toward awakening the vision you hold for yourself and humanity at large?

TWELFTH HOUSE—THE HOUSE OF THE UNKNOWN. Aries dwells in the final house of your chart, indicating the end of karmic cycles. At times your very sense of identity may feel alone or lost in this world. Know you might sense Aries to be quite more ethereal or mystical than the rest of us. How might this exploration of Aries inspire you to let go through imagination and creative visualization? How does Aries energy evoke within you a connection to spirituality and otherworlds?

ARIES AS A CHILD

WHEN BABIES ARE born, they most often enter the world headfirst. Upon their entrance, they let out a cry. This sound of screaming tears is eagerly awaited, as it signals the newborn's ability to breathe on its own. On a practical level, the crying activates and opens the lungs. On a spiritual level, this moment comes to represent the miracle of new life! Parents and family members begin to laugh and cry themselves. This mysterious otherworldly moment of incarnation holds the great power to shift our consciousness into a state of universal compassion and love. Many parents agree that this moment marks a major shift and upgrade in their lives. From this moment forward they will never be the same.

Connecting to incarnation relates to the story of Aries. The astrological wheel can be observed from start to end as the phases of a human's life. Aries as our first sign of the astrological journey is connected to birth, incarnation, and early childhood. This topic of Aries as child is very informative to understanding the Aries soul path. For starters, each astrological sign rules over and is connected to a different part of the body. Aries rules over the head, so this headfirst entrance into the world comes to act as a metaphor for the entire life span of Aries. Thrusting forward into new life, the Aries is adventurous and courageous.

Then followed by the entrance through the birth canal, we connect with the loud cry signifying the baby is breathing. This connects us to the importance of Aries expressing their emotions. Often thought of as quick to anger, Aries feels intensely, as if it is the very first time they've ever experienced a particular emotion. In the same way a baby might be crying one minute and laughing the next, the span of emotion for Aries is often expressed quickly and resolved, like a short fuse on a small bomb. Just as it's important for the baby to cry to activate the lungs, emotions activate an Aries's life and become a sacred compass pointing Aries in the direction of their life's purpose. But as the Aries grows and matures, the impulse to act out on emotions by letting out a screaming cry tempers through patience and nurturance. This is when Aries learns to become their own mother. The image of a mother now cradling her newborn comes to represent the different parts of an Aries. We can feel into this evolution by meditating on Aries evolving through its polar sign of Libra, which connects us to balance, symmetry, internal peace, and relationship.

And then finally, and perhaps most importantly, is the part of the birthing process in which follows baby's first cry. This is the spiritual moment in which the room is filled with laughter and tears, "It's a miracle!" This, above all else, acts as the most profound connection Aries holds to birth. The Aries incarnation is one in which, through the power of their own sense of individuality, they come to serve as a symbol for the collective as the hope for new life. It's through Aries that we are all reminded of the preciousness of the here and now. We are filled with a sense of wonder, that on this new day, with this new birth, the potential to live a full and expansive life is boundless and unlimited. It's through the vessel of the baby, or Aries, that we are gifted a clean slate for new beginnings. Families join together in joy. Old hurts and wounds are forgiven. Without the newborn baby, perhaps there would be no reason to gather at all, no reason to continue forward. Aries gifts us a reason to wake up in the morning. Aries gifts us a reason to live.

Aries children are energetic, spritely, and brave. In the same way the Knight of Wands (the court card in the tarot associated with Aries) takes life by the reins, Aries is proactive and forward-moving. As soon as an Aries can move they will likely reach out and grab something. When an Aries child is able to walk, and often they will learn to walk on the earlier side, Aries is unstoppable. Their connection to spring and to the physical inertia of Mars gives Aries as a child a certain thrust of momentum. The image of a young toddler tilted forward, charging forward as if walking from their head, comes to mind. Aries children experience the world from their own individual perspective. So on one side this becomes a child who is independent and confident. They may want to be first in line and will actively ensure their place both at home and in the world. It is so important to keep an Aries child challenged both creatively and intellectually. Aries children need to be provided many opportunities to problem-solve. This helps to build up their confidence in themselves. Offering them praise is also wonderful, but be wary of too much praise. If the Aries child is not kept stimulated, they are more prone to impatience, temper tantrums, and bullying.

It is important to note that Aries children are deeply sensitive to their home/parental life and government/school life. They also often feel a heightened or intensified connection to conflict and violence, with the drive to optimistically move forward. Legendary Aries and Japanese artist Yayoi Kusama, born March 22, 1929, offers an example of this. Kusama's mother was physically abusive, and her father was described as a womanizer. Her childhood was also greatly influenced by the events of war, and she claims that during this period she began to value notions of personal and creative freedom. Although these events could have happened to anyone, an individual with an Aries soul path will greatly feel the resistance from their square to Cancer (volatile family situation) and Capricorn (political/public climate). The karmic relationship to violence, both in the home (Cancer) and war outside in the political arena (Capricorn), is made more palpable and noticeable to the Aries child. This is because of Mars's influence, the planet of war and violence. These experiences will often feel heightened or intensified for the Aries, which is part of the tempering process that fuels Aries forward on their path of individuality.

In a similar scenario for example, a Gemini child would likely react in a completely different way. Take for instance legendary Gemini Anne Frank. Also experiencing karmic ties to violence and war, Gemini views the world from their personal air qualities. A communicator, writer, and storyteller, Gemini's soul expression often manifests in their unique ability to perceive duality in their immediate surroundings and communicate about darkness in an airy and uplifting manner. The square for Gemini is not found between Cancer and Capricorn, but rather between Virgo and Pisces. This square for the Gemini indicates a karmic relationship to entrapment and fantasy (Pisces) and work, service, health, and details (Virgo). Anne Frank experienced confinement (Pisces), which led to a wild imagination (Pisces) that helped her channel her Gemini gift of words into great detail. Her journaling practice became a tremendous service to the world (Virgo).

When observing the lives of legendary artists/writers Yayoi Kusama and Anne Frank, we feel the difference the astrological sign makes in relation to their ways of expressing grief toward war. Kusama, in carving out a path of her own, moved to New York City at a young age and found herself involved in activism, fiercely devoted to bringing equal rights to women. Growing up in a family and culture that did not value gender equality, Kusama activated her cardinal right as an individual to stand up for

CARING FOR AN ARIES CHILD

If you are a parent, guardian, or teacher for an Aries child, you might benefit from reflecting on the following questions:

✳ In what ways can I more lovingly support and encourage my child's freedom to express their identity?

✳ How might I better nurture my child's sense of individuality while teaching the importance of cooperation, and communication (Libra)?

✳ How might I soften those expectations and truly listen to my child's natural gifts, tendencies, and callings?

other women who might have experienced similar injustices.

This is not to say that all Aries children will experience violence and war or abusive relationships to father and mother, nor is it to imply the Aries child will always experience difficult upbringings. This is however an opportunity to understand the soul agreement of an Aries. Whatever it is an Aries experiences in their childhood, it will likely act as fuel for their purpose. The Aries child wakes up early on in their journey to the importance of their innate birthrights. Although they may not be conscious of it at the time, they will be able to one day look back at their life and realize just how informative their childhood was. The very path before them was divinely unfolding all along, leading them to the expanse of their greatest potential in this lifetime—to be fierce survivors, warriors, and pioneers.

All of this is wonderful and expanding, but to take it back to our opening metaphor of the baby being born into the world, is the baby (Aries) conscious of how profoundly they inspire those around them? On one level, we could say no. The baby (Aries) is just simply being. The focus for the newborn is literally first just survival. The baby at this point hasn't even met their parents and is just solely trying to breathe. Yet this cry of the baby represents so much to those in the world around it. Aries may find themselves projected onto at different moments in their lives. What symbol does the Aries individual serve for others? And how might those individuals loosen their expectations? Aries does not want the pressure or the sheer weight of responsibility that comes with serving this function. Aries is in fact just trying to breathe, to survive as an individual here in this world. If too much pressure is put on Aries to fulfill someone else's destiny, their rebellious nature may arise—the kicking-and-screaming temper tantrum. If Aries is not given permission to be their own sovereign self, independent from the projections, expectations, and conjectures from parents, family, and society, the Aries can become excessive or deficient. The excessive Aries child grows frustrated, impulsive, careless, hyperactive, competitive, enraged, aggressive, and even violent. Whereas on the other end of the spectrum, the deficient Aries child can manifest with a victim mentality—low self-esteem, shame, self-blame, poor focus, repressed emotions, lack of energy, self-hatred, or depression.

An Aries child who is told day in and day out who they are supposed to be and how they are expected to act will likely do their best to be obedient, as our current culture in many ways rewards complacency. But over time this obedience may begin to make the Aries feel trapped, blocking the Aries from expressing their soul's longing—individuation and the expression of their innate birthrights. So the once-respectful child, when told to follow the rules one too many times, may act out in a fit of Aries excess, which can also be sensed and felt by connecting to the Tower card in the tarot, the respective correlating tarot card for the planet Mars.

To help better make sense of this, let's think of a classic example. An Aries child told to color within the lines may scribble destructively all over the page. The Aries child perhaps rips the page out of the book and screams or cries. The moments to follow will depend on many factors, but the Aries child will often feel confused by their sudden reaction. Since they are new to this planet and this human experience, they most likely will not be conscious of the root cause of their frustration. This confusion can lead to externalizing or internalizing the experience. When the Aries child externalizes, it might look like they're blaming the eruption on others: "You messed me up" (Aries swinging into its polar sign Libra blames others). When the Aries child internalizes, they might be really hard on themselves: "I am an idiot."

What's important to consider with the Aries child who may have a volatile reaction is that it isn't necessarily the instruction to "color within the lines" that is causing the Aries frustration, for that would be far too shallow of an interpretation. "Coloring within the lines" acts as a metaphor for the deeper psychological instructions children receive every day. "You're a boy, you should be tough. You're a girl, you should be sweet." This overload of pressure and rules placed on a child can be very intense for a child whose soul purpose is to carve out a path of their own. So the scribbling on the page outside of the lines is a subconscious outlet for the sheer frustration of not being supported by parents or by a society that nurtures the child's innate gifts.

The cardinal cross reflects all of these themes. Aries squares Cancer and Capricorn. This reflects childhood restriction with mother/father, home/public life, and nurturance/authority. The Aries opposition to Libra reflects obstacles around one-on-one relationships and karmic experiences with cooperation and fairness, particularly as they relate to the balance of masculine and feminine energies.

Whatever is the cultural conditioning beneath the surface, particularly as it relates to expectations of the child's public persona, home life, and expected gender roles, the Aries child will eventually release those expectations. It's important to note that if the Aries child retaliates it is not out of disrespect, but rather a freeing up of stagnant energy. When Aries becomes excessive in their expression (anger, outrage) it is a natural inclination to free up space for their deficiency (entrapment, lack of identity). The Aries child who seems unreasonable for throwing a fit over coloring within the lines is in actuality communicating something much deeper beneath the surface. This is an indicator of Aries—reclaiming respect through an intuitive journey of self-realization.

An Aries child who is not given permission to express themselves fully, perhaps because of the harsh rules of authority figures (Capricorn) and parents/family (Cancer), over time could internalize this through self-blame ("I am not capable") or self-hatred ("I am stupid"). These internalized involuntary beliefs will eventually lead to both deficiency (low-energy and depression) and excess (irritability and aggression). On the other hand, if the child is given full permission to be themselves but lacks the appropriate support from authority figures and family, over time they could externalize this through delusions of self-grandeur ("I am the most important person here"). These externalized involuntary beliefs will eventually lead to both deficiency (lack of purpose and direction) and excess (recklessness, bullying, teasing, and violence toward others).

This serves as a reminder to parents with an Aries child to let go of the need to mold your child into the person you think they should be. Allow your Aries child to explore these questions, "Who am I, separate from my parents? Who am I without the expectations and projections that have been placed upon me by society?" The phrase for Aries is "I am." It's imperative that Aries is given the space and freedom to discover their own personal connection to their sense of individuality.

ARIES IN LOVE

Do you believe in love at first sight? Can you recall a time when you felt such an intense, immediate attraction to another human that your heart started pounding while your thoughts ran a mile a minute? Just even the simplest touch from this other person might cause your whole body to shiver. We might say and do things we would not normally do. We might feel youthful again, even giddy, tripping over our words. Our body language might even change altogether. An immediate attraction to another person can be so visceral that we even start to tell fables or white lies in an attempt to impress them. When we feel this intense physical draw toward another person, our whole body reacts. According to scientists, chemicals in our brains (the part of the body connected to Aries) are released that induce the feeling of falling in love, all within a matter of seconds. This release of hormones can create a sense of euphoria.

When exploring Aries and its relationship to love, connecting to the initial spark of attraction, the moment when we fall in love, connects us to the energy of Aries in love. In my own life, I recall an immediate heightened attraction I felt with another individual. This person, who unexpectedly swept me off my feet within seconds of us meeting, just so happens to be an Aries. "Uh oh, I'm in trouble," I remember thinking to myself as he walked toward me. Before I knew it, he asked me my favorite place to bike in New York City. There wasn't even time for me to think, let alone answer. He interjected and swept me off to his favorite place to bike in all of NYC: Times Square.

Next thing I knew we were pedaling full speed ahead over the Williamsburg Bridge and into the heart of the city, to one of the busiest commercial intersections in the entire world. "The thrill-of-adventure, the magnitude of the noise, the bright lights, people from all over"—these are just a few of the things I recall this adrenaline-junky Aries spouting off as reasons why he loved to visit here daily. "It's like being in the center of the entire Universe," he said matter-of-factly. Never had I felt so inspired and uplifted on a first date... never had I felt so in love. Our date continued on until the wee hours of the morning. "Where have you been hiding all my life?" he whispered to me as our lips met for the first time. My entire body lit up. How could I be falling in love so hard and so fast with someone I just met?

In the weeks that followed, we continued to hang out with the same eagerness and fervor. I felt renewed with a sense of hope for life. The world around me suddenly felt brighter. He empowered me to start writing again and to share my gift of spoken word. There was a new hop to my step. I felt invincible. But underneath the buzzing sensation of heightened newness and attraction, I also sensed an imbalance (Libra opposition) that I had never quite witnessed within myself before. I felt a kind of jittery obsession or addiction. If we weren't together, he was texting me compliments, counting down the seconds until we'd meet again. If I didn't respond right away, I'd receive a flood of texts asking me if I was okay. This wasn't normally something I would find attractive in another individual, but coming from him, an Aries, it felt endearing, and I have to admit I was enjoying the passion and the attention for a change.

As quickly as our heated romance caught aflame, it suddenly died out. I didn't hear from him for a few days. Those few days turned into a few weeks. He was nowhere to be found. I was heartbroken. I would inadvertently wait by my phone. When a text message would appear, I'd check to see if it was him. When it wasn't, my heart would drop. In the rare moments he did text, I'd promise myself I wouldn't respond, but somehow I always would. I didn't recognize myself. My shoulders were rounded, my head lowered down toward the ground. I couldn't even think about writing, let alone being a spoken-word poet. How was it that I had swung so far, going from the top of the world to down in the dumps? What was it that made me so affected by this person I barely even knew? The next week I ran into him in the West Village. He was holding hands with another person. I sensed between them the same rush of excitement of falling in love for the first time, the very same feeling I had experienced weeks prior. We made eye contact and his face said it all: "You caught me."

> **Aries harness the sensational ability to make you feel fully seen and appreciated for all of the glorious gifts you have to offer.**

This anecdotal story is not intended to typecast Aries as the ardent heartbreaker, but it is intended to call to mind moments of falling head over heels for another person while also highlighting the high-vibe and low-vibe characteristics of Aries in love. Aries as a Fire sign is romantic and passionate, with a zeal and love for life. As a cardinal fire sign, Aries might be impulsive or quick to act. Aries is bold and sensuous, humorous, and even charismatic in their approach to love. Their appetite and hunger for love is strongly felt. They know what they want in a relationship and how to get it. Their confidence in the matter draws people to them because knowing what you want is *sexy*.

Aries harness the sensational ability to make you feel fully seen and appreciated for all of the glorious gifts you have to offer. Aries in Love feels quickly and intensely. With a pure presence, warmth, and charming frankness, their flames harness the fervor to light up your whole world, make you feel alive again, and bring out the best qualities that you, as an individual, possess.

Aries in a higher expression can make you feel on top of the world. Those lucky ones who get to experience life in a relationship with Aries will surely tell you how incredible it feels to be both desired and held in the same moment. For the lover of an Aries becomes everything—the center of their universe.

With this charged energy in relationships, Aries, as in all astrological signs, has its lower manifestation. Aries may at first only consider their own perspective and emotions. Their need to continually experience newness may make it a challenge for Aries to commit. Prone to diving in headfirst, Aries may also find themselves deeply infatuated with another person before genuinely getting to know them. Because of their red-hot magnetism, they can pull people into the magical world they've created without considering the consequences. Consider our current culture's glorifying of love and marriage. The willful ambition of Aries can lead them into perceiving romance as something to obtain, which in turn can make them prone to fantasy, disappointment, or burnout. If strongly under the influence of ruling planet Mars, the focus can be heavily situated on their physical attraction to another, with a strong urge to fulfill their sexual desires. This can get quite complicated, because Aries may be able to experience physical relationships without attachment more easily than other signs, especially Earth and Water signs. It's so important for Aries to learn the art of clear and *conscious* sexual boundaries so they do not fall into outdated patterns of seductive manipulation and sexual acting out. If Aries can commit to working on this while also learning how to communicate (Mercury) their physical needs and desires in a collaborative way with their partner (Libra), it will earn them greater respect from other people as well as from themselves. It will also help to prevent breaking someone's heart or even breaking their own. Because just as much as Aries appears to be on the individual's path, immune to the heartache of love, their polar sign Libra begs to differ.

With an opposition to Libra, there can be a great deal of challenges for Aries in relationships. All signs are subject to swinging into their polar sign if they become off-balance. For the Aries, this may take the form of creating an identity around their partnership. This can lead to an attachment to their partner and even codependency. The pendulum swinging into dependency might have Aries feeling triggered or confused. This is because of their natural mode toward an individual's path. Aries may feel overly concerned with their partner to the point that one or both of them feels smothered. An example of this might find Aries unable to attend a social event without their partner there with them. If this pattern becomes habitual, on one end Aries may become passive-aggressive. On the other end Aries might lash out, saying hurtful things that just aren't true. Either way, both of these scenarios are an attempt at expressing an underlying need for autonomy. It is imperative that both Aries and their partner understand the importance of independence in their relationship. If they can find themselves coming to this balance, then Aries learns not to swing into Libra, but rather to evolve through it with peace, balance, and consideration.

Since Aries evolves through Libra, the sign of committed partnerships, Aries greatly benefits by being in a one-on-one relationship. This invites Aries into a place of sweet balancing of *self* with *other*. Libra is about patience and peace, so meditating on these attributes when Aries is starting to feel excessive in their approach to love will prove beneficial. It is imperative that Aries creates space in their schedule every day to be alone with their breath and to relax. This helps to guide Aries into a more centered and peaceful state in love. Whether it is a new

sign	stage of relationship	themes and attributes
Aries	Attraction	Initial attraction; first date; heated, fiery passion; infatuation; intense sexual attraction; focus is on the individual; subject to burnout
Taurus	Commitment	Steady dating; sensuality and exploration of body; flowers, gifts, money, food, and nature; makes a commitment; shares values; reality sets in
Gemini	Communication	Intellectual communication; long conversations; social interest and events; introduction to friends; explore the neighborhood; read books and write letters; learn about partner's "hidden" side
Cancer	Home/Family	Spend time at one another's home; emotional, moody, and protective; potentially move in with one another; introduction to family; nostalgia and memories
Leo	Romance	Passion and romance; enjoy one another's company; creativity and playfulness; talk of children and pets; first fight; aggression
Virgo	Service	Encouragement of work-life; there for one another during sickness; supports health; deeply nurturing; acts of service; cleanse, diet, exercise; criticism
Libra	Marriage	Halfway point of relationship; collaboration, compromise, and balance; compassionate communication; learn one another's love language; place expectations and opinions on each other
Scorpio	Transformation	Intense emotion; rage and jealousy; empathetic awareness; psychological healing and transformation; death of a loved one or relative; emotional support; couples therapy
Sagittarius	Vision	Cultural expanse; world travel; honeymoon and vacation; philosophical and religious values; visions for the future; faithful support
Capricorn	Morals	Become parents; stability, responsibility, reliability; renewal of vows; long-term planning and commitment; career support; retirement plan; mortgage
Aquarius	Awakening	Children leave home; renovations to home; early retirement; expansion and space; objective point of view; free from social norms; eccentric nature emerges; hopeful for humanity; childish wisdom; stuck in ideologies
Pisces	Spiritual Release	Complete trust and surrender; retirement; death of self or partner; end of karmic cycle; deeply emotional; mental illness; Alzheimer's; reflection and release; spiritual connection

relationship or a long-term committed relationship, Aries benefits by taking a moment to pause, both for themselves and when interacting with their partner or potential new love. For instance, to take it back to the beginning of this section, if Aries feels a strong attraction toward someone, how might the Aries stop for a moment, take a deep breath, and consider what they might have to communicate to the other? Libra as a cardinal air sign doesn't discourage Aries from being an initiator, but it does invite Aries into a much slower, more thoughtful approach. For example, instead of riding a bike full speed ahead to Times Square, what might happen if the Aries waits for a response from their partner? What Aries just might find is that their partner guides them to a reflective secret haven along the river, a place they would have never found on their own. It's here that the bold heart of the Aries Ram will soften as they learn that this thing called life doesn't have to be conquered alone.

For Aries in love, the importance of family and career greatly supports the Aries mission. With the balance of partnership, Aries aligns their pioneering nature with the purpose of helping create momentous change. They do this for themselves and to help guide the individual rights for their family (Cancer) and the community at large (Capricorn). Having a loving, supporting partner (Libra) who believes in the Aries's mission is imperative for the Aries, as Aries does best when supported by another. With that, Aries could arguably be considered one of the most romantic and loving in the zodiac in one-on-one relationships. With its polar sign as Libra, Aries is the most balanced when in a committed, loving relationship. Aries as they grow into adulthood hold enormous potential to form solid, long-lasting relationships that stand the test of time. The soul-growth card for Aries in the tarot is the Emperor. This encourages Aries to learn the art of commitment and safe boundaries.

Aries inspires us all to not only be fierce individuals but also to love with all of our hearts.

ARIES AT WORK

IMAGINE YOU ARE awakened by the sound of an alarm clock on the first morning of a new job. If you feel prepared, a sense of readiness for the day erects the spine. You are well rested and confident. You might use this early morning time to stretch and yawn, drink hot lemon water, and reflect on the day to come. Maybe you even look in the mirror and say to yourself, "You got this!" Partaking in morning rituals like these helps to ground and realign you with your confidence. Now imagine what it might feel like to wake up late, not feeling prepared for this first day at a new job. There may be a sense of urgency or anxiety from a night of restless sleep. Dashing toward the kitchen to brew coffee, you hurriedly get ready for the day, tripping over your pants as you recklessly sling them on. Both of these scenarios in their extremes connect us to the higher and lower forms of Aries at work.

The first day on the job is the vibration Aries carries with them throughout their experience of working. When their heart is fully aligned with their work, Aries is fully present and committed. Their ambition and willpower make them attentive and truly alive when working.

With an enormous amount of energy and initiative, Aries drives projects forward, searching for new ways to achieve. Their ability to work at an accelerated pace under pressure combines harmoniously with their exploration of self-identity. This makes Aries perfect for entrepreneurial endeavors or solo projects. When a challenge arises, Aries might be the first to raise their hand in the air to volunteer. Aries is confident they will get the job done and enjoys working alone. There is a naivety to this bold, warrior-like spirit that allows them to bravely try on many different hats. While one individual might mull over their options for a few days, Aries has already tried out numerous different ways of approaching the situation. With dynamism and quick thinking, Aries is on the edge of their seat, ready to greet the world with new, brilliant ideas. Their mind is sharp and holds the enormous capacity to retain facts and information in a short amount of time. Their ability to let go of information when it no longer serves them also allows for a productive and forward-moving momentum. Aries exudes just the proper amount of confidence and enthusiasm needed to make others believe in their leadership. If you want to succeed, just look to an Aries to lead the way. They navigate the world headfirst. This is exactly the bold spirit needed to achieve greatness.

However, there is a downside to the fiery determination of Aries. Their brisk pace and eagerness to achieve might make them a bit reckless in their decision-making. Quick to strike the match, Aries may be careless with details, thought, and action. This might manifest by taking on too much or not heeding warnings. If Aries finds themselves activating from a place of urgency, they may lack the bandwidth to follow through with their projects. This could eventually lead an Aries to place an enormous amount of pressure on themselves to produce the best results. If Aries is taking on too much, they can become stressed out or flustered and even resort to anger or aggression. This might look like them sending a volatile email to a colleague too quickly or perhaps launching a project too soon. Aries may even be immediate in their reaction to agree to take on a task that they aren't quite fit to deal with. Their optimism and ambition may oftentimes be bigger than their skill level or experience. These scenarios are sure to dwindle the flames of the Ram. It's important for Aries in their relationship to work to remember to step back and pause.

> **Aries brisk pace and eagerness to achieve might make them a bit reckless in their decision-making.**

As Aries learns to ground their energy and trust in their power, they learn to move from their personal fire perspective to an expansive objective perspective. How do the Aries's day-to-day tasks fit into the greater grand scheme vision? Aries benefits from this long-term vision. Aries in its highest is most fulfilled when their work contributes to their own individuation process and acts as a catalyst for inspiring the collective to own their individual rights. This makes the Aries great in career paths involved with activism, leadership, individuality, and adventure. All of these career paths allow Aries to activate their traditional ruling planet Mars with physical vitality and life and empowerment. However, Aries should never be limited to or typecast by these obvious career options.

ARIES CAREERS

Some of the career choices most resonant with the Aries include:

- producer
- executive
- entrepreneur
- professional athlete
- firefighter
- emergency medical technician
- life coach
- sports coach
- physical educator

Aries is on a path of self-discovery and may find their vocation and career going through many different changes throughout their life. Perhaps these more obvious career paths connected with Aries act more as metaphor, because the career Aries chooses to align themselves with is more fulfilling when they find themselves taking on a heroic role. For instance, take the firefighter as an example: brave, dashing, daring, efficient, driven, and forward-moving. In addition, the firefighter is not self-focused on their own personal gain and ambition, but instead is here to support the community. Having a cause to focus their ambition toward is very important for Aries so they can give back to society, and this does not always have to manifest with physical careers.

When Aries activates from esoteric ruling planet Mercury, this elevates Aries toward mental activity and intellectualization when working. Aries holds the great capacity to multitask and to hold on to quite a bit of information. When Aries drops out of the need to physically be moving or asserting themselves forward with a thrusting ambition, Aries begins to learn the art of strategy and discernment. No longer does Aries see the world as a place of competition, but rather begins to witness those around them as co-collaborators on a journey toward actualization. When Aries allows themselves to drop the egoic belief that they have to prove their self through their accomplishments and understands themselves to be a powerful agent for manifesting great change for the collective, Aries becomes inspired and inspirational. By looking at the life of many famous Aries, the physical vitality and bravery holds true for Aries, but often they activated from Mercurial planes of divine wisdom. Take for example legendary Aries Gloria Steinem, a radical feminist, journalist, producer, and social political activist who became nationally recognized as a leader and a spokeswoman for the American feminist movement in the 1960s and 1970s; or legendary Aries Maya Angelou, a pioneering voice for the African American community as a poet, best-selling author, memoirist, and civil rights activist. The planet Mercury elevates the Aries toward more intellectual career paths that inspire us all to live our best life. This might look like an inspirational teacher or poet, a fierce life coach radiating authenticity, an investigative journalist, or an incredibly empowering speaker advocating for social justice and equality through spoken-word activism and intellectual discourse.

ARIES AS AN ADULT

ARIES'S ENERGY INSPIRES us to take life by the reigns, but if we pay attention to nature we will find that, in the beginning of spring, life goes on and keeps on keeping on whether or not we will it into creation. Every day the sun will rise. Every spring the flowers will bloom. The Aries adult who has successfully moved through the very initiatory phases of early childhood, as often connected with the Aries experience, will find themselves softening into this realization. No longer does life seem to be a war zone or a place to claim space or territory. No longer does the individual need to exert their sense of identity and ambition. Instead, a tremendous amount of trust ensues. The survival mentality or flight-or-fight response often activated for the Aries slows down.

Aries may find themselves becoming an adult at a young age or actually desiring to be an adult before it is their time. The cardinal fire energy of Aries gives Aries the ambition to pursue something with faith and vigor. So when it comes to adulting, Aries may find themselves in some way glorifying this experience. This forms quite a juxtaposition, however, to Aries being the first sign of the zodiac, because Aries is also connected to youthfulness. Because of this, on the high end, Aries may really have their act together. Aries has learned how to stand up for themselves and how to take the initiative. But if Aries falls too into the role of authority or responsibility (Capricorn square), Aries is cutting off their gift of being sprightly. Aries as an adult needs to be given continual permission, perhaps most often from themselves, that it is okay to not be the typical adult. Just like in all areas of life, Aries carves out their own path and way of interacting with the world, so Aries as an adult becomes just as individual as the rest.

As a personal fire sign, Aries is on a journey of self-discovery and self-identity. Don't be surprised if Aries as an adult feels just as explorative as a teenager. This might involve Aries shaving their head out of nowhere or completely switching jobs, moving homes, or booking a flight last minute. To some, these actions might feel like impulsive decisions or unthoughtful antics. It's important to remember that these sorts of actions are what fuel Aries and give them new life and a continual journey of self-exploration.

Referring back to the cardinal cross, Aries squares Cancer and Capricorn. As a child, this often manifests as karmic relationships to home, family, and mother (Cancer) and society, school, and father (Capricorn). These experiences left in the subconscious will often continue to play out into adulthood. Thus, now as an adult, the Aries's experience mirrors that of its childhood. For example, the Aries child who experienced an abusive relationship to parents may now carry this pattern on into adulthood by sabotaging home and living situations. Or the Aries child whose individuality was squandered because of a rigid societal upbringing, like by attending a private school with a strict code of ethics, may now carry this pattern onto into adulthood, seeking a career that limits their potential by playing out a submissive role to authority figures. Aries may even find themselves with a compulsive dependence on familial approval or support, living out their parent's dreams or expectations with little satisfaction or few tangible results.

When subconscious and conscious realities are in misalignment, they often manifest as some sort of form of self-sabotage. This tendency to neglect home and family can result in Aries swinging into a compulsive focus on career and achievement, with little satisfaction. In order for Aries to set themselves free from these karmic trappings, Aries as an adult must be ready to meditate on its inconjunct pairings—Virgo and Scorpio. Aries's inconjunct signs are on the opposite side of the wheel without being the oppositional or polar sign of Libra. The exploration of subconscious and superconscious reality can take many different forms for the Aries adult, but it will in some way always connect back to an intuitive journey of self-discovery. The Aries adult will often find themselves attracted to new experiences that enrich their connection to the world at-large. This journey of self-discovery into the internal world can be observed by Aries meditating on Scorpio and Virgo.

> **The Aries adult will often find themselves attracted to new experiences that enrich their connection to the world at-large.**

Scorpio rules over psychological healing, transformation, death, and rebirth, and it is connected to practices such as psychotherapy and esoteric arts. As a Water sign, the exploration of Scorpio pulls Aries into the mystery of life. When Aries learns to let go of the egoic belief that they are in charge of the life they are manifesting, they come a long way in relation to facing their fears of the unknown. As a fixed sign, Scorpio teaches Aries to stay focused and committed to the task at hand. It's through the exploration of Scorpio that Aries begins to trust in their intuition and touch base with their desires, bringing healing to their psychological processes. Any practice able to shine a conscious light toward the subconscious realms is Scorpio in nature, including practices such as tarot and astrology. It's through Scorpio that Aries learns to hold space for their emotional nature, to honor death and release, and to trust in their capacity for ambition which transmutes or transforms internally from within.

With the help of Virgo, Aries channels its ambition into productivity by humbly offering their services to the world. Virgo rules over holistic health, purity, cleanliness, and volunteer services and is connected to mastering one's work. Instead of the plight toward prestige and approval, Aries learns humility. As an Earth sign, the exploration of Virgo teaches Aries to be connected to the body and material and to move forward with a sense of resourcefulness and practicality. When Aries as an adult learns to humbly bow to this human experience, Aries softens into its more nurturing side. This might take the form of Aries experiencing some health crisis, slowing them down. As a mutable sign, Virgo reminds Aries to adapt and improve. It's through Virgo practices that Aries is encouraged to refine their gifts and to commit to being the leader they were born to be. By focusing and channeling the Aries ambition toward a holistic, service-based offering, Aries learns to practice modesty and patience when manifesting. This process allows Aries to go deep within to assess their purpose for channeling their fire for the benefit of others, so that Aries may come to offer a great service to the world.

Without exploration of the inconjunct signs, the fiery flames of Aries are subject to dwindling or combusting. Aries may find themselves repeating old patterns. Once Aries explores the darker recesses of its prior experiences, whether they're from childhood or from previous incarnations, Aries begins to shine a light to

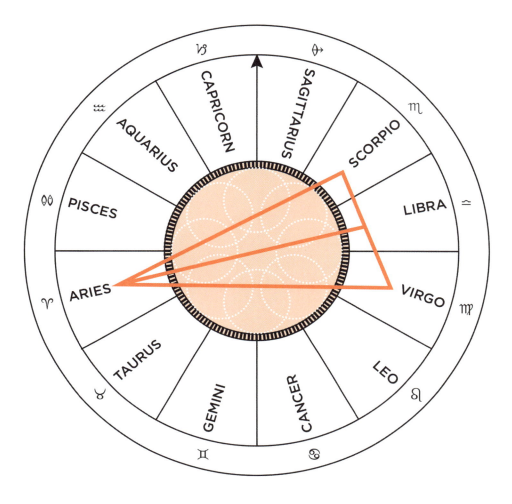

its subconscious motivations. Once Aries takes the time to channel their drive into productivity, Aries awakens to its potential as a beacon of light unto the world. Through the help of Scorpio practices (psychotherapy, tarot, etc.) and Virgo practices (volunteer services, holistic healing, mastering of one's craft), Aries as an adult becomes aware of their shortcomings. If the Aries makes contact with Virgo and not Scorpio, they may channel all of their ambitious fires into their work, running themselves into the ground. If Aries makes contact with Scorpio but not Virgo, their ambition goes into overdrive with a ruthless and even malicious competitive edge. The Aries adult learns to integrate both of these practices, thus leading to a reparenting of themselves through psychological healing, service, and health.

Through these newfound discoveries, Aries releases the need to channel their cardinal fire ambition toward external achievements or seeking approval from parents. Instead, Aries owns their rights as an individual to channel their ambition and creative life force toward their heart's longing and soul purpose. This will often tie back in some way to their upbringing and the discoveries made from exploring both their square and inconjunct signs. It's through this work that the Aries brings their conscious talents, skills, and gifts into alignment with their subconscious desires and emotions, thus opening themselves up to the alignment with a *higher calling—superconscious reality.*

This connection to a higher calling emerges when the Aries individual forms a union between their conscious/subconscious reality and their superconscious reality. Without superconscious awareness, Aries is centered solely in the ego-self. Before the Aries individual makes contact with superconscious reality, they might often impulsively charge ahead with determination and ambition. To more gentle souls, this version of Aries can appear to be competitive and self-absorbed. The Aries adult with no connection to superconscious reality will often still achieve greatness in the world but may often feel the world to be a cruel, unjust, or unforgiving place. This individual charters a path of their very own and has learned to depend on no one else but themselves. They know what they want and how to move forward in order to bring their vision into manifestation, but they lack the clear interpersonal relational skills to bring harmony and balance to their life.

If the Aries continues on this path without attuning with higher spiritual awareness, Aries will eventually burn out. For example, say an Aries individual who grew up in a strict family moves away from home as an adult and focuses their ambition toward their career. They may even become conscious of their subconscious motivations to seek parental approval and prestige in their career, but the Aries individual uses this pain as fuel to catapult themselves even further, channeling their heartache into their work. Without the support from and connection to superconscious reality, the Aries's relationships may suffer tremendously because of their hardening beliefs and attitudes. The Aries's relentless spirit can continue down this path for quite some time, answering to themselves and only themselves. Eventually, without the connection to superconscious reality, the Aries loses contact with their purpose for incarnation. Aries finds little spiritual fulfillment in their quest if it does not involve a higher connection.

In order for the Aries adult to self-actualize, they will have to make contact with superconscious reality. The astrological wheel offers continual insight into ways to bring loving balance to an individual's life. The signs on the opposite side of the wheel provide a balancing

new perspective and outlook on life. Aries's oppositional sign Libra, as well as inconjunct signs Virgo and Scorpio, can help Aries make connections with superconscious reality. For some Aries, this might look like a devotional offering that channels their services to the higher power or for the higher good of all (Virgo). For other Aries, their gifts are awakened by fully committing to another person through marriage or by connecting to equality through a cause for social justice (Libra). Aries can often find themselves connecting to a higher power when they dive into their depths and transform their darkness into light (Scorpio) potentially becoming great healers, intuitives, or mystics. Often though, the soul-centered Aries awakens when they have fully made contact with all three of their polar signs: Virgo, Libra, and Scorpio.

A new sense of freedom arises as Aries begins to trust in themselves ("I am me"), other people ("I am you"), and in the human experience ("I am life"). The embodiment of one's birthrights emerges forth through the Aries capacity to become their own mother or their own father, separate from the expectations placed on them by society. The Aries adult learns to trust in the human experience: "I am life." The Aries adult upgrades when they are rightfully so in the flow with life. They become incredible conduits for universal energy.

Tarot is one of the greatest visual tools when connecting with astrology. For the purposes of this chapter, the connection between these two practices is for the visual component of symbols and archetypes, not for divination. Each astrological sign and planet is paired with a correlating Major Arcana tarot card. The astrological signs appear in numerological order in the Major Arcana, starting with the Emperor (Aries) and going to the Moon (Pisces).

THE EMPEROR
Soul-Growth Card For Aries.

The Emperor, at a very base level, shows himself as a reminder of the importance of structure and order—not in a way to control or to gain power but rather as a holder of sacred space. As the number 4, the Emperor speaks to the importance of creating structure, reflecting Aries's maturation into responsibility, authority, and reason. However, the essence of the Emperor extends well beyond these traditional traits of embodiment.

Aries is the spark of creation. Not only does Aries connect us to the beginning of spring and the start of our astrological journey, Aries in essence represents the beginning of time. The Emperor connects us to the Ancient Wisdom of Aries. Stephen Hawking in the lecture "The Beginning of Time" states, "All the evidence seems to indicate that the universe has not existed forever, but that it had a beginning, about fifteen billion years ago." True soul-centered Aries/Emperor is the voice of the ancients, connecting us to our long, distant path. The soul growth for Aries is reflected by this.

The phrase for Aries is "I am." The stages of consciousness for Aries can be thought of in three phases:

Personal—Individuation Process: "I am me."

Interpersonal—Evolving through Libra: "I am you."

Collective—Soul-centered Aries: "I am life."

When Aries is grounded in its connection to the ancient past, Aries becomes like the Emperor, expanding beyond the personal toward the collective. It's here that Aries the Emperor reminds us to honor the sacredness of the land and to respect its natives. Aries/Emperor declares the importance of taking responsibility for our brutal past while encouraging us forward: the Love Warrior—ruling from the dominion of the heart. Soul-centered Aries transforms the ego, "I am me," to the ancient wisdom, "I am Life."

conscious, personal, and cardinal nature of Aries: ambitious, proactive, forward-moving, and confident. He invites us into an empowering space where we learn to harness our fiery energy to create, explore, and follow through with our dreams. Meditating on this image will help align you with the Aries principles of self-recognition, individuality, and the declaration of creative and ambitious goals.

THE TOWER
The Tower Connects Us to Aries's Ruling Planet Mars.

One of the most misconstrued cards in the tarot, the Tower is infamous for bringing up fear, panic, and confusion. What we see on the card in the Rider-Waite-Smith-Centennial version is a tall stone tower placed on the top of a narrow, craggy mountain. Out of the dark and stormy sky lightning strikes the top of the tower. An oversized king/queen's crown pops off the top of the tower, reminiscent of a cork when you crack open the top of a champagne bottle. Then, out of the burning tower, two individuals (one appears to be a Magician-like figure with a red cape on, and the other appears to be a royal Emperor-like figure with a crown on) leap

KNIGHT OF WANDS
Cardinal Fire (Knight = Cardinal; Fire = Wands).

The sixteen court cards in the tarot can also be used as a meditation on the twelve astrological signs. The Knight of Wands reflects the

headfirst from the windows. The Tower scene depicts a moment of complete chaos, destruction, and tragedy, but when following the Fool's journey from beginning to end, one will observe its symbolic meaning.

The Tower represents a moment of subconscious energy being set free from conscious reality, expanding into superconscious reality. This is a similar trajectory to the personal-interpersonal-collective evolution of "I am me–I am you–I am life" mentioned previously with the Emperor. However, instead of the external relationship to reality, the Tower speaks to the internal journey of Aries. Connecting to the physical inertia of new life, Mars/Tower reflects the physicality and innate courage of Aries to fearlessly face life. Imagine the amount of effort it takes a seed to push through its pod and break through the soil, or the amount of energy it takes for a baby to be born. These moments of friction, resistance, and heat are all symbols for Aries, and they reflect the three levels of consciousness depicted in the Tower: conscious–subconscious–superconscious.

These three levels of consciousness are not separate, but rather interwoven. For example, the baby entering this world is guided by a conscious desire to be born, the subconscious need to survive, and the superconscious longing for soul evolution. In order for a birth to be successful, all three levels of consciousness need to occur simultaneously. With Aries and the Tower, if one of these layers of consciousness is out of alignment, then the Tower will feel devastating and life-shattering. If conscious reality isn't in alignment with superconscious reality, Aries may feel as if they are alone in the world, with no help from spirit/higher power. If subconscious reality is in misalignment with conscious reality, this may manifest for the Aries individual as self-sabotage through limited beliefs or destructive pattern behaviors often connected to early childhood or inherited trauma. And finally, if the superconscious is in misalignment with the subconscious, the Aries individual may be taken over by wild primal emotions like rage, grief, violence, or depression. The charged creative life force must find a way to be discharged.

The Tower also offers a meditation for Aries on the relationship between the layers of external reality (personal–interpersonal–collective) and internal reality (conscious–subconscious–superconscious). For example, an Aries individual who holds enormous potential as an author of mind-expanding new thought works for decades in an unsatisfying job that pays well. The conscious decision to work this job for practical money-related issues masks the subconscious decision to commit to a limiting job out of the fear of failure. Conscious and subconscious realities are in misalignment (limiting belief patterns).

In addition, the individual has no clear connection to a Higher Power or to their soul's longing for evolution and expansion. Conscious and subconscious reality are both in misalignment with superconscious reality (feelings of helplessness/overtaken by emotions). The internal reality (that which dwells inside the Tower) now interacts with external reality. The individual bricks of the Tower come to represent the varying degrees of life decisions—the "I am's" of life. Perhaps each brick represents every day this individual shows up to a job not in alignment with their highest expression. Now the Tower is so tall after years of showing up to this job that that which dwells on the inside no longer matches that which dwells on the outside. The external life manifested is in misalignment with the internal realities.

If internal reality is in continual misalignment with external reality, a Tower moment is sure to ensue. The Tower comes to represent the moment of destruction/creation. Perhaps the individual shows up to work depressed day in and day out and is fired from their job. This is a Tower moment. For some, it may feel totally and utterly devastating. For others, it may crack them completely open—a cosmic breakthrough. These moments arise as a realignment with our life's path. We all will experience Tower moments in our lives, but perhaps the Aries will feel and connect to this energy more prominently. The Tower serves as a continual reminder for Aries to check in with the varying layers of themselves in both their internal and external realities. With the Aries's enormous amount of creative life force, Aries holds the potential to be continually creating anew.

THE MAGICIAN
The Esoteric Ruling Planet For Aries Is Mercury, As Represented By The Magician.

As number 1, the Magician is the initiator of the tarot journey. This connects to Aries as the first sign of the astrological wheel. The Magician, like Aries, symbolizes the spark of creation and continues the reflection on the relationship between conscious, subconscious, and superconscious realities. As the co-collaborator with life and Spirit, the Magician is a conduit for universal energy. The Magician realizes the interplay between conscious intention, subconscious desire, and superconscious expression. The individual self—"I am me"—dissolves with the cosmic truths of collective self—"I am life." The Magician knows the individual is not solely responsible for manifestation, but instead works with and honors spirit (as symbolized by the crown Chakra infinity symbol halo above the head) and the four elements. On the table rests a symbol for each of the four elements: *sword* (Air), *wand* (Fire), *pentacle* (Earth), and *cup* (Water).

The Magician serves as a continual reminder for Aries to drop the egoic belief that they are responsible for what is being manifested. Aries symbolizes creation, but Aries is not the creator. The Aries individual is just the magical conduit through which this incredibly charged life force is moving through. Aries rules the head, and here the Magician reminds us of the sacredness of this connection. For Aries, when they make meditation a regular practice and find ways to get out of their own sense of individuality to connect with God, they bring themselves into a flow state. This is how Aries elevates their consciousness into personification. Like the Magician, Aries acts as a force for great change and creation.

Aries must remember: it's not the seed sprouting on its own. It is the co-collaboration of many factors. The great Winds or Hand of God (Air) that gently placed the seed. The great Earth that nurtures and cradles the seed. The great sun (Fire) charging the seed with life force. And the great waters that rain upon it. The Magician/Aries is not solely responsible for the magic of new life. The Magician/Aries is just a conduit in which the beautiful manifestation of all the elements comes together in human form to infuse and inspire heightened spiritual and intentional awareness into every act.

ARIES TRAITS

The manifestations of Aries have been distilled into five soul-centered Aries traits:

1. Deeply honors individuals of the past by courageously moving forward
2. Acts with Divine Intention as a conscious agent for equality
3. Pioneering spirit paves a pathway for future generations
4. Reclaims respect through intuitive journey of self-realization
5. Embodiment of soulful wisdom connects the collective to their birthrights

CONCLUSION

THE JOURNEY OF Aries, traveling from child to the world, is an inspiring story of perseverance. The hero and the protagonist, Aries sets forth on a path of personal empowerment and learns to see past their own individual struggle. Aries emerges out from a place of fear-based ego; releases outdated patterns in relation to violence, oppression, and war; and learns to activate from the higher octave of the Aries incarnation. The archetype of Libra becomes a guiding force for Aries throughout their lifetime. Through the many themes of Libra, Aries learns to bring a balance to its personal fire nature through the interpersonal air elementation of Libra. When Aries carves out a path for the individual self, Aries may leave others behind. Libra reminds Aries to consider the other, to practice the art of collaboration, and to bring others along with them toward expansion. It is through Libra that Aries upgrades to the soul-centered attributes of its nature. Aries, as the individual, innately connected to the ownership of birthrights meets Libra and learns to channel its ambition not just for itself but for a world in need. Through the balance and symmetry of Libra, emboldened Aries learns to take a deep breath into the heart to connect with the peaceful energy of the Goddess. Libra teaches Aries the importance of compassionate communication, intellectual discourse, and social inclusion. It's the Scales of Justice and the Sword of Truth of Libra that awaken Aries to a heightened spiritual awareness—one of activism, intuition, and soulful wisdom. By evolving through Libra, Aries learns the art of collaboration, communication, justice, and rightful relation. Through this journey of individuation, Aries connects with a higher power or a uniting Universal Truth. This opens Aries up to acting with Divine Intention as a conscious agent for equality.

APR. 20–MAY 20

text by Courtney O'Reilly

element — EARTH

symbol — THE BULL

modality — FIXED

house — SECOND

ruler — VENUS

LYRIQUE

INTRODUCTION

WHAT AN HONOR and thrill that you picked up this book and decided to read it; thank you from the bottom of my heart. *Zodiac Signs: Taurus* was my first book, and I suppose that as an astrologer I shouldn't be surprised by the timing, but I am nonetheless. At the time I signed on to write about Taurus for this series, the planet that rules astrology, surprises, and exciting out-of-the-blue change, Uranus, was on top of my natal sun in Taurus to the exact degree. I am thrilled to be a part of this wonderful series on the zodiac. Throughout this chapter I break down key components of what makes Taureans tick in all the different areas of their lives—childhood through adulthood, in love, at work, and in the world at large—in an easy-to-understand way with lots of examples. If you are a Taurus, I hope this serves as a helpful guide on your path to shine your very brightest. If you are reading to gain a better understanding of a particular Taurus in your life—perhaps a lover, dear friend, or boss—I hope it sheds light on your questions and offers greater insight. My highest goal with this chapter is to help you understand yourself and those around you a bit better with the hope of increasing compassion for both yourself and others through the lens of astrology.

Astrology is the study of possibility, not to be confused with predestination or religion. It is the study of planetary cycles—their placement at our birth and their continual motion thereafter, known by astrologers as transits—that affect our lives in ways both large and small. It is an invaluable tool used to explore our innate nature and understand those who orbit us in a more intimate and integrated way. For this reason, astrology is also a study in compassion, for once you see the scope of what an individual is working with, it's almost impossible not to feel compassion for that individual's situation—astrology is broadening and enlightening in this way. Astrology reveals the climate and condition, which we then can use to make more conscious decisions on how to make the most of what is in order to thrive and live the best life possible. We have free will, and you are the captain of your ship at all times. Astrology simply reveals potential we may have otherwise missed. It helps us maximize and make the most of our gifts and work with more intention and clarity through the challenges that surely will come.

> *Astrology reveals the climate and condition, which we then can use to make more conscious decisions.*

Astrology has deep roots dating back to ancient times, with the people of Babylonia (present-day Iraq), Central America, India, Egypt, Greece, and China all developing their own methods. Those methods later mixed and blended, evolving over many years into astrology as we know it today. In his *Handbook for the Humanistic Astrologer*, Dane Rudhyar said, "Astrology is a language. If you understand this language, The Sky Speaks to You." It really does feel like translating another language at times—astrology is a rich and wonderful mix of ancient study infused with mythology and rooted in math and symbology.

We as individuals are a reflection of the cosmos at the moment we are born through what astrologers call a natal chart, or natal horoscope. We each carry within us the imprint of the luminaries: sun and moon, as well as all eight planets and each sign of the zodiac, spread across the twelve houses, which show how we relate to specific areas of our life such as love, career, and parenthood. You may be interested to learn that among the eight planets, the inner planets—Mercury, Venus, and Mars—along with the sun and moon, relate most to our personality, and Jupiter and Saturn, the two planets considered to be in between the inner and outer planets, show major trends of the time. The outer planets (Uranus, Neptune, and Pluto) are related to generational trends, since those planets are much farther away and move far more slowly than do the inner planets. While astronomers now classify Pluto as a dwarf planet, many astrologers still consider Pluto a planet. We see how potent Pluto's affect is within the chart. The slower a planet moves the longer it stays in one sign and area of your chart, which leaves a lasting impression. Pluto's powerful affect has not altered, and so in relation to astrology you will notice Pluto is still referred to as a planet. There is a series of sacred texts called the Hermetic Corpus written by Hermes Trismegistus, which includes the Emerald Tablet. The Emerald Tablet details one of the defining concepts of astrology—"As above, so below"; or in other words what occurs above (sky) affects below (Earth). Similarly, our inner workings affect our outer world and vice versa. Astrologer and author Betty Lundsted brilliantly explains this concept of "as above, so below" in her book *Astrological Insights into Personality:* "In an ancient religious manuscript, the author discusses the concept that the entire zodiac represents a person. The macrocosm and the microcosm reflect each other. 'As above so below.' In order to realize the full potential of personality and creativity in a lifetime, all the signs should be integrated within the individual. This integration process will make us 'whole.'"

Let's explore a few fundamental foundational points as you dive into this chapter and the others in this book. The first is that we all have two charts: what's called a solar chart, which is based on your sun sign, and a natal chart, which is based on your precise birth information. You can (and should!) read the two chapters in this book for your sun and rising signs. When you read horoscopes, you may want to read for the sun and rising signs as well. This will offer you a wider scope of understanding of yourself and current planetary happenings. Your solar chart is based on where the sun was when you were born and is what nearly every person you encounter will know about astrology: "What sign are you?" "Taurus!"

Your solar chart is an extremely important part of your personal astrology and nature, just as the sun is the center of our solar system. In the same way, it is the core within you. It illuminates the center of your essence—how you shine in the world, your vitality, and your ego identity—and offers great insight into your purpose and what you will enjoy and thrive at doing. This is why horoscopes are written for your sun sign—there is a reason all the other planets in our solar system dance around the sun and not the other way around. It is our brightest light and the life-sustaining source of energy for our planet.

If you were born between April 20 and May 20, you are a Taurus. If you were born very close to either the beginning or the end date listed, it's of critical importance that you find your exact time of birth to calculate whether the sun was in Aries or Taurus if you were born at the beginning of the season (April 20), or in Taurus or Gemini if you were born at the end (May 20). The sun changes sign at slightly different times each year, so if you were born on April 20 or May 20, there is a chance you are not a Taurus at all. You may have heard others refer to being on the "cusp"; what this really means is that you're born on the day the sun changes from one sign to the next. However, the sun cannot be in two places at once, so you're either one or the other. You must find your exact birth time to reveal the sun's precise placement at the moment of your birth. Locate your birth certificate, ask a parent or trusted relative who would remember, or alternatively, if you were born in the United States, you can contact the Bureau of Vital Statistics in the capital of the state in which you were born to purchase the long-form copy of your birth certificate, which includes birth time if it was recorded. Once you have the time, there are several resources online to calculate your natal chart for free. To calculate your natal chart, you will need your birth date, including the year; your exact time of birth; and your birth location. This chart will not only confirm your sun's placement but also determine what sign you have rising, or the sign that was coming up on Earth's eastern horizon when you were born. Your rising sign sets the layout of your completely individual natal chart. Your natal chart is unique to you and you alone—no two will be exactly the same.

Perhaps you've asked yourself, "How can it be that astrology divides all of humanity into twelve signs? Surely we are more individual than that." It's true! We each have the sun, the moon, and all eight planets manifesting their energetic pull within our lives. To further understand the complexities of your natal chart as it pertains to all of your planetary placements, seek out a skilled astrologer for a one-on-one consultation. In this chapter, though, we will be focusing on Taurus as a sun sign. If Taurus is your rising sign, this chapter is equally important for you, and I invite you to read it for a more rounded understanding of your deepest, truest nature.

Astrologers study the planets' movements through the twelve constellations the ancients deemed most impactful for us here on Earth. We are interested in the planetary conditions under which an individual was born, because depending on these conditions, some planets will be particularly impactful for that person. Each of the twelve signs has a planetary ruler, with Venus overseeing both Taurus and Libra. Yes, it's no surprise that sweet, sensual, earthy Taurus is Venus's child.

In Latin, Taurus means "The Bull": symbolically Taurus is represented by a circle (spirit) with a crescent moon on top (soul) that looks like the bull's horns. Taurus is strongly linked to agriculture and represents the time of year when the Earth is fertile and lush. We can also look to the mythology of Venus (Roman) and Aphrodite (Greek) for greater understanding of Taurus's motivations. Across cultures, Venus is considered the goddess of love and affection, receptivity, beauty, and friendship. Venus oversees all social interaction; anything she touches is softened and has an angelic glow. Venus imparts joy and fun! With Venus's guidance, a Taurus is good-humored with a magnetic allure that is hard to deny and a tactile style of affection that is simply irresistible.

Astrology is complex, but fortunately it offers us a few subsections to help explain the nuance and variation from sign to sign. These are known as the elements, modalities, and houses, with all the signs evenly divided within each subsection. We have four elements: fire (Aries, Leo, Sagittarius), earth (Taurus, Virgo, Capricorn), air (Gemini, Libra, Aquarius), and water (Cancer, Scorpio, Pisces), also known as triplicities, with three signs falling under each element. There are three modalities:

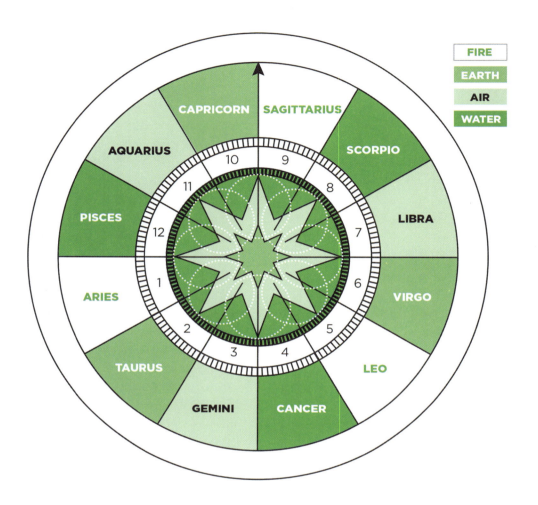

TRIPLICITIES

cardinal (Aries, Cancer, Libra, Capricorn), fixed (Taurus, Leo, Scorpio, Aquarius), and mutable (Gemini, Virgo, Sagittarius, Pisces), also known as quadruplicities, with four signs under each modality. Finally there are twelve houses, with each sign traditionally claiming ownership of one house. The elements add texture to the quality of each sign; the modalities correlate with nature and align with the seasons; and the houses, which the twelve signs of the zodiac fall within, emphasize the different areas of our lives. Your natal chart reveals the layout of the zodiac around the twelve houses and thus shows which sign you have rising or which sign was on Earth's eastern horizon when you were born, as well as where the sun, the moon, and all eight planets fall within each of your natal horoscope's twelve houses.

Taurus is the fixed-earth sign of the zodiac, and like all the fixed signs, Taurus sustains the mid-part of its season, which is spring, with Aries (cardinal) initiating the season and Gemini (mutable) ending the season. You can look to nature for information on every sign. Consider spring for a moment: Mother Nature is in full bloom, flowers greet us in abundance, trees are full with foliage that seems to have come to life overnight, as if

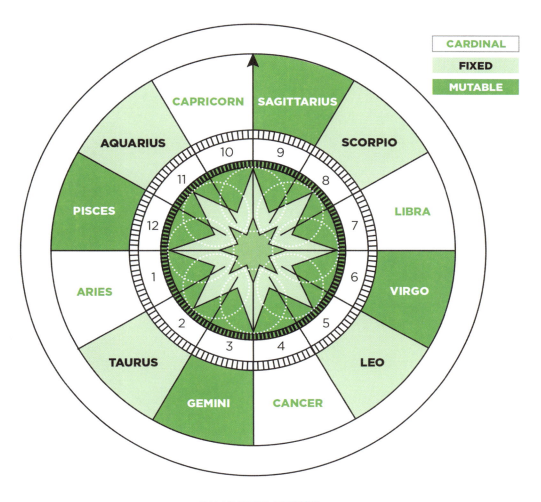

QUADRUPLICITIES

they had not been bare just days before. There is a general lightness and a welcome warmth in the air. It's not the beginning (Aries; cardinal) or end (Gemini; mutable) of the spring—it's smack-dab in the middle (fixed). Taurus sustains all that's been initiated before releasing into the end of the season. In the same way, if you are a Taurus or have Taurus Rising, you carry the sustaining qualities of a perpetual spring within you. Just as nature can't be rushed and steadily builds to bloom right on time, so it is with a Taurus.

Traditionally, the second of the twelve houses is Taurus's natural domain, with a focus on values, possessions, money, and self-esteem. This area of the chart offers insight into what we value most. We can learn much about our own self-esteem from the second house in both our solar and natal charts. It also offers insight into how we relate to material possessions and how we manage and leverage the resources available to us. Remember, Taurus is an earth sign, and so Taureans live in the practical realities of this world and are deeply enmeshed in pinpointing the task at hand and building it into a tangible reality. For this reason, the second house also correlates to ways in which we may earn monetary income.

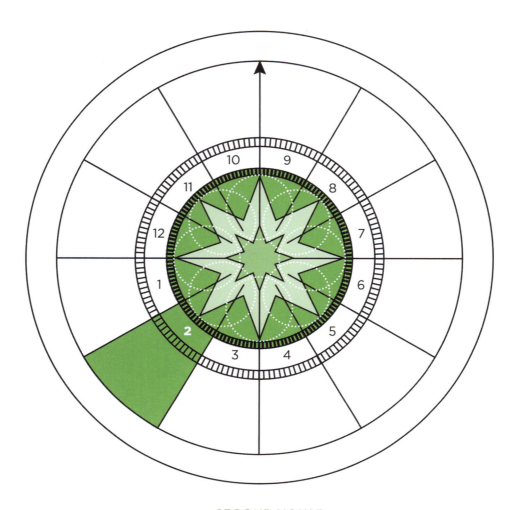

SECOND HOUSE

After all, money is a tangible resource, as any decent Taurus will gladly remind you.

Remember, if you are a Taurus or have Taurus Rising, you are a child of Venus, and so you are affected by her movements more than are the other signs, save for Libra, as Venus rules both Taurus and Libra. For this reason, pay close attention to when your favorite astrologer discusses Venus changing from one sign into another, which happens about every three and half weeks, especially when Venus retrogrades, which is once every eighteen months, to last approximately six weeks. Mark these dates on your calendar, as they will be periods in which you're especially sensitive to the energetic shifts at play. With Venus retrograde, you'll want to note that it is not a good time to launch a business or something you hope to be financially fruitful or for anything beauty related (think cosmetic surgery or drastic changes to your appearance).

Now that we've covered those fundamentals, I truly hope you enjoy your time spent exploring the sections that follow. May this chapter spark joy, produce "aha" moments, and assist you in solidifying your understanding of the zodiac's most down-to-earth sign, Taurus.

TAURUS AS A CHILD

To explore a child's experience of their unique astrological makeup requires a different approach than one used in exploring the chart of an adult, whose life is much farther along in the layers of its unfolding. Children's charts offer exciting insight into the seeds of their potential; their character is considered malleable and not yet fully formed. Children are still in the beginning stages of their lives, and thus everything related to a child's chart is an opportunity to root into. As a parent, investing in understanding your child's astrology will offer a wealth of knowledge about how to best guide and develop your child's innate gifts and skills and also will provide helpful information on navigating areas in life that may be a little tougher for your wee Taurus. The idea is to nurture and guide your child toward activities, teachers, and resources that may help them grow into their unique potentials and flourish on their path. Astrology can be such a helpful resource for parents! In this section you will learn more about what it means to have your little one's brightest light, their sun, in the sign of Taurus.

The child whose sun or rising sign is in Taurus is sensitive to their surroundings, as Taurus is the most sensual and sensory-oriented sign of the zodiac. These are the children who while playing outside will stop along the way to literally smell the roses, run their tiny fingers along a brick wall as they find the texture exhilarating, or sing along and dance with musicians and performers on the street. They are completely enthralled with worldly delights and have an uncanny knack for effortlessly finding them wherever they go. They also may be more attached to physical items as a source of comfort than are children of other signs: a blanket, a stuffed animal, or the tactile comfort of sucking one's thumb. I myself am a Taurus and admit I sucked my thumb until I was seven. It was an impossible habit to break. I found a deep sense of comfort in sucking my thumb or gently running my finger along my eyelid or the top part of my ear to fall asleep. Something about the texture and connection to habit itself was soothing. I also had a small purple blanket sprinkled with tiny sparkly silver stars (the foreshadowing!) named Blankie that I would take everywhere. I couldn't leave the house without it, and if I couldn't find it, I would be completely distraught until it was located. To say I was attached is to put it lightly. I was so in love with Blankie that I refused to allow my aunt and grandmother to make me a new one despite their pleading. I loved on Blankie so hard for so long that by the end it was in tatters. Even after I no longer needed Blankie, I didn't have the heart to toss it and so held on to it in a little box for years; its remains were mostly polyester stuffing with a few scraps of ratty purple fabric dotted with long-since-faded stars that I literally tied back together in knots as pieces fell off. I share this to show how deep Taureans' attachment can run to an item or habit we hold close to heart.

The planet Venus is Taurus's guiding light, and that imbues these children's nature with tenderness. Taurean children tend to be quite charming. They are warm and affectionate, bestowing you with an abundance of hugs, kisses, cuddles, and "I love yous"—they are sweet as can be, a true joy, and overall their temperament is easygoing. However, when they get upset, they're likely to be physical, using tough little fists and feet in protest, and probably forceful too—Taureans tend to have a sturdy build and a naturally strong constitution.

In the body, Taurus rules the neck, throat, vocal cords, and ears, and that gives these children a natural attunement to music, particularly singing and the performance arts in general. They are the children most likely to be your backseat entertainment (aside from Leo, of course), loving to sing along in the car, belting their tiny lungs out to today's greatest hits, not missing a beat and surprisingly on key. They also enjoy being sung to, so be sure to join in. Taurus is an exceedingly creative sign—there is a love and appreciation of art, dance, and music.

Thrilled by worldly delights and generally relaxed, they have an affable nature that ensures that they naturally make friends wherever they go. Their inclination toward physicality means a good run around the playground or a soothing drive in the car will have them out like a light, fully surrendering to naptime, in no time. This is not to say that they don't have a stubborn streak, which they surely do as one of the four fixed signs of the zodiac, the others being Leo, Aquarius, and Scorpio. Natives of the fixed signs are built to sustain, and so once they've made up their minds, redirecting them may prove to be a true challenge. Taurus children who have set their sights on something and have been told no are likely to dig in their heels and raise their fists in solid protest. Their will is so strong that they're likely to tire you out with their steadfastness rather than the other way around. Explain in practical terms what you're asking rather than making blunt demands—they'll eventually come around when they feel it was their own decision to do so. They have a strong will and attach to material things and loved ones deeply. Because of this, a kind of possessiveness may pervade them; as a young person, their sense of security is still forming, and so a parent or teacher requesting they share their most prized toy with someone else may throw them for a loop. However, Taurus children are typically generous as long as it's understood that the precious possession in question belongs to them at the end of the day.

Taurus children are delighted when it comes to mealtime, and they love to go out to eat—the whole experience feels like an exotic thrill. From real flowers on the table and the feel of the tablecloth to deciding what to order, they love the sense of community gathering around the table to share something delicious has the power to create. There is deep comfort to be found in a shared meal with people you love; it's one of life's simplest and most profound gifts. Food unites, nourishes, and comforts. A friend

> **Taurus children who have set their sights on something and have been told no are likely to dig in their heels and raise their fists in solid protest.**

whose younger brother is a Taurus shared that when the siblings were young, the brother would randomly shout, "Apple pie!" He'd wake up and gleefully announce, "Apple pie!" or walk into a room and declare, "Apple pie!"—it became a kind of official proclamation on the celebration of food and the joy of dessert within their family. His love of food, and clearly apple pie, was loud and clear from a young age.

Taurean children are tactile learners. They do well with immersive experiences to accompany their book learning and school assignments. This will help solidify their understanding through being able to get their hands dirty, build, touch, and fully experience the information introduced with all their senses. For this reason, they're sure to love recess and field trips. Recess offers a chance to get outside and experience the glory of nature, and school field trips to the aquarium, the museum, and historic sites offer the chance to learn in the hands-on way they really thrive with and adore.

On a similar note, teaching them early on the value of their effort, time, and resources through helping out around the house with chores is great for young Taureans. If they seem a little bored or are leaning toward laziness, give them a task! They'll perk right up at the chance to do something to be helpful—they relish the experience of seeing a project through and flourish on the appreciation that comes with a job well done. Offer an allowance for their effort, even if it's small. Since this is one of the signs most naturally inclined toward finances and managing resources, starting them off with a strong foundation around earning and saving will set them up for success and fine-tune their natural ability to accumulate wealth and manage their financial security later in life.

Taurus children do well with routines that are stuck to. They're not big fans of change, so introducing a change too quickly would likely have you in a standoff with a small person that may very well outlast you—Taurus kids can hold firm till the cows come home! They crave the comfort of what is known and familiar—they are creatures of habit. They find their routines soothing and steadying, which is important to them, as this is a security-oriented sign. Change is a necessary part of life, but when introducing it to a young Taurus, you will have more pleasant results for all parties involved if you do so slowly and over time whenever possible. Remain solid and consistent yourself, showing by example that all is well and that change is completely natural and nothing to fret about. Speaking of habits, ensure that good ones are set in place and try to nip any poor habits right away, as these little ones latch on to consistent habits quickly and it will be arduous to break a bad habit once they become accustomed to it.

As a Taurus child, I loved to put on little shows for my baby brother. I would set up the living room as my personal stage and dance around and maybe share a little impromptu song I was making up in the moment. Actually, as far back as I can remember, I have always loved to dance and sing, and singing in the car was my favorite! As a child I was obsessed with Whitney Houston—I knew every word of every song she sang. Her voice is perfection, and my Taurean sensibilities have always known it. You may be surprised by your little Taurus's natural sense of pitch at a young age. My friends and I were constantly putting together dance routines and loved competing in the lip-sync battle as part of our homecoming festivities in high school. My two besties, another Taurus and a Gemini, took it very seriously, putting together elaborate choreography and costumes and rehearsing to perfection for months in advance, every detail in place. We placed in the top three every year, with our senior year an all-out extravaganza to Michael Jackson's "Thriller," complete with a dozen other classmates as zombies popping out of seats in the audience. We were good too, so good that we had teachers trying to get us to spill what we'd do leading up to each year's competition, with other classmates spying on us to see what we had planned. Years later on a visit home, I ran into the band teacher at a coffee shop, and he told me that after we graduated the lip-sync competition was never the same. This is one of a Taurus's greatest skills: combining their talents with their above-average diligence to achieve a level of excellence through consistent effort, which inspires others around them to do the same.

TAURUS AS AN ADULT

THE TAURUS SUN or Taurus Rising person has a soothing, steady presence. These individuals radiate a natural sense of calm wherever they go. When they are with you, they give you their full attention. Making those around them feel seen and heard is a rare gift of theirs. They are the friends of the zodiac who will gently touch your arm rather than speak to make their presence known, are generous with hugs at both hello and good-bye, and hold your hand tight when sharing an emotional story. You can trust your steadfast, devoted Taurus friend to be there to comfort you when you need it. Not only will Taurus friends be there, they will arrive with wine in hand, a perfectly paired cheese to match, and a willing ear ready to listen. Their attention is fully focused; they are great listeners and do not rush you—you will have their undivided attention. Their patience is admirable and is part of what makes them so likable. They exude grace and charm and have an easygoing way about them, and they tend to get along with most people. They are sure to make you laugh and feel loved, all with a little twinkle in their eyes; they enjoy spreading joy. They have a warm glow about them, thanks to Venus, the planet of love, affection, and friendship that governs their sign.

Taureans are patient and persistent; they take their time to make a decision, but when they do, they make it with their whole will and heart. You can count on them to follow through on what they've said they will do. Exploring the world with a Taurus is a luxurious experience, as this is the most sensory-oriented sign of the zodiac. Each of their senses is heightened, and that gives them refined tastes. Want to experience the best the world has to offer? Befriend a Taurus, and they will lead the way. They'll take you to the best new restaurant in the neighborhood, a gorgeous part of the park you hadn't noticed before, or an exceptional music venue featuring unparalleled talent—their taste is impeccable. Their finely tuned senses won't allow them to settle for less, and so they won't let you, their dear friend, colleague, or lover, settle for less either!

They are also some of the most reliable people you will ever meet. If they commit themselves to a task, you can bet your bottom dollar they will follow through. They are thorough too; they may be slow moving, but trust that what needs doing will be done with the utmost care and attention. Taureans have a strong sense of their own values. They are rock solid, and that is one of the greatest benefits of knowing and loving them. This quality can be frustrating at times, however. I say this because Taureans are so steadfast, they can end up a bit stuck in their ways. They are the fixed-earth sign of the zodiac, after all. I like to say, "A Taurus in motion stays in motion." This means that once they are set on their course, they are unlikely to change because you have told them to or have suggested another way of doing things. Taureans much prefer to deal with change on their own terms and in their own time. Just like the bull, they are slow and steady and unmovable until they decide it's time to move. Offer your insight, then give them time and space. They will come around once they have had time to consider all the options and realize you have a good point. They are security-oriented creatures, so change is no thrill for them. They much prefer the known tried-and-true way of doing things. Why rock the boat? Why fix what isn't broken? They have a reputation for clinging to habits, and so veering from the known is unsettling to them. However, their steadfastness is what makes them such loyal lifelong comrades, and they will prove time and again to be a stable anchor through some of life's most rocky moments. They aren't the ones who flee when the going gets tough. This is not to say that Taureans don't have limits—they do. They just have a wide threshold, as they're very tolerant. Still, a Taurus pushed too far is no joke. It takes a lot to rile them, as the bull is stable and unmovable, but when they are provoked too hard, you can have quite the fury on your hands.

Taureans are sensual souls, using all their senses to navigate the world around them. They make spectacular lovers for this reason. There is a transcendence in their touch, a tranquility innate within their voice, and a radiant warmth to their aura. Because they are ruled by the planet Venus, their affections are infused with a level of grace and warmth completely individual to their sign. There will be no doubt you're cared for when you date a Taurus. They'll wine you, dine you . . . and, well, you get the picture! When they care for you, they invest in you through the selfless offering of their time, energy, and resources. They're true-blue loyal to the ones they love and thrive on appreciation in return for their efforts. Taurus is a receptive sign: Taureans give love openly but also need this kind of openness in return. They tend to stay present in the current moment rather than dwelling on the past or fretting about the future—as their heightened senses keep them connected to what's happening in the moment.

Taurus is all about values with a capital V. They carefully and thoughtfully select their things, think big purchases through, and take pride in their wardrobe of hand-selected prized pieces made of the finest fabrics in beautiful shades. To give a personal example, when I traveled to Greece, there was a miscommunication concerning my luggage. I was headed to Crete but first had a layover in Athens, and the attendant checking my bag heard only Athens. When I arrived in Crete, I watched as hundreds of bags were carouselled out. Being the good little Taurus I am, I waited patiently as the crowd eventually thinned until there were only two of us remaining, with no more bags. After about an hour of waiting, the panic set in. Oh, no! My precious, carefully curated things! As I filled out the claim to find my bag in Athens and have it sent to Crete, I did mental gymnastics,

> **Taureans much prefer to deal with change on their own terms and in their own time. Just like the bull, they are slow and steady and unmovable until they decide it's time to move.**

thinking of my favorite pieces—some of them irreplaceable should my bag not be found. This cataloging of possessions is a classic tactic I subconsciously revert to as a means of protecting myself, to make sure I am safe—because as you now know, we Taureans are a fixed sign, and we hold tightly to our perceptions of security. We like to stick to what we know works. When a wrench gets thrown into the mix, it can make our whole system go haywire. My travel buddy, whose sun and rising signs are mutable, or flexible, signs, was cool as a cucumber, saying this had happened to her twice and both times the bag was recovered, no problem. Once, she told me, it even happened hours before she had an appearance on television! I was horrified at the thought, though she was able to laugh about it and seemed unconcerned. This is an excellent example of why we need an eclectic mix of people of all signs in our lives. Her flexibility in the moment was enough to shake me loose from my tight fixed grip on the situation and make me consider a different way of reacting. They found my bag and returned it to me the very next day. Crisis averted. I share this story to show how we Taureans are so attached to the physical. Our sensitive sensory system makes us more attuned to the tangible world around us, and so we attach meaning to and place special emphasis on our prized possessions. Oh, and by the way, one such prized possession in my bag that day was a one-of-a-kind vintage silk blouse, the most delicate pink with a hand-painted rose on it—can you get any more Venusian than that?

In their careers, Taureans take a pragmatic approach. As security-oriented beings, they like to know what's expected of them, and of course, being ruled by Venus, they are focused on finances. Figuring out how to grow their nest egg is important to them, as well as feeling valued for their time and efforts. Venus rules love and relationships. It is considered what's known as a "benefic planet," as whatever Venus touches tends to have a beneficial outcome, including aspects of our lives related to money. With Venus as their planetary ruler, Taureans have a leg up when it comes to financial savvy. As one of my beloved mentors, Susan Miller, likes to say, "Taurus is the sign most likely to be at home on a Friday night with nice glass of wine, reviewing their bank statement." They are naturally skilled and practical when it comes to taking an idea, shaping it into something tangible that can turn a profit, and then making that profit multiply through diligent planning, saving, and investing. They are particularly adept when it comes to finances and managing resources to maximize results. Taurus traditionally oversees the second house, the area of the chart related to earned income, and so with wise decision making, Taureans are likely to accumulate wealth throughout their lifetimes.

Venus's influence assists Taureans in finding success in a number of fields, such as the performing arts, dance, and especially singing; they are often gifted vocally, with many well-known singers being Taureans. They also do well in professions that entail managing money, tending to the land, or working with food, such as banking, financial planning, real estate, farming, and landscaping, or in the culinary arts as a chef or sommelier. They may have great success in trades that involve caring for our physical form, including bodywork such as massage and in beauty-related professions such as a perfumer.

TAURUS IN LOVE

TAURUS IS RULED by the planet of love and affection, Venus. Under Venus's tutelage, a Taurus native has a magnetic allure that is impossible to deny and a tactile style of affection that is simply irresistible, not to mention that Taureans are overall easygoing with a great sense of humor. Taureans are some of the most affectionate and receptive people with whom you could hope to pair. Their delicate sensory abilities steer them straight toward the finest wine, first-rate restaurants, fine chocolates, soft floral perfumes, and dreamy lush locales for vacationing. You are lucky if you love a Taurus, as you'll reap the benefits of accompanying them on their elevated sensory adventures.

In the introduction to this chapter, we discussed how each of the signs has an element and modality with which it correlates. Since Taurus is the fixed-earth sign, Taureans find common ground and harmony with other earth signs, which are Virgo and Capricorn, and also with the water signs: Cancer, Scorpio, and Pisces. If you consider the elements and the ways they may blend, it's easy to see that earth and water are a natural duo, with earth absorbing water and the combination creating the perfect climate for abundant growth. Taureans may feel a strong bond with the other fixed signs as well, as there is a sense of kinship in their abilities to sustain and see something through. Fellow fixed signs are Leo (fixed-fire), Scorpio (fixed-water), and Aquarius (fixed-air). I should also mention that there is potential for some butting of heads with the fixed combos, as each stands firm in its own right.

TAUREANS' COMPATIBILITY WITH THE OTHER SIGNS OF THE ZODIAC

I am asked all the time, "Are there signs I should avoid or signs I shouldn't be with?" I believe any two signs can work together romantically or otherwise with a little love and effort. Every relationship offers us an opportunity to grow, and so I would never recommend dismissing people because of their signs. Please don't do that, because you will close yourself off to such a wide pool of experience and potentially wonderful connection if you do. Each of the signs is equally valid and has its own wonders, gifts, and complexities to uncover and learn from. Don't limit yourself!

This is of course in reference to an individual's sun sign, so also keep in mind that you each have several other factors to consider as they relate to the complexities of your charts as a whole. The combinations with Taurus below can be interpreted from a romantic perspective, though the descriptions can easily apply to friendship and business relationships as well. Just adjust the wording to suit your situation for helpful clues to how Taurus works together with each of the other signs. Now, let's take a look and see how Taurus plays with the rest of the zodiac.

TAURUS WITH ARIES
(cardinal-fire)

These two are quite different: Aries thrives on initiation, action, and loves to go, go, go, whereas Taureans much prefer to take their time and work slowly toward a goal. Perhaps you will butt heads on this from time to time, but Aries reminds their Taurus companion to take change in stride and get out of their comfort zone, and Taurus has an anchoring effect for Aries.

TAURUS WITH TAURUS
(fixed-earth)

A pair of Taureans are right at home together. You're on the same page; you just get each other. You have the same Venusian sensibilities and share a love of the arts, music, delicious food, and life's comforts. This is a double dose of fixed-earth, however, which means it may be easy to fall into the same old patterns and routines together. You'll have to intentionally find ways to spice it up from time to time to keep things fresh!

TAURUS WITH GEMINI
(mutable-air)

Geminis are mentally astute and quite clever, with varied interests. They tend to enjoy a detached way of living, which may prove a challenge for a Taurus. Taureans much prefer the comforts and security that a forever home, stable job, and attached relationship bring. The gift of this combo is that Gemini may teach Taurus the joys of letting go and wandering where one's curiosity leads, whereas Taurus shows Gemini the benefit of seeing an interest through and the joy of mastering a skill because of one's steadfastness.

TAURUS WITH CANCER
(cardinal-water)

This is a very sweet combo. Taurus and Cancer are both quite sensitive, and they both love the security of home, family time, cooking, and cuddling and are equally protective of what they've created together. Cancer is connected to matters of home and establishing a place that feels warm and loving, whereas Taurus works hard to create a sense of security that stabilizes and maintains that home life. You'll want an invitation to their dinner parties!

TAURUS WITH LEO
(fixed-fire)

Leo and Taurus really know how to have a good time. The two share an affinity for luxury, fine dining, and being an active part of the local cultural scene, not to mention that both are extremely creative in their own right. Their fixed natures create a mutual understanding, although from a different perspective, there is the potential for both parties to be quite headstrong when there's a disagreement. Taurus needs affection and appreciation, and Leo needs attention and respect. If both can learn to meet each other on those things, they'll be on their way.

TAURUS WITH VIRGO
(mutable-earth)

Taurus and fellow earth sign Virgo get along beautifully, as they share a desire to build something of worth and integrity and are each naturally humble. Virgo is the mutable-earth sign, whereas Taurus is the fixed-earth sign. Virgo's flexibility helps Taurus see the value in pivoting when necessary so that things don't get too rigid, and Taurus's ability to follow through on promises made is reassuring to Virgo.

TAURUS WITH LIBRA
(cardinal-air)

Libra is a super-social sign and is most at home through connection to others. Social interactions stimulate their airy qualities assisting them to explore perspectives outside their own, which they enjoy. Taurus is not antisocial by any means but doesn't need the level of social stimulation Libra may want. Taureans like to sit with an idea, mull it over, and come to their own conclusion, whereas Libras like to get everyone's opinion to determine what makes the most sense based on varied perspectives. They do share Venus as their planetary ruler, and that creates harmony between them. They are truly a pair in their warmheartedness and softness and in their commitment to the ideals of beauty, grace, and pleasure.

TAURUS WITH SCORPIO
(fixed-water)

This combo proves that opposites really do attract. Polarity is the word used to describe opposing signs, or signs that sit 180 degrees across the wheel from one another. Scorpio is the sign that sits opposite Taurus. It may sounds counterintuitive, but actually opposing signs have a natural affinity for each other—they tend to balance each other. Taurus and Scorpio are both fixed signs: Taurus is the fixed-earth sign, and Scorpio is the fixed-water sign. They each have a staunch attitude thanks to their fixed natures, and their elements—earth and water—create the ideal alchemy. Earth absorbs water, creating the perfect environment for life to grow and flourish. Both are determined and aren't easily steered off course, and that could potentially create competitiveness—though they tend to see eye to eye, but from opposing perspectives. Scorpios approach a situation by using their intuition and emotional intelligence as a result of their water influence, whereas Taureans take a more logical and grounded approach because of their earthy qualities.

TAURUS WITH SAGITTARIUS
(mutable-fire)

Sagittarians are freedom loving and changeable, and their untethered nature can feel unsettling for a Taurus, whereas a Taurus's set ways and inflexibility can feel a bit too prohibitive for a Sagittarius. The two will need to be dedicated to understanding the other's perspective and compromise to accommodate the other's needs. The beauty of this combo, however, is that Sagittarius will inspire and ignite Taurus to action, and Taurus will offer Sagittarius practical advice that gives their big-picture dreams a firm footing.

TAURUS WITH CAPRICORN
(cardinal-earth)

Fellow earth sign Capricorn is a natural fit with Taurus. Taurus admires Capricorn's tenacity and hardworking nature. Their ability to set a goal with practical steps to achieve it is a real turn-on for Taurus, whereas Capricorn's sometimes doubtful nature appreciates Taurus's tender heart, honesty, and encouragement to stay the course. The two also have similar goals in regard to building their assets, bank accounts, and list of accolades for their hard work. There is mutual understanding with these two.

TAURUS WITH AQUARIUS
(fixed-air)

Aquarians have their sights set on the future. They're more interested in where we're going than in where we've been, whereas Taureans prefer to remain squarely in the present. Taurus may have a hard time understanding why Aquarius wants to re-create what's already been established, and Aquarius will be perplexed by Taurus's attachment to material things and immutable concepts of security, much preferring a detached mode of being. There will be challenges to meeting each other in the middle, though they are both fixed signs—Taurus is the fixed-earth, and Aquarius is fixed-air. There is respect for each other's commitment to a cause but sometimes conflicts in working together to achieve it.

TAURUS WITH PISCES
(mutable-water)

Taurus and Pisces make for a dreamy duo. Both are highly creative, and their earth and water combo is fertile ground for inspired artistic pursuits. There is a shared love for film, the theater, dance, and definitely music, and they'll never be at a loss for activities to do together. Pisces is more detached from earthly necessities than Taurus. Pisceans are not materialistic and don't care much for money or the mundane realities of life, whereas Taureans care deeply about the material world, and creating a sense of tangible security through their home and financial resources. Differences in this area may baffle both partners, but there are helpful connections within these differences. Pisces's fluidity and flexibility remind Taurus of the importance of giving back and being charitable with their resources, as nothing is permanent, whereas Taurus's stable rootedness assists Pisces in making more of their inspired visions tangible realities than would be the case if they were on their own. There is a softness to each of these signs that ensures a tender, gentle, and loving combo.

TAURUS LOVER

When a Taurus loves you, you will know it; there will be no question about it. Their affection will be apparent in the kindness and tenderness of their words and touch; they can be quite sentimental and poetic as a result of their creative inclinations. As Taurean and queen of jazz Ella Fitzgerald said, "I guess what everyone wants more than anything else is to be loved. And to know that you loved me for my singing is too much for me. Forgive me if I don't have all the words. Maybe I can sing it and you'll understand." Their love is clear, honest, and genuine. There's not a lot of game playing or confusion (assuming there aren't any complicated aspects to their natal Venus or moon, for example). There is a kind admirable simplicity to a Taurus's affection—it's warm, sensual, and unwavering. It may take Taureans a while to decide you're the one for them, but don't take offense; this is because they are careful. They're not likely to rush into something or make rash decisions about the gift of their affection, but once they decide, they are all in. Taurus is one of the most devoted partners you could ever ask for and will stand by your side through and through. Loyalty is major for Taureans. Once they've decided you're the one for them, they become deeply invested and will do almost anything for you. To be clear, they expect the same kind of loyalty and commitment in return and don't handle a breach or lack of it well. They are loyal almost to a fault, at times staying the course when it would be best to leave. However, if a lack of loyalty is clear from the get-go, they're likely to back out as the connection just won't feel sustainable to them.

When you are dating a Taurus, consistency and follow-through really get their heart rate up. Ask them out and follow through, with no rescheduling multiple times, no flaky hard-to-get games; show them you're interested and then see the plan through. As this is an earth sign, their preference leans solidly toward in-person dating as opposed to long distance, since they crave the comfort of tactile experiences, especially with their love. It would be burdensome to not see or touch their beloved for long periods. They are well versed in body language, and no amount of video chat or texting could replace that for them. Taureans are sensualists; they enjoy physical affection, and that transfers to the bedroom as well—Taurus is inherently gifted in regard to sexual prowess. They aim to please and be pleased and are not shy with the gift of their attention; they enjoy doting on their lovers.

A fun first date for a Taurus may include going to an acclaimed restaurant with rave reviews, a walk in the park with fair-trade locally roasted coffee in hand, finding a cozy garden cafe to sip wine and lose yourselves in intimate conversation, or sharing your favorite art exhibit or museum with them. These experiences will make them feel seen and cherished and are a surefire way to impress them.

TAURUS PARTNER

When the time comes to take it to the next level with a Taurus, such as moving in together, you can be sure that the lease will be reviewed in full, mail will be forwarded ahead of time, the moving truck will be booked well in advance, and utilities will be scheduled to come on upon move-in.

They are thorough people. Although they move at their own pace and cannot be rushed, you can trust that all will be accomplished as a result of their thought-out methodical approach. You'll enjoy an upgrade to your living space too thanks to your Taurus love's inclination toward all that is luxurious and comfort-oriented. Think soft lighting, lush fabrics, comfortable furnishings with beautiful natural finishes in hardwood, and lots of plants in an effort to invite nature indoors.

In dating and marriage alike, Taureans are loyal and true. Their close relationships are precious to them, and so they work hard to provide a stable and secure home life for themselves and their loved ones. They are present and attentive as well as supportive of a partner's goals. It really feels like a team effort when you're in it with a Taurus.

TAURUS AT WORK

TAUREANS ARE HARD workers; they sometimes get a bad rap for being lazy, but they actually love to be useful. They will be the ones to ensure that a project is seen all the way through, beginning to end, with all the boxes checked. They are thorough through and through and much prefer something done well over time to something done at half quality but completed quickly. As the sign that sustains the season of spring, they aren't concerned with rushing. As Lao Tzu said, "Nature does not hurry, yet everything is accomplished."

In the body, Taurus rules the throat, vocal cords, and thyroid as well as the ears. Taureans are sensitive to sound—as a sign ruled by Venus, they have a refined ear for music and often have quite skilled vocal abilities. They adore the arts and may be drawn to pursue them through careers as performers, dancers, artists, and vocalists. They may also have much success in beauty and healing services that incorporate the body, such as an esthetician or massage therapist. My lifelong best friend Cassandra, another Taurus, born the day after me, April 26, is a dancer and yoga teacher. Her yoga classes are very hands-on and almost always include essential oils on her warmed hands for students to inhale during the final Savasana, or final relaxation pose, and usually incorporate a little neck massage too, ensuring that her students release fully into a relaxed state. Her area of expertise is restorative yoga and Yoga Nidra, variations meant to slow one down and calm the nervous system. How Taurean is that? She once shared with me that she often finds it easier to express herself through dance, using her body rather than spoken words. It makes sense, doesn't it? With their heightened sensory abilities, it seems Taureans have easier access to expression through the body—touch, smell, taste, and sound—as opposed to words alone, which rely on logic, to get their message across.

On a similar note, one of the loveliest facials I've ever received was with an esthetician who had Taurus Rising. It incorporated facial massage that was downright intuitive, and everything down to the dimmed lighting and music at precisely the correct subdued volume was just right—Taurus knows how to create an atmosphere. Their ruling planet, Venus, has much to do with their atmospheric discernment. Venus rules the sensual but doesn't stop there. As I mentioned earlier in the chapter, Venus also oversees finances, and so Taureans may very well be skilled in banking and finance positions as well as real estate. Their earthy nature means they may thrive in fields that deal with food, such as gourmet grocery and catering, as chefs or sommeliers, and in farming.

Venus also relates to women and women's causes, and the divine feminine nature within all of us (which we all have regardless of how we identify in terms of gender), and so Taureans may be drawn to work that champions women's interests, causes, and rights. It's also important for Taureans to feel they're working toward something that matters to them. They can really build something solid through their efforts, though if they can't see the point, it will be much more difficult for them to maintain motivation. Janet Jackson, a singer, dancer, and Taurus, said, "If I wasn't singing, I'd probably be an accountant." I find the juxtaposition interesting in relation to something Harry S. Truman, the thirty-third U.S. president and a Taurus, said: "If I hadn't been President of the United States, I probably would have ended up a piano player in a bawdy house." Both Jackson and Truman, each a well-known Taurus in different positions at different times in history, said if they weren't pursuing their profession, they'd be doing something seemingly on the opposite end of the spectrum but still equally Taurean in its own right. With Janet—if not music, then finance; with Truman, if not being entrusted with one of the highest responsibilities, then music. Both encapsulate the full essence of their sun sign, Taurus.

Taurus has a fascination with value and consequently money. On a nine-hour international flight, I was in admiration of the attendants' ability to remain cheerful while serving two meals, including cleanup, in tight quarters, all while zipping across time zones. I then caught myself thinking, "They must get paid well." And then, "Oh, God, I hope they get paid well!" Believing proper compensation plays a large part in the acknowledgment of a job well done, a Taurus will always see the value in compensation that matches the time and effort. Also, this is not the first time I've caught myself in that thought, in true Taurus fashion. I am always curious about what people do and the value attached to it—it's an innate curiosity about how people earn and then what they decide to do. A big part of Taurus's sense of security is tied to these concepts, and so I suppose it's no surprise my Taurean instincts go there.

Taureans are not afraid of hard work whether it is in the arts or at a bank. They give it their all and quite enjoy it if they can see the value in what they're doing. There is a specific kind of pleasure that comes from exerting yourself and getting to see the fruits of your labor. Taureans are deliberate about how and when they spend their energy. You've probably seen mentions on the internet about Taureans being lazy. I've never fully bought into that, as it's a little too vague; I think this stereotype may have more to do with motivation than with sheer laziness. Why should Taureans budge from a comfy seat if they don't see the value of the effort? When they do decide to commit, they're all in, and they give their fullest—and they'll also require the rest that is their due once they're done. A Taurus can't be rushed once they sit down to relax. Everything has its time and purpose when it comes to this sign.

A Taurus at work is a doer. They like to know what's expected of them and then get to it. Taureans also tend to do well under pressure and take challenges in stride; they're steady by nature, and so it takes quite a lot to unsettle them. A Taurean tends to be a steadfast force in the workplace and a calming presence. I have a dear friend, Linda, a Capricorn and private chef, whom I've helped on some very high-end, high-stress intimate dinners and parties over the years. I felt so much pride when she told me I was one of her favorite friends to have help because she found my presence in those situations calming; even when there was chaos or demanding clients, I managed to stay steady as a rock. I take so much pride in this compliment! This is not to say we Taureans never get stressed, but it's fair to say that when we do get stressed, we tend to dig in and root down, which definitely has an anchoring effect.

Taurus is a security-centered sign. Change is not their favorite thing in the world, as it may threaten to rock the boat of their precious stability. They like to know where their paycheck is coming from, how much, and how frequently. For this reason they prefer jobs that have stability and room to grow, with a consistent and reliable paycheck. Truth be told, they'll do whatever they set their minds to, though jobs at which variables are flexible, such as sales or working on commission, are not likely to be their first choice. Taking big risks regularly in their business affairs is not for them.

A Taurus in a senior position makes for a fair boss. They are clear and direct, and they expect you to do what you've said you will do. They are patient and prefer that things be done well and so are willing to invest time and money in your training. They'll expect you to be on time, give your very best, and follow through. They appreciate honest, genuine people and want them on their team.

Taureans in junior positions won't mind answering to their superiors. They understand that it takes time to build a career and reach the higher ranks. They're happy to launch right into their assignments and will work hard to earn their way up. Taureans do well when they

> Janet Jackson, a singer, dancer, and Taurus, said, "If I wasn't singing, I'd probably be an accountant."

have a clear understanding of what's expected of them, while unclear direction may cause frustration and lead to doubts about their superior's judgment.

Taurus employees are diligent and will accomplish every task asked of them, but once they find their routine, they won't appreciate it being changed much. It's true that they can be stubborn and set in their ways: If it works, why change it? It's unlikely that they will be persuaded to change easily. It has to be their idea, so provide them with clear-cut facts and a little time and they'll soon come around.

CONCLUSION

ASTROLOGY OPENS OUR perceptions to a world brimming with potential within ourselves and also within each person in our lives, extending outward into the world. It broadens our view, enables us to see a situation from a new angle, and is a source of great compassion as it increases our empathy for not only our own situation but also the situations of the people around us, as well as offering invaluable insight into current events.

As you now know, astrology is much bigger than any one sign alone; its true value lies in the understanding of the sum of all of its parts. Each sign of the zodiac holds special significance

> **Learning about your personal astrology will open a world of opportunity to you.**

in and of itself, but no one sign is better than any other, just as no one person is an island. As I said in the introduction to this chapter, "As above, so below—as within, so without." We are intrinsically linked to all of nature. We each have a responsibility to ourselves to strive to be the best we can be, and that has a reverb effect that extends much farther than ourselves. There is a dignity and great responsibility within the study and practice of astrology, my hope is that you will take this to heart and continue to expand your understanding.

The ancients were clearly on to something, as we still use astrology to inform greater understanding today after thousands of years. From its early beginnings in Mesopotamia to modern times, astrology has persisted because it works. Astrology is not predestination or a religion but rather a tool to help us navigate our lives and make more conscious decisions that are based on our unique challenges and strengths in any situation. We have free will and choose how to participate with the cosmic climate every step of the way. When you begin to study and use astrology in practice, that is when it really comes alive, and you reap the benefits within your life. It takes some time and commitment to learn, as astrology is a complex study, but I can assure you from my own experience that it's worth it! In fact, I never in a million years thought I would be working as a professional astrologer. Years ago a friend suggested that I take my now mentor Rebecca Gordon's beginner astrology course, and it was all over from there. It's true that astrology finds you.

If you are curious, if astrology's concepts stir excitement within you, keep going, keep learning, commit, and really go for it! I think each of us is a skeptic, and rightfully so, until we take the time to learn and see how astrology actually works. Astrology is the study of planetary cycles and possibility, an exploration of the synergy at play between the sun, the other luminary—the moon of course, all eight planets, and all twelve signs of the zodiac, as well as the twelve houses that the planets and the signs of the zodiac fall within. All parts must be integrated to best understand the whole. Most are aware of sun sign astrology, horoscopes in the paper, for example, and for good reason—the sun plays an extremely important role within our personal astrology and is the base of our solar chart. It's the core of who we are, but the scope of astrology in fact stretches much farther beyond your sun sign alone. Learning about your personal astrology will open a world of opportunity to you. The natal chart, based on your exact birth information is completely unique to you, your cosmic fingerprint. It will reveal intimate details such as your rising sign, as well as your sun, moon, and planetary placements within the signs and houses. The inner planets relate to your personality (Mercury, Venus, Mars)—the midplanets, Jupiter and Saturn, affect trends of the time—and your outer planetary placements (Uranus, Neptune, Pluto)—relate to generational influences. The outer planets move very slowly, staying in one sign for years at a time, and for this reason have a generational influence, whereas the inner planets make their trip around the sun quickly, thus change sign more frequently, and so relate more to our nuanced personalities in studying a natal chart. These factors are also the reason why you can meet another Taurus who has much different characteristics than you do but still has a similar guiding principle and sense of purpose.

It's important to integrate the chart as a whole in addition to learning about your sun sign. Also, if you have your birth time, you can calculate your chart through many free resources online. You will need your birth date, including the year; your exact time of birth; and your birth location. You will be prompted to enter your birth information; these sites will tell you what sign was rising on Earth's eastern horizon when you were born. The rising sign is also known as the ascendant (ASC). If you're unsure of your birth time, flip back to the introduction to this chapter, where I give some handy ways to procure it. Once you know your rising sign, or sign on your ascendant, be sure to read the chapter for that sign as well. You can also read your favorite horoscope column for both your sun and rising signs, and I hope you do! You'll get a much better idea of the big picture when you do.

Taureans are intrinsically linked to the planet Venus; they are some of the most affectionate, genuine, and reliable people you could ever hope to know. Right from the beginning straight through to the end, from childhood to adulthood, in all facets of life, it's clear that Taurus is a sensual, stable, loyal, and calming force through and through. Want to enjoy life's pleasures more? Date a Taurus. Want someone to stand by you with a steadfastness that verges on the spiritual? Befriend a Taurus. Want someone you can trust completely to help build your business into a solid empire? Hire a Taurus. My hope is that through reading this chapter on Taurus you now have a deeper understanding of Taureans' nature, what drives them, and how to best utilize their natural gifts at work, in love, and in living life to the fullest.

You read this chapter and made the decision to expand your knowledge of Taurus in all its beautiful intricacies, so that is a great start! I hope you'll explore the other eleven chapters as well, rounding out your understanding of the entire zodiac for the best results. The more we actively invest in learning about ourselves and one another and in experiences outside of our own, the more we foster an environment for compassion and understanding to thrive. This has a unifying ripple effect within our closest relationships, our community, our city, state, country, across the world, and beyond. As the spiritual teacher Ram Dass said, "We're all just walking each other home." I thank you with all my heart for taking the time to read this chapter.

MAY 21–JUNE 23

text by Colin Bedell

element — AIR

symbol — THE TWINS

modality — MUTABLE

house — THIRD

ruler — MERCURY

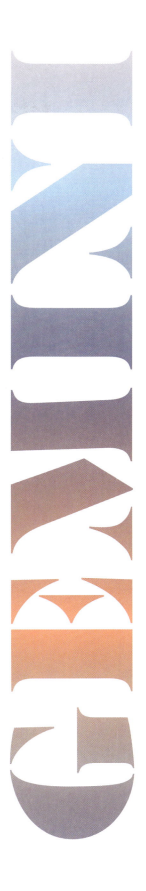

CEYLON

INTRODUCTION

AFTER THE SLUMBER of winter and in the midst of spring's full flowering, a Gemini is born. At the moment of a Gemini birth, the sun shines behind the constellation of the Great Twins, and a soul enters the Earth armed with the knowledge of how to change a heart, which is the intelligence that can change the world.

The zodiac year begins on the spring equinox, when the universe honors Aries the Ram. This first sign in the zodiac teaches us how to explore our identity, power, divinity, passions, and lovability. Then, on April 21, Taurus the Bull gently stewards us out of Aries's Martian fire and into the Venusian Eden of aesthetics, pleasure, personal security, and clarity. Aries helps understand what follows after "I am . . . ," and Taurus places the answers to "I have . . ." in our hands and heart. On May 21, the zodiac calendar follows the first two animal signs with human twins. Building on the foundation of the Aries fire of identity and the Taurus groundedness that keeps us secure and in pleasure, Gemini points to our mind and mouth to help us answer the question, "I think . . ."

When the planets shine behind Gemini, we're all asked to think critically, exercise adaptability, sharpen our verbal communication skills, concentrate on active listening, cause a bit of friendly mischief, and—as the symbolism of the Twins teaches us—interpersonally connect with others. Those born between May 21 and June 21 and/or carrying other personal planet aspects in Gemini—from the rising to the moon, Mercury, Venus, and Mars—are the messengers assigned to lead these crucial efforts and teach their successful application so the rest of the zodiac can learn from them.

That's likely you. If you're the one holding Gemini in your hands, then you likely have Gemini as your sun, moon, or rising sign. If you are a Gemini, then you probably already deduced that within each one is two. You have two power sources for the price of one. You have twice as much mental agility, speed, versatility, and skill to explore in this life than the other signs. You make life management and success look easy. Your ruling mythological story, planet, modality, and element help you fly to the heights you dream of, while you inspire others to do the same.

Many ancient cultures, from the Norse countries (named Freyr and Freyja), to Nigeria (Ibegii—the twins of joy and happiness), to Egypt (Nut and Geb), have a myth of the Great Twins, though the archetype for Gemini was largely inspired by the ancient Greeks. Twins named Castor and Pollux were born to the queen of Sparta, but Castor was fathered by a mortal while Pollux was fathered by the king of the Gods, Zeus himself. Myth tells us that these fraternal twins were inseparably loyal to each other, especially on heroic adventures searching for the Golden Fleece among carnage-ridden battlefields. Tragically, mortal Castor was lost in battle. When his immortal twin, Pollux, begged his divine father, Zeus, to reunite them, the Olympian king placed Castor and Pollux into the Gemini constellation, where they live together to this day.

I think it's important to take this myth with us throughout the rest of this chapter. This story is told through the lens of relationships, love, and loyalty. If Gemini is the first of two zodiac signs iconized by humans—the other being its Mercury sibling, Virgo the singular Maiden Woman—it is also crucial to hold in our heads and hearts that the first sign appears as two figures. Humanity begins

Castor and Pollux

with connection. Social theory reminds us that human beings are hardwired for interpersonal relationship. Couples therapist Esther Perel regularly shares that the quality of our relationships determines the quality of our lives.[1] As we'll explore later in the third section, "Gemini in Love," the Gemini archetype and function aren't just arcane knowledge, but are actual forms of energy that exist between two people, from the most casual to the most intimate of connection, when they feel seen, understood, and loved. Prioritizing relationships and engaging in the communication practices that sustain connection enhance the quality of our lives. If this connection is absent in relationships, suffering, addiction, anxiety, and depression can grow. So it's important to see the Gemini Twins as teachers of connection, as that's how they appear intentionally in the zodiac.

Every sign is ruled by a planet, which seamlessly matches the energy of the sign itself. Mercury rules both Gemini and Virgo, given their relationship to cognition, communication, transportation, technology, and active intelligence. Since Mercury is the first planet next to the sun, it is the celestial subject of superlatives, as Mercury is the smallest, closest, quickest, and hottest planet in our solar system. This demonstrates the superlative possibilities available to Gemini, who's invited to be the quickest, funniest, most agile, most controversial, and most energetic person in whichever room, relationship, office, or campus they find themselves in.

Returning to ancient mythology, Mercury was the messenger god who flew between the highest heavens of Mount Olympus and the lowest depths of the Underworld, ushering critical information between these diametrically opposed forces, and even ferrying souls from the realm of the living to the realm of the dead. His Greek namesake, Hermes, means "persuasive tongue." While the shadow side of Gemini can manifest as a person who only wants to keep it heavenly and light-filled *or* hellish and cynical, high-minded Geminis allow themselves to soar to both the highest realms of thought that consciousness can allow, but also develop a perspective capable of discovering the deepest wisdom of heartbreak and suffering. This sophisticated ability to comprehend both extremes of human nature is inherent in Gemini's dualism. Society, on a personal and global level, fails when it can't hold space for that nuance. If Geminis are brave enough to convey the truth in these observations, then they can use their words to righteously inspire others.

One of the easiest ways to understand the dimensions of a zodiac sign is to remember that each one is a unique combination of two astrological concepts: an element and a modality. In order of appearance throughout the zodiac, the four elements are fire, earth, air, and water. Chronologically, the three modalities are cardinal, fixed, and mutable.

Gemini is the zodiac's mutable air sign. Born while spring transitions into summer, Gemini possesses the vitality of the evolution into a new season after another has come to a close. Geminis hold all of this transition's elegance, grace, and beauty in their lungs. As the first mutable sign preceding Virgo, Sagittarius, and Pisces, Gemini theoretically has a high level of psychological comfort with the in-between moments of the human experience. It teaches us to accept the painful but helpful paradoxes, juxtapositions, uncertainty, impermanence, change, and pivot points that are necessary for us to engage with in order to live a meaningful life.

The air element represents our analysis, perception, socialization, and conviction. Air signs Gemini, Libra, and Aquarius help us choose how to think, what words to use, which relationships to engage in, and to what high-minded principles we should aspire. The air signs also remind us who we are without principles, ideas, and philosophies. Gemini represents our first curiosities, which allow us to engage with the experiences ruled by air. As the first mutable and the first air sign in the zodiac, Gemini helps us make sense of life, the questions we ask, the words we choose to explore, and the messages we feel compelled to share as a storytelling species.

You've probably read the shallow interpretations and unnecessary—though sometimes funny!—Gemini slander all over the internet. In an effort to correct the misunderstandings on Gemini, this chapter explores the archetype in its many incarnations—from child to adult, parent to lover, and in daily life as well as in the world.

Up first is Gemini as a child, where we learn just how fast a young Gemini can talk, crawl, walk, and then talk some more. From infancy to adolescence, Gemini children are two handfuls for parents. So I've included helpful suggestions on both affirmation and the right amount of discipline so Gemini understands boundaries, ethics, and follow-through from an early age.

Some Geminis do make the choice to grow up, and do it well. I cover common adult expressions of Gemini in the second section, and highlight areas in which Gemini has the opportunity to own moral authority in various life arenas, with cautionary tales about where they are most likely to miss the mark.

Even this freedom-loving sign can absolutely commit to the right romantic relationship partners, and the third section illuminates the Gemini heart in love. Nobody demonstrates the fact that the most important romantic and sexual organ is the mind quite like the Gemini. So I summarize the way to the Gemini's heart across all pairs of the zodiac. Don't worry—I don't believe in bad compatibility, especially with Geminis who can actively learn how to connect deeply with anyone if they so choose.

Once Geminis commit to an industry or profession that is evolving, interesting, intelligent, and of service to the collective, their work ethic shines. In the fourth section, I offer a list of helpful professions and industries, suggestions for finding your niche, and ideas that can aid the sometimes-indecisive Gemini walk a more helpful path toward merging their purpose with profit. From the communication industries to entrepreneurial adventures, there are few spaces where Geminis can't be of service.

It's my hope that this chapter can help all Gemini-influenced souls look at their twin ruled planets through a lens that clarifies, strengthens, and motivates them on their path toward discovering the truth of who they are, how they love, and what their function in this world really is. The Gemini soul understands Geminis' special mission, their function in the zodiac's collective, and how they can apply their natural gifts and abilities to healing the world.

There's no higher art form than living a soulful life, and astrology is a tool that all signs can learn from. The wisdom of the zodiac helps Geminis understand who they are, why they're here, who they're meant to love, and what they're astrologically ordained to do. When thinking of all the wonders that a Gemini can work in the world, it's easy to become overwhelmed and ask yourself if you can do it all. It's important to remember that the universe gave you Gemini energy, but it's equally crucial to understand that you're meant to be successful in its expression. It would not be reasonable to assume that you have Gemini gifts without the means to bring them to fruition. So together, let's get started.

GEMINI AS A CHILD

LOOK WHO'S TALKING! Odds are, if Gemini children are in the room, it's them. Often at a precociously early age, the Gemini child learns how to use their hands for communicating even before they learn to crawl. Lovingly parented by Mercury, Gemini children are born to be messengers. The earlier Gemini children start learning how to observe, critically analyze, gather information through research, listen, and talk—the *better* for their adult development.

Whereas one twin of the Gemini child's sign is the scholar in training, the other twin is the mischief maker. This dynamic is sure to keep their parents on their toes! Gemini children love learning the reasoning behind the rules, then figuring out the loopholes in the logic to break them. With two children for the price of one, little Geminis quickly demonstrate to their parents that children need dualism to thrive. A happy Gemini child is one who experiences both familiarity and adventure, reliability and surprise, logic and the arts, disclosure and mystery, black and white and color.

The Gemini child will get themselves into a bit of trouble as they develop the skills to manage the paradox between these seemingly irreconcilable needs. I'd argue that the Gemini child doesn't mean any harm as they figure out how to allow the new and the familiar to coexist side by side. They're tasked with exploration, innovation, disruption, and change, which isn't an easy or, often, a culturally supported objective. They'll miss the mark every once in a while in an effort to find the bond between seeming opposites, inadvertently causing chaos. But don't forget that these machinations are generally not mean-spirited.

Beginning in infancy, it's very likely that the Gemini will show a special connection to Mercury-governed communication through an avid appreciation for talking, storytelling,

> **Gemini children love learning the reasoning behind the rules, then figuring out the loopholes in the logic to break them.**

reading, listening, or appreciating the visual arts. Within the heart of each Gemini child lies a message, and one of the most helpful acts a parent can perform is providing that child with a pen, paintbrush, or other means of sharing that message. It's equally beneficial to surround the Gemini child with masterful storytellers, from those in their own family of origin to those found in popular culture, including in literature, music, and cinema, as well as in academia. Creating this kind of environment will leave an incomparably positive impact on the Gemini child, allowing them to integrate the skills of presentation so that they, too, can become a teacher or storyteller when their time comes.

Gemini children bond most meaningfully to their family through verbal communication. Families of Gemini children will want to make their little ones happy by turning into audience, interviewer, and interviewee while talking to the Gemini child. Demonstrate to the little Gemini what it means to actively listen without interrupting, but rather with thoughtful questions, mirroring, and validation of the experiences and stories being told. The junior Gemini will learn through what's modeled by parents in dialogue and will soon apply those lessons when their age allows it. If you want to make a Gemini child happy, share some stories. From family oral histories to ghost stories to the lyrics of a song, anything that involves a plot, exciting characters, and wisdom will catch their attention. Since they're quick studies, you'll be amazed by how the Gemini child learns the art form of verbal communication. While watching other children and adults, they'll want to mirror the intelligence, creativity, and excitement they observe in conversation.

Gemini children will let their imagination enchant their life in magical ways. They can tap into fantasy, surrealism, and other planes of existence with rapid-fire speed. Gemini children will create universes entirely of their own making, and their self-directed personality enables them to express these universes without the help or permission of adults. With a hunger for information, Gemini children will allow their curiosities and adventurous longings to take them to other worlds inside their own head, and in their own life, too. Daydreaming should never be interrupted, because you never know what the Gemini child will find in the land of pure imagination and bring back to our world so desperate for enchantment.

Appropriate discipline does have a place in the home and in the Gemini child's life. When boundaries are crossed or improper choices are made, parents will want to spend time with the Gemini explaining exactly why their choice was irresponsible and why the appropriate consequence is being enforced. It might seem like the Gemini is talking back or pushing too hard, but these conversations are critical for their Mercury-ruled cognition. Geminis need to understand the reasoning, morality, and ethics behind parental discipline so they can draw lessons from their mistakes and make wiser choices in the future. Gemini children don't have to learn the "hard way" if their parents are willing to help them learn important life lessons from their own experience and share them clearly with the Gemini child.

As siblings and cousins, Gemini children will want to socialize often with their family. Even at a young age, Gemini children strive to be helpful, imaginative, joyful, and sometimes hell-raising influences on their generational cohorts. As air signs, they're born highly relational, with a precognitive knowledge of the language necessary to talk to others. So family relationships mean a great deal to this sign, since Gemini, as the Twins, is born in the energy of relationships. They'll know how to talk and listen to the words of the other children they're living with and will enjoy beginning to understand some of the interests they have in common. This process can build meaningful bonds in the Gemini's family of origin, where most children learn about emotions, communication, and other life-defining experiences.

In early education, Gemini children usually access language and speech either through a high aptitude, like an advanced reading level, or an impairment like dyslexia. These diametrically opposed reactions make sense for the divine fraternal twins. If a Gemini child's school highlights their language and speech as a strength, and then tailors their education to enhancing that proficiency, they have a head start toward winning the Pulitzer. If they need extra help in this area, this can still serve the Gemini's long-term success. If a Gemini child is aware that they have a communication issue—for example, a stutter or a speech impediment—they will become more sensitive to the outsider's plight throughout life. In the right therapeutic scenario, the Gemini will soon find the technique that helps them overcome the impairment, but the experience of being on the outside looking in will leave a permanent mark on their heart, making them more empathic toward and mindful of others.

A Gemini child is likely to have a wide range of passions and interests, so their family should help the Gemini taste-test all these intellectual cravings, while also encouraging a specialized focus on specific areas as they come of age. The Gemini child is a lifelong multidisciplinary student. As they mature, they'll find the common thread among their seemingly opposing interests, as long as they're not forced to choose or commit to one prematurely. Because of their mutable air quality and because they're ruled by Mercury, Gemini children are often self-directed in education, so fortunately all teachers and parents need to do is just listen to what's captivating them and provide the right resources to help them learn even more.

In school, the Gemini child will inevitably be scolded for talking too much. Authority figures will want to encourage and sometimes mandate a lengthy period of contemplation for Geminis, so other children can have a chance to participate. Learning to wait before talking is an annoying—but helpful—experience for the Gemini child's long-term development. Because the mind of a Gemini child moves rapidly, if they engage in contemplative activities first thing in the morning, like a mindfulness, meditation, or exercise routine, it'll enable them to let off some of their hyperactive steam. Taking some of that pressure off first thing in the morning gives them a greater ability to concentrate and contemplate throughout the day.

In adolescence, Gemini's aptitude for learning really begins to take flight. By their teen years, Geminis are most likely serving in leadership positions in extracurricular activities, dodging detention with their charm, ranking at the top of their class, and alternating between athletic responsibilities and their role as the star of the drama production. There's little they can't do, so they try it all.

Gemini youth should be celebrated for their "soft" skills of social competence and diverse curiosities. The dominant culture assumes that soft skills are easy, but as we all know, getting along well with others is tough. Gemini makes it look effortless. Highlight the specific behavior that helps Gemini connect to others, and celebrate their gifts. Your attention gives Gemini an opportunity to teach through demonstration, showing others how they do things differently. Our culture often encourages specialty, focus, and linear thinking, which feels like a straitjacket on the wings of the Gemini. Instead of trying to force them into the established way of doing things, parents of Gemini children can enable them to develop their strengths.

GEMINI AS AN ADULT

THE SECTION OF the astrological chart associated with Gemini is adolescence. What's the state of being for the eternally youthful in adulthood? From an astrological point of view, adulthood begins during the Saturn Return, which occurs when a person is between twenty-seven and twenty-nine years old. Additionally, there's a celestial school of thought that says we shine into our sun sign throughout our thirties and midlife. This section will explore how Gemini maintains a youthful disposition in the years after their Saturn Return, while they simultaneously assume the responsibilities of adulthood.

The secret of the Gemini in adulthood is they don't take themselves too seriously—but they take life *very* seriously.

Adult Geminis aren't concerned about taking themselves too seriously. By maintaining an adolescent, ethereal quality, they feel they don't need to impress others by focusing too heavily on perfectionism and performance. However, if adult Geminis are unbalanced between freedom and accountability, they'll need to do some personal growth work in order to live their lives more fully.

Geminis are light on their feet because they're not weighed down by self-seriousness. They don't waste time caring about what the culture demands of them, and they're able to sidestep critics, jerks, and others filled with mean-spirited energy. The adult Gemini gets the joke. The critics and jerks are committed to misunderstanding them, so the adult Gemini can be as playful, focused, vulgar, sophisticated, creative, literal, and vulnerable as they want. Those low-level energies approach the Gemini with a foregone conclusion in mind, but Gemini doesn't need their regard and can easily ignore their judgment. Would-be antagonists who have already decided what they want to believe before they start investigating it aren't worth a Gemini's time. An adult Gemini repudiates single-minded criticism every time they bravely demonstrate the capabilities of the divine Twins within and change their mind. Every person, regardless of sun sign, is given the freedom of thought and transformation. Gemini, however, is divinely set up to be the one who initiates it.

Would I call an adult Gemini carefree? Not necessarily. Again, the adult Gemini takes life seriously. More than that, Gemini recognizes that "life" is so much bigger than the insignificant and meaningless things within their own purview. This is why they're seriously interested in "the other," the unknown, and the sunset that lies beyond their horizon.

You'll see Gemini gravitas in all their intellectual pursuits and how they apply wisdom in areas beyond the personal, like their family, friendships, and romances. In their professional lives, they work hard to be of service, along with their employers, to the outside world. It's easy to assume that we all think beyond ourselves in relationships and career, but remember: Our culture tends to give us permission to use relationships and work for personal gain only. Geminis see the transcendence in these experiences.

An adult Gemini can easily lighten up, as long as they are holding on to values in their heart that keep them fully engaged. In an interview with Oprah Winfrey, Dr. Brené Brown pointed out that wholehearted living requires clear values and convictions.[2] The adult Gemini will want to choose two to three values that are most important to them in order to make good decisions. Gemini should promote qualities like courage, integrity, connection, and creativity, combining them with their strongest personal convictions. They should also avoid becoming unhealthily attached to a specific end result.

A pitfall the adult Gemini may fall into is moving too fast, saying too much, and acting too soon without this clarity. As such a hyperactive, fast-moving, mental sign, Gemini's gifts need to be concentrated ever so slightly before this sign can become centered. I cannot encourage an adult Gemini enough to spend time contemplating what values they cherish before they make big decisions. If the decisions they'd like to make are in line with their core beliefs, excellent. The adult Gemini is on their way to flying to the peak of virtue. If not, they need to pause, reflect, and reprioritize. One of the most frequent critiques of Gemini is a lack of depth. This is common if the adult Gemini moves too quickly and can't bear to stick around long enough to acquire sufficient focus and carefully review all the details in a particular circumstance or relationship.

The adult Gemini will always want to maintain vigilant awareness of the power of their words. As the adage reminds us, great power carries great responsibility. So Geminis will want to remember that when they speak, people do listen, so they need to make sure they're choosing their words carefully. If they don't take the time to be mindful of what they're saying, Geminis can be master manipulators: emotionally violent, disruptive, and suffused with the poisonous side of the Mercury element. Given the influence of their language, they can shape others' perception of reality very powerfully. So if Geminis fail to find a positive way to direct their prodigious mental energies, they can turn toward deceit and even fraud.

Some helpful strategies to promote intellectual and vocal impulse control are a morning meditation practice and any therapeutic practice. A daily stillness exercise, like meditation, keeps fear-based, frantic thinking at bay, and introduces more mindful, tranquil energy, which can only uplift the Gemini's life. A therapeutic practice can provide the Gemini with helpful tools that prevent them from inventing stories without fact-checking them. Without that self-editing, Geminis can concoct masterful conspiracies that exist only in their own heads. They have a talent for confabulating the truth—which is the act of telling lies honestly. Since the Gemini is convinced of their own view of events, they'll believe their own conspiracies as honestly true, engage in self-deception, tell everyone else, and thereby spread false information.

In adulthood, the Gemini's adaptability, detachment, and flexibility work as their saving grace.

Remember: While they're not too weighed down by self-seriousness, Gemini can use their cognition, mischief, lightheartedness, messages, and creativity to create catalysts for joy and change. In a holy book of ancient Chinese wisdom, *The Tao Te Ching*, mystic Lao Tzu wrote, "All things, including the grass and trees, are soft and pliable in life; dry and brittle in death. Stiffness is thus a companion of death; flexibility a companion of life. An army that cannot yield will be defeated. A tree that cannot bend will crack in the wind. The hard and stiff will be broken; the soft and supple will prevail."[3]

In the passage above, Geminis are given permission to stay flexible in pursuit of their passions and the wind beneath their winged sandals that keep them flying above "foolish consistency," a phrase immortalized by Gemini Sun Ralph Waldo Emerson, who wrote that it is "the hobgoblin of little minds, adored by little statesmen and philosophers and divines."[4] Not taking yourself seriously, but taking life seriously, gives you the elegance, social proficiency, and intelligence not only to keep doing what's working, but to adapt progressively with wisdom and competence when things are going awry.

The human experience is characterized by dualism and the law of opposites, so the adult Gemini's most crucial responsibility is to demonstrate to the rest of the zodiac the mind-set, language, analysis, and adaptability required to engage with contradiction. The adult Gemini's secret to this is thinking beyond themselves. By looking past the horizon, the adult Gemini teaches us the value of play, creativity, education, communication, emotionality, and relationships.

GEMINI IN LOVE

LET'S BEGIN THIS section on love with what a Gemini loves—definitions. We say and write "love" often, but we do really know what it means? Dr. Brené Brown defines it this way: "We cultivate love when we allow our most vulnerable and powerful selves to be deeply seen and known, and when we honor the spiritual connection that grows from that offering with trust, respect, kindness and affection."[5]

Can a Gemini not only profess love but practice it along these lines? Of course. So can the rest of the zodiac. It's important to disclose here that I don't believe in the binary of "good" or "bad" compatibility. Like all signs, Gemini can learn how to connect to the entirety of the zodiac with the right amount of willingness, work, and understanding.

Love begins in the Gemini's life through the mind. And as Shakespeare (a Venus in Gemini) wrote, "Love looks not with the eyes, but with the mind . . . And therefore is winged Cupid painted blind."[6]

When a Gemini feels a romantic spark, a longing, or the heat of desire, it's because their partner showcased the best of their intellect, curiosity, and verbal communication skills. Only then will the Gemini begin their initial descent from the skies that rule their sign.

When in love, the Gemini will want to honor their natural abilities to maintain a sense of wonder and to focus attention on their partners.

Love survives and thrives when partners continue to pay attention to each other, and when a Gemini's in love, hardly a detail about their beloved escapes them. Their partners will relish knowing and feeling that that they're seen, cherished, and understood by their Gemini partner.

Additionally, Gemini will want to maintain their intrinsic sense of autonomy and freedom. It might seem antithetical to love, which appreciates closeness, but it's important to maintain the possession of self, for Gemini or otherwise. Without self, intimacy can become intrusion and an unhealthy codependency. As the sign of the Twins, Gemini knows when one ends and the other begins. They'll want to be as upfront as possible in the beginning stages of the relationship so their partner knows what love story they're coauthoring.

Lastly, given Gemini's social popularity, it's possible that a partner could feel intimidated or unsure of how much they matter. Tending to this is a twofold process. First of all, Gemini needs a village: They can't put all their expectations, needs, or demands on one romantic partner. Second, the Gemini should find out what their partner desires in terms of validation so that Gemini can provide it without compromising their robust social network. To ask a Gemini to give up relationships in order to provide security is a fool's errand—it will make Gemini feel resentful and insecure, and foster the kind of codependency any relationship should avoid.

Geminis look for a relationship in which commitment doesn't feel like a violation of their freedom. As the sign of dualism, Geminis hope for adventure, novelty, spontaneity, joy, education, stability, and friendship in their romance. To house all these qualities requires a delicate balancing act, but it can be done, and hopefully the result is that Gemini will be able to see their partner as both home and the unknown—both comforting and exciting.

Oftentimes, Geminis can provide the exhilarating thrill of riding a wave, but not the safety of the anchor in a relationship.

So the Gemini will be drawn to a partner imbued with structure, consistency, reliability, and accountability in order for the relationship dynamic to survive and thrive. Generally speaking, they'll align with a partner who's more comfortable initiating the anchor role. In the best-case scenario, Gemini will be receptive to and grateful for this security. When Geminis see mutuality as a helpful—as opposed to a restrictive—quality in the relationship, they can let the anchor partner sit back, relax, and take the lead in tending the solid ground beneath them. This builds trust and reliability. Variety and contrast keep the dynamic exciting and make the relationship a great environment for mutual growth and transformation. Also, Gemini will want to get out of their head and into their body, heart, and soul to access some of the most meaningful experiences when it comes to eroticism, intimacy, and love. This kind of grounding allows the relationship to go deeper than it normally would have, given Gemini's tendency to rely on physical senses to see and experience what the heart knows to be true in love.

Another possible blind spot for a Gemini in love is their tendency to interpret the worth of their partner by the words they say. It's critical for the Gemini to remember the so-called Mehrabian rule and understand that language, their specialty, is only around 7 percent of the entire communication continuum. The rest is all in the body language, tones, social cues, and seemingly limitless number of nonverbal messages being broadcast in the invisible ether. So to gain the most holistic understanding of who their partner is, Geminis need to expand their perception to hold space for everything that's being communicated nonverbally. They need to work hard to master fluency in this language, too.

As noted previously, I don't believe in inherently good or bad compatibility, because the nature of relationships is in managing complementarities and the paradox of love and desire. I've outlined below all matches Gemini can have with other signs in the zodiac, informed by the research conducted by couples therapist Esther Perel in her book *Mating in Captivity: Unlocking Erotic Intelligence* (Harper, 2017). Perel argues that love and desire are separate entities that can be reconciled carefully in romantic relationships. As in Dr. Brown's definition of love, the roots by which love grows need to be tended with closeness, affection, warmth, understanding, and safety for them to thrive. Maintaining sexual desire requires the complete opposite, as its power is born of distance, mystery, longing, intrigue, and adventure. It's a good thing that Gemini, as the sign of sophisticated dual thinking and paradox management, can hold these two energies in harmony without choosing one or the other as more valid for relationship health. It doesn't have to be either/or when both/and is available!

GEMINI & ARIES

Between Gemini's air and Aries's fire, this is a match that is romantic, friendly, and lights up each other's lives immediately. When Gemini and Aries become romantically involved, it's entertaining, passionate, and supportive. This pair can blend the best of both affectionate love and exciting desire. Still, it'll be hard, and this speed-loving match will want to pace themselves appropriately so as not to burn out the excitement too soon. Since these signs are known for relatively short attention spans, it will keep the couple longing for each other. Aries's cardinal fire leadership skills will help Gemini focus all their energy in powerful places, and Aries will take the Mars-ruled action inspired by Gemini's Mercury-ruled ideas. Gemini will help Aries work on their impulse control and carefully consider their words or actions before speaking or acting.

GEMINI & TAURUS

When the Gemini Twins hop on to ride sweet Taurus into their Venus-ruled romantic garden, an unlikely love affair begins. This dynamic often has a wonderful sense of fondness, admiration, and wonder for each other. As a match between Gemini's mutable air and Taurus's fixed earth sign, it's a friendly competition between preservation and progress. This neighboring match has the right amount of contrast to keep the spark alive. It'll require a comprehensive conversation on how they understand and practice love, however. Gemini must learn the high art of follow-through and focus from their Taurus lover, whose concentration levels are second to none. Gentle Taurus will need to learn how to become more flexible as Gemini teaches Taurus how to navigate risk, uncertainty, and discomfort.

GEMINI & GEMINI

If there's two for the price of one in every Gemini, I hope four isn't a crowd in this pair! When Gemini falls in love with another Gemini, the enthusiasm, vitality, and adventure between them keep this more detached sign closely held in each other's embrace. The connection thrives in conversation. While they're all there, it's important to disclose what love means to each and then get to it. Given their hunger for information, they'll want to reveal their respective worlds slowly, because desire needs mystery to maintain its spark. In this same-sign match, both partners will bolster what comes to Gemini naturally in love, like friendly mischief, curiosity, conversation, and spontaneity. To sustain this powerful dynamic, they'll want to join forces to create a structure of consistency, affection, and trust, which will strengthen the pair.

GEMINI & CANCER

It's a match of the head and the heart! As two neighboring signs, cardinal water Cancer and mutable air Gemini offer the best of the Mercury-ruled head and moonlit heart in this relationship. What possibly started as a connection grounded in mild annoyance and intrigue turned into a power couple. As a tag team, know that the affection and the power of love is Cancer's domain, whereas novelty and the mystery of desire is all Gemini. It'll be a delicate step up, step back waltz, but if you see it as the key to unlocking relationship success, you'll be happy to do it. Gemini will learn the language and experience of the emotional realm from Cancer, which helps Gemini transcend the rational world they love so much. Cancer will learn logic and emotional regulation, which will help them retain their power and succeed with Gemini by their side.

GEMINI & LEO

If larger-than-life is your favorite size, this match is a perfect fit. As two generative, dynamic signs, the fixed fire Leo and the mutable air Gemini can create an exciting life together, full of affection and adventure. Ruled by the sun, Leo infuses a great deal of warmth, power, and excitement into the Mercury-ruled curiosities of Gemini. For the foundation of love to be secure between the zodiac's Royal and the Jester, Gemini will want to give the Leo extra-special attention and affection. However, Gemini's inherent need for privacy and mystery requires breathing room, which the Leo will want to step outside of their castle comfort zone to deliver, because space protects their shared passion. For this union to function successfully, Gemini will learn more about creativity, confidence, and courage, and Leo will need to develop relational skills to make others feel included and understood.

GEMINI & VIRGO

Nerd alert! You two brainiacs are a cerebral pair, enchanted by an intellectually stimulating love. In fellow mutable earth and Mercury-ruled sign Virgo, Gemini finds a partner who's a mental match and performs the ultimate magic trick: holding their attention. In Gemini, Virgo's disarmed by a sophisticated ability to think deeply and optimistically. Whoever's more comfortable with emotion will take the lead in building a home for love and affection here, whereas whoever's more comfortable with intrigue, uncertainty, and risk will coach the other on seduction and desire. In this connection, Gemini concentrates and commits to specific life and relationship strategies that Virgo will help them specialize in. Meanwhile, Virgo will watch and learn from Gemini in exercising their innovation, creativity, and ability to embrace imperfection.

GEMINI & LIBRA

Love's in the air! When two air signs align in a match, it's harmonious, comfortable, and pleasurable. Ruled by Venus, Libra, as a cardinal air sign, has social and artistic skills supreme enough to catch the Gemini's attention. In Mercury-ruled, mutable air Gemini, the elegant Libra finds another smooth talker whose passion for play turns this indecisive sign into one who's utterly committed. Love is Libra's domain, so they'll want to initiate the dialogue on love as practice for clear communication, which leads to inspired action. Desire is Gemini's bailiwick, so the Gemini will want to make the familiar unfamiliar—and more physical. Gemini will learn the Libra balance of emotion with intellect and how to navigate social spaces more elegantly. Libra will learn how to overcome the disease to people-please with the direct Gemini.

GEMINI & SCORPIO

This match can be a bit of heaven and Armageddon. In Pluto-ruled and fixed water-governed Scorpio, Gemini falls in love with a partner who's psychology runs the deepest. In Mercury-ruled and mutable air-influenced Gemini, Scorpio finds an imaginative and intelligent lover who keeps the match passionate and educational. The differences between them can create hellish circumstances without flexibility, however, which is why Gemini's assigned the task of providing love and affection. Scorpio has a penchant for seduction and desire, so they'll keep the mystery alive, since they don't like revealing anything. Gemini will learn how to receive, observe, and feel more deeply without an attachment to the intellectual world. Scorpio will work on adaptability and how to leave the devil they know for the angel in the unknown.

GEMINI & SAGITTARIUS

Opposites attract! These two are opposing sides of the same axis, but they have more in common than meets the uninitiated eye. Jupiter-ruled and fellow mutable fire sign Sagittarius loves to ferret out the wisdom in the data that Mercury-governed Gemini finds in their airy research. Sparks fly in this match, because it's complementary, intellectual, and passionate. Sagittarius will know how to keep the seduction alive, as they're more freedom-loving and space-needing than Gemini. Meanwhile, Gemini will coach Sagittarius on the proximity, affection, and stability that love needs to emerge. Gemini will learn how to use fewer words and more wisdom from Sagittarius, whereas Sagittarius will learn how to infuse more compassion and curiosity into their lives from the relational Twins.

GEMINI & CAPRICORN

Meet 'em at the top! This match between ethereal Gemini and mountain-climbing Capricorn is highly visionary, as they connect where the mountain meets sky. In cardinal Earth- and Saturn-ruled Capricorn, Gemini's impressed by the stature and moral authority of this dutiful sign. Capricorn slowly finds that the Mercury-ruled Gemini has more than jokes up their sleeve, but critical thinking, too. Love and affection would be Capricorn's mission to demonstrate here, as the love between these signs needs consistency, structure, and trust. For the desire to stay seductive and passionate, Gemini will want to keep the mystery, play, and seduction in the relationship. Gemini will be inspired to emulate Capricorn's morality and long-distance dream planning. From Gemini, strict Capricorn will learn how to lighten up and enjoy the pleasures of life.

GEMINI & AQUARIUS

Put it in writing! An exciting match between two air signs, Aquarius and Gemini will never run out of things to talk about or stories to write in a love letter. Ruled by innovating Uranus and with a fixed air heart, Aquarius loves to ask Gemini, "Have you thought about this?" Mercury-governed with a mutable air heart, Gemini has a love that soars when it encounters the brilliant and disruptive cognition of Aquarius. With their relational skills, Gemini will want to take the lead on the structure and reliability that love needs to breathe. Aquarius loves the unknown, so they'll teach Gemini all about longing, seduction, and desire. Gemini will learn how to stay true to their convictions more from the principled Aquarian, and Gemini will teach Aquarius how to disagree without dogma or divisiveness.

GEMINI & PISCES

Two fish in every Pisces, and two people in every Gemini. In this dualistic match, contrast, change, and novelty uplift and secure the couple. Neptune-ruled and fellow mutable sign Pisces brings to the relationship creative, empathic, and healing skills that inspire Gemini. Pisces is charmed by Gemini's Mercury intellect and mutable air communication skills. Gemini also helps Pisces look on the brighter side when Pisces becomes too bogged down in introspection. Gemini will want to facilitate conversations on how love needs the structure of consistency and reliability. Because Pisces's natural self is so mysterious to Gemini, they'll preserve the passion of this relationship as they strive to learn more and more about each other. Gemini will evolve in their nonverbal fluency and how to read a room, as instructed by Pisces, who will conversely learn the value of straight talk for clear understanding.

Now that we have reviewed all the matches in the zodiac, let's begin the ending of this section with how it opened. Dr. Brown wrote on love, "Shame, blame, disrespect, betrayal, and the withholding of affection damage the roots from which love grows. Love can only survive these injuries if they are acknowledged, healed and rare."[7] How can Gemini best acknowledge these injuries through their governing practice of verbal communication when they are upset with their romantic partner?

When we talk about love, it's crucial that we also talk about how to help love survive injuries through acknowledgment and healing. In other words, we can't talk about love without talking about how to apologize. Given Gemini's imperfect state of being, they'll make mistakes. We all do. So let's explore leading ideas on apologies and forgiveness so Gemini has the emotional strength to acknowledge an upset and take steps toward healing the wound.

A very helpful method for navigating such situations is nonviolent communication (NVC). A system invented by Dr. Marshall Rosenberg, NVC encompasses four steps not just for the Gemini who loves a framework, but for all us. The first step is observation—where the Gemini is encouraged to describe what they observed neutrally and without interpretation. The second step is the emotion that the Gemini feels when they observed the behavior from their partner. It could sound like this: "I noticed that when you walked into the room without saying hello, I felt upset..." The third step is identifying the need. So the Gemini will want to identity what they need from their partner. In continuing this example, the Gemini can say, "I need to feel that you see me; otherwise, I feel like I don't matter to you." And the last step is the request. The Gemini can request what they need specifically to not feel disregarded: "So when you walk in next time, can you greet me, and give me a few minutes of your time, so I can feel more connected to you?" It's important to provide the recipe for success to our partners when it comes to connection. The four steps, again, are: observation, feeling, need, and request. This is especially useful for the Gemini, but can be applied to all relationships.

I spoke with another Gemini Sun recently. Without even asking him directly what Gemini can do to improve the quality of their relationships, he said, "All a Gemini has to do is say, 'I'm sorry.' Period." He's right. As a highly intellectual sign, when Gemini hears that their behavior caused pain, they'll often run into explaining it away to the person who's experiencing the upset. That's generally the last thing the upset party needs from Gemini—more of their words. When my Gemini friend mentioned the need for an apology, I knew I needed to explore how to properly apologize.

Dr. Harriet Lerner is a Sagittarius Sun—Gemini's polar opposite sign, which has perfect vision on them, since they're across from each other on the zodiac—and a clinical psychologist who specializes in improving family and work relationships and methods for apology. Not only do many of us avoid apologizing, but we assume that we're born knowing how to do it. Dr. Lerner's techniques include avoiding add-ons to our apologies like, "I'm sorry if" or "I'm sorry but." In an interview with *Forbes* magazine, Dr. Lerner said, "High-stakes situations call for an apology that's a long-distance run—where we open our heart and listen to the feelings of the hurt party on more than one occasion." What Gemini stands to learn is that there's nothing more precious to the upset party than their gift of wholehearted listening to the kind of anger and pain they're being accused of causing without defense, justification, or explanation. The upset speaker wants to know that the Gemini listened carefully to their feelings, validated their reality, feels genuine remorse, is willing to carry some of the pain, and is committed to avoiding an encore of the behavior that caused the upset.

I'm of the opinion that astrology can strengthen our relational intelligence and skills. With ethical understanding, your Gemini selfhood can be improved through the context of your relationship with others. It's important to remember that one sign cannot exist properly without the other. That's why the symbol of the zodiac is a circle, because each sign has a responsibility to the other, a continuity and a belonging. Each sign offers something special to Gemini, and Gemini offers something meaningful to all twelve signs.

GEMINI AT WORK

IT CAN NEVER be the same day twice for Gemini on the job! With vitality for variety and a gift of gab, Gemini needs a career where they can put their intellectual skills to work in industries that celebrate innovation and change. As a sign governed by Mercury, which rules the media, communication fields, technology, commerce, education, and transportation, Gemini needs to interact with others and especially appreciates using modern technology to send the messages they were born to deliver. On the job, Gemini is a student and a teacher. Whatever they know, they share. What they want to know, they ask. Along with their prodigious social skills, Gemini can uplift the bonds among coworkers through facilitating conversations and thereby promoting collaboration.

In any communication industry, Gemini can research, analyze, speak, and write because they know the power of the word. From editor to journalist, commentator, and author, Gemini can use their versatility and language skills at work with ease and to great success. Think of the works of Gemini wordsmiths like Anne Frank, Walt Whitman, and Nikki Giovanni. As student and teacher, Gemini thrives on self-directed education and finds it essential for their professional trajectory. Their work will benefit tremendously if they keep researching, learning, and attending professional events, like industry-related conferences, where they can stay current on all the latest research and theory. That way, Gemini's flexibility can move their industry toward innovation, progress, and the culture of the future.

You'll definitely find many a Gemini in Silicon Valley and other tech hubs, as Gemini is adept at using technology as a problem solver. The inventor of the World Wide Web, Sir Timothy Berners-Lee, is a Gemini. Naturally! Given their bright-eyed, alternative-possibility-loving, and yet highly mechanistic way of thinking, you can find Geminis in cutting-edge technology spaces in a range of industries, from health care to entertainment, transportation, and education. What makes the Gemini special in these spaces is their ability to humanize technology and remember how it serves people, and not the other way around. If Gemini blends the best of relational with technological in these industries, they can be among the most valuable employees on the job.

In any kind of sales or commerce field, Gemini can sell just about anything. Using their Mercurial persuasive tongue and (hopefully) nonmanipulative strategies, they can help consumers understand why their product fits the consumers' need. Within each Gemini mind is a public relations expert, copy editor, marketer, and strategist. They can utilize this range of skills to understand what the market needs, how to tell the story, and who to tell it to. Sales is another area where relational skills are essential for the bottom line, and it's Gemini's ease in communication, and perhaps their popularity, that makes them shine in this role.

In education, a Gemini can find a professional sanctuary. From kindergarten teacher to college professor teaching graduate students, a Gemini academic, with their adaptable intelligence, can figure out what each student needs to learn effectively. Based on their ability to think, speak, and listen in diverse settings, they know how to individualize the teaching styles and curriculum to fit the students' most effective mode of learning. Geminis love the magic that happens between teacher and student as they alternate roles and explore, disagree, validate, and expand on preexisting theory together.

Now that we covered how Gemini uses their intellect in communication, tech, commerce, and education, let us review the deeper, more universal meaning of why they feel compelled to contribute to a range of industries. Gemini has an obligation to harness their intelligence in an effort to heal others. According to the solar chart, Gemini is situated at the first house of identity, which then makes Pisces the ruler of their tenth house of career. This placement means that Pisces's creative sensibilities, artistry, and soulful approach to life's trajectory extend to the Gemini's career.

It's too simplistic to just connect Gemini's career path to how smart and communicative they can be. Given Gemini's mutable energy, they can contribute a range of skills and styles to their career beyond just intellect and language. Gemini has to blend the mental and emotional with inspirational Pisces, inspiring their highest mission.

The mutable receptivity of both Gemini and Pisces means that it's important for Geminis to spend enough time in contemplation so they can identify the deeply held personal beliefs behind their choice of career. The Twins have an open mind, so they can almost be easily persuaded to pursue inauthentic and ultimately unimportant paths if they're not following their own genuine personal convictions. Their career path might be completely traditional, nontraditional, or a combination of the two. To know which one is in alignment with their truest self, Geminis need to spend time alone to think. Then they'll know how their gifts and abilities could best contribute to compassionate healing.

Since we covered a great deal of what Gemini does well on the job, let's discuss where they

> Gemini's verbal fluency is top-notch. What they need to practice is listening to the nonverbal—and there's no place like work to practice how moods, subtexts, body language, and cues can really tell a story.

have opportunities for growth. First, with all their Mercurial energy, it's difficult for Gemini to focus on one thing at a time because they can multitask like magic. However, there's a time and a place for their multitasking and for concentration. In order for Geminis to be all they can be on the job, it's crucial for them to finish what they start, own what they can't, or delegate it to someone else if they can't undertake it themselves. One of the most difficult scarlet letters to wash off at work is a reputation for unreliability or inconsistency. Unfortunately, Geminis can fall into those habits if they're not carefully concentrating on or committed to the completion of a task.

Gemini is smart enough to know when they're distracted, instead of focused. That's why it's especially important for them to enforce mental boundaries on the job so as not to interrupt their work flow. Whether that means blocking social media sites on the internet browser or moving the phone far enough away not to read unrelated texts, a few preventive measures go a long way. Given Gemini's ability to do it all at once, another helpful habit for Gemini is asking whether or not a particular task is a time-sensitive priority. Since they're so fast and so agile, they can work well under pressure, assuming they know what tasks need to be completed more urgently and which they can put on the back burner.

Gemini will want to ask supervisors and colleagues, "What's the time line on this? What needs to be done by when?" This helps them understand the expectations at hand. From there, Gemini can agree, negotiate, delegate, or refuse the assignment, based on their skills, current workload, and projected turnaround time. Having straightforward conversations at work is hard, but they're necessary to develop trust among colleagues. Gemini's honesty, clear communication, and questioning identify them as reliable because their cognition is so focused; they can prioritize specific tasks, helping them deliver on those expectations.

Another skill Gemini will want to pick up on at work is the ability to see, hear, and feel with their inner senses. As mentioned, Gemini's verbal fluency is top-notch. What they need to practice is listening to the nonverbal—and there's no place like work to practice how moods, subtexts, body language, and cues can really tell a story. So for Gemini to acclimate and adapt to their work culture, they'll want to honor their language skills while practicing hard at seeing, hearing, and feeling all the things that aren't being said. It's Gemini's responsibility to identify what's not being said and apply language to it at work. It could begin as simply as this: "Hey, [insert colleague name here], I noticed in the meeting that your body language shifted a bit when I presented and shared my idea. I don't want to make any assumptions, but is there something we need to clear up?"

Utilizing the best of their emotional and intellectual communication skills, Gemini can proactively defuse any possible miscommunications. It's not easy to see the future, but Gemini's mind can come close to anticipating possible professional pitfalls if they're willing and brave enough to step in with strong communication after observing colleagues' emotional discomfort. We're living in a time when it's no longer just the bottom line that's a nonnegotiable, but also the employee's relational intelligence. So Gemini will want to showcase the best of their mind and heart on the job.

Last but not least: listening. Just because Gemini is ready to talk does not mean their colleagues are ready to listen. A Gemini will want to make sure the environment is right for discussion by beginning with a few polite bids for their fellow employee's attention. Gemini can start by saying, "Hi, [Name], I had an idea I want to run past you. Do you have about ten minutes so I can review this with you?" If they say no, Gemini will want to ask when they'll have time, and then follow up later on to confirm.

When Gemini's the listener and not the speaker, the most effective way to ensure accuracy in the dialogue is to mirror back. It'll seem a little clunky at first, but you might as well lean into this discomfort before the error is made. Gemini can say, "Let me make sure I understood you. So you want me to [identify the task and action] by [date and time]? Did I get that right?" This is essential, because studies on listening show that we often have a 13 percent accuracy rate, which means we miss 87 percent of vital information. This mirroring exercise increases our accuracy and efficiency. If it is done well, the speaker will confirm. If not, hopefully they'll clarify. You'd be amazed at how kindly people take to Gemini when they showcase the best

of their cognition, listening, and language skills with these techniques.

Pisces, as the ruler of Gemini's career, imbues Gemini with a soulful professional mission. If Gemini sees their work as a ministry that comforts the afflicted and disrupts the comfortable, they will be successful professionally. Geminis measure their professional value by asking themselves, "Did I do my part to make people feel seen, heard, and understood? Did I listen carefully and not interrupt?" If the answer is yes, the Gemini constellation will shine even brighter in their honor. If not, it's never too late to start again.

CONCLUSION

AFTER COVERING GEMINI as child, adult, in love, and at work, it is my hope that you can grasp the identity of this air sign with a bit more clarity. This sign of transformation and uncertainty often sends critics into a knee-jerk rejection without meaningful contemplation on the necessity of Gemini's traits—positive and negative.

We covered Gemini as child as highly curious, mischievous, and with quicksilver energy who wants to immediately understand and experiment with their environment. The Gemini child needs to talk their ideas out, which doesn't change as they become adults. When Geminis reach their maturation in adulthood, their social competency and relational intelligence shine. When their Mercury communication skills allow the Gemini to facilitate thoughtful dialogue and discernment, Gemini can moderate between speaker and listener. This leads the way in creating a space for connection through communication to emerge, because Gemini knows how to interface with a variety of people and help them transition from separation to union.

Naturally, these skills extend to their parenting. Gemini is both fellow troublemaker and moral authority to their offspring. Their inner child never truly grows up, since the age most thematically associated with Gemini is early adolescence. Gemini never forgets the perils or joys of youth so, on the positive side, they can be a space that allows for becoming. With a healthy mode of detachment—since Gemini, as twins, knows that not everyone is them—the Gemini parent can raise children without expecting their lives to look just like the parent's.

When it comes to partnership, I firmly believe that, like all signs, Gemini can learn to love and forge connections with the entire zodiac. Astrological consciousness has expanded beyond the binary of good versus bad compatibility, especially when it comes to Gemini's relational history, which isn't either/or but always both/and. As long as Gemini and their partner understand relational theory, how to manage the paradox of love and desire, ideas on growing together, and they use the relationship as a context for healing, they'll be two little lovebirds sitting in a tree.

Though not widely known as a "hard worker," Gemini can passionately throw themselves into their work and contribute extensively to the healing of the world. The task for the Gemini is seeing their knowledge as cumulative, as well as understanding what platforms allow for their multidimensional talents. Since Pisces is the ruler of Gemini's career sector, Gemini's mission needs to be focused on service. If a Gemini doesn't feel like they're making a difference in the lives of others, their minds or hearts won't be in their chosen vocation. When they can see how they're improving the experiences of other people through their intelligence, artistry, or any other healing modality, the Gemini will feel gainfully employed and work hard to keep it that way.

An eternal student, ruled by Mercury, Gemini is gleeful in the classroom. From lower to higher education, school offers these bright-eyed students the place to focus their mental energies. Gemini will sample, mix and match, pick up, and then drop their interests along the way, a practice that should be encouraged. Gemini shouldn't feel pressured to pick a course of study until they find the school of thought that allows them to be and do all they want. School is also the laboratory for Gemini to apply their strong social skills, and they can quickly rise to leadership positions as their campus recognizes their ability to inspire others.

When it comes to food, parts of the body, and more, Gemini can choose particular habits that enhance their life. Given Gemini's brainpower, Gemini needs to set aside an hour first thing in the morning, of uninterrupted focus, concentration, and/or a meditation exercise, so their most powerful tool is working at peak capacity throughout the rest of the day. Once every light on their mind is on, Gemini flies through life with enchantment, curiosity, a sense of humor, and the social graces that connect people to others. They just need to be careful not to do too much all at once; otherwise, they overpromise and underdeliver, which creates a difficult reputation to repair.

After I explore anything astrological, I like to leave the reader with some ethical guidance so they can use this power responsibly. Geminis, as the sign of the Twins, are a symbol of enormous connection. Twins have a sacred bond. And this union is the key ethic for all astrology.

Now that you're more familiar with Gemini, please remember to use what you know to connect to others more deeply. High-minded astrology posits that we all incarnate to understand love more carefully and practice it more compassionately. Gemini has no more or less capability to do just that. As the sign of partnership and connection, it's the Gemini imperative to use their social intelligence and communication styles to help others feel that they're less alone. Loneliness is a public health crisis throughout the world. Gemini is a sign very qualified to ameliorate this crisis and teach us the skills that allow us to avoid it.

The highest purpose of astrology is as a tool for relationship success. So I invite you to see it as a way for others to be as connected as the Gemini and to try to avoid any weaponizing, shaming, or seeing yourself as separate from the rest of the zodiac. Remember: The zodiac wheel is a symbol of awareness of our connection and oneness. We are each other. Gemini represents this truth, and helps the rest of the

> **Though not widely known as a "hard worker," Gemini can passionately throw themselves into their work and contribute extensively to the healing of the world.**

zodiac understand how the quality of our relationships affect the quality of our lives.

Thank you for immersing yourself in the quest of self-discovery and seeking answers to the questions of why we are here, what we are here to do to, and with whom. May you as a Gemini and/or the Gemini you love feel worthy and courageous in the pursuit of your or their highest expression. May your curiosity, intelligence, communication skills, and connections uplift your life and take others with you on the adventure of bringing the heavens to earth.

NOTES

1. Esther Perel, "The Quality of Your Relationships Determines the Quality of Your Life" (February 12, 2019). Retrieved from https://youtu.be/LmDPAOE5V2Y.
2. Brené Brown, Rising Strong (Audio blog interview). (n.d.). Retrieved from https://open.spotify.com/episode/7ngz5mzi8FnnIXfPwbLlLL?si=xxLgKhj3Ss64oz7OvXGkag.
3. Lao Tzu and Tom Butler-Bowdon, "Tao Te Ching," in *Tao Te Ching* (West Sussex, United Kingdom: Capstone, 2012), 29.
4. Emerson, Ralph Waldo. *Self-Reliance, and Other Essays.* Dover Publications, Incorporated, 1993.
5. Brené Brown, *The Gifts of Imperfection: Let Go of Who You Think You're Supposed to Be and Embrace Who You Are* (Center City: Hazelden Publishing, 2010).
6. Shakespeare, William, et al. *A Midsummer Night's Dream.* Simon & Schuster Paperbacks, 2016.
7. Brené Brown, *The Gifts of Imperfection: Let Go of Who You Think You're Supposed to Be and Embrace Who You Are* (Center City: Hazelden Publishing, 2010).

CANCER

JUNE 21–JULY 22

text by Alice Sparkly Kat

element — WATER

symbol — THE CRAB

modality — CARDINAL

house — FOURTH

ruler — THE MOON

CYCLE

INTRODUCTION

I READ STEREOTYPES OF Cancer and instantaneously feel like we have all forgotten about the strength of Cancer. And why not? They cry readily, except when they don't, and they're easily agreeable, except when they're not. They're soft and tender, except when they're hard and fierce. They never seem to make up their minds and go to and fro like crabs on a beach—except when they do, and sparks light up because they're angry at you.

You may have memories of Cancers: There's the girl who once suddenly screamed in class as blood ran down her arm before another student took her to the nurse's office. There's my friend who forever talks of pining for his homeland, a place where he did not grow up, stocked with relatives he does not know. He mails me postcards decorated with pictures of homemade bread, with messages such as "You broke the ocean in half only to meet nothing that wants you—Immigrant" scrawled on the back. There's the person in your friend circle who knows just about every other queer person under the sun and around whom everyone flocks without even realizing it, like dust to gum on the sidewalk; they're attracted to them not because they have so much clout, but simply due to the sense of ease they give to those in their vicinity. There's the activist who undertook the impossible feat of organizing a group of sarcastic twentysomethings for a cause, who let the masculine-presenting people in the room take the spotlight in meetings because they spoke louder but who was the person everyone knew held the entire event together in the unglamorous late night and early morning hours.

And being an immigrant and being a Cancer? Being diasporic and being a Cancer? Having no homeland and being a Cancer? That's like having a perpetual case of homesickness that you forget about until it hits you with another case of nausea and misplaced nostalgia.

The signs are defined relatively. Language is in its location, and astrology, like real estate and climate change, is a language of location, location, location. Cancer sits on the zodiac wheel across from Capricorn, at odds with its cardinal sisters, Aries and Libra. The Cancer-Capricorn axis is this: nationhood defines the familial unit and vice versa. Our microscopic senses of belonging that we associate with every whiff of cooking from the homeland can be rebranded as a sentiment of nationalism. Cultural activities center around food. There is nothing more American than apple pie. Barbecue sauce calls to mind hot summers on the Fourth of July, and Chinese propaganda outlets want you, lost child, to go home and eat dumplings with your family and keep the nation together. Food and patriotism give us a sense of belonging. This is the sticky axis of the zodiac, where drama, regulation, and blood ties come together to take us hostage. The Cancer-Capricorn axis isn't just about fitting in socially like the Leo-Aquarius axis, which tries to connect your sense of individualism to the group. Cancer-Capricorn is about blood, heritage, and loss. The Cancer-Capricorn axis is your inheritance. It's in your biology, or your nation, and you have no choice in the matter.

All water signs have to do with death, after all. Pisces, symbolic of your own death, is anticipated but never experienced. Scorpio—representing those who die within your lifetime—is felt, and deeply. Cancer, the sign of those ancestors who have already died and survived in order to make the event of your birth possible, is only remembered and memorialized.

I think that we call Cancers the crybabies of the zodiac because we often have a romanticized view of the family, and especially of Mom. We want to see our families embodying that special place where we are protected from the reality of the world. We want to see Mom as that special someone who never judges us and defaults to understanding. We want to find our heart at home. We want to see home as soft, and so we choose to see Cancers as soft.

But home is often unyielding. Home often has mothers who don't speak the same language as you, mothers who starved through their childhoods and will beat you and drag you by the hair before they see you doing the same. Home has uncles who become monsters in the night. Home has siblings who want to eat or beat you, and home often doesn't protect you from reality because it is already reality. Home is often a hard lesson. It is a place that carries the trauma of having survived and the remembrance of death.

I won't say that Cancer is more hard than soft. That polarity is a game of gendered terms, and privileging one over the other doesn't do anything. Astrology itself is not a game of personality traits adapted to the modern age. Astrology is a set of archetypes adapted from certain ecological patterns and mapped for your reimagining, and Cancer is the archetype of the home. In the twenty-first century, home is often an imagined place more than a lived experience. "Nostalgia, once regarded as a symptom of extreme homesickness, has become a key term to describe the modern and postmodern cultural conditions... Nostalgia is no longer what it was under modernism—the empiricist representation of a historical past; in the postmodern age, it has become the appropriation of 'the past' through stylistic connotation, conveying 'pastness' by the glossy qualities of the image. Mass advertising thus often represents 'imagined nostalgia' by which people are driven to yearn for a mediated world they have never lost," writes Koichi Iwabuchi in his book *Recentering Globalization*. It is a place that exists in images of home cooking in ads and in rom-coms about the modern family. More than that, it's a nostalgic place even when we have never experienced the place the nostalgia refers to in the first place. I have often watched images of 1950s families on television and felt nostalgic, even as a first-generation Chinese person living in the 2000s, for an America that I've never experienced and that would have kept me out. Home is a social construct. It is a racial place and a gendered place. It produces a longing, and it is this longing that is exactly the stuff Cancer is made of.

In this chapter, we will talk about how the archetype of Cancer influences a variety of social roles—roles such as child, parent, worker, lover, and country. We will talk about how the longing for homeland, the nostalgia for history, and the inheritance of memory have affected these social roles in the twenty-first century. We will talk about Cancer as an archetype and define an archetype as that which produces meaning and a frame that encompasses an infinite number of symbols. To give you a little technical knowledge about Cancer, it is the sign on the summer solstice in the northern hemisphere, which is where the western zodiac originates. This is the warm and sticky time of the year, and warmness and stickiness are things that we attach to Cancer. It can be hard to breathe during the heat, the same way it can be claustrophobic to breathe in a tight-knit family.

The animal symbol of Cancer is the crab, which is the collector of shells on a beach. Like its opposite, Capricorn the seagoat, Cancer is between the land and the water. It is soft and yummy on the inside, but it wears a hard shell. Its claws know how to close around the object

CANCER ARCHETYPES

Some symbols for the archetype of Cancer follow.

- bed
- belonging
- birth
- collection
- comfort
- consumption
- domesticity
- family
- femininity
- home
- homeland
- homesickness
- home cooking
- kinship
- luminance
- the masses
- matriarchy
- menstrual cycle
- milk
- mom
- nostalgia
- ocean
- primordial soup
- the proletariat
- reproduction
- salt
- security/insecurity
- soup
- source
- tides
- womb

of its desire but almost never open voluntarily. Like Mom, it has you and it never lets go.

Cancer is the cardinal water sign. Cardinal signs begin seasons and are represented by the thirty days after a solstice or equinox. Cardinal signs often have tunnel vision about whatever it is they want, and Cancer can be singular in its vision. Water, the primordial substance, dissolves the weight of history. Water holds our genetic memory together.

Our moon rules Cancer. The moon is responsible for the powerful waves that crash around you when you get to the ocean. It's responsible for cycles of warming and cooling. The moon changes its shape every day and makes a cycle every twenty-eight-and-a-half days. It is a luminary, borrowing light from the sun and making brightness luminescent instead of direct. When it is new, it follows the sun and rises during the day. When it is tilted to be full, it has its own reign at night. The moon is a satellite of Earth and often a symbol of our final frontier. In popular sci-fi novels, we often imagine the moon as a site of colonization, a place to grow when Earth has been consumed (with Mars as a source of invasion). Thus, Cancer, the swallower, has to do with cultural colonization, consumption, and consumerism.

In Hellenistic astrology, the moon is associated with fortune. Fortune, in those days, was a bit different than how we think of it now. As opposed to spirit, fortune in Hellenistic times governed the physical body in all its yearnings and satisfactions. The body is the changeable thing.

The full moon that happens during Cancer season, the thirty days of each year when the sun is in Cancer, is always in Capricorn. Cancer's qualities are reflected by Capricorn, qualities such as what security may mean and what one's place in the world is. We glimpse Cancer in the myth of Saturn, who stands for Capricorn, when he swallows his children.

In the Thema Mundi, which is a theoretical chart that was used as an educational tool to learn astrological concepts that symbolized the beginning of the world, Cancer is on the rising sign. The birth of the universe has a Cancerian face. Thus, Cancer is connected to the beginning of all things.

The Harry Potter character with a Cancer Sun is Dudley Dursley. Dudley, in the narrative of Harry Potter, represents the child who overcomes the prejudice of the parents. In the beginning of the story, he is clearly insecure and defined only by the values of his family. By the end of the books, he gives Harry a small and heartwarming symbol of nurturing in the form of a teacup left outside his door, despite said insecurity. In this, we learn that Cancer's movements are not flamboyant. They are small yet packed with meaning. We learn that Cancers become strong when they choose to define the family, rather than perpetuate its cycles of trauma.

We will use these technical pieces of information to talk about Cancer through various social roles. More than that, we will read Cancer through the politics of the home. The home, the domestic sphere, is often that place where labor is taken for granted and boundaries are never enforced. It is often a place of tribal identity that replicates gendered norms. When we talk about parent, about child, about worker, and about country, we won't talk about *should*s or about things that you're supposed to be. We'll ask questions about how things have worked and should work, wondering like true Cancers about just what kind of memories this forever nostalgia and our ever-increasing desire for authenticity create.

CANCER AS A CHILD

CHILDREN WITH THEIR sun in Cancer are conceived during "cuffing season," the winter months when partners often "lock down" their relationships in order to have reliable companionship. Cancer-influenced babies, whether Cancer shows up in the sun, moon, rising, or another part of their natal charts, look for security. Some find it in family, others in friendships, and still others in routine. Parents may find it hard to get away from these babies. They want to be next to you, following you around from room to room like cats. They don't like to try new things until they've actually tried them. They don't like to leave the house until they do. Then it's hard to pull them away from what they're doing and talk them into getting on the bus again to come home. Cancer is attachment.

Once, over Malaysian food, I had a friend tell me, almost as if she were confiding a stolen secret, "I don't have boundaries because I am Chinese." But not all of us who have poor boundaries can say that it is because we are Chinese. We say that we don't have boundaries because we are Spanish, because we are only children, because we are first-generation immigrants, or because we grew up without fathers. We all have reasons we refer to when apologetically explaining why our boundaries are so poor. Often, these reasons are a nod to the patterns of homeland. The implication is always this: that boundaries are a profoundly Western experience and rooted in individualism. The key points are that boundaries are learned, not inherited, and we must force them into our biological ties for the good of all.

We repeat the word *boundaries* like a mantra. We fear our boundaries becoming too rigid. We feel self-justified in having boundaries. Boundaries, boundaries, boundaries.

If a boundary is closing a door and knowing that it will remain closed, what happens if you live in a one-room apartment with your grandmother, aunt, and mother and there are no doors to close? If boundaries are the ability to say no to the family's needs in order to discover your own, then what happens when it takes three generations working in tandem to buy a home? What happens when your mother doesn't take your need to raise your child in your own way, apart from her, seriously because she had both your grandmothers to help her raise you, and it's so ingrained in her that raising a child takes the whole village that it never occurred to her that you would try to do this incredibly difficult thing on your own in the first place?

Are boundaries a privilege? Cancer, the homeland, seems to know no boundaries. We strive to set breathable boundaries. We seek to make our boundaries, like skin, keep in what we prefer to assimilate, keep out what we do not want to absorb, and keep in what we want to keep precious. We rarely think to set boundaries to our inner worlds, between our past and present selves, to stop our brains mid-anxiety-spiral when we don't want to lose track of ourselves.

Capricorn, Cancer's opposite, can have boundaries; Cancer rarely feels allowed to. The Capricorn myth of Saturn swallowing his own children is a warning: don't let your family swallow you whole. Capricorn hears and listens. Meanwhile, Earth is engaged in a game of mutual absorption with its satellite. Moons can either be swallowed by whatever they're orbiting or they can choose the fate of slowly but inevitably drifting away. Our moon has chosen to leave us. It used to be bigger and closer to Earth. After the passing of millennia, it will sink into space. Other moons are not so lucky and cannot resist the gravitational pull of their main bodies. Their fate is to become one with the planets they are orbiting.

If Capricorn is our knowledge that, without boundaries, we will become too angry and too resentful and too taken for granted, then Cancer is that perpetual question of why that keeps boundaries soft and living. Why do my boundaries look the way they do? Have they become a defense mechanism, or are they still healthy? How can I let my culture and family still move within me while maintaining my sanctity of self? When making my boundaries, how do I ask the question of what to let in?

Parenting a Cancer child or re-parenting your own inner Cancer child can be a lot of fun. It can take an extraordinary amount of tears, some angry temper tantrums, and even more sidesplitting laughs. The moon, ruler of Cancer, is a messy and strong planet. Artemis of the moon was the wild goddess. The moon makes us nonsensical, and it makes the wolves howl. At the end of the day, Cancer is a very raw zodiac sign. Your relationship with a Cancer child may be tough, and it may be volatile, but it will always be real.

CANCERS, BIRTH, AND BABIES

The symbol of Cancer, two wells conjoined to shape a womb, is the container or vessel. Like a walled garden, Cancer is often seen as cold and separated from the outside world but also spontaneously wild and full of life on the inside. This makes Cancer a contradictory sign, one that seems uninhibited to those who know them well but withholding to those looking at them from the outside. In the birthing process, which is another symbol for Cancer, this contradiction is represented by the umbilical cord. While Cancer, our root, is tethered to the ancestor, the event that symbolizes Cancer best is the moment when the baby leaves the mother's body—that first breath of individualization.

Another symbol for Cancer is the seed. Cancer season is seeding season. The seed, in its smallness, contains all the information of the world. The seed is life. The seed is a symbol of raw potential that needs a little nurturing, water, and sunshine to get started.

Because all of a Cancer baby's time is spent with the parents, this is when their wild and unpredictable side comes out. Cancer babies need—with a vengeance. They are hungry, want to sleep against your body, and scream when they don't have safety. Because Cancer babies are feeling creatures, not emotional creatures, they react to everything and anything that they touch, see, smell, taste, or hear. What Cancer needs is to feel the intimacy of the parents so that they can feel free to pull away on their own terms.

Cancer, like the moon, is the sign of *goo*. This is an impressionable sign, and one that can never quite follow any strict rules no matter how hard they try. Cancer has an ingenuity all on its own, with a raw intuition that is best listened to—or else.

Cancers are comfortable as babies and toddlers. This is the best time for them, because they're free to be who they want to be without pressures or expectations. This is a time for them to learn how to be taken care of in the primordial sense, which is integral to the Cancer heart. When a Cancer baby understands that there is beauty to failure, that you will still be there for them if they want to play in the other room, they will be the crab willing to leave its small hole and look for the shoreline. When the crab finds the ocean, the source of inspiration, they're able to go almost anywhere they please, but only if they know that their way home is guaranteed.

CANCERS AS KIDS

Because birth is the symbol of individualization, Cancer wants to simultaneously flee back into their parents' arms and push away, yelling that they are their own person already. This is the contradiction within all Cancers, because Cancer is about release from genetic ties while remaining tethered.

In childhood, you have more rules to follow. You find that there are expectations for who you're meant to be. You start being social and, with that, begin to discover social problems.

Too often, our society tells kids to be good and, especially in the case of girls, to be neat and pretty. Cancers may wistfully imagine themselves to be pretty, but Cancer is too uncontrollable to be simply "pretty." There's just too much going on. Cancer is meant to be genuine, to be untamable, and to be unguessable—there's too much beauty going on for Cancers to be reduced to something as trite as prettiness.

The most difficult thing for a Cancer is accepting change. Children only individuate when they feel that it is safe out there, not when the things that happen are unexpected. Because the crab seeks security, Cancers will do all they can to avoid changing the situation they already know and can predict into something where anything could go wrong. They can play mind games with themselves, imagining the worst possible outcomes, just to be prepared. Without actually going through change and finding that they do have the strength to survive it, Cancer can become quite pessimistic. The thing that a Cancer kid must do is make sure that they are prepared for things, which means resisting spaces that make them feel safe but closeted.

Around seven years old, we all go through our first hard Saturn aspect. Transiting Saturn—that is, Saturn in the sky—makes a ninety-degree angle to the location the planet was in when we were born. This transit is a hard reality check. This is often the age in which kids, going to school for the first time, are faced with non-familial authority figures and time away from the home. It's a big change.

As a kid learning how to be a social animal, Cancer's shyness kicks in. Before they go out and have friends of their own, when they're living in the comfort zone of the family, Cancer is an outspoken personality. As kids who are expected to cultivate their own friendships and carry responsibilities for building trust in their groups, Cancers suddenly find that they need their own space much more than before. Because they are not fully grown—since none of us are ever fully grown—they need to bring the free space of early childhood with them no matter where they go. Cancer develops a large headspace and an active imagination. In their heads, they can play all the roles. Inside, they're in control of all the pieces and can safely explore emotional dramas without the risk of getting hurt. They make collections of their favorite objects, because holding and counting the things they understand and know makes them feel as if they can own parts of the world.

It's common for Cancers to find a close friend or two to play games of pretend with. They will choose someone they trust, and they will create characters that they may feel embarrassed to show the outside world and outsiders who may judge them. It can be easy for Cancer kids to put all of their emotional eggs in this one basket and rely solely on one close friend who makes them feel safe for companionship. It is better for them to come out of their shells a little at this age and to realize that there is more security in a community of different personalities.

If your Cancer kid is the only kid of color they know, go out of your way to find some other kids who look like them to play with. If they're not neurotypical, find other kids on the spectrum. It's important to encourage Cancer kids to cultivate a group over one friend, because it will teach them that safety is more likely to come from group accountability than friendships with secret conflicts and languages. As adults, they will be less likely to rely on one relationship for all of their emotional needs.

While Cancers know innately how to keep a group together and how to make everyone feel special, what they need a little help with is how to make a new member of the group feel welcome. Cancers are loud and funny and hospitable until a stranger walks into the room. This is when Cancer shyness is often interpreted as intimidation. Encourage your Cancer kid to say hi to the stranger first and see what happens—not to keep secrets from those who haven't proven their allegiance to the group yet but to extend an invitation to teach them the game that everyone else already knows how to play. Show them that a group is not broken when it is changed, but that it becomes stronger when it is able to change.

CANCER AS A TEEN

It's hard for anyone to be a teenager. The category of the adolescent as a type of human experience began around World War I. The idea of the teenager in the social imagination has always been associated with discipline, whether it's a so-called hooligan in need of some rigid rules or a well-trained young man preparing for war through ritualized sports. After World War II, the white teenager more often embodied rebellion, and youth culture as we know it today became widespread alongside a consumer culture that realized no one else was speaking to young people with free time and money to spend. However, brown and black kids are often still cast in the role of the prewar teenager in the American imagination, relegated to prison or the military and associated with either discipline or public malice.

The discipline that teenagers are subjected to is difficult for Cancer to endure. The pressure of impending adulthood as less free time is a constant threat to developing Cancer consciousness. Today's regimented teenaged schedule, often beginning at the crack of dawn before school begins, is hard on a body that just wants to stay in bed for a few more hours to dream what needs to be dreamed. We demonize teens, thinking of them as superficial and numb, and forget about the vulnerability of teenagers, especially oversexualized, overworked, and overly policed teenagers.

Some Cancers will take what they have learned in childhood and build a world of imagination that protects them from the world that wants to discipline them. They will learn how to quietly rebel and to do unorthodox things while appearing to be "good." This is why so many Cancers become good at the arts and writing, because drawing and writing are quiet acts of rebellion that look like obedience from an outsider's (often a teacher's or parent's) perspective. Before being sexual people, Cancers may explore what desire means to them in a notebook or sketchbook. Before choosing an area of study, Cancers will fantasize about what success looks and feels like to them without consequence.

Don't read your Cancer kid's journals. Don't make them share if they're not ready. Give them their own space. When they shut the door, even if it's with a slam, let it stay closed.

Remember that Cancer, to keep itself tender, wears a hard shell. It's not that your Cancer teen suddenly stops trusting you when they go through puberty. It's that this is the age when they're supposed to be learning the hard task of boundary setting.

Setting boundaries is a frightening prospect for a Cancer. Their friendships are close and intimate. They have a hard time saying no. They want their friends to think that they belong. They will often practice setting boundaries with family members first, because they know that family won't go away. They'll also do it in all the wrong ways before they get it right. They'll let you identify with them and project your own anxieties onto them until something explodes and they shout that they're not your property before storming away. They'll keep unimportant secrets just to see if they can get away with it and dangerous secrets to play with the idea of being dangerous. This is Cancer not knowing how to recognize their need for boundaries yet and putting them up wherever they can just to see if something sticks. Remember, Cancer is where impulse and tears come together.

But, eventually, Cancer will notice when their boundaries are respected. They will learn to recognize the thing in themselves that says "enough" when someone asks more of them than they're prepared to give. They'll learn that it doesn't take a breakdown to communicate their discomfort. They'll learn to choose the people who listen to their quiet and solid no so that they don't have to later scream them into a void. They will learn that setting a boundary is an attempt to grow a relationship, not shut one off.

Respect is the hardest lesson of all for Cancer to absorb. This is because Cancer is read to throw off all need to be respected if it makes others feel a little closer to them and if it makes them more palatable to a group. They'd rather be the friend whom everyone jokes about and invites to all the parties than the stick-in-the-mud whom everyone knows isn't down for certain things because they have too many principles. This prioritizing of acceptance over respect can be damaging in early relationships, both in new intimate spaces and in existing friend groups.

What saves Cancers in their teenage years is their knack for building the kind of friendships that remain real despite all of the social pressures. The thing about Cancer is that they stick with their childhood friendships. Cancers can go through hell in their teenage years, but they will have at least one friend who sticks around even after they say no to pressure from a romantic partner and are teased for it or speak out against a group of friends who are out to do something stupid. The thing is, Cancer isn't out for coolness or social acceptance as much as real and genuine care. If all the kids in their grade turn on them, Cancer will still know how to prioritize the friends who stay by their side because they've always been more hungry for real love, even when it's not pretty, than superficial acceptance.

CANCER AS AN ADULT

WHAT'S THE DIFFERENCE between adulting and being an adult? When we think of adulting, we think a lot about paying the bills, doing the laundry, washing the dishes, and undertaking any of number of other mundane and routine tasks that no one ever seems to have enough time to do in a complete and satisfactory manner. Adulting is often the shame of being incompetent at the simple task of being a human. In Anne Helen Petersen's article for BuzzFeed titled "How Millennials Became the Burnout Generation," she describes why millennials, who are not kids anymore but fully grown adults in their thirties, become paralyzed at the thought of a simple task. She claims that technology, scattering our attention and blurring work with life, creates emotional exhaustion that makes everyday, routine tasks that maintain our state of affairs feel unworthy of our care and attention. We sit down to plan a project, but we find it impossible to go to the post office.

In contrast, being an adult, that magical year of turning eighteen, is a graduation from childhood (a state of dependency) and the introduction to becoming a full, self-governing citizen. We're supposed to move out and go to college. We are expected to start being productive members of society, to vote for our interests. We are expected to participate in democracy. To be a full citizen, which adulthood is supposed to grant us, we are entitled to the preservation of life, liberty, and the pursuit of happiness.

What really happens when we turn eighteen is that many of us take out student loans to afford college—a lifetime of debt. Turning eighteen means that we enter into a contract with finance. Turning eighteen means that we can be arrested, tried, and incarcerated as adults. However, in non-Western cultures, adulthood is not a move away from the home but is a different commitment to the ancestral home.

Many heroes' journeys feature a protagonist who, in some way, does not fit into society. For example, Chinese folk hero Mulan wasn't the perfect daughter, and Greek hero Hercules was an outcast. During a hero's journey after leaving the community, the hero often encounters a villain, who represents the parts of the self that the hero must overcome. Often, the hero receives supernatural help, which symbolizes the will to overcome what feels inevitable. Once the hero has conquered the villain, they are allowed to return to the community and reintegrate in a socially responsible way. These are stories about growing up. The process of becoming an adult is a story about committing the self to the collective. However, solar heroes' journeys, about ego and validation, tend to center on victory, while lunar ones, about dependency and response, more often value self-sacrifice.

Adulthood is the stage of life during which the individual must answer to and become responsible for the community. When we are kids, the community invests in us. As teens, we can blame everything on society and dwell in apathy. The process of growing up is one of civil responsibility—one in which we discover our own power as well as social injustice. It is a process of taking ownership over the society we find ourselves in and summoning the will and agency to enact change.

CANCER AND JUPITER

Jupiter is frequently seen as an adolescent planet, full of experimentation and general messing up, but it's still considered one of the slower-moving planets. Jupiter is exalted in Cancer, which means that Cancer embodies Jupiter characteristics very well.

To put it simply, Jupiter is the planet of knowing things will end badly but doing them anyway because you just want to see what happens. It is the *Superbad* or *Booksmart* planet, to use two popular teen comedies as examples. Cancer embodies Jupiter well, because, at the end of the day, Cancer has but an insatiable appetite. This means that Cancer's exceptionality comes from its ability to mess up many times, absorb every loss, and still feel alive.

Jupiter is the planet of making mistakes, which is an important part of becoming an adult that, sometimes, we forget to have patience for. It is the planet of staying up super late to watch Korean dramas, even though you have work in the morning (and, in the process, finding out that you have an interest in storytelling), getting

> *Cancer is considered the funniest sign.*

too drunk at a party and making yourself look stupid (which reminds you not to take yourself too seriously and helps you gain a set of friends who don't judge you), and accidentally talking loudly about your boss while she's within earshot (and making her aware of some problems she's been taking out on the employees that she hadn't considered). The thing is, we can do all these things when we are adults because we are adults. Like Andy and April from *Parks and Recreation*, Cancer knows that there's no point in being an adult if all you do is pay bills. You're supposed to do all the things that you wanted to as a kid but couldn't do because you didn't have money.

Because Cancer is the glue that holds a community together, Cancer is also elastic. Out of the entire zodiac, Cancer is considered the funniest sign, and this sense of humor is what makes Cancer bounce back. In order to be their true and comical selves, Cancers make every place, even the workplace, a different type of home. In doing that, Cancers create a safe environment for making mistakes. You don't worry about mistakes when you're at home and you feel safe. Cancers never hide their inadequacies but seek to create an environment in which everyone feels safe to be less than perfect. In Cancer's realm at home, you're willing to show your work and your errors, which makes others treasure you when you do it well, and you earn respect through your imperfection. That's what the Jupiter exaltation in Cancer, a mature sense of how to mess up, is about.

CANCER AND SATURN

Before that highly anticipated Saturn return (the time when transiting Saturn returns to where it was when we were born) hits, we receive two Jupiter returns, and Jupiter is exalted in Cancer. The thing is, Cancer is a rather childlike sign and likes to experiment. It does exceptionally well when it can do whatever the heck it wants.

Saturn is the planet that rules Capricorn, while the moon rules Cancer. Saturn and Cancer naturally seem a bit opposed to one another. While Cancer is carried by the changing appetites through the course of a day, Saturn is set on long-term planning. Like the crab, Cancers like to change their minds a lot, unsettling plans and settling others. Saturn discourages this type of activity. While Cancer is about the familiar places, Saturn is about growing up and growing pains.

How your Saturn return looks depends on the condition of your Saturn, the person you are, and the world you live in. It is different for everyone. However, those who are Cancer-aligned often have Saturn returns and rites of adulthood that deal with the insecurity felt during large life changes.

In some ways, Cancer, pre–Saturn return, is a sign that is very good at doing adultlike things, such as keeping a secure job, taking care of others, and making sure that the home is livable (if not tidy). This is because Cancer is the sign that feels in control of the internal self and not in control of the outer world. Thus, Cancer can latch onto a clear career trajectory, already validated professional standards, and institutions that feel like they take themselves too seriously to fail.

But adulthood is about making your own decisions and owning them. It is about feeling in control of your life and your circumstances.

Often, the Saturn challenge for Cancer-aligned people is watching something they thought was bigger and more stable than their personal subjective realities fall apart. It is the realization that no one really knows what they're doing, not CEOs of big companies and not mothers having their third kid. It is the realization that no amount of credentials will make a person daring and wise enough to not need other people to tell them how to be them. It is the realization that change happens to everything and that you have the ability to make it happen but not the ability to control every aspect of it.

Saturn is about big decisions. If we take Cancer as the archetype of community, then the Saturn return to community is telling it that it must be able to swallow change in order to justify its own existence. It reminds us that groups that cannot adapt to the times and that culturally stay in a safer time period have no utility.

When challenged by Saturn and forced to grow, Cancers need to make a move toward big change of their own initiative. They need to understand that no larger structure, institution, corporation, or family can save them from the authority to make choices, stick with them, and know the consequences. Often it is a time of taking risks and making decisions that we don't know will pay off in the end.

CANCER AND URANUS

Trans-Saturnians is just another word for Uranus, Neptune, and Pluto (and Eris, if you use dwarf planets). I like to call them invisible planets.

Uranus, Neptune, and Pluto don't have rulership in traditional astrology. Rather, they are generational planets that describe whole generations, time periods, and zeitgeists. When we get Uranus returns, around the time we turn sixty-four years old, we learn to identity with our generational purpose. Humans don't get Neptune or Pluto returns, because we don't live long enough, but subcultures, family trees, and nations do. As humans, we do get Neptune and Pluto oppositions and squares, which is when transiting Neptune and Pluto form important angles to the places they were when we were born and define larger life transitions.

Uranus, in mythology, was the first rebel and was castrated by his son. When we get our Uranus return, that can be a time when we define our generational struggle not only from where our parents left off but also from where the next generation begins. We are aware not only of our own generation's challenges but also the limits of our children. We see the ways in which they perpetuate the same cycles of trauma that we are caught inside. Some of us get grandchildren around this time.

I can't talk about Uranus returns from an insider's perspective because I've never had one, but I can give an example. When my grandpa was sixty-four years old, his daughter decided to immigrate to the United States. Now, my grandpa is an old-school socialist and a devout believer in the anti-imperialist ideologies that the Chinese Communist Party created. Throughout his life, he witnessed a nation define itself against the West, against American dominance, throw off its roots and tethers, and create a new nation with no heritage and feverish industrialization, that burns resources and people all in the name of proving third-world merit. Even today, he talks about American schemes for world power and the destruction of the third world. His own child's choice to forfeit all of that political fervor marked a certain point in the timeline of our lives. It marked a period in which mistakes were made, became history, and could no longer be changed. The realization set in that a younger generation will not make different choices because of that history.

Uranus challenges to Cancer are about a change in culture. If Capricorn is the nation-state, then Cancer is the state of the nation—the culture within the nation that is just a container. Cultural changes don't happen statistically but through the changes in a mother-child relationship, a grandparent-grandkid relationship, or a peer-peer relationship. It is a change in feeling. The other thing about cultural changes is that, like Uranus the god, these changes defy existing cycles of trauma and create new cycles in which the old are overturned.

If adulthood is about becoming a free and political agent of change, then it's only fitting that we end our discussion of it with Uranus. You see, Uranus is the change of upheaval and revolution. It is the rebel's star. However, as the philosopher Hannah Arendt writes, revolution is only a turning of the stars. Revolution, in the root of the word, has an astrological meaning, and makers of revolution (especially in the period during which Uranus was first discovered in the late eighteenth century and Age of Revolution) were aware of this. For them, revolution and upheaval were natural parts of the turning of time. Take a step back and revolution is just one part, frame frozen, of the never-ending cycle of change upon change.

CANCER IN LOVE

"Love is patient (except when it's not), love is kind (except when it's not). It does not envy (except when it does), it does not boast (until it does), it is not proud (but sometimes we want to shout it from rooftops). It does not dishonor others (but sometimes it does), it is not self-seeking (but love starts from the self), it is not easily angered (but we are easily angered in love), it keeps no record of wrongs (except that we, in love, often do). Love does not delight in evil but rejoices with the truth. It always protects, always trusts, always hopes, always perseveres."

—1 CORINTHIANS 13:4–7 (PARENTHESES ARE MY OWN)

CANCER AND SELF-LOVE

Love starts with the self. Cancer's main challenges to unconditional self-love lie with their ability to hold a grudge down with their teeth until their gums are bleeding. This is true even with their own mistakes. Often, Cancers blame themselves for things they can't blame others for. Often, Cancers let things go in others because they feel more in control of their inner world than the outer world. Often, Cancers let their control of their inner world become rigid and unflinching, full of blame for things they wish they did just a little better, because they sense that it's easier to be soft and unassuming to those who are unwilling to change for them. Cancer, after all, is a similar type of control as Capricorn but exercised over the internal. All the tropes we hear about Capricorns—of being too authoritarian, too punishing, and too controlling—are also true of Cancer. It's just that these are the ways they treat themselves inside their own heads.

Love is ruled by Leo. Leo is the sign after Cancer. The sign immediately following the first is the sign that nurtures the first into being. The second sign reminds the first to take a break from being itself once in a while. The second sign is one that the preceding sign can find hard to grasp. Love can be hard for Cancer to remember. Love reminds Cancer to stop lying in its bed playing games of blame in which every culprit wears Cancer's own face. Leo reminds Cancer that love takes courage, and that it provides necessary nourishment. Astrologer Dane Rudhyar describes Cancer as a feeling sign and Leo as an emotional one. Feeling is mostly a biological response, while emotions are a social expression. Astrologer Alan Oken says that, because of this, while Leo expresses love regardless of what the other person does or feels, Cancer watches for signaling and will only express love while they trust the exchange. Cancer feels and ferments, but Leo is here to teach them that expression is important. Cancer can withhold—Leo wonders, what's the use of that?

Self-hate is safe. When bad things happen, it is easier to blame past versions of yourself, even publicly. It is easy to call yourself out on errors that you committed six (or more) years ago. It is easy to know all the things you did wrong and duck behind them like a mask that keeps your true self invisible and unknowable. It can be easier to say that your internalized racism keeps you from finding yourself beautiful, that you will never be smart due to institutional invalidation, that you have been taught learned helplessness due to your gender, and that this is why you can never be brave than to figure out how to be brave despite all of these things.

Self-love is harder. Self-love is forgiving your younger self for your mistakes. It is having the audacity to make new selves, and believe in the self you present to the world even when you know that there's a very big chance you're wrong about a lot of things. It is the understanding that while your hindsight bias makes you wish for perfection in a past that you will never be able to change, you still wouldn't change anything because your mistakes have created an accidental self that is worthy of love. Self-love is saying yes and no with some doubt, but meaning it anyway.

For Cancer, self-love starts with coming out of the shell. It is easy to blame yourself for everything when you are in your own inner cave and all you have to blame is yourself. Start seeing the larger societal trends underlying your problem: Are you really poor because you spent $6 on a lunch that you're beating yourself up for, or are you poor due to systemic oppression? Are you really depressed due to your own failures, or have your paths as a human in the world neglected to teach you some important coping mechanisms?

CANCER AND PLATONIC LOVE

The thing about Cancer is that they can be guilty of throwing all their emotional needs into one romantic, sexual relationship. But Cancer, as the sign that rules the clan, is not about one-to-one relationships. The Cancerian need for security simply cannot fit into a single relationship; that relationship would become fragile and break. Cancer is the village.

The difference between cliques and communities is one of security. Cliques are, by definition, the product of insecurity, and they perpetuate said insecurity. They contain members of a similar age range with similar interests and competing drives. They are insular and rigid. They keep new members out, treat their members as disposable, and hoard social capital.

Communities, in contrast, are built to protect their members from the insecurities of having children, falling ill, and growing old. A strong community replaces the need to hoard wealth with this social security. Communities contain babies and elders and have rituals for new members to build trust, as well as processes for those who seek to leave, knowing that leaving doesn't completely sever the connections that hold all of us together. Communities don't care about passing whims and whether you like someone in one moment and not in another. Communities care about building structures that support one another economically, socially, and emotionally.

Cancer, the sign that feels another's hunger as if it were their own, is absolutely necessary to a community. Cancers are needed because, without feeling one another's hunger, we feel isolated in our own. Without feeling one another's hunger, we would never learn to farm and cook. Without feeling one another's hunger, we forget that meals are best when shared.

In a clique, Cancer feels the insecurity of other members and gets lost in the socially paranoiac atmosphere of keeping up a nonthreatening appearance while constantly undermining others in a constant race for resources. In a clique, Cancer becomes cutthroat. Cancer's empathy doesn't disappear but instead becomes

CANCER LOVE LESSONS

1. Learn your own expectations. Often, Cancers have expectations when dating but lack the self-importance to divulge them honestly, feeling that they are asking for too much. Love becomes a battleground when resentment festers. No one knows what's going on with you unless you tell them.

2. Stop going for the safe option. The most available people often seem like safer choices and, when frustrated, all Cancer wants is someone who is at their house all the time. But, if you're choosing someone whom you're not that into just because you're afraid to hurt, you'll disappoint yourself. We're talking about love here. Go big or go home.

3. Don't give up everything that you have in exchange for commitment. While both Capricorn and Cancer want commitment, Capricorn really wants authority, while Cancer wants to feel needed. There's a difference between support and offering yourself up as a crutch because you're afraid that someone could go away.

a constant projection of learned desire that obfuscates what is really needed.

Cancer can feel what you need—exactly what you need! They can sense your every insecurity, even the ones that you don't want to show anyone! Isn't that a truly powerful thing? In a competitive society, this ability becomes a threat that must be hidden away in a disguise of polite smiles and playing nice. In a cooperative society, there is hope, because it's exactly this ability that makes it possible for us to feed each other while feeding ourselves.

CANCER AND ROMANCE

Cancer's brand of love is defined by hunger. All the water signs are boundless, because water always flows into the fabric of whatever it touches. Pisces lacks boundaries because it can project its self-image onto another person. Scorpio's love is expressed through desire, which looks for personal meaning through another person. Cancer is love that craves. Cancer love can be a vicious type of love, because its hunger is never satisfied. Often, Cancer falls in love more with yearning itself than with any person.

Cancer is a big gaping hole—a mouth that takes it all in and wants more and more. In love (can it be true?), Cancer is kind of... dirty? Cancer is a spiritual bottom. Once you are digested, you are part of them for good. *I want to accept you for all that you are. Bring me all your dirty trodden poor and I will make them whole again. Come to me in all that you already are and I will take you in as you are (except for the three months when I play hard to get, but not really that hard to get).* Think of Cancer as a huge, open pit. You may be a bit afraid to fall in, but once you do, you'll forget what it's like not to be under the spell of Cancer's gravity.

Love romances with Cancer are all about the mundane moments. The most romantic things for Cancer include seeing one another's puffy faces after waking up, being able to wear the old pajamas with holes on the bottom around each other all day, and cleaning up each other's messes, figuratively and literally. It's about having inside jokes that make no sense to anyone else and signing to each other in your own language.

Cancers aren't impressed by expensive dates, and their gut intuition just can't be fooled by some whimsical gift. They stalk you not because they will ghost you once they find your dirty laundry, but so that they can accept you for the imperfect person you are. They know if someone they're seeing really and honestly cares for them and is in it for the long haul. They have a sixth sense for whether someone's future plans include them or not, and, if it's the latter, they will bail without telling you why.

CANCER AND SEX
(Trigger Warning: Consent)

I'm not going to talk about what is the best way to have sex or how to have sex. Everyone has a different body and kink and likes sex a different way. Some people don't even like sex that much. All of these things are okay. What I am going to talk about is consent. If you choose to have sex, consent is key.

Sometimes, Cancer is a sign that wants too desperately for others to accept them. They are forever willing to please others, and nowhere can this get more dangerous than in the world of sex.

We've all had encounters where we didn't say no, not because we were unsure whether we wanted sex, but because we were unsure whether the time was right to say no. No is a hard boundary, and Cancer sometimes wants these boundaries to be implicit rather than explicit. They want sex to already be a place of mutual understanding without having to communicate with a single word.

> Sometimes, Cancer is a sign that wants too desperately for others to accept them.

The best thing for Cancers, in sex, is to practice saying what they want out loud so that their partners can hear them say it and ask questions if they need further explanation. Consent is not a single transactional statement or built into sex itself. It needs to take place as a constant negotiation that both partners engage in willingly. Consent can be fun. It can be fun to talk about all the things we want and refuse all the things we don't want.

Cancer, don't confuse sex with commitment. Don't confuse sex with giving all of yourself because someone who loves you wants to take you whole. Don't settle on having sex that you don't want to have because you're afraid of alienating the other person. Instead, make your desires explicit. Make boundaries for what you can give so that others value what you choose to give them. Make commitment a goal if you want it, but don't confuse that conversation with the conversation about your sexual desires. Choose to have the sex that you enthusiastically want, and only the sex that you enthusiastically want.

CANCER AT WORK

Because Cancer is associated with enclosed spaces and home, it's also associated with the domestic. Much of the labor in the Cancer (domestic) sphere has been unconsidered and unpaid. Think for a moment about how much it takes to keep a familial unit running. The trash has to be taken out, the mustard has to be replaced, the kids must be taken to the doctor, the rodents must be expelled, and everyone must be loved just a little at least once a day. And someone has to keep track of all of this. The French comic *The Mental Load* by graphic novelist Emma explores how the job of "project manager" at home is already a full-time mental load even if one doesn't take actually doing the chores into account. Outside of the domestic sphere, there is always a person in every office who remembers birthdays, cleans the microwave, and notices when a colleague is going through a difficult time.

Mars, the planet of action and doing things, is considered to be in the dignity of fall in Cancer. It's unrecognized in Cancer. Mars, the planet of getting things done, is Cancer busy doing the invisible forms of emotional labor—of settling disputes, of compassionate work, of doula-ing, and of doing the cooking and cleaning that no one considers when they define work in a broader sense. Mars in Cancer can end in feelings of resentment and disrespect. Mars can end up feeling *humiliated* in Cancer when it sees everyone else in the office getting raises and promotions while they're holding the entire thing together after everyone else has already left the office.

The thing is, our economy cannot run without someone doing the cleaning, without someone doing the childcare, and without someone feeding the hungry. It just can't.

CANCER AND THE FREELANCE ECONOMY

I remember one of the most valuable pieces of advice a career counselor once told me about working in today's economy: "You need to start thinking of all your jobs as projects. Once you finish a project with one company, you might get hired again for another project. You might not. Your projects are your expertise."

It is hard for Cancer to operate with the precariousness that a freelance economy demands. Cancer wants to make a home out of the job. They want to know what they will be doing next month, and preferably five years from now. They want their jobs to make them feel that they belong somewhere, and they want to feel emotionally validated by the work they do. They will accept low wages and a lack of benefits in order to do work that feels good to their heart, working for very little in social services or the nonprofit sector. In a project-based job market, Cancer can't help but feel betrayed.

In addition, Cancer may feel alienated by the push such a job market demands for its participants to network, network, and network. Cancer can be a shy sign. They have trouble going out of their way to meet people, especially if the meetings ring of inauthenticity.

However, it's exactly these traits that may help Cancer survive in the workplace.

The thing is, Cancers keep close the people they know to truly advocate for their work. Cancers do the work they do because they've followed their heart, not because they've researched the best employment options for people with their skills. They will not leave a place of employment just because it is less than ideal. Instead, they'll stay until their magic has made it better.

It's hard for young Cancers to start their careers and swing from one place of employment to the next—this is true. However, the value of Cancer is that, in their older years, their years of work experience have not only given them a good CV, but also a *tight-knit* group of friends and comrades. These friends know *intimately* what Cancer is good at, have been through struggles with them, and will advocate for them even when they make mistakes. Cancer has friends who will send them jobs and put in a good word not because they seem to be currently winning but because they're in a moment of hardship. They are able to approach jobs not as just another candidate in a pool, but as an individual who truly understands the work and the people already behind it. They can handle the environment of ruthlessly competitive capitalism and somehow create their own microcosm of a kinship network inside of it.

This helps Cancer survive.

You see, Cancers always build security in their own ways. They may not do it by attending elite institutions, crafting intimidating résumés, having flashy work histories, or even knowing the "right" people. They do it by knowing the people they know, building trust over the years, being there for their friends, and knowing that, with a group around them as emotionally bonded as their circle, there's no way Cancer will be left in the dust.

CANCER AND MONEY

The thing is, if you have Cancer somewhere in your chart, and especially if you have the moon in your second house, your finances are going to be motivated by security. It's a place where you may have worries about the future, a place where you hang onto what you have tightly, and a place where you can have trouble letting go.

For Cancer, money is not luxury or freedom. It is security. It's protection against questions of what happens when you fall ill or grow old. It's a buffer against precariousness.

Cancer likes to save and save. Money, in this capacity, isn't a tool anymore. It can easily become a psychological complex. If you feel like you don't deserve to pursue your dreams until you have a certain dollar number in the bank, that number will keep growing higher and higher as your spending levels increase with your income, and you will sit down one day and realize that you were never brave enough to step out of an unhappy comfort zone. Money can become neurosis.

Of course, that's not anyone's fault. This is a social problem. People tend to feel like they need to hoard resources when we lack adequate social security.

The thing I've noticed with Cancers is that they can lack the ability to invest their resources into things that turn into wealth in the long term. This is because they respond intuitively to the economic climate of the day. The moon moves signs every two days, after all. When the economy feels secure, Cancer can consume their feelings. They buy things that make them feel good and spend more than they accounted for. When the economy is austere and resources feel scarce, Cancer becomes scared and starts to put more in the bank as a psychological comfort and without an adequate long-term plan.

This can be true of how Cancers feel about their skill sets as well. They respond too easily to market trends, burning themselves out so that when the trend dissipates, their workflow does as well. In this state of mind, capital becomes something that manipulates the lone Cancer, who can only scramble to respond to a capricious market.

Cancer needs to learn how to think of money as a plan. Money is a plan for the future, not

DO

* Create real relationships with people you work with, even if you don't make friends with everyone. Prioritize the friendships you can take with you after the job is over.

* Follow your heart. You will not be able to stay in a job field that you don't care about for very long.

* Commit to your dreams. You will only see them pay off when you stop half-assing them and start believing in them.

* Make joint investments. You will feel safer about them, which will give you a more level head when it comes to maintaining them.

* Invest in your community. Your independent work ethic will not pay off nearly as much as mobilizing for wealth as part of a larger collective.

DON'T

* Isolate yourself when you're in environments that aren't good for you instead of looking for the one or two people you can team up with.

* Prove yourself right about not being able to do something by choosing work that you never wanted and won't be able to sustain.

* Change your mind about what you want too early, using it as self-justifying proof that you can never excel.

* Let employers tell you that the market is bad to justify paying you less than you're worth.

* Let market trends freak you out about your long-term commitments in the moment, leading to overreaction and betrayal of your purpose.

---

just what you eat today or tomorrow. They need to start building wealth. Inequality does not exist due to differences in income or work ethic. It exists due to the different histories of wealth. Fighting for income equality means that you're fighting for the opportunity to work for a living your entire life. Fight for wealth equality instead. This takes more and steadier hands on deck.

You'll never feel that it's the right time to stop what you're doing and start your own apothecary business if you rely on business insights to tell you when. You will know it's the right time when you focus on your own requirements in the moment and what you need to grow. You'll never feel like it's the right time to invest, because either the market is doing too well or it's doing too poorly. You will know when it's right based on your own savings, age, health, and commitment to meeting your goals. Make your own financial plan for yourself and stop googling things in an effort to try to outsmart the market. You can't and will never be able to, because the market is fundamentally unpredictable. Use your income to build wealth slowly and incrementally. Use your skills to build value at your own pace. Don't let peer pressure break your resolve and make you change your mind about something that you felt was right yesterday. There's no such thing as the wrong decision so much as decisions given up on too early in the game.

Water is a temperamental and fluid thing. Financially, it can make loss and gain unpredictable. Water does well mixed with a bit of earth, which is solid and unflinching. Cancer should take care not to let employers or so-called experts psyche them out about their own financial realities or employability. They need to embody a little earth when it comes to financial stuff and exercise a self-understanding so strong that they know bad advice from their own intuition in one glance. Did you buy into a market when it was on the decline and lose money the very next day? That's not necessarily a bad thing, unless you get scared and sell at a loss before things pick back up again.

All this said, while a rock-solid mentality can be helpful when it comes to exorcising the anxiety of money, the reality is that money is oppressive. There are things you can't overcome with saving. If you do more feminized forms of labor, like social work or work in the beauty industry, you may not get paid as much as people who choose industries that are more likely to be characterized as masculine, like finance or tech. There are ceilings that have not been broken yet. There are communities that have been robbed over and over again, and that inherit more debt than wealth.

This is where Cancer's best qualities kick in. It is far better for Cancer to invest in the people they care about—and I mean that literally—because Cancer understands relationships better than money. Because Cancer is a pack animal that looks for other people, they often feel safer in joint investments than in solo ones. This is good, because we come up together or we don't come up at all. Cancers innately put money into their community because they understand that relationships bring more security than a good portfolio any day.

It's better to be creative with how you can build wealth if you can't afford to invest in anything by yourself. Get a bunch of people together and commit to a joint investment plan. Make plans to stop renting by seeking out those who would like to purchase property as a large group. If you want to start a business and can't do it on your own, find other people who want the same things as you and go in together. Make it a community-led initiative. I'm part of the millennial generation, which has inherited considerably more debt and less stability than our parents. We will not be able to invest in retirement in traditional individualistic ways. We will need to work together. We will need to make our communities strong so that when money fails us we'll have people to fall back on. And we need Cancers in the mix to remind us of the power of collective strength.

There's a saying that's applicable in this situation: "If you want to go fast, go alone. If you want to go far, go together." Money, like living, is a lifelong affair.

CANCER AND THEIR DREAMS

Cancer is a dreamer. It's a sign that never feels comfortable fulfilling conservative expectations. Cancer has an intuition about what they are good at, and they excel when they allow themselves to be creative. They need to do what satisfies the heart. They dream of being a famous young adult novelist, of being a world-renowned artist, of being a niche stand-up comic, and of opening their own restaurant—all at the same time. However, Cancer can be a fearful dreamer. Their dreams feel so real to them that they often inhabit them instead of reality. Their fantasies can be a placebo until the day reality checks in and they realize that they're unhappy postponing real action.

Cancer is also a tremendously capable and talented sign. They're literally able to do all these things that they dream about. They're fantastic at building sentiment through writing, at creating new aesthetics, at making people laugh when they're not expecting it, and at building environments in which people like to gather. Cancers bring tremendous value to the table by just being themselves.

The thing that gets in the way of Cancers making their dreams into livable realities is the constant to-and-fro motion of nervous indecision. Cancer is like the beach. On the beach, you never know when the next wave will hit. Things disappear if you leave them there too long.

Any time Cancer spends worrying over whether they are making the right decision is time wasted. Stop asking whether a decision is the right one. Start asking yourself whether it is a decision that you can *commit* to. The advice to follow your heart is well and good, but what if your heart is constantly changing?

Again, there is no such thing as the wrong decision for Cancer. As a water sign, they are too in touch with their intuition to really forget it. They will always know the right decisions for themselves. Difficulties come when their intuition changes direction every few days. Decisions that were right at one moment go wrong when they hesitate. In the end, decisions are just decisions. Any decision becomes wrong when it is given up on too easily or too quickly. Any decision becomes the right one when you put in years of commitment and dedicate yourself after you make it.

The mistake Cancers can make is that they put their toes in, testing the waters, when it comes to living their dreams. They half-ass things because they're scared to get their hopes up. They're afraid to go all in, and they pretend not to care how things turn out. They set themselves up for failure.

Did you once dream of being a concert pianist but didn't give yourself the time to develop your skills because you were scared of what would happen if you failed? If you feel this way, you will fail, because you'll never give yourself a shot in the first place. Do you consider doing comedy but also starting your own tattoo studio and decide to try both to see which takes off? If you do this, you will end up feeling so split in terms of time that neither venture will pay off.

CONCLUSION

WE HAVE TALKED about two types of Cancers in this chapter, or viewed Cancer through two frames. One is Cancer as an archetype, which every person that participates in culture is both influenced by and influences, and the other is people who have strong Cancer placements, meaning that they're doing the work of remixing the Cancer archetype actively. Astrology is a cultural science, which means that, like art or language, it is just a way to describe social complexes. What distinguishes astrology from the other cultural sciences is that it focuses on the archetype, which is something that is both inherited and reproduced.

There is a branch of astrology called evolutionary astrology. Evolutionary astrology tells us that, by constantly striving to detoxify and improve yourself, you can "evolve" as a Cancer and rid yourself of negative Cancerian tendencies to embrace the good traits. Evolutionary astrology, influenced by Darwinism, often forgets that genetic change doesn't occur at the scale of an individual's lifetime. It happens through lifelines. It happens through history.

Ultimately, astrology is talking not only about biology but also about the intersection of biology and society. When we get into the murky waters of genetics, we must remember that trauma is inherited generation after generation.

Sometimes, we forget that the word *generation* has two meanings. One refers to a stage of human life or age group, while the other refers to the magical capacity to release an idea and change the world. These two meanings are not too separate. They only seem different when we think of our ability to create things as limited to the self.

Astrology's mantra is "As above, so below," but the other half of that mantra, the less repeated half, is "as below, so above." The stars are not something that shine down on you and tell you who you are, thereby controlling your fate. The stars are a mess of lights that contain multitudes of stories that every human generation has passed down to their kin. Astrology tells us that we can change the stars to remind ourselves that the grand narratives about the world, ones that seem bigger than the world, are changeable by yours truly.

I disagree with much of evolutionary astrology not because I think that people can't improve but because I don't think that improvement can be done by yourself for yourself. Evolution is not the pursuit of making yourself into a better Cancer, which relies on the same stereotypes and social complexes. It's about committing yourself to join other people who strive to change how the social complexes exist in the first place.

For example, much of Cancer's negative traits have to do with insecurity, clinginess, and hysteria (a type of female craziness coined in the nineteenth century and thought to be caused by a wandering womb). These traits are deplored in Cancer because Cancer, having to do with the moon and thus the menstrual cycle, is associated with femininity. Moon goddesses, in the West, are often female. In response, our reaction should not be to try and figure out how to be a better type of woman while using all of our willpower to resist being the bad sort of woman; it should be to figure out where these social complexes are coming from, who is in charge of telling the stories, and what social needs these behaviors may be responding to. We may find that female insecurity comes from having less political power, that clinginess happens when the community is uprooted, and that hysteria contains symptoms of unbelieved trauma. This is what it means to evolve, and it doesn't happen through individual productivity. It happens through the social movements of history.

All archetypes change over the years. The moon is especially hard to track because of the multitudes of deities. Once, the moon, because of its fast motion, was imagined to be a goddess who sought to conquer the sun, a male god, chasing him down to make him submit by taking his light into herself. As the role of women changed in a more militant and bureaucratic society, the moon became a more passive body that only received the sun's rays. By Roman times, Artemis, the goddess of the waxing moon who represented the older version of the moon as a female hunter, was replaced more and more by Hecate, the goddess of witchcraft. During industrialization, witches were stigmatized, persecuted, and burned. Likewise, lunar and nocturnal things acquired a sinister association. Mythologies are not contained by distinct cultures but echo each other. In both Japan and Brazil, there are stories about the rabbit in the moon—evidence of how far stories can walk when humans wander.

But storytelling has not died. It is less useful to look at the lunar myths of yesteryear than at those being circulated and received today. Looking at the moon in modern films and media is more useful than referring to Chaldean or Roman stories because we can understand them more. They speak to the symbols of our current day and they speak to our own subconscious. Myth is not dead. We watch and read myths on our televisions, phones, and tablets, disbelieving and subscribing more than ever.

MODERN MOON MYTHS

Science fiction, which originated as an extension of the Western as a genre of fiction, tended to view the moon as a place where further colonization could happen, from penal colonies to military bases to eugenist elites. In the Cold War era, the moon represented possibility. If we treat their fictions as mythologies, we find that the archetype of the moon in classic science fiction represents the final frontier. The 1969 American moon landing, happening in real life but a story as large as a myth, is heralded as a symbol of American pride.

In a more recent publication, fantasy author N. K. Jemisin creates a world with unpredictable seasons and no history in her Broken Earth trilogy. Later in the books, we find out that the volatility of the world is due to the loss of its moon. Without a moon, the orbit of the planet becomes unstable. In this work, the moon is a symbolic anchor. Its lack is the evidence of history lost.

The moon is a vastly different symbol in the Broken Earth trilogy than that of older science fiction stories. The moon is not somewhere you can go, as it was during the Cold War, but a thing that should not be touched or disturbed, lest the world turn to hell. In the Broken Earth series, the moon represents the sanctity of nature.

If the moon represents our home in archaic mythology, then Cold War–era storytelling imagined the expansion of that home through military and scientific endeavors. N. K. Jemisin writes of the lost moon as a symbol of a lost home, as a warning against what we have already done to Earth. Hope, for her, comes not through expansion but through restoration.

Outside of the United States, the moon continues to haunt us. Teresa Teng's pop song "The Moon Represents My Heart" is considered the anthem of diasporic Chinese. This song has been heard everywhere in China, but only after the Communist Party became more open to Western influences following the Cultural Revolution, which erased much of China's cultural, ancestral home. Teng, a Hong Kong pop star, expressed a feeling of nostalgia not only for the homeland missed by diasporic Chinese living overseas but also for the Chinese cultural history lost in revolution. The song itself, characteristic of *gangtai* Cantonese pop music, blends modern Western musical sounds with instrumental Chinese folk influences to create a new but familiar sound.

In the story of the anime *Neon Genesis Evangelion*, the moon is a mostly monstrous, larger-than-life threat to humanity. In the First Impact, the Black Moon collided with Earth and killed most of the world's population. In the Third Impact, the murdered angel Lilith is so gigantic that her blood stains the moon. This impact is what dissolves the rest of humanity, turning everyone into primordial soup via the singularity, or uploading of human consciousness, into a virtual space.

In the story of *Neon Genesis Evangelion*, the enormous threat of the moon is meant to represent the United States as a nuclear power, according to literary critic Hiromi Azuma. The impact of the moon is what shocks humans to dissolve into the primal human source. As a result of the moon's impact with Earth, every human's consciousness loses its individuality and joins together into a mass consciousness. Speaking from a post-Hiroshima Japan, Azuma is talking about globalization. In his narrative, the cultural parts of the world do not retain their distinctness when impacted by globalization but instead become a cultural sludge. In contrast to Cantonese pop music, Japanese animators tried to create a feeling of cultural odorlessness in their work by emptying it of Japanese and Asian elements. This odorlessness, or *mukokuseki*, is relevant to a global audience.

In Teresa Teng's music, the pop cultural moon conjures a pining for a home that feels vastly different from the home imagined by the Communist Party's patriotic folk songs. In *Neon Genesis Evangelion*, the moon is the colonizing culture that melts cultural distinction. In both media experiences, it is impossible to imagine a home that is uninfluenced by colonization or globalization because it is impossible to imagine a nation with no nationality.

In all three examples—the Broken Earth trilogy, the lyrics of "The Moon Represents My Heart," and *Neon Genesis Evangelion*—the moon no longer references a specific ancestral homeland but instead the feeling of nostalgia as provoked by anxiety over the future. Within this nostalgic feeling is also the feeling of anxiety. In the Broken Earth trilogy, the anxiety is about climate change, and loss is experienced out of respect for the land on which we live. For listeners of Teresa Teng, the nation is lost due to disillusionment over nationality, and anxiety comes from the inability to define a place of cultural belonging. In *Neon Genesis Evangelion*, the anxiety is over nuclear catastrophe, and the loss is over self-sovereignty. In a postmodern age, the moon, and Cancer, become the sour feeling of cultural loss.

NOSTALGIA AND NATIONALISM

I want to bring Saturn and Capricorn back into the discussion, because every lunar and Cancer meaning has a reflection and another meaning through the lens of Capricorn. Capricorn, an agricultural king, is the land itself. The god Saturn was worshipped in archaic times with the casting of dice, which was a game peasants played when their work of sowing seeds was done. By gambling, peasants symbolized the risk of relying on nature to fill their needs even when seeds had already been sown and little else could be done except to wait and see whether they would grow. By respecting our gamble with Saturn, we learn to respect the capriciousness of nature.

In his 1624 poem "No Man Is an Island," John Donne writes that "no man is an island entire of itself; every man/is a piece of the continent, a part of the main." For Donne, people do not exist independently of their nations. Every part of our culture and sense of self comes from the continent to which we attach ourselves. Our home and our lands are not separate. I am American, we say, and I belong in America. In this statement, we're not only referring to the land we live on but also to the nation as a cultural symbol. Nostalgia and nationalism, then, are as linked as Cancer and Capricorn. The ethnic nation-state and its nationality have historically been built on a feeling of nostalgia for a lost cultural golden age. While Capricorn seeks to describe the limits of every nation concretely by its physical borders, Cancer takes on the much more nebulous task of describing the ends and beginnings of a national identity through yearning, loss, and the anxiety of nostalgia for the home.

In this chapter, we talked about the crab as a symbol for Cancer. The crab not only wears a hard shell but also lives on our beaches, the literal ends and beginnings of our continents. If you go to the beach, it is a place where everything is transitory. No structure erected on a beach, not a sandcastle nor a building, lasts without continual renovation. The line between the water and the land is not clear or predictable but changes with the appetite of the tides and the flow of the moon. Our literal borders are not immobile. Rather, they shift each and every day.

There is a threat to our borders and a threat to our land. This threat is a danger to our basic sense of security. This threat, which will erase our beaches, is rising sea levels due to climate change. Because we have industrialized our agriculture, you could say that we have ceased to pay respect to Saturn, the old god and his tendency to gamble, trying to make him something that he is fundamentally not—predictable. We have begun to see nature as something to be controlled instead of honoring the inherent risk of playing games with it. This creates a backlash, happening as slow as time and with the force of a tsunami.

Evolving the archetype of Cancer is not about being less needy, emotional, or hysterical. Evolving the archetype of Cancer is about rethinking what our borders, our homes, and our kinship networks mean in the twenty-first century after globalization and with certain ecological disasters on the horizon. There is no astrologer who can provide you with your own answers to these questions, but a good astrologer will ask you questions that provoke you to arrive at your truth. Living life as a Cancer means that you are in charge of playing with, remixing, and narrating this archetype of Cancer with your own voice at the forefront.

In Stacy Simplican's book *The Capacity Contract,* she describes two types of communities: communities of strength and communities of vulnerability. Communities of strength exclude those who are not fit to prove themselves worthy by the standards imposed by the group. In contrast, communities of vulnerability seek to include members on the basis of need. While a community of strength is actually very fragile when met with change, a community of vulnerability becomes stronger through change because its boundaries are flexible. Cancer, because it is an empathic sign and one that responds to needs urgently, can be a community of vulnerability when it is strong enough to give safety back to itself. Climate change brings up uncomfortable questions about who we can depend on if our systems stop working. Despite our borders, despite our cliques, and despite our exclusivity, the work of a Cancer is to remind us that real communities last forever by never staying static.

Challenge those who make you feel that you must belong to them or with them. Exercise as much criticality around the things that make you comfortable as the things that make you uncomfortable. Create challenging and flexible boundaries. When in doubt, always leave the house. This is the work of living life as a Cancer.

JULY 23–AUG. 22

text by Bess Matassa

element — FIRE

symbol — THE LION

modality — FIXED

house — FIFTH

ruler — THE SUN

INTRODUCTION

COME CLOSER. PUT your hands on your own sun-kissed skin and feel the pulsating magenta of the bold blood that courses beneath. The zodiac's "Glitter Kitten" is composed of equal parts fluff and fire, a relentlessly tender sparkler made to sport their pumping heart on ruffled sleeves. Custom-built for a lusty lifetime of recovering and relishing in their own true colors, no matter the cost, Leos are here to show themselves and the world that they were absolutely born to be this way.

Paving the sequined way back to innocence and fueling a thirsty quest for their personal disco balls, these fancy felines are lifelong proclaimers of the message that it is all right to trust this life, exactly as it is. It doesn't mean they'll never get hurt. It doesn't mean they won't want to shut it down, draw the curtains, and throw in the beach towel altogether. In fact, developing some tolerance for the darker shades of experience only makes their glow even glowier, because these summertime astrobabes are ruled by the relentless rise of the scorching sun. Cultivating the willingness to come at it again and again is the magical mission of a lifetime for this warm-blooded cosmic creature, kissing cynicism straight on the lips with cherry balm glitter gloss and a healthy dose of hedonism.

I will love again anyway, says Leo. I will show up at the doorstep of life clad in my finest frocks, regardless of what receives me. I will sport diamonds on the soles of my shoes and glow no matter the weather, pulling the plants out of their dormancy and toward my gorgeous, goddess-given heat. I will open wide to exactly what's here and take it into my heart. I will let myself be moved by the world, so that it will be moved by me.

LEONINE PLEASURE PRINCIPLES

These guiding lights shape the Leonine lifestyle, both as reasons for being and dynamic calls to embrace.

HEAT

Signaling the sweat-soaked center of summertime in the Northern Hemisphere, Leo "season" is literally the hottest section of the astrological year (running from late July through the heart of August). As we strip ourselves down to bare skin, shedding our layers and slipping into teeny-weeny swimwear, Leo energy reminds us of the potential seamlessness between our environment and ourselves.

Imagine cocktail hour in the sizzling tropics after an epic day spent frolicking in the hot sun. Whether at high noon or midnight, Leo weather is stable in its temperature. It's connected to its sign's consistency and loyal sense of self-expression. Clad in the same soul clothes no matter the hour, Leos are here to literally close the gap between themselves and the world, reaching out to touch and be touched by the humid air with a delicious sense of reciprocity and a generously seductive availability for exchange.

The second of the fire sign trinity (preceded by engine-revver Aries from late March through April, and followed by wild pony Sagittarius from late November through December), Leo is the roaring beach bonfire to Aries's lit match and Sag's Olympic torch. While the first sign of each element is here for the self (Aries) to initiate and explore, the second is here to "express" that element, collide with the collective, solicit feedback, and divine how to creatively contribute. While the Leonine mission is intensely focused on shining on, no matter what, this sign is also constantly learning how to focus these beams in order to both avoid burnout and best inspire.

In a deep dance with the generous spillage of their one and only selves, Leos' light must also be channeled into coaxing all the little flowers that surround it to burst into full bloom. Leos have literally been incarnated to harness their eternal flames to heat up the world. They must figure out how to share their tropical sensations and contribute to the world without compromising a drop. Think of the energy of a delicate marshmallow roast, where there's both a celebration of toasty open flames and the careful consideration of how to turn all sides golden brown rather than a burnt BBQ. These kittens are here to serve up their signature snacks with honed heat, ensuring that everyone at the bonfire gets to taste the smoky sweetness.

EXPOSURE

Just like how summertime strips away our scratchy layers and brings us back to the beautiful basics of slick skin, Leos are here to work with the principle of "exposure." Contrary to popular belief, this isn't necessarily connected to extroversion. Leos come in all shapes and sizes of loudness and shyness. This process of self-display is less tied to a sense of spectacle than to a willingness to bring whatever part of themselves is most vulnerable to center stage.

Cultivating the capacity to skinny-dip in broad daylight and show themselves no matter what is a constant process of ego rock tumbling that blends unapologetic self-expression with the call to dive deeper into self-awareness. There is an unabashed clarity to the midday sun, which sparkles while illuminating cracks and fissures. Leos are here to bless it all with warmth. The willingness to come ever closer to the core of their being with both celebratory fervor and realistic self-assessment brings them into alignment with their heart's true mission: lasting and luminous self-acceptance.

In the tarot's Major Arcana, Leo's patron saint card is Strength, often depicted by a being clad in glorious white robes approaching a lion's open mouth with open palms. This willingness to come at the world unarmed and heart-first lives at the core of the Leonine call for expo-

In the tarot's Major Arcana, Leo's patron saint card is Strength.

sure. Whenever this little love cat has lost its way, the secret is always to summon a palms-up approach rather than a Napoleonic pretentious defense. Showing up in softness to face life's most seemingly ferocious beasts is this sign's greatest act of courage.

Swapping "I'll show you mine if you show me yours" for simply letting it show, Leo's "me-first" attitude can be channeled into a willingness to "go first" no matter what. Here to teach the rest of the world that dropping our armor is not only possible but highly desirable, these acts of disarmament bring Leos deeper into the dance of core self. Valuing their own humanness allows them to extend this generous acceptance to every person they meet.

Considering their carnivorous nature (alongside the Scorpion, the Lion is the only other explicit meat lover in the zodiac), this willingness to soften may seem paradoxical. Yet Leonine landscapes contain both the jungle cat and the well-tended house pet, reminding us of the sign's capacity for fancy-feasting on all flavors of ferociousness. Even huntresses can consider the humanness of their prey, giving thanks to the succulence of the treats they consume and licking their chops with satisfied satiation. And when Leos choose the path of more fluff and less exhausting force, literally letting the muscles of their mojo relax, they can forge entirely new concepts of success. When these love cats gain confidence in a lifelong capacity to catch their next meal, sweaty moves to stay "on top" need never be the endgame.

REALNESS

Softening into the sunbaked range of their selfhoods brings Leos into communion with a sparkling destiny forged through relentless realness. Following the lead of their compulsive drives to be exactly as they are at all times, Leos are perpetually brought back to the heart of their own circumstance, compelled to check in with their own personal beats at every turn.

And while what is "real" for them is certainly subject to evolutionary appetite change, there's a remarkable constancy to the Leonine lifetime.

You can almost always spot a Leo, whether it's thanks to their stylistic flair, the swagger of their strut (which definitely deserves a theme song), or the feeling that you would still be able to see them even in a darkened room. No matter the situation, Leos seem to carry a signature scent. When the world turns cold or they feel like they've lost their way, returning to this essence is essential, no matter how small the gemstone glint of this proprietary pulsation.

While "cardinal" signs initiate the start of each season (Aries, Cancer, Libra, Capricorn) and "mutable" signs slipslide us into the next (Sagittarius, Pisces, Gemini, Virgo), "fixed" signs (Leo, Scorpio, Aquarius, Taurus) hunker us down into the center of the Tootsie Pop and work with the solid fullness of willpower, stability, and desire. The "eternal flame" of the three fire signs, Leos must follow what truly lights them up, relentlessly pursuing their heat sources regardless of how they are perceived.

The Queens of un-guilty pleasures and full-bodied passions, Leos are tasked with igniting their entire beings with an all-or-nothingness-fueled appetite. Living, breathing proof that the heart wants what it wants, the Leonine lifetime is best lived from the center of the chest rather than the neck up. Not one for half measures, these bright beings are here to let their realness spill up and over the sides of their cups, learning to banish the shame around "too muchness" and to quite simply bring it on.

SPECIALNESS

While this persistent focus on their own interests can sometimes morph into blind self-obsession, at its core it is connected to the kitten's mission to celebrate how special it is at all costs.

As the fifth sign of the zodiac, a number associated with the magic and majesty of laying claim to what we've learned through experience, Leos take the first steps toward truly considering their tastes. Leo marks the moment in our soul's development when we leave the safety of our private lair and step out into the world. After the highly personal journeys of Aries, Taurus, Gemini, and Cancer before it, Leos are built to let their brushes with others refine what they consider beloved. Think of the Leonine lifestyle as a kind of teenage locker left open, papered with band pullout pages and little vanity altars to treasured moments.

The question of their specific incarnation and its contours is perpetually on their hot pink lips, demanding constant attention and incantations that bring it into being. Learning to believe that the world can savor their distinctive flavor with no effort is the kitten's growing edge. When out of alignment, this little fluffball can puff and plump aimlessly, grasping at their bigness as a cover for lurking feelings of less-than-lusciousness.

More than any other sign, Leos are driven by a sense of personal destiny, convinced that they have graced the earth for a carefully chosen purpose ordained by the heavens. And they are absolutely right. Their sparkle and shine is unparalleled in the zodiac, and good goddess do we need their glow. But at the heart of the matter (where a Leo always longs to live), this meet-and-greet with destiny must be a midnight chat between Leo and whatever they deem their god to be. Always checking first with their internal heat source is the key to creating sustainable fire. And when synched up seamlessly with their special flairs, Leos learn that they don't have to break a sweat to become irreplaceable. They simply have to *be*.

CREATION

Whether or not they're actual artists or performers, all Leos are here to work with the process of creation, learning to understand the specific sparkle that animates their DNA. Often pigeonholed as the zodiac's crowd-pleasing, jazz-hands performers, Leos actually undergo very subtle processes of show-and-tell. Regardless of whether or not the seats are filled, Leonine acts of creation must first and foremost bear witness to the self. After the watery inner world of Cancer, the sign that directly precedes it, Leo is here to give birth to these private fantasies. These creative acts are akin to a second heart that lives outside the body, and Leos must match the blood type of this second heart in order to thrive.

Indeed, their entire lives must consist of creative acts, and Leo returns us to the original dictionary meaning of the word romance: "a quality or feeling of mystery, excitement, and remoteness from everyday life." Extending far beyond simplistic visions of red roses and white weddings, romance is connected to our capacity to inject magic into the mundane. The notorious Leonine capacity for "drama" is actually connected to this magical mission, and Leos are here to remind the rest of us that our existence is worthy of epic mythology. A life worth living is worth living larger, whether that means strutting down the street to an imaginary soundtrack or hairspraying their notorious manes to high heaven.

At its highest octave of expression, this pleasure-soaked, color-saturated vision can inspire Leo's traveling companions to sparkle and glow alongside the kitten, which in turn can help Leo find the courage to simply sit back and enjoy. Passion must go hand in hand with compassion, which literally means "to feel with." Uncovering the poetry in every gesture and the star-studded quality of every sensation leads Leos closer to both their own hearts and the humanity of others. Leo thus provides a soul train of dancers to help keep the beat for whatever other style is shimmying its way through the center of the crowd.

Leo's curvaceous sign symbol is part lion's mane, part playground equipment, and urges those born of the kitten to dive heart-first into its ice cream swirl, arms up and completely alive to the present. For Leos, play must become a form of prayer. Strategy is swapped for a full-throttle trust in the aliveness that courses through our veins. Stripped down to its barest skin, the Leonine lifetime keeps rhythm with a deceptively simple heartbeat: the cosmic call to become more and more of the selves we long to be and already are. Leos must sport their truest colors, no matter the cost.

This journey into the leopard-print luminosity of Leo's lair is set to a mash-up of Céline Dion's "My Heart Will Go On" and Madonna's "Express Yourself." It is clad in gold lamé, hot pink, and whatever saturated, signature shades your soul wants to sport. It also comes served with plenty of succulent snackables: think mangoes on sticks, overripe juicy tomatoes, and bubblegum bubbles ready to burst. Truth be told, Leo is bombastically emboldened and gaudily gorgeous in its unapologetic urge to just be.

So strap on your roller skates, slather yourself in suntan oil, and get ready to shake it to your own bedazzled beat.

LEO AS A CHILD

IMAGINE AN ENDLESSLY idle summer afternoon, complete with the heady scent of honeysuckle, poolside cheese curls, ice cream truck soundtracks, and absolutely nowhere to go and nothing to do but be, be, be.

The perfectly plumped orb of the orange creamsicle sun, Leonine energy embodies the very essence of childhood, exuding the sheer excitement and unstoppable animation of our original life force. Leo is here to celebrate vitality and remind us that our mere existence is always more than enough reason to walk this earth with majesty. In childhood, we all catch a glimpse of what it means to carry this credo. For Leos, the trick is to never stop courting this mistress of miniature-me magic.

For Leo children, this life is a delectable treasure to behold and adore. They clutch it close to their hot little hearts, tucked in and tender. Filled with the pulse-quickening spirit of unquenchable hope, life arrives in their upturned palms like a birthday present, complete with shiny ribbons and glittery wrapping paper. During the perpetual process of self-exploration, Leo children learn how to harness the power of the personal, how to lay claim to their turf, and how to inject their strongest rainbow-sherbet-saturated sensations into even the most mundane of life's moments.

THE PATRON SAINT OF PLAY

Whatever the age of the Leo, the sign itself is the patron saint of childhood, and this patronage is deeply connected to acts of play and creation. The Leo child is the embodiment of the verb "to play," and is most fully themselves when deep in the flow of gushing expression and unstructured freedom. Quite simply, Leo youth just wanna have fun. And they are undeniable proof that play is the worthiest of all art forms.

Take a moment to consider the onomatopoeic sound of the word "Leo." Just three letters and ending in a vowel ready to embark on a Mediterranean holiday, Leo is the simplest sound in the zodiac. It's a straightforward sparkle that feels as luscious to roll in the mouth as a hard candy with a liquid center. In childhood, Leos must harness this open-endedness and stripped-down sense of self. Over time, they learn how to constantly recreate themselves through acts of make-believe. Every moment becomes proof of their own deep magic. When they embrace the magic of each moment, no matter how minuscule, they remember to treat life like a grand inheritance they've been gifted.

The act of play invites us to fearlessly bring forth our own whimsical inner landscapes. It's a reverential ode to the sheer joy of being alive. This act is successful not because it's recognized by others or because it results in some tangible reward. Rather, the reward is the process of becoming more and more ourselves. To play is to put strategy aside. To relax our defenses. To believe that life wants to lift us and catch us and swing us up and over the bar. To remember that we are not an accident. To understand that life is here and waiting for us to enter it. And for Leo children, everything must conspire to support this belief.

Although play doesn't need to bear any tangible results, as they engage in these guileless acts of joy, Leo children inevitably develop some attachment to seeing how they affect the world that surrounds them. The key is to encourage play while also making sure they don't become overly dominant in their surroundings. The results of play should always be pure, with greater emphasis placed on the "being" rather than the "doing." At whatever stage of development these young cats find themselves in, they must surrender to the moment of creation, when the maker lets go of what gets made. Whether it's as low-stakes as a backyard mud pie or as intense as their first serious homework assignment, Leo children thrive when they are focused on the motions of the action itself rather than the action's results.

Yet these acts of creation must always bear the signature of the self. When the process is deeply aligned with what the Leo child hopes to create in the first place, there is seamlessness in the sparkle. But when they inevitably run into external rules and authorities, these little love cats simply must find ways of adding their own bit of flavor and flair, no matter the limitations. As they enter adolescence, finding their flair becomes even more vital. Perhaps more than any other teen sign, they need to seek out new ways of letting their creativity shine. Whether it's bumper sticker proclamations on their rides or signature streaks of pink through their hair, Leos are built to leave a glitter trail through the high school hallways. Even if it's simply penning a heart-shaped dot above the decimal mark in an all-too-linear math equation, making their pizazz known is critical to their development.

CINEMATIC CHORE LISTS

The fire function is forever larger-than-life, and this plumping-up process begins early on for Leos, who may feel actively oppressed by the limits of the mundane world almost from the moment they arrive. And while some Leo children might follow the rules if they get to be the leader, in their hearts they often seek escape in a more exotic realm.

Preparing a young Leo for a lifetime of colliding with the mundanity of existence means making sure they are equipped with the most vibrant color palette possible. If they're engaged in chores that feel oppressive, they might need to find a way to transcend this experience. Imagining that they're playing a starring role in a show called "Life," which occasionally requires them to make the bed or wash the dishes, can help these love cats find the epic in the everyday. Such a skill set will be useful well into adulthood, when everyday drudgery can often feel endless and inescapable.

Leonine children can sometimes have a startling sense of immediacy about them. They may appear constantly on the edge of the next big feeling, ready to burst into tears, rage, or a song and dance. At the core of these cravings is the desire to be adored. To be held by this world in constant awe. Even the most introverted of Leos craves this kind of glory, and if they're not tap-dancing and tugging on your wrist to get you to watch, they will still harbor secret longings to be looked at in some fashion.

Indeed, at this most tender of times, teaching the Leo babe how to grapple with the full range of their feelings is critical, as they tend to ride the roller coaster of extremely high highs followed by bottomed-out lows, especially as they enter their teen years. Chasing the intensity of "solar" hits starts to pattern itself in their youth, as Leo kiddies hungrily seek out dramatic moments of self-mythology and expression. Learning to navigate these slopes starts by fully supporting their most heat-saturated pink and turquoise sensations. As they weather their own emotional intensity, they build faith in the belief that these colors are part of their very soul's palette, available at any moment.

Telling a Leo child they're "feeling too much" or to "stop that crying" signals a kind of soul death that will echo throughout the rest of their days. Allowing young Leos to emote the rainbow without reprimand affirms their fundamental right to spill over the edges and beyond the lines. Additionally, young Leos should be gently encouraged to spend quiet time amidst their feelings. This will help them learn to live with the fluctuations without immediately demanding a reaction. Channeling feelings into finger paint, choreographing a private dance number in the basement, or strutting down the neighborhood block can replenish and restore a young Leo's soul, providing proof of their Technicolor while teaching them how to cope with and celebrate every shade of emotion, all on their own.

> **Allowing young Leos to emote the rainbow without reprimand affirms their fundamental right to spill over the edges and beyond the lines.**

RULERS OF THE CASTLE

Whether they're doling out dolls to the neighborhood kids, deciding who will play with which one and creating backstories for each Barbie, or staking out a certain area of the house as their own little kingdom, Leo youths are always looking to assert their right to inhabit their own lair.

With a reputation for sometimes taking on the role of a dictator, it's important that their parents and mentors help guide these urges for rulership early on, to ensure that the young Leo leads with love rather than force. When they feel secure in their own signature flair, there is no child in the zodiac more generous with their heart space. It's most often the Leo child who's willing to extend a bejeweled hand to lift others up onto the top of the fort for heaps of fierce fun.

Leo children are best supported when they're given the right to enact self-dominion, even when it comes to mundane situations. If you bear a Leo babe, letting them exercise their personal appetites grants them an everlasting key to their castles, whether it's picking out their lunchbox snacks or the outfit they'll wear to a family function. To be seen and felt is of the highest importance, complete with signature color palettes. In fact, playing dress-up can be a prime arena for self-exploration and self-determination, and Leo children truly flourish when diving into a closet of fantasy frocks. Whether they choose glittering gemstones, a spandex superhero suit, or simply a piece from their parent's work ensemble, the act of slipping in and out of threads is a powerful part of their process of self-empowerment.

Whether or not the Leonine youth is a born performer doesn't matter. Any chance to experience the self's reflection and be "received" is highly desired. Whether it's locked in the closet recording a personal podcast or watching footage of themselves dancing in the backyard, the process of solitary mirroring is a critical one for Leo children. Even before their gifts go out into the world for feedback from humanity, these early, more private exchanges help Leos build an unshakable trust in their own identities that can stave off feelings of not-enoughness that might come later. Filling their own cups with the strength and security of their self-expression at a young age will ensure that the little love cats are able to lick their own wounds and celebrate their own victories.

SENSITIVE STUFFED ANIMAL PILEUPS

Playfully reflective self-awareness and megawatt feelings are part and parcel of the little Leo's deep desire to get closer to this world. Like the love cats they are, Leo children want to rub up on the furniture and leave their scents. They want to make sure they are *felt* by everything that surrounds them. While Earth signs (Taurus, Virgo, and Capricorn) are known for their deep sensuality, Leo youths also love to touch and be touched. If conditions are right and they feel supported, they can be some of the most affectionate youths on the astro block, clutching whatever they love close to their hearts. As they pet their fuzzy stickers, comb glossy purple pony hair, dive into plush pink stuffed animal pileups, or emblazon their bestie's neck with a golden "Forever Friends" heart, Leo children are constantly attempting to close the gap between themselves and what they care about most.

This desire for closeness and magical mirroring means that Leonine youths often have a rather animistic view of their surroundings. They can be passionate about their most beloved toys, often naming them and giving them full life histories that include birth certificates. A Leo child might even go as far as to worry about a lone piece of pasta in the trash that has no traveling companion. This process of injecting the material world with narrative should be lifted up and celebrated in the young Leo and never deemed silly. Leonine hearts are pumping outside their bodies after all. If encouraged, this youthful tendency toward animism can strengthen the generosity of their spirits.

In Carl Jung's (who also happened to be born under the sign of the love cat) primary psychological functions, fire energy is connected to the intuitive function. At its core, this function is proof of our capacity to believe in the beauty of our own existence. The belief that we mean something and that we can sense, in our wildest moments of freedom and flow, a larger connection to all that exists. That we are not separate from this world. For Leo children, this connection is vibrant and alive. Every object that they see, whether it's a blade of grass or a plastic Barbie slipper, reflects themselves and their self-expressive stories.

LEO AS AN ADULT

AS YOUNG LEOS prepare to leave the plush pink of their bouncy castles for the harshness of the wider world, the transition into adulthood can be a startling one. Playground power struggles lead to higher-stakes encounters with authority later on, and the key to a full adulthood lies in stoking and tending the eternal flame.

With time, the gap between the jungle cat and house cat identities can widen, and Leos may find themselves swinging wildly between voracious, leopard-spotted grasps at power and prowess and rhinestone-collar retreats into the kitty cup for petting and grooming. Growing up seems to necessitate ferocity first, and the inner softness and tenderness of the fluffball can start to wither.

The answer lies, as with all things Leonine, in a simple but potent act. As the Leo ages, the call home to their central mission gets more and more vital: to live heart-first. In fact, more than any other sign, Leonine beings are asked to "grow down" as they age. This means they must remember their core selves at every turn.

THE TWENTIES:
Hungry, Hungry Kittens

As young Leos first head out into the world, their central focus is often on maintaining the sense of "specialness" they developed as children. Their experiences as young adults can be direct reflections of how much or how little they were adored and affirmed.

In either case, the usual romantic fervor of any sign's early twenties is amplified a thousandfold in Leos, and they come at the world hungry for vittles to boost their vitality. These ravenous youths can often find themselves in the throes of dramatic obsessions, sometimes shifting their notorious forces to another being or beings who they believe are necessary to confirm and stoke their flames. And as they enter into their first serious partnerships and begin to let the world's limitations in, a harsh skin sometimes starts to form over their soft hearts, which plump and puff in reaction to all this new criticism.

Astrologically, this time is leading the Leos toward their "Saturn Return," a cosmic comeuppance that occurs around the ages of twenty-eight to twenty-nine. Connected to the earthy pragmatism of the sign of Capricorn, this period can feel like a reality check for Leos in particular, as their sunbaked tropical island light starts to look more like the harsh exposure of the morning after. The lifelong question of how to collaborate with the contours of life as it is gets activated, and the young Leo is asked to envision this time as a kind of spiritual haiku. They must learn to dance in whatever room is available, no matter the size, and paint with whatever colors are currently on hand.

Gifted with extremely potent life forces, the question of which way to point their love beams is always of the highest importance. And as the late twenties crest, Leos start to become aware of their true prowess on a durational level. They come to understand that the promise of their specialness is here to incarnate on the earthly plane rather than to just be chased into the clouds for its addictive highs.

THE THIRTIES:
Taste the Rainbow

Following the Saturn Return, a core piece of the Leo's being has been recovered, and there can be a sweet feeling of getting scooped out and washed clean. Leos find themselves all the way back on the shores of a more settled sense of self, and this can never be taken away. As Leos enter their thirties, they start to stand proudly and firmly at the center of their bouncy castles and catch glimpses of a glittery mission that is truly meant to warm the world.

During this decade, Leos first start to come into communion with the concept of channeling. Creative actions come through them, and they don't have to push so hard on the pedal of proving. As they start to release into relishing passion projects, guided by instinct and intuition, they can begin to creatively marinate projects and partnerships. They can now also trust that their essence will flavor whatever gets tossed into the frying pan without having to make sure that their names are explicitly listed on the menu.

Toward the end of this decade, the Leo gets their first hit of the "Pluto Square" astrological aspect, and this underground planet can take the burgeoning fluffball straight into the belly of its beasties. For Leos, this means starting to truly explore questions of power, success, and sustainable strength, and to consider swapping gold stars and carefully autographed names for a curiosity about the star-studded stuff they contain. During this time, the young Leo starts to explore how to "stay with" every feeling that arises, rather than instantaneously translating everything into larger-than-life emotions that must be immediately strung up in neon lights.

Pluto is also the planet of deep feeling integration. It takes us to the bottom of our wells and the undersides of our logs in order to examine all of our creepy crawly impulses. A successful mission to the underworld is evidenced by our capacity to feel rather than our ability to fix. The unstoppable glow of Leo's headlamp can help reveal this. This is a time for Leos to start probing exactly what they are made of and to consider the snackability of all their shades, rather than favoring only the ripest tomatoes and summer fruits.

THE FORTIES:
Sparkle and Shine Symphony

The dawn of the forties can signal a period of tumult for the glamour pusses, as they begin to sense the physical limitations of the bodies they inhabit. No matter where they sit on the spectrum of vanity, Leos will start to come up against the gnawing sense that they won't be the first souls to live forever in the fullest glory of their Texan-sized manes.

> **In their forties, Leos are called to carefully consider the menu options. They become choosier in their selections of partners and projects.**

But rather than a plastic-surgery-fueled frenzy to hungrily grasp at forever young, this decade offers Leos the chance to revise their beauty standards and learn to truly "behold" themselves as their bodies shift and change. The forties love cat is invited to celebrate whichever aspects of their physical selves feel most on fire. And this can become a quietly insular, self-seductive process, with the forties Leo staying home at night for epic sessions of self-massage.

This decade is about understanding appetites and desires. In their forties, Leos are called to carefully consider the menu options. They become choosier in their selections of partners and projects. Rather than simply stalking prey out of animalistic instinct, forties Leos learn to banish this scarcity mentality and to trust that, if they pass on a certain snack, there will certainly be more soul food on the way.

Astrologically, this era is dominated by the "Uranus Opposition," a planetary transit that wakes us up and shakes us up (commonly part of the notorious "midlife crisis). This planetary shock jock invites Leo to integrate its opposite sign of Aquarius, the cosmic queen of panned-out perspectives and collective consciousness. While Leos start to get hits of creative "channeling" in their thirties, the forties Leo begins to deeply grasp what it means to "play their part" in a complex symphony. They become more concerned with collaborative efforts rather than merely waiting for their next solo. If they can rise to the occasion, the Leos in their late forties learn about their vital connections to the whole. By doing less and being more, their presences alone can become some of the most powerful creative forces imaginable.

THE FIFTIES:
Life in the Shade

Armed with a newfound concept of sustainable glamour and a growing trust in the vital role of their symphonic instruments, Leos enter the fifties with a nocturnal trail of glitter in their wake. The thought of going "softly" actually starts to bring out even more of their notorious sparkle, and it is here that Leos begin to learn to truly integrate their call toward tenderness. They recover that original "Strength" tarot card mission of disarming themselves and coming at the world palms-up.

Astrologically, this era is dominated by the "Chiron Return," an event that calls for deep sensitivity and a willingness to access our feelings no matter how much it hurts. Minor planet Chiron

Uranus

is the zodiac's softest spot, a little package we've arrived with that may not even be ours to carry. This archetype is the gateway to our humanness, a reminder that there are things that can only be felt and not fixed. And for the Leonine pride, this can be a tall order.

Trusting in this process of self-tenderizing is Leo's deepest work during the fifties, and the love cats are called to truly consider what an internal experience looks like. They come up against their factory settings of a life forever lived in the full light of day. Yet there are untold treasures tucked into these shadowy places, and the maturing Leo is asked to get a little loony with it all. At this time, they may find creative inspiration in the midnight hours as they craft their own particular brand of silk-robed sensuality. They're invited to come into communion with these glamourous ghosties rather than trying to push away any darkness that arises.

THE SIXTIES:
The Inner Throne

As the fifties close, Leos come into their second Saturn Return, which beckons them into a brand of boldness that will shine bright for the rest of their days. This is the time of deepest "earth" element integration for the sign, and the call is to develop a profound trust in their inner authority. They have the chance to step out into this decade clad in precious metals and soul alignment.

"Who's really calling the shots?" asks the sixties Leo. "And what does a life well lived truly look like for me?" As they begin to walk the rooms of their castle at this juncture in life, the answers they find may surprise them. Initially, this can lead to scrambled attempts to rectify anything that doesn't seem to be in soul-shaped order. Another common feeling is a profound sadness over what's been "wasted." On the surface, the early part of this decade may appear to bring on the blues, especially as the Leo reflects on the accolades and achievements they have earned in life. While these may have provided initial satisfaction, it's possible they haven't proven to be sustainable sources of sparkle and glow.

Yet this is all part of the rainbow integration of feelings for the later-in-life Leo. It's designed to push them toward that internal source of heat and power that can never be tamped down. Before they hurtle toward the psychiatrist in search of prescriptions to shut off the sadness valves, they're called to sit steadily with these feelings, to integrate them, and to let them lead to an assessment of their truest sources of pride.

What have they created that they'd be willing to risk their bodies for in a house fire? In the long process of "growing back down" to meet their original sources of ignition, the sixties signal a decade of pageantry and regality. In the hopes of creating a legacy that's built to last, the sixties Leo seeks only the most sustainable sources of diamonds to mine.

THE SEVENTIES AND BEYOND:
Return to Source

Following the emotional diamond-mining and throne-claiming of the sixties, the seventies arrive as a breath of candy-coated air. The original package of presence Leos were handed as youths is promptly regifted to them. This mature Leo has the deepest capacity to harness the heat that originally ignited their birth. The Leonine generosity of spirit starts to spill over during this decade as the little love cat settles in, gives it up, and turns it loose to a higher law.

This is the moment when the abundant sense of sparkly treasure really flowers, and these felines come into their own as cosmic coaches and cheerleaders for all those mere mortals who surround them. Genius guidance counselors and emboldened blood transfusers for whatever has gotten stale and sepia-toned, these wise Leos are all spryness and sparkle, lit up as though from the great beyond. The key word during this decade is "bask," and it's here that Leos learn to lie down in whatever sunlit patch is close by, full up with the feeling that they've got nothing to lose and everything to give.

Astrologically, if the Leo makes it into the eighties (and they often do, for no other sign loves the sheer exuberance of existence quite like this sign), they hit their "Uranus Return," a cosmic transit that electrifies the relationship between their personal identity and collective gifts. While the energy builds toward this moment, whatever simply succulent, straightforward sensation first opened their hearts as youths must be uncovered and recovered. As their whole lives flash dance before their wide eyes, these wise kittens see, suddenly, that it was all for the love of it, whatever it was. And it was never in vain.

LEO IN LOVE

WHILE TAURUS AND Libra may be the signs ruled by rose petal planet Venus, Leo has the cosmic corner on lavish love, which is lit by the eternal flame pulsations of the midday sun. The lust of Leos is quite literal, and they were born to live it (with just one more letter, Leo becomes the word *Love*). The zodiac's everlasting romantics in the classical definition of the word, these fancy felines are perpetually poised for mutual adoration fests and heavy petting, letting lovers lap them up like sweet cream. They carry their paramours across their big cat backs with unwavering passion.

The growing edge for these little love kittens lies in learning to receive. They must open their arms to their lovers as separate beings and magnetize what they desire with sweet allurement rather than blind dominance. Hyped up on their own heat, Leos can sometimes plan the whole Hawaiian vacation before checking in with their traveling companions about their choice of luxurious locale. But when Leos learn to disco dance in time with a true give-and-take, they liberate even more of their precious hearts. This can turn them into hot tubs full of healing waters, ripe and ready for anyone who wants to take a dip.

TELL IT TO MY HEART
Crushes and Courtship

As with all flame-on fire signs, Leo comes at love in plain sight. But unlike the sometimes-painful obviousness of phallic Aries or the wildly elusive stylings of fly-by-night Sag, Leo has a profound urge to demonstrate its fancy flair. Thus it can transform the crushing-and-courting process into a chance to exercise its creative muscle.

More than any other sign, there's something of the classic sweetheart in Leo, and at any stage of life, the early throes of a love affair can carry the body spray scent of teenage mall infatuation. The Leo is convinced that they are the first one to ever get all hot and bothered. They feel as though love has never been lived quite like this before. That the pavement underneath their feet is lighting up like a personalized dance floor, or that the birds have broken into pop music ballads composed just for them.

A perpetual prom night of personalized passion, early-stage Leo loves are injected with melodrama. Even the most minimalistic Lion (if there truly is such a thing) will engage in some pumped-up proportions in the throes of romance. Like a neon Miami Beach night or a high-rolling weekend in Vegas, there is an irrationally over-the-top quality to Leo's infatuations. And whatever the response by their chosen beloved, the love cats can run on the fumes of the love drug like no other sign, full-up on the life blood of a new affair like a romantic tick. And while this quality is part and parcel of the Leonine capacity to love through the apocalypse, gentle reminders that their love drug is brought on by the presence of an actual complex human with a history can help the Leo evolve beyond the next hit of hedonism.

Regardless of the outcome of dating explorations, Leos are encouraged to celebrate their capacity for trust at all costs. This can be tough and tender medicine for little Leo, as the end of affairs can bring them into some of the darkest depths of any sign. Their capacity to hop into the hot tub and start making promises is directly proportionate to the innocence they lose. But to learn to love again anyway, raising their lighters high above the ashes, is exactly why Leos exist in the first place. Their heartbeat beneath the heartbreak stands as a testament to their strength.

ETERNAL FLAME
The Long-Term Leo Lover

The Leonine lover is built to last—a solid-gold nugget that nestles into a beloved's arms for the long haul. Regardless of the form durational partnerships take or the gender identification of the little love cat, there is something of the *Brides Magazine* happily-ever-after that shapes their spirits. Even in the unhitched Leo, there's still a flavor of serial monogamy that takes root, transforming even one-night stands into epic poems scratched into bathroom walls in bubble letters.

In long-term affairs, the generous potential of the Leo is magnified, and in these partnerships they evidence their incredible solar-paneled staying powers. "Devotion" is the guiding light for these long-haul Leos, and they can require a bit of upkeep to feel solid on their romantic thrones. Leaving little love notes and packages around the house helps keep Leo's emotional pillows fluffed. And when they feel safely loved-up-on, the Leonine commitment is unparalleled, renewing its wedding vows through daily acts of devotion.

Long-term Leos are urged to come closer to their romantic growing edge: accommodating inevitable carnal change and opening up to separateness. To last through the night, Leos must learn to understand their lovers as evolving planets in their own right rather than solar-powered satellites fueled only by the Leo's core desires. Cultivating the capacity to remain curious is vital, and Leos in long-haul love are urged to present options to their partners rather than signed, sealed, and delivered statements. "I've booked the tickets to Belize, we leave at 7 p.m.," might be swapped for something like: "Right now, all I can think about is us prancing through humid jungles in matching unitards. Is that something you'd be interested in?"

And when they face up to their fears of waning affection and wounded pride, long-term Leo lovers can find the space for self-driven pursuits that keep the internal flame bright. If their partner isn't feeling their particular heat at a given moment, Leos are urged to take "love vacations" by engaging in acts inspired by their affections without having to demand their partner's full-throttle participation. Taking a romantic getaway for one or crafting a letter to their beloved that they simply read to themselves can bring the Leo back into communion with the point of all this sweet ardor: to maintain their lusty life force by filling their own love cup from the inside out.

RIDE OR DIE
Lion-Sized Friendships

The intensity of Leo's romantic love affairs spills over into their more platonic friendships. They are often playful in their pulsations, ready to radiate outwardly and touch everyone who surrounds them with sunshine. Minus Leo's itchier insecurities of amorous adoration, friends of Leo can benefit from the love cat's oversized heart.

Central to these friendships is a sense of soul recognition, and a Leo who feels truly seen and understood in their essence can return the favor times a billion, beaming their love lights onto others in a mutual melt of delicious appreciation. There's a buffet-style quality to these exchanges, as both parties are allowed to bring more and more of themselves to the table. This results in second and third servings of support, with whipped cream on top. And if the Leo has extra cash to spare, they love to fête a friend, planning impromptu shopping sprees and weekends with besties, and going all-out on the bubbly.

Regardless of their level of social-butterfly status, all Leos thrive with a core group of ride-or-dies, and they're usually ready to literally donate their organs to whoever has pledged allegiance. And when they're careful to cultivate qualities of deep listening, paying close attention to the nuances of their friends' narratives, they can tap straight into their pals' bloodstreams. Choosing love over judgment is always the answer, and when they let themselves be fully present with friends rather than preachy, they become champions of virtually any cause they recognize as heart-centric.

Deep Leonine friendships are 'til death do us part, and the greatest triumph of a Leonine life can be the epic party at their funerals, complete with endless toasts to the person they really and truly were. To capitalize on the festivities, a Leo might even stage these kinds of celebrations of self before they actually depart, honoring thresholds in soul development the rest of us might be too shy to feast on. Whatever the occasion, the Leo comes ready to get down, and the earnest emotion in their party-starting will forever fuel their companionship conga line.

ELEMENTAL EROTICA:
Sign-by-Sign Collisions

Astrological pairings go far beyond good/bad binaries, and every cosmic collision has worthy treasures to mine. Check out the following descriptions for quick-and-dirty tips on what kind of lusty learnings the Leo is in for with each of the signs.

ARIES: Fellow fire sign Aries comes on just as fiercely and fully in love as little Leo, with a straightforward sexual focus that fans Leo's

desire for tantalizing transparency. Battles for getting "on top" can produce growth when they learn to let each other take turns in the lead. Leo's more leisurely glitter shines when Aries is allowed to handle the heroic logistics. This leaves Leo content to trust in their right to regality. The undying innocence of both signs can blossom together, as their clear carnal commitment reminds them of their shared capacity for trust. Transcending heart break and personal history, these two hop back into the ring together, ready to keep it lit through thick and thin.

TAURUS: Both of these signs are of the "fixed" modality, signaling a penchant for rooted entrenchment and profound underground power sources. Taurus flowers open in the wake of Leo's seemingly unending rays, and Leo is magnetized by Taurus's sweet stability. A rock-solid partnership that can veer toward the staid, the gateway to growth comes through body knowledge, as each helps the other to trust their gut. Both signs are scratch 'n' sniff, touchy feelers, and unabashed sensuality is a carnal cause for celebration. From breakfast in bed to elaborately prepared dinner platters to simply rolling in the sheets and rubbing up on each other, it's a beautifully basic, skin-and-bones affair.

GEMINI: These signs can be both circulatory and full of spring, and there's something fresh and ready about their partnership, which perpetually promises the eternal elixir of youth through its rainbow of possibilities. Whether hitting the club or hosting house parties in their lair, these two thrive on colliding with the world at large, relishing each other's emotionally perceptive reads on the souls of those they meet in the streets. For fixed Leo, Gemini's butterfly wings can sometimes spark fears about lack of loyalty. And Leo's unwavering affection can leave the bee searching for a way out of the cloying honey. But with open telephone lines of communication, these two proverbial teenagers can always talk it out, reigniting their passion through carefully penned love letters and shared secrets.

CANCER: On the surface, Cancer's internal waters and Leo's externalized flame don't appear to mix and mingle, but together, this can be a deliciously loony, midnight-skinny-dipping trip into the pools of personal passion. Cancer's wild inner world finds a friend in Leo's plush romantic visions. The two signs conspire to become co-creators of a shared artistic process, finding the wellsprings of support to vulnerably expose whatever's being held close to their chests. Both loyalists to the core, durational partnership is a possibility, and as the zodiac's archetypal Mother and Father figures respectively, these two members of the same soul family can heal ancient wounds.

LEO: Leo-on-Leo action has all the makings of a sequined showstopper, as both parties take to the floor in their finest frocks. Both are lit by the never-ending belief in love after love after love. At its best and brightest, this dynamic duo can bring out the inherent generosity of spirit embedded in the sign. If they allow love to lift them up to where they belong, they can become cosmic cheerleaders of each other's every move. The key lies in remembering that there is always room for their twin flames, and they must work to stoke each other's specificity while soothing fears of being put out. When in doubt, letting stalwart support take center stage results in trampoline-sized leaps in mutual heart expansion.

VIRGO: An intricate union and ritualized affair, each can profoundly expand the other's trust in what they're here to contribute. Virgo's realism helps Leo hone its unending energy for creative participation in the world at large. And for Virgo, Leo's immediacy and obvious *joie de vivre* help soothe Virgo's hard edges, heating up a forgotten sense of play that doesn't need to be analyzed. They connect through a shared sense of integrity, bolstering their respective allegiances to unwavering inner sources of intuitive knowing. Together, their partnership is self-possessed and teaches both parties that they have the right to just be, in all their perfect imperfection.

LIBRA: Both visionaries in the sack, Leo and Libra seek romantic aspirations to tack to their mood boards. While Libra's intellectual approach can sometimes feel a little too minty cool for cinnamon-blooded Leo, at its best, this creative companionship can skyrocket both toward their greatest capacities for ideal love, with each acting as the other's perpetual artistic muse. Placing each other on pedestals is common, and both are urged to be careful about the inevitable fall. They must grow to accept each other in all their messy complexities rather than chipping away to create Greek-sculptural perfection.

SCORPIO: The only out-and-out carnivores in the zodiac, the appetites of this pair are insatiable, and sexual expression can reach deliciously sordid heights. Even in friendship, there can be something feverously frisky about this duo, as they erotically co-conspire about their next carnal pursuits or swap locker room stories about last night's conquest. The capacity for soul-deep transformation through collision is profound. If both stay open to clear negotiations of power and demonstrate their unending affection straightforwardly to soothe suspicion, they can take each other to emotional depths and developmental heights previously unimagined.

SAGITTARIUS: This larger-than-life collision is perpetually decked out in the oversized baubles of a love that liberates both of these fire babes from the mortal coil they long to leave behind. Fueling each other's sometimes-manic fires and self-scripted mythologies, the key can be learning how to stoke the flames without getting consumed in the carnal candle. While Sag's notorious need for ever-expanding horizons may threaten the little love cat's sense of loyalty, the wide-open vistas of the zodiac's wild pony can teach the kitten a thing or two about a love without borders. Leo learns to trust in holding a Sag's heart when the Lion learns not to keep it under lock and key.

CAPRICORN: Both embodiments of the archetypal "father figure," this paternalistic pair ignites themes of power, authority, and self-sufficiency. With Leo sometimes playing the eternal child to Capricorn's buttoned-up headmaster, the key to happy cohabitation lies in learning to protect rather than parent one another. No matter their walks of life, both of these signs have a penchant for opulence and an inherent desire to take to the throne of their own majestic birthright. Together, sensual indulgences can be a source of liberation, helping to build a shared belief in their diamond-encrusted worthiness.

AQUARIUS: On an oppositional polarity together in astrology, this pair can magnetize across a crowded room. They are co-conspirators in the search for unapologetic self-expression. The learning for this potent pair lies in the question of attachment, with the Leo forever pulled by its heartstrings and the Aquarius singing a tune crafted straight from its cerebellum. Aquarius's panned-out gaze helps draw Leo out of their sometimes self-centric experience, and the kitten's fluff and buff reminds Aquarius that they must have a heart beneath it all. Together, the duo comes ever closer to their shared vision of using their singular creative forces to light up the planet.

PISCES: A partnership that coaxes Leo into the silk sheets of its most sparkly dream life, this duo is all soft-lit romantics and mystical healing. Both parties' urge to escape into each other's arms is amplified, and if the pair commits to mixing their cloud life with some reality checks, the resulting relationship can bring heaven to earth. Leo gives structure to Pisces's loose edges, reminding the fishy that they have a right to ask for what they want directly, without a trace of shame. And Pisces beckons Leo into the deep end, soothing the Lion's endless appetite for ego expression and helping the love cat grow an everlasting trust in their specialness that never needs to be proven.

LEO AT WORK

ONE OF LEO'S greatest longings is to gift their heat to as many plants as possible, watching flower petals open wide to greet their regal rise. And their capacity to spread this seed of sun-kissed selfhood can find magnanimous manifestation in their professional pursuits. More than any other sign, Leo must come at their careers heart-first, redefining the phrase "passion project" and collapsing the work/life divide. And as with all things Leonine, the question of fulfillment lies in harnessing the spark of their specialness to shine all the way to the back of the filing cabinet. They tend to do best when they feel confident that what the world needs now is more of the selves they already are.

Believing that they've been "chosen" to execute a mission bequeathed upon them by their personal god, Leos must commit to the credo that they were put here on the planet for a signature songwriting experience. This sign is encouraged to consistently create from the professional place that feels the most instinctively "true," cultivating a relationship of self-driven rightness that may fly in the face of external markers of success. If a Leo isn't coming into the boardroom completely alive and fully lit, they may as well have called in sick. No matter what professions they choose, Leos must follow their heat at all costs.

When they seem to have lost their connection to this career god, the key for the working Leo lies in holism. The Leonine obsession with authenticity finds both challenge and promise in the workplace as they seek to craft creative continuity between every piece of their glittering lives. Not ones to adopt a work persona that wouldn't be recognizable off duty, Leos shouldn't be afraid to exercise their right to match their life in the sheets with their work in the streets. They can find career ease by doing away with professional packaging and shedding the uniforms and suits cramping their styles.

And when their personal lives and professional pursuits find alignment, there's no other being that can light up a creative conference quite like a Leo. Aspiration, inspiration, and appreciation must travel hand in hand for these love cats. They will find balance through the feedback loop of personal dreams and collective needs. Impassioned speakers, inspired actors, and cosmic cheerleaders for their most downtrodden colleagues, Leos are here to transform glass ceilings into circus tents, reminding the rest of us that the journey to "make it" in the material world should be fueled by the magic of a profoundly personal mission.

FOLLOW THE SUN
Choosing a Path

Like all fire signs, Leonine beings are lit from the inside out. They're invited to chart their career course from an inner code and concept rather than from the predetermined path society may have pushed them toward. Deciding a path must be born of pure desire, and wherever they find themselves on their journey of professional unfolding, Leos are urged to divine their guiding concepts first before getting mired in the specificity of skill sets.

When searching for a job or looking to renew their relationship to their current career, a Leo gets lit by choosing emotional rallying cries over already-posted job descriptions. Starting any job search by stating what they are here to bring to the world will ensure that their Leonine labors are truly connected with their luminous life forces. Stating something as simple and potent as "I am here to bring the romance," or "I want entering the office to feel like sinking my toes into the sand," will lead them closer to their career destinies. The panned-out, tagline portion of their resume is always more vital than the specific accomplishment details. Function should follow the feline form.

From the time they are wee ones, Leos cultivate strong aversions and attachments, and even seemingly innocuous hobbies and interests can dictate their career paths. It's not uncommon for a tiny Leo who spent hours smoothing Barbie locks to become a stylist, or for a sommelier to emerge from afternoons sniffing juicy fruits in the backyard. When feeling lost, a Leo is always asked to return to these early images and sensory experiences when their heart first opened up. They must study the poetic traces

> More than any other sign, Leo must come at their careers heart-first, redefining the phrase "passion project" and collapsing the work/life divide.

of these life worlds to ensure full body and spirit alignment with their chosen path.

And while there certainly isn't an established list of careers that Leos should or shouldn't embrace, the key to crafting a purposeful path lies in the concept of customized creation. Whether it's a bespoke piece of parsley placed atop a cafeteria dish or tiny initials carved on the underside of an assembly-line item, Leos must know that whatever they're making in the world bears some resemblance to their own specialness. Whatever their line of labor, Leos are invited to find the mythos in the mundane and trail their glitter through even the most corporate halls.

BEDAZZLED DESKTOPS
Leo's Professional Style

As the cosmos' party-ready playmate, the muted tones of duty can present a particular set of challenges for the Leonine spirit. Whatever their chosen path, their professional environment must feel like a kind of artist studio, and the laboring Leo is encouraged to transform their workspace into a living, breathing mood board. This space should spill over with personal flair to keep the flames lit. In even the most rigid of corporate dress codes, ensuring that a pair of undies or a tucked-away pendant is personally chosen provides Leos with an anchor of authenticity that keeps their core self secure and ready to find creative flow.

> Some Leos will remain in a role that's not as regal as they're worthy of out of fear that, by putting their full selves on the line, they might lose it all.

For Leonine beings, their work, like the rest of their lives, is a constant act of creation and re-creation. Once established in a given role, the Leo both longs to lord over their lair, secure in their sense of competence, and perpetually prowl, chasing the next ambitious hit like a cat in heat. This is the paradox of "potential" that Leos will dance with all of their professional lives. They grapple with the rollercoaster concept of success and seek to define a custom-cut inner code to guard against the fear of perceived failure. Many Leo laborers will memorialize a particular creative high, convinced that they will never again be able to reach this professional pinnacle. And at the other end of the professional party pool, some Leos will remain in a role that's not as regal as they're worthy of out of fear that, by putting their full selves on the line, they might lose it all. In either case, there's a kind of high school football-star quality that can afflict career-driven Leos. They cling to the remembrance of championships past, which leaves them ravenously hungry to relive that one moment of stadium-sized magic.

To grapple with these swings between perceived potential and bottomed-out loss, Leos are invited to develop a sense of unshakable personal pride. Early on in a job, the love cat is tasked with creating their own form of performance review that exists outside the confines of their so-called superiors. Developing a kind of self-possessed "safe word" can return them to center during moments of professional turmoil. Whether it's a selfie they love tucked under their desk or a mantra as simple as "I am worth it" whispered under their breath, Leos must become their own authorities and acknowledge themselves first before seeking out external accolades.

When feeling satisfied with their own work, Leos transform into artistic visionaries perpetually greenlit by hot red passion. They can be delightfully playful thinkers, content to let the future unfold from the present. In brainstorming sessions, they splash around for the sheer joy of possibility. And when focused on an end goal, they tirelessly labor to realize their professional desires, outlasting many of their cosmic colleagues through their life force alone. As long as Leos can see a part of themselves reflected in what they produce, the labor is reward enough, and a Leo will fall in love with whatever career creature pops out.

WET 'N' WILD WATER COOLERS
The Leo Coworker

The Leonine dream is a kind of perpetual Employee Appreciation Day, with Leo standing at the ready to receive a new Girl Scout patch or holiday bonus. When they can gift this sense of accomplishment to themselves, their potential to lift up their cosmic colleagues is immeasurable.

Leos often find themselves in leadership roles, fueled by seemingly unending sources of heat that others instinctively gather around. And as much as Leos long to feel their personal distinction, they can transfer this passion for particularity to others by inquiring about the bios and flavor palettes of each member of their work force and rallying each to surpass their own goals. As with any Leo in a position of power, Leo leaders are cautioned to "lift" rather than "lord over." At every step, they must ensure that their vision is fit to serve and be served by the whole, and they need to pay careful attention to the specific sparkle of each team member. And even if they don't bear the literal title of boss, Leos should always embrace their place and play their passionate part to the hilt, letting the contours of their turf keep the creative fires alight.

While fire can sometimes consume people who want to get close to its warmth, Leonine light is meant to be shared. Generosity grown through teamwork is highly encouraged. In the workplace, Leos can find themselves in fierce competition with their coworkers. If left unchecked by collaboration, this may lead to hungry grasping for turf. To combat this potential career cannibalism, a Leo should commit to growing their capacity to receive criticism. They must check in with core motivations to notice when attempts to swallow an effort through singular possession are actually stifling the joys of creation.

Leos are encouraged to explore the energetic concept of "ghostwriting" in their teamwork, learning to relish their individual contributions to the soup while also sitting back to savor the deliciousness of the full meal. Growing toward their "opposite" sign of Aquarius in the workplace will serve a laboring Leo well, and they're asked to experiment with gifting their creative efforts to a larger whole. This professional generosity allows them to see the shining faces of their colleagues as they experience the aftereffects of Leo's labors. When Leos strive to become Secret Santas instead of showstoppers, they'll be surprised at the delight produced by the precious presents they release into the wide world.

ALL THAT GLITTERS
Making Money

Like its fellow fixed signs (Taurus, Scorpio, and Aquarius), these kittens have incarnated to explore the concept of value, both inside and out. Rather than sweaty efforts to have and hoard, Leos learn to magnetize their gold through the sheer force of their own goldenness. Over the course of their professional pursuits, Leos are asked to probe this relationship between being and earning. Money must be the natural result of their creative impulses, rather than raison d'être. And when these high rollers are in full flow and immersed in their own pleasure process of making what's aligned with their heartbeat, the emerald oceans will open wide.

As Leos earn, they're consistently called to check in with their sense of deservedness, paying attention to moments when their desire to amass wealth or accolades borders on "lack" mentality. When feeling unworthy or unloved, the professional Leo can develop an envious streak that feeds on a sense of fundamental

LEO QUESTIONS

- **HEAT.** When do I feel the sensation of complete warmth? What triggers this feeling?

- **EXPOSURE.** What does it feel like when I show myself completely? When I hide instead, what am I protecting?

- **REALNESS.** What am I made of? What would it mean to become more of this?

- **SPECIALNESS.** What is my signature? What is the one thing that only I can bring forward?

- **CREATION.** What wants to come through me? What is my personal definition of success? How can I support my own birthing process?

- **PLAY.** How can I return to an absolute innocence that lights me up from the inside out? When do I feel alive without strategy?

- **PRESENCE.** Am I ready to risk trusting this life completely? What does it feel like when I'm simply here, now? What parts of my life, and which people in it, can I accept exactly as they are?

unfairness. In these moments, Leos tend to focus on others who seem to somehow "have it all." Most Leos secretly harbor a desire for a full life of leisure. They want to stretch their paws out on the couch and wait for the next platter of treats. In times of financial fear or spiteful hedonism, a Leo is always encouraged to return to sweetness. They have to realize that they are their own greatest treasure, and there's nothing wrong with them loving up on their presence like a precious diamond.

Whether or not a Leo appears particularly glamorous on the surface, they often harbor dreams of a lavish lux lifestyle. Rather than dampen these desires or dismiss them as superficial, Leos are encouraged to deeply enjoy the fruits of their labors and let the juice drip down their chins. Experiencing ample, full-bodied pleasure always paves the way to securing sustainable wealth. Licking the plate clean and

> **Whether or not a Leo appears particularly glamorous on the surface, they often harbor dreams of a lavish lux lifestyle.**

savoring the feeling of their bodies sliding into newly purchased pieces of clothing like second skins lets them see the shiny dazzle of their inner world made material in all its majesty. By bringing their entire presence to this process of spending, Leos fuel trust in the very realness of their contribution.

CONCLUSION

Now that you've brushed up against all the bedazzled facets of this sun-scorched feline fluffball, it's time to take it to the streets. Whether you're a Leo Sun sign who's looking to renew their commitment to their personal mission or simply an aficionado craving more Leonine light in your life, refer to the energy checklist that follows to power up your fiery force.

THE HOUSE RULED BY LEO

Check out the pie slices of your chart and look for the Leo symbol. This is the arena of life in which you're invited to enjoy a Leonine approach. Over time, you'll cultivate greater trust in its contents and learn to savor its tastiness.

THE SIGN RULING THE FIFTH HOUSE

The fifth pie slice is naturally ruled by Leo, and as the house of "creation and re-creation," it symbolizes the artistic process and all shades of romance. Whatever sign you have here is key to unlocking your birthing potential. It governs how you fall in love, raise your children, shape your creative clay, and find faith in your particular flavor of self-expression.

YOUR SUN SIGN

Literally ruled by the sun, Leo energy reminds us that we are all custom-built stars on a personal mission to sign our hearts on the dotted line. Whatever your sun sign placement, it's here where you're meant to shine. Consider it both a marker of what you already are and an unfolding destiny you're asked to dynamically develop.

LEO SEASON

As the sun travels through the entire zodiac, it spends about a month in each astrological sign. Each of us has the opportunity to celebrate and integrate these twelve powerful archetypes. As Leo season dawns in late July and August, it's a heightened invitation for everyone to leap back onto the dance floor, claim our true colors, and shimmy with the sweet knowledge that all we have to do is become more of what we already are.

LEO IN YOUR BIRTH CHART

Whether or not you were blessed to be born under the sun sign of the kitten, Leo light is for everyone. Here's how to feel the heat, no matter your sign.

LEO PLANETS AND PERSONAL PLACEMENTS

When you look up your birth chart, you'll discover that you're not just your sun sign. Rather, you are composed of an array of celestial cuties, each symbolizing a different part of your life force and personal cosmic story. Explore if you have any other planets or placements in the sign of Leo.

* **LEO RISING:** The rising sign is the kind of packaging we arrive in. It indicates the energy of our approach (the lens we use to view the world) and calls on us to take this sign's principles to a deeper level. Leo Rising signs are invited to show up in every sense of the phrase, syncing their inner and outer presentations on a more profound level.

* **MOON IN LEO:** The moon is a tucked-in shellabration of our inner worlds. It's symbolic of how we feel and what makes us secure. For Leo Moons, emotions run high and can't be hidden, as the sun is literally shining through the moon and sporting its heart on its sleeve. Stability is found when they learn to lick their own wounds, which then enables them to give even more of their generous hearts.

* **MERCURY IN LEO:** Quick-footed Mercury is the zodiac's butterfly, ruling perception, communication, and how we relate to everyday change. Mercury in Leo uses words to delight and dazzle, enamored of its personal poetics and custom credos. Opening up to more varied viewpoints is a growing edge. This placement is asked to learn the art of adaptation, rather than always firmly anchoring.

* **VENUS IN LEO:** Pleasure-petaled Venus rules all kinds of receiving, from money to food to sex. It describes how we take in the world, content to magnetize rather than force our mojo. In fiery Leo, the ante is upped for adoration, and this sign placement craves heavy petting and fixed attention. Growth comes from accepting the inevitable ups and downs of love and seeing objects of affection as more than just materials.

* **MARS IN LEO:** Mars is our red-hot muscle and mojo, the source of both our sexuality and success drive. In Leo, the engine revs are related to the heart-center, and passion projects are an absolutely vital source of sustenance. These jungle cats are also learning to trust in their irreplaceability. They're still figuring out that they no longer need to sing for their fancy feast—the world will come to them.

* **JUPITER IN LEO:** Jupiter is the planet that blows open our windows and doors, beckoning us to expand beyond our constrictive beliefs and risk connecting to our wild natures. In Leo, the party rages on, and this sign placement is both gifted with an ability to

land forever sunny-side up and asked to bring greater consciousness to its personal definition of true happiness.

* **SATURN IN LEO:** Saturn is the planet of limits and laws, a sometimes hard-knocks school that paves the way toward lasting competence. In Leo, there can be a kind of schoolyard push and pull between the urges to play and self-critique. With effort and attention, Leonine exuberance can break free, and this sign placement's secret superpower lies in birthing creative projects through pragmatism.

* **URANUS IN LEO:** This rule breaker and change maker shakes it up, interrupting our usual societal programming and urging us to travel beyond the mapped roads. Uranus in Leo is a living, breathing embodiment of originality, here to reshape the very concept of identity and risk eccentric expression to rally the troops.

* **NEPTUNE IN LEO:** A generational planet that shifts signs every fourteen years, Neptune is the zodiac's dream queen, an escape hatch that takes us into the mystical world and symbolizes where we crave transcendence. Neptune in Leo builds faith through force, bowing at the altar of creative expression and personal significance.

* **PLUTO IN LEO:** The outermost generational "planet," Pluto is ruler of the underworld, a jet-black metal detector indicating where we must enact karmic change. In Leo, self-expression is associated with incredible intensity and high stakes. With this Pluto placement, family legacies may have to be explored so that we can unearth whether or not our specialness is truly being supported.

* **CHIRON IN LEO:** This touchy-feely planetoid is ready for healing. It asks us to develop deep sensitivity and awareness in its sign placement without expecting immediate fixes. In Leo, there's a tenderness connected with fully and vibrantly just being us—a call to develop deeper compassion in regard to our very natures.

* **NORTH NODE OR SOUTH NODE IN LEO:** The Nodal axis connects us to past lives and future promises, as we're asked to integrate both our North and South Node signs to come closer to our soul's purpose. With one of the Nodes in Leo, and the other in Aquarius, the work lies in balancing between the heart and the head, and in understanding both individual expression and collective participation.

AUG. 23–SEPT. 22

text by Bess Matassa

element — **EARTH**

symbol — **THE MAIDEN**

modality — **MUTABLE**

house — **SIXTH**

ruler — **MERCURY**

ARGO

INTRODUCTION

BOW DOWN. GET low. Sink your hands into the dirt and touch the life force that teems beneath the surface. Let yourself receive the subtlest shifts in the breeze. Pressure-gauge the preciousness of the plants and their readiness to rise. Know your season. Lean into the cracks and the fissures. And embrace the willingness to feel that all this perfect imperfection is just a conduit for the liberation of even more light.

Poised on the threshold between our innately beautiful bodies and how we will use them, Virgo marks the place where we pledge allegiance to our essence and divine our craft. Where we see ourselves with clarity and consciousness, standing alone and apart. Standing whole. Where we commit to the long road ahead with a tough and tender knowledge of exactly what we're here to bring, in both its contoured limitation and untamable libido. Where we decide, with complete devotion, that we cannot waste one single drop.

Often misunderstood and maligned in astro write-ups as anal, critical, and anxious, Virgo's energy is too subtle to be sound-bited, marking a pivotal moment in the process of self-development. Following the bombastic hot pink splashes of Leo's self-expression spillage, and preceding the plunge into partnership of Libra's "we-ness," in Virgo we must reckon with the edges of our selves. Who are we really, when stripped down to bare skin, sans artifice or pretense? And what do we have to give? In Virgo, we cut our teeth and slough off the excess, coming into communion with the very matter that we're made of, turning it over in our hands. Assessing and refining. Learning to love it. And learning to put it to good use.

The so-called virgin of the zodiac is not a prudish perfectionist, but a self-contained sensualist who moves to the backroom boudoir beat of their own inner code. Reigning over natural cycles and right timing, Virgo serves as both a bellwether and barometer for microcosmic shifts in the mundane. Here to remind us that heaven is truly a place on earth, this sign gives as much reverence to the ant colony as to the castle. Ushering us to grow fierce and full with our crystal-cut capacities, Virgo energy marries us to the regalness of realism.

"What kind of witch are you?" whispers Virgo, from a cabin in the deepest woods. Work your magic, whatever its flavor, divining exactly what you stand for, and what you won't fall for anymore...

"What kind of witch are you?" whispers Virgo, from a cabin in the deepest woods.

VIRGO PLEDGES OF ALLEGIANCE

These carefully crafted credos and committed principles guide Virgo through a lifetime of subtle shifts.

INTEGRITY AND DISCERNMENT

Virgo occupies the critical sixth slot amidst the twelve zodiac signs, waiting to usher us from the self-awareness of the astro wheel's first five energies and into the collective. Separating the wheat from the chaff, this sign of the apprentice is learning first to see itself as separate so it can be poised to participate, knowing its true skill set like no other cosmic cutie. Virgo's lifetime of labors is a kind of culinary art, isolating essences to divine what's most vital to the dish. But for Virgos to serve it up on a perfectly aligned platter, they must first serve themselves. And the process of tastily contributing to the world's feast begins with a deep knowledge of their own spice.

While the sign is traditionally associated with winged planet Mercury, co-ruler of buzzy, communicative Gemini, at its core Virgo pledges allegiance to the asteroid Vesta. A symbol of sensual and creative wholeness unto the self, this autoerotic aesthete is a closed carnal circuit. To develop integrity means to become integral, understanding what does and doesn't align with gut instincts. Virgo's deep dive into its own animal essence helps the sign to remain whole during the blending process, figuring out precisely what makes it tick. And developing a single-pointed focus of self-knowledge sticks Virgos to their very bones, ensuring integrity as they serve their treats to the world.

Also connected to the tarot's Hermit card in the Major Arcana, Virgo's discernment process often necessitates some real or metaphorical solo getaways, taking to a cabin in the woods to recommit to an inner knowing. There's something profoundly solitary about the Virgoan journey, even though they certainly aren't destined for isolated lives as monkish outliers. Committed at all costs to the inner sanctuary of the self, Virgos' plunges into privacy help them understand exactly what their packages contain. Knowing their contents ensures that Virgos can contribute with a sense of celebration, rather than tightly tying strings in an attempt to get it right.

Armed with an understanding of their essence, Virgos function like a fine-mesh sieve, employing a subtle filtration system as energies enter their orbit. Artfully identifying exactly what an item is made of, and how to put it to good use, Virgos must take time to turn tastes over in their mouths, touching their tongue against the "thisness" of things. Raising their noses to the world like a master sommelier, Virgo proves that their reputation for critique is actually evidence of an ability to sort the lineage of all that enters, as they apportion ingredients like members of a tasty team and play each one's essence to the hilt. Against Virgo's palate, each tasting note is an act of loving realism, and consciously delineating what's there creates pairings that bring every element into resplendent relief.

RHYTHM AND RITUAL

Virgo season (running from late August through most of September) marks a moment when a certain form of elemental energy both reaches its pinnacle and begins to fall away. Signaling the shift from summer toward fall in the Northern Hemisphere, and winter into spring in the Southern, Virgo energy carries us across a threshold and asks us to adapt and learn. All mutable signs (Gemini, Virgo, Sagittarius, and Pisces) are apprenticing themselves to the elements, seeking to understand and integrate what has come to pass, and opening wide to what's just beginning to glimmer on the distant horizon. As with all earth signs, Virgo's adaptations occur on the material plane, showing up through the artful honoring of the body, the physical environment, and all that encompasses real, tangible life here on land.

> **Deeply aligning with the markers of nature helps Virgo fulfill its mission, both through their internal bodies and the external wheel of the year.**

Knowing what season of their lives they're currently in is key to Virgo's orientation and development. Deeply aligning with the markers of nature helps this sign fulfill its mission, both through their internal bodies and the external wheel of the year. For these subtle earth babes, a ritual like spring cleaning or winter hibernation can take on heightened, visceral meaning, as Virgos learn to balance cues from the environment with their inner rhythms. More than any other sign, Virgo energy asks us to pause preciously, decide our own pace and quality of movement, and commit to an unfolding that's as subtly timed as viticulture, letting ourselves remain in process until we're perfectly ripe and ready to be plucked.

The Virgo reputation for overscheduled planners and overstuffed filing cabinets is actually evidence of this process of physical attunement, as they learn to constantly check in with their place on the world clock. And when Virgos get too caught up in the agitation of constant nervous system response to these fluctuations, they're always asked to realign with nature rather than their iCals. Syncing with the cycles of the moon or following the lead of a site in the body that's holding tension helps Virgo to feel the rightness of their life force and to learn to let it fully flow through them.

When they're deep in the flow of this rhythmic responsiveness, Virgo's ritualized energies can become an ode to divine detail rather than OCD. For the aligned Virgo babe, God shows up everywhere, and the lowliest dust bunny deity is just as vital as an angel on a cloud puff. And when they surrender their need to fix anything to their capacity to let go and let flow, the entire world becomes animated with a magical life force. As Virgo notices, separates, and seeks to refine from a place of compassion rather than harsh critique, this sign reminds itself that it fits perfectly in the wild puzzle, granting each life form its precious place as part of the organic whole.

WITCHERY AND WILDNESS

Understanding the secret lives that animate the seemingly rock-solid material world grants Virgos their status as the zodiac's earth witches. Here to harness the elements for the highest and best, for Virgos to become good witches, they must learn to both read the environment's needs and honestly assess their own capacities. Working their own particular brand of magic is a process of purification rather than perfection, transforming raw matter instead of trying to make right. When focused on compassionately drawing capacities to the surface, Virgo artists can perform the highest form of alchemy, using their mettle to transform metal into twenty-four-karat gold.

Early on, Virgos must carefully consider where to aim this alchemy, elevating their sometimes ego-effacing energy through reciprocal exchange. Rather than simply refining any rough-edged stone that crosses their path,

focusing their consciousness where it's most needed also means figuring out where they feel most alive. Called to preserve the connection to their preceding fire archetype of Leo means Virgo must find a way to keep their own cauldron lit. Remembering that they have a right to feel their own heat and benefit from their own carefully loving attention ensures that Virgo's magic doesn't drift into martyrdom.

When out of alignment, some Virgos will try to do it all, standing vigil day and night and serving at altars at the expense of any sense of self. To avoid complete obliteration and behind-the-scenes burnout means Virgo must commit to becoming a conscious channeler rather than a muted medium. When they feel like they've started losing themselves in the mix, Virgos are always invited to return to the altar of their beautiful bodies. Are they constantly angry when the wind picks up? Can they read a room through raised hairs on their arm? Checking in with these carnal weather reports helps Virgos read the subtle signals of their own skin before they blindly start putting skin in the game.

As they connect with the subtlety of their bodies, Virgos are able to harness their

> **When out of alignment, some Virgos will try to do it all, standing vigil day and night and serving at altars at the expense of any sense of self.**

high-functioning nervous systems for true healing work. Rather than the sign's usual association with health nut hypochondria, Virgo's fullest flower is found in the "like heals like" language of homeopathy. When concerned with paying an ode to what's here and understanding through holism rather than a nitpicky inventory of symptoms, Virgo can unleash a lusty love for all functions of our humanness. Seeing the medicine in every moment, whether astringently bittersweet and prickly, or holy honeyed, reminds Virgo that it's all part of it. And that they're a part of it too.

When Virgos learn to bless their natural appetites and embodied urges, these vestal vixens can return to the center of their own pantheon, swapping stake-burning exile for lasting self-sovereignty. Holding both the lock and the key to their own chastity belts of "shoulds" lets this sign unleash their wildness in the service of an even higher law. To know the windiness of wind on their skin. The fierceness of the flame. Or whatever their chosen flavor. To let things be exactly as they are, in all their perfect imperfection and divine discomfort. And to marry themselves to what lives inside of them, attending to the tiny biosphere of their beings with sweet, soft devotion.

This ode to Virgo's intricate intensity and subtle shifts is brought to you by the sands of the American Southwest. By latticework and lace. By the most sensitive wine grapes and the essential wholeness of butter on bread. By the sparkly specks in the pavement cracks and each distinctive star in the sky. Everything matters, says Virgo. And everything is made of matter. It's time to bring exactly what you're made of to this feast.

VIRGO AS A CHILD

LIKE BABY ANIMALS, Virgo children read the world's complexity through environmental secret language, registering shifts in the weather with their fur. Both vigilantly tapped in to all that is, and fully alive to the physical sensation of having incarnated in the first place, little Virgos are encouraged to stay little as long as possible, leveraging their youthful maturity with a less structured sense of play.

First and foremost, Virgo babelettes are observers of the natural world, other children, and themselves. After the excesses of Leo, the zodiac's previous sign, Virgos step aside from the hot-blooded playground power moves to catch some shade. And whether burying their noses in a book, or themselves in the sand, these kiddies can have something of the invisible about them. At its most beauteous and free, this invisibility cloak is evidence of an undercover privacy pact that the little witch makes with the world, and staying low to the ground lets Virgo love up on the Universe's signs and signals more deeply. But the Virgo little must also connect to a sense of unbridled wildness that comes from claiming their place on this planet, letting themselves remain a rough-cut gem that's valuable no matter its state of polish. Virgo children are encouraged to notice when they're getting pushed aside, swapping out a firm sense of self in favor of letting the other, more obvious, kids take center stage, and losing their "I" in the process.

In childhood, Virgo's relationship to "craft" gets carefully created, and these littles can think of their youth as a kind of sorcery school. Forging a relationship to the mystery of it all is critical and will lay the groundwork that keeps Virgos wondering and wandering through the world with ease, rather than anxiously breaking a sweat sorting it out. Supporting a Virgo child's body knowledge will keep them forever close to the ground of inherent instinct, a careful campground scout who both learns to respond to nature and can celebrate their capacity to start the fire.

ALL CREATURES BRIGHT AND BEAUTIFUL
The Making of a Little Witch

A kind of child-size magic mushroom trip, Virgo's lifeworld exposes the inherent aliveness of all beings. As Virgo look around them, they notice even the smallest pulsations of plant life, attuned to the desires of the actual dirt and the screams of broccoli stalks as they hit the frying pan. For a Virgo youth, even bacteria can be beautiful, and early celebrations of organic processes help these little witches build deep trust in their own natural selection, the appetites and attitudes of even the trees serving as evidence that they, too, get to take their place amidst the pageantry of the seasons.

This "aliveness" can course through a Virgo kiddie's veins when they are left to their own devices, as they literally dig in the dirt with glee and put their hands on things, sorting the natural world into the sign's notorious categories as a way to celebrate their own corresponding desires and needs. Whether on campgrounds, in natural history museums, or simply having an imaginary tea party in a backyard thicket, this process of whispering to the world reminds little Virgos of their necessary place within it. As they prepare for the harder edges of adult critique in later years, these early encounters with an animistically supportive environment help young Virgo develop a core sense of self that's in conversation with all creatures bright and beautiful.

To further support the Virgoan creation of self, the little witch must seek to balance scientific inquiry into the how and what of the Universe with a lusty, full-bodied immersion in the experience. Often, Virgos will catch themselves mid-play, placing an analytical distance by creating elaborate taxonomies or staging a step-by-step experiment. And although there is nothing inherently wrong with this more measured process, evidence of Virgo's desire to understand each creature's singular specificity and contribution to the whole, bolstering the earthier aspects of inquiry keeps these little witches connected to their own instinctual navigational system. Balancing trips to the science section of the bookstore with all-out wilderness expeditions helps Virgo remember that beneath the facts, there is the fullness of life force that animates this earth and their own desires within it. Exchanges with the earth's creatures build Virgo's compassion muscle, as the sign sensitively extends a hand to a paw, looking to walk through this world, with this world. Like the anthropomorphic household items that support Belle in *Beauty and the Beast*, Virgo longs to both help and be helped by the matter that surrounds them.

DOLLHOUSE DIVINITY
The Virgo Child's Microcosm

When they focus on letting the details wash over them, rather than trying to lock them all down, Virgo children have a veritable Polly Pocket™ of pleasure awaiting and can give themselves over to cracking open nutshells, taking apart clocks, peering through dollhouse windows, and turning over logs. As they gaze inside and underneath, Virgos gain further evidence of the very stuff things are made of, and how they function. Taking apart, putting back together, and rearranging remind little Virgos that they, too, are intricate systems. There is a deep interiority to this sign, and at this stage of development, mini curios and miniature worlds are both symbolic of their capacity to find divinity in the detail and a source of support for Virgo private lives. Yet rather than trying to micromanage these miniature worlds, or fix parts that appear broken, building trust lies in simply relishing the life that exists inside. Experimenting with acts like shaking a snow globe, rather than painstakingly picking out dollhouse curtains, can remind Virgo that Fabergé egg treasures await their tender, ecstatic touch more than their attempts to perfectly play God.

Seeking to ensure that each creature has its own clear-cut place reminds Virgos that they have a plot to possess within this pantheon. Virgo kiddies benefit deeply from divining their own spatial contours and having their own mini turf to tend at home. Whether an Easy-Bake® Oven re-creation of their parents' kitchen, or a secret spot under the stairs where they store their most prized possessions, a personal domain helps Virgos regain their center and stave off some of the overwhelm that can come from the wildness of the macrocosmic world. The "too muchness" of it all is mitigated by their mini habitat, and prideful possession ensures that the critical impulse doesn't extend into other family members' closets.

And as the little Virgo moves out from these more private places under the stairs and behind the bookshelf, a sense of tending turf continues to keep them steady. Young Virgos come alive when watching over microcosmic plots of land, delighting in window seed boxes, veggie garden plots, and sea monkey colonies. The classic grade school egg baby project, where partners incubate an almost-hatched creature, was designed for Virgo youth, and in this endeavor the sign discovers that the capacity to care for is just as vital as being careful. These kinds of natural world management assignments satisfy some of Virgo's desire to both tweak and refine, but ultimately remind the little witch that there is a wild inevitability to nature that they must bow to, moving rhythmically with what is forever untamable.

NURSE'S OFFICE SOVEREIGNTY
Building a Virgo Child's Body Knowledge

The Virgo child is a deeply feeling creature, affected by the most nuanced changes in their own and the collective's proverbial skin. These tiny zodiac babes are vessels and lightning rods, running the whole of existence through their bodies without the Virgo adult's finer-tuned filtration system. Rather than writing off a young Virgo's sensitivities to scratchy fabrics and strong smells, these can be used as kinds of scavenger hunt points of inquiry, letting Virgos learn where their bodies end and the world begins.

Unfortunately, because we tend to immediately pathologize many forms of body knowledge, these little environmental readers may end up in the nurse's office, convinced that their earthy sensitivities are a sign of sickness rather than their own burgeoning capacity to heal. To keep the Virgo babe from getting locked into a hypochondriacal cycle of illness and treatment, they're encouraged early on to find ways to read the language of their bodies beneath the noise and to speak these secret signs into being. Is the grumble in their gut really evidence of a stomachache? Or is it telling them that they don't want to play this game anymore?

Building a body language reminds young Virgos that operating from their gut is always better than short-circuiting clear signs to avoid creating a mess. *Everybody Poops* should be on every Virgo kid's bookshelf, a reminder that venerating all parts of their humanness liberates self-compassion and soothes self-critique. As they get closer to the carnal, Virgo kiddies remind themselves of their right to instinct and appetite, staying close to their wildness without having to treat it. Even if these little cosmic cuties might not pull an all-out fire sign tantrum, or bite playground arms like a Scorpio, Virgo youths are invited to let the tears flow freely without needing to constantly contain themselves. Moving bigger feelings of anger or sadness out from the background can help Virgo's litany of allergies and body ailments start to heal all on their own.

For those who parent them, it's critical to attend to this child's instincts by not forcing them to engage in activities where they evidence strong aversion. While developing some risk tolerance is vital to avoid becoming the boy in the bubble, responding to intuitive hits not to plunge into the kiddie pool headfirst or ride the roller coaster helps young Virgos find their rudders. Pleasure rests in powering up with a private definition of play, rather than getting tug-of-warred into submission. Whether through solitary play or long, idle afternoons spent tea-partying in the woods, Virgo's overtaxed nervous system is soothed when self-governed, wedding these wee ones to their own forms of fun.

LEMONS INTO LEMONADE STANDS
Balancing Play with Pragmatism

Virgos' inherent desire to be of use can come on strong at an early age, and they may take a special delight in dressing up in their parents' work clothes, setting up shop in their rooms, or running a neighborhood library out of their own book stacks. These microcosmic experiences of future labors are certainly something to be celebrated, evidence of the pure pleasure a young Virgo can take in sorting and serving. But they're also prime opportunities for learning to sort the difference between the tiny Virgo's sense of the external world's shoulds and a deeper inner authority. Knowing that they don't have to make good to be good ensures that the little Virgo can play the proverbial "game of life" with a more relaxed panache, delighting in rolling the dice as much as they do advancing through the stages.

Balancing these energies can start with injecting some color into household chores. Even on summer vacation, these littles love a to-do list. As they delight in polishing a bathroom mirror or carefully laying out the cutlery, they're encouraged to bring their own signature sense of artistry to this process. Whether it's creating abstract shapes out of the cutlery, rather than having to lay out the pieces in the proper order, or leaving a note etched onto the corner of the mirror's fog, finding themselves reflected in their work at a tender age ensures that they remain devoted to their own process, choosing to engage in labors of love rather than constrained by soul-dampening diligence. And while wee Virgos certainly shouldn't be forced to shut down their paper routes, saving a space for more outright forms of play lets them start to surrender to some of the mystery without having to map it all out.

Young Virgos are encouraged to remember that they can choose their own adventures rather than always following the box. Repurposing household items as toys or staging treasure hunts where they craft the clues, instead of having to seek and find, reminds Virgos of the delight in the unfolding. By choosing to occasionally forgo organizing the sock drawer in favor of making a sock puppet instead, Virgos learn that the existence of all things, including themselves, is a gift to be cherished rather than a surface to be polished spotless.

VIRGO AS AN ADULT

AS THE LITTLE witch leaves sorcery school and starts to work more mature forms of magic, there can actually be a sweet sigh of relief. Young Virgo's sense of seriousness doesn't always sync with the playground antics of youth, and for some of these sensitive souls, the boundarylessness and "searching" quality of early life can feel like a deluge of infinite possibilities for their sieve to sort. As the constraints of time and space close in, Virgos can relish treating their life like a self-driven haiku, each adult decision a chance to refine their careful filtration system. Whether picking out the curtains for their new apartment or deciding definitively to leave a lifelong habit in the dust, Virgos find increasing serenity in the solidity of their hard "nos" and full-on "yeses." Aging gifts these beings the opportunity to drop into alignment with their very bones.

Amidst the endless responsibilities of adulthood, the Virgo delight in daily divinity takes even deeper root, and the sign savors both what it can do by itself and for the world. From refining the grocery list by their own hand to growing herbs in the garden in conjunction with the shifting temperatures, adult Virgos dance between inner examination and self-selective service, building increasing trust in their competence when meeting external conditions. Adult Virgos are constantly calibrating, checking to make sure the outer matches their inner code, and the process of maturation finds them increasingly employing their sieve, sifting through the dirt to pan for precious metals and deciding exactly where to send their efforts.

At its most gorgeously expressive, Virgo adulthood is a viticultural process, with Virgo's heart and soul-shaped grapes spending a lifetime gaining specific terroir. How will Virgos move with the rhythm of the unfolding seasons? What flavor profile will they take on as they expose themselves to the elements? What experiences will alter their chosen altars? What essence will remain? And how can they trust that they'll gain value and sheer deliciousness by simply exposing themselves to the weather that's there, harnessing whatever arises in the name of beautiful usefulness? In the end, successful Virgo adults are the sorceresses who know how to take a sit down at their own tables, complete with goblets full of juice from the grapes they've so carefully grown.

> *Virgo adults are the sorceresses who know how to take a sit down at their own tables, complete with goblets full of juice from the grapes they've so carefully grown.*

THE TWENTIES:
Choosing the Curtains

As young Virgo heads off to college or into the workforce, the first tastes of freedom contain an interesting paradox. On the one hand, this sign can embrace young adulthood in all its finery, leaping to fulfill the role by staging elaborate grown-up murder mystery dinner parties and caretaking more careless friends. This flavor of Virgo growing up may seem startling to those who've known them as a child, as Virgos seize any opportunity to exercise more bold forms of control. In their twenties, Virgos are sketching the floorplan of their lives with increasing detail, and they can take intense care making sure to set it up just so, convinced that where they put the coffee table is the secret to burgeoning success.

This flavor of Virgo young adulthood carries all the markers of Virgoan majesty, as the sign shapes and sculpts its world, finally getting to make strong aesthetic choices in their spaces and their lives. But there is also a wildness that lurks beneath the surface, moving at its own pace and in accordance with private pleasures. While the twenties Virgo might not always be given over to all-night ragers in quite the same style as their fellow young cosmic bucks, they can have a quiet ferociousness in their calls for freedom at this time. This young wolf will often stray from the pack with a self-contained silence that answers to no one, finding endless joy in disappearing for a secret weekend love affair or diving fully into a cryptic new hobby turned obsession that consumes them completely.

Virgo's late twenties lead toward the notorious Saturn Return transit in astrology, a cosmic moment that asks us to reckon with the structures we've inherited and created and decide how to live our lives with increasing consciousness and self-sovereignty. For the earthly attuned Virgo, this astro event might not rock the boat as fiercely as it does for some of their zodiac compatriots, already gifted with the ability to see the contours of their lives with clarity. But no other sign is so quick to make do with whatever conditions are here, powering through with pragmatism and doing what must be done. And at this crossroads of young adulthood, Virgos are invited to take this moment to reflect on exactly what gets their sweet loving attention, examining the true function of the flames they're beginning to tend.

THE THIRTIES:
Feeling Themselves

As Virgo slides out the back end of the Saturn Return, there can be a flavor of retreat that characterizes the early thirties. Virgos know something secret about their insides at this juncture. They've seen glimpses of their bits and pieces on the cutting room floor. And they understand how to better calibrate their carnality and creative force, choosing what's intrinsically right for them, rather than blindly doing the right thing. This distinction is critical during the early thirties, as Virgos are asked to return to their gut instinct navigation systems, using their notorious sensitivity to follow their own form toward function.

Whatever work they've chosen gets called into question at this time, and the early thirties Virgo is invited to really examine the legacy they're starting to craft. For the Virgo who has remained relatively behind-the-scenes during the first part of life, this can be a moment to consider stepping out onto the stage, speaking up in an important meeting, and finally penning their name to their carefully executed work. The rote machinations of service without specialness start to taste stale, and thirties Virgo is called to remember that they have a right to exist in the first place, using their voice to ask for what they want, need, and inherently deserve.

As the late thirties dawn, Virgos enter into the Pluto Square astrological aspect. The planet of underground power struggles and purging past patterns can expose where Virgos have given away their potency, bowing down to a cause or fellow creature possibly not worthy of their bootlicking devotion. Depending on how carefully a Virgo has attempted to keep life clean of messy carnality, these more animalistic urges might feel like an unleashed team of beasties busting out from under the bed. But if Virgo can let the impulses arise, curiously greeting them like any other crawler in their garden, the late thirties can serve as a very human reminder of their right to have an appetite. As Virgos learn to ride the waves of their emotional impulses like a Texas bull, they can find freedom in the shameless sweet feeling that absolutely nothing needs to be fixed.

THE FORTIES:
Fit to Be Queen

Armed with even more of their humanness, the early forties Virgo is perfectly poised for some healthy hedonism. Whatever impulses were repressed in their youth can come out to play in full force at this juncture. For Virgos, the forties are an opportunity to bow at the altar of their beautiful bods, loving up on how they're cut and contoured and what their cravings reveal about their very essence. Whether partnered or single, there's something autoerotic about this time, as Virgo syncs their skin back to their very bones, starting to finally believe that the reason they've incarnated is simply to relish all of existence.

This is also the moment when Virgos truly start to make good on their mission, understanding that their contribution is not a list of boxes to be checked, but an energetic willingness to come to the table as themselves. The question of "enoughness" that often plagues this sign has the opportunity for soothing here, as Virgo starts to understand their essence as vital and irreplaceable. There is something queenly to this era, and the forties Virgo is invited to claim their power as inherent, rather than proven through what they produce.

This era is also marked by the Uranus Opposition aspect in astrology, part of the midlife crisis suite of cosmic events. For Virgo, there can be a deep deliciousness to this upset, as the lists get burned and the libido unleashed.

For this sensitive creature, the key to navigating these electrical hits lies in remembering their witchy capacity for environmental adaptation. Content to channel what's there, rather than try to control the direction of the winds of change, the forties Virgo can make magic out of whatever weather patterns arise.

THE FIFTIES:
Breakfast in Bed

After the electrical hits of the sensual forties storm, there can be quite a bit left on the ground, and the fifties Virgo is urged to stay with and abide what might seem broken rather than immediately trying to sort. In whatever state Virgos find their house, the fifties is a profound moment to start trusting the process. At this point in their life cycle, Virgos have come up against their own form of serenity prayer, beginning to poetically parse out what they can and cannot change. And as they loosen their grip, they turn increasing attention toward how they might actually enjoy the ride.

While Virgos may have spent a big part of their existence plumping others' pillows and serving breakfast in bed, it's during this era of their lives that they're asked to consider what they've done for themselves lately. For a sign that's so deeply body conscious, Virgos can sometimes be remarkably estranged from more profound exercises in self-care, and it's here that they are asked to dive beneath the symptoms and to "treat" their entire systems with tenderness and affection. By committing to repair any ruptures in the body and spirit that have occurred as the result of overly harsh critiques, the process of softening to themselves can become a Virgo's greatest act of service.

This decade is marked by the Chiron Return, and this touchy-feely planetoid's release into Virgo's life reminds them of their sensitive emotional bodies, and the things that must be felt rather than fixed. And though it can feel like the floodgates are opening to all things beyond their conscious control, there can be a relief in washing themselves in these tides, as tears, laughter, and other big emotions come out from under wraps and wrap the maturing Virgo in a cloak of many colors. "Allowing" is the guiding light at this juncture, and the Virgoan credo to honor every creature's process must always include themselves.

THE SIXTIES:
Essential Essence

Virgos enter their sixties with a stripped-down sensibility, back from the fifties spa of self-care with a newfound crystal clarity. This also marks the decade of the second Saturn Return, and, depending on how fully a Virgo reckoned with the first one, questions of soul alignment and outer security are up for review again. But as Virgo looks around at the contours of their lives in the light of day and starts to consider making changes, there's a shift in the rhythm of these adjustments. No longer content to just focus on the grains of sand, sixties Virgos start to explore the larger castle of lasting self-worth.

The sign's deep interiority becomes even more apparent during this era, and no matter their family situation, there's something of the hermit about the sixties Virgo. Wandering an unmarked trail into their own backwoods, Virgos are returning to the seat of themselves at this time, paying close attention to their private process and to the learning that can only come from staying close to the ground of their chosen lives. And although there's not anything bombastically rebellious about this sign's energy, it's during this moment that the fierce fealty to their inner code gets most amplified, as Virgo begins to police their plot with a ferociousness, no longer content to leak energy or love toward projects and people not 100 percent in alignment.

This is the era of essence for Virgos, and if they stay close to their own code, shoring up boundaries and exercising firm "nos," they start to understand what's essential on a soul-deep level. Releasing worry in favor of their flavor of emotional minimalism, sixties Virgos start to drop off what they no longer want to carry and pack only the feelings that keep them most alive. This may even take a very literal form, with sixties Virgo gifting away possessions in search of their cosmic capsule collection. This streamlined Virgo can feel freer and lighter than ever before, adopting an energetic and emotional uniform that is closest to their very skin.

THE SEVENTIES AND BEYOND:
A Place Among The Stars

For a sign that is often wise beyond its years when wee, this stage of Virgo's incarnation can feel like a long-awaited homecoming. Whether curled up with their collections, or out in the world reading to children at their local library, this fine wine Virgo pairs careful intentionality with experiential knowledge and is poised to share their expertise with a wider audience. During this era, Virgos find ease in their craft, and creative flow trumps endless tweaking, as the sign lets efforts come through them, seasoned by their channel's distinctive form of magic.

As Virgo enters the seventies, exfoliating extraneous matter from their lives can feel remarkably graceful, and whatever is already receding in the rearview mirror simply slips away. This relationship to change is amplified by the Uranus Return astro aspect in their eighties, and a Virgo of this age range can find that any attempts to manage their lives are gleefully tossed out the window in favor of the sheer feeling of the top-down wind through their hair. For a sign that's notoriously sensitive about their physical bodies, Virgos can actually be quite content to age. As they watch themselves evolve, shifts in their physicality serve as evidence of their participation in the world around them, their bones an inevitable gift from and to the dirt on which they stand.

There is a kind of porousness to this time, as the maturing Virgo opens wide to the whole of the physical world and lets themselves be moved by matter rather than carefully mapping their place. Whether wandering at the base of momentous mountains or slipping barefoot into the aliveness of an early morning meadow, these Virgos are sanding the last of their hard edges and embracing their opposite sign of Pisces's urge to merge. Trusting so firmly in their distinction that they can lose themselves to the whole, this ultimate Virgo becomes a glittering dot in a blanket of stars.

VIRGO IN LOVE

THERE IS ARGUABLY no area more misrepresented in pop astrology than Virgo's love and sex life. And the intricate complexities of the zodiac's harvest maiden reveal that their so-called "virgin" status is anything but prudish. This woodsy witch is romantically self-possessed, filled with a coiled, self-contained potency that stirs her own carnal cauldron first and doesn't give it away freely. In love, Virgo's key word is *devotion*, and whether choosing to literally bow down in a BDSM-infused affair, or approaching the altar of monogamy clad in white, Virgos must consider exactly to whom and to what they are serving up their hearts.

Before the symbol was coopted by the patriarchy, Virgo energy was steeped in the goddess, an archetype that simply meant "whole unto herself," rather than chaste. Virgo's notorious choosiness is further evidence of a fierce inner code, and high standards certainly don't rob this sign of sexual libido. In fact, when Virgo energy is fully connected to its carnal center, there can be a full-on feast of the body's functions. Collapsing the categorical divides between virtue and vice, this ripe-when-ready harvester celebrates the organic urges and delicious quirks of the human animal in love.

Choosing an appropriate altar for their ardor can be the work of a lifetime, and in all partnerships, there's some degree of sweet solitude to Virgo's journey. For any friend or lover who lives by Virgo's side, understanding this loner status is critical to sustaining their collision. While it may not make itself explicitly manifest through literal getaways and disappearances, there is a part of Virgo that will never belong to another being. And once both Virgo and their beloveds embrace this most personal locket that lives inside the sign, they are gifted with a devoted partnership that lets both of their hearts live, coming together through the separateness of two selves that are truly seen.

JUSTIFY MY LOVE:
Dating and Courtship

Because of the sign's more subtle heart songs, the fast food of modern dating can sometimes feel abrasive. Virgos crave carefully crafted companionship and elaborate tasting menus, and swiping right and then showing up to an amorous job interview often feels remarkably boring. But as the single Virgo navigates the dating wilds, they're asked to balance between their high-end selectivity and a little bit of spontaneous fun, letting even bad dates become natural history experiments. While a dating Virgo doesn't have to completely relax standards, allowing for the possibility that a future lover might arrive in an unexpected package lets Virgo loosen the controls and discover what actually turns them on.

When they're attentive to urges that lurk beneath societal trappings, Virgo's inner code can sometimes lean decidedly kinky. Even inside the white wedding Virgo dreamer, there can be something deliciously sordid, and Virgos are encouraged to connect to this sex-positive carnal knowledge, dropping out of amorous analysis and between their sign glyph's carefully crossed legs. As they embrace a fuller range of sensual flavors, following their bodies instead of their heads, Virgos learn to move beyond the binaries, and can forge relationships that are delightfully non-normative.

Whatever partnership shape and size they decide on, the process of defining a relationship must feel personal. And any Virgo heart explorer is urged to exercise some healthy restraint when swallowing inherited love stories. As parents, friends, and popular culture urge this sign to adopt tried and true pathways down the proverbial aisle, Virgos must always walk their own way. When this sign is single, they're often scapegoated at family functions, as a pushy uncle or cousin keeps asking them why they haven't yet found "the one." In these moments of pressurized constraint, Virgo is asked to assert their amorous code, reminding themselves that love comes in as many forms as there are lovers to feel it.

Once Virgos have identified an object, or objects, of their affection, the devotional acts begin. This sign's fully focused, careful attention to a lover can sometimes lean toward the critical, skipping the honeymoon phase and heading straight into the harsh light of day. Under the Virgo gaze, a lover can become yet another candidate for refinement, evidence of potential rather than personhood. It's especially vital that Virgos in the early stages of love remain open to encounters with their own and their partners' humanness, cultivating a willingness to stay with any messy emotions that arise. When their attention is focused on the mysteries of the flesh rather than the fixable cracks and fissures, there is truly no sign better equipped to understand the intricate chambers of the human heart. Filled with the sacred act of giving themselves and receiving another without judgment, Virgo finds their higher love.

LABOR OF LOVE:
The Long-Term Virgo Partner

A mash-up of riding-crop leather and Victorian lace, Virgo's relationship to domesticity is decidedly complex. On the one hand, the sign may harbor hardened honeymoon visions of idealized long-term partnership, creating impossible standards for potential betrotheds who are forever falling short. But even these standards can actually be evidence of the more untamable qualities of the sign, as the endless search for the elusive "one" frees Virgo for spending time in solitude. Whatever their path toward enduring partnership, Virgos must be careful to own this seeming paradox, balancing devotion to another with sustainable self-love, checking in at every turn to ensure self-sovereignty rather than blind servitude.

As the sixth sign of the zodiac, arriving just after Leo's signature flair and before Libra's deep mirroring, Virgo represents the last moment we truly have to ourselves. No matter the style of long-term love affair they enter into, there is something of the singular bachelorette or dashing widower to this sign. While they're not necessarily inclined to wander sexually, preserving this inner flame in some form is vital for

> Wherever they identify on the introversion/extroversion spectrum, many Virgos will keep a close-knit crew of friends, selecting their team members like superheroes fit to survive the apocalypse.

the sustenance of their longer affairs. Keeping a proverbial backroom, basement, or boudoir on hand as evidence of their own secret world lets Virgos know that there is part of themselves that will forever remain self-wedded.

If the Virgo partner can learn to see their union as self chosen and perpetually in-process, they can create lasting trust that comes from a ready willingness to do the work rather than an oppressive sense of duty. Even in marriage, retaining the concept that both parties are showing up daily rather than being bound for life can feel like liberation, as Virgo remains curious about the unfolding instead of martyred to the cause. Any Virgo who enters into a long-term affair must feel into the evolutionary aspects of their relationship, relinquishing some of the urge to keep score for the feel-good flow of give-and-take. Celebrating self-development milestones instead of externally imposed markers of relationship success can keep Virgos connected to the heart of the matter, gifting compassion instead of china, and passion instead of paper.

WITH A LITTLE HELP FROM MY FRIENDS:
The Virgo Pal

Their friend zone is a vital extension of this give-and-take romantic tango, as Virgos learn to live and let live, transforming their harshest inner critic into a compassionate cheerleader for their besties. While they can sometimes remain blindly devoted in romance, in friendship, Virgoan sensitivity can flair up. As a Virgo pal confronts their friends' distinctive life choices and beliefs, they sometimes read their pals' self-chosen paths as betrayals of what they believe to be right. But rather than cut and run, they're asked to stick around and reckon with these differences. Learning to voice their hurts cleanly and clearly, and to trust that each pal's life path is as valid as their own, is the way for Virgo to earn and keep lifelong comrades.

When they commit to listening to their pals without prejudice and holding space for their wholeness, Virgo friends have the opportunity to activate their potential as profound healers. Remaining careful not to ride the gossip train or give unsolicited advice, Virgos help friends make sense of it all, sorting through the pieces of their lives with surprising softness. Able to identify when friends are straying from their own inner codes, Virgos can also lend a steady hand to bring pals back to center. And as long as they remember to do so with a beating heart, rather than the stern projections of their own harshest inner critic, Virgos become beloved slumber party BFFs from dusk 'til dawn.

Wherever they identify on the introversion/extroversion spectrum, many Virgos will keep a close-knit crew of friends, selecting their team members like superheroes fit to survive the apocalypse. And although the depths of these unions don't need to be discouraged, Virgos are invited to hit the streets from time to time, embracing the partygoing circulation of their fellow Mercury-ruled sign of Gemini. Making sure to balance their urge to curate with some human curiosity, colliding with people from all walks of life helps build Virgo's faith in forging their own highly personal path.

ELEMENTAL EROTICA:
Sign-By-Sign Collisions

Astrological pairings go far beyond good/bad binaries, and every cosmic collision has worthy treasures to mine. Look to the following for a primer on all flavors of Virgoan partnership.

ARIES: This collision of cardinal fire and mutable earth is complex, to say the least, and growth lies in exploring the concept of aligned action. Virgo is floored by the obviousness of Aries's unapologetic intentions and is here to harness some of the Ram's unanalytically bold moves. And while Aries may be baffled by Virgo's urge to serve, the Ram learns to let Virgo help them channel their flame for the greater good. Together, they bond by fully supporting each other's fiercely self-directed agendas.

TAURUS: These two earth babes love to bed down, finding comfort in simple luxuries and subtle touches. For Virgo, Taurus's full-on abundance mentality is a balm for their sometimes nervous souls. And for Taurus, Virgo's urges toward improvement can help awaken the cow out of too-stuffy pasture patterns. Together, it's an exercise in sensual stability and carnal change, letting body language tell them when to root down into their relationship, and when it's time to till the soil of stuck grooves.

GEMINI: The quick-footed planet Mercury rules these two signs, and a partnership invigorates their nervous systems and accelerates change in both parties' lives. For Gemini, Virgo teaches the winged one that endless bits of info can add up to an inner credo, encouraging the butterfly to trust in their own voice. And for Virgo, Gemini keeps the sign spry, reminding Virgo that the shifting nature of life is cause for curious celebration. Together, they're invited to soften the urge toward over-analysis and learn when to sit back and simply let their love be.

CANCER: A decidedly internal affair, these signs slide into their seashells easily, supporting each other's desires for self-protection. Virgo is invited to take a skinny dip in Cancer's emotional waters, learning to ride the tides without an overly analytical life jacket. And Cancer is asked to come in for a landing, adopting some of Virgo's more detached perspective on their highly personal feelings and cultivating an increased ability to ungrip their crab claws. Through sharing their secret diaries, they find strength in sensitivity.

LEO: As neighboring signs in the zodiac, these two lovers represent the process of vulnerable exposure, and together they're here to explore the feedback loop of self-expression and societal recognition. For Virgo, Leo's spontaneous urges for self-possessed play can soothe the harder edges of the sign's self-critique. And for Leo, Virgo gifts the over-the-top kitten greater self-awareness, helping them understand how their fiery force is received. Together, the creative contributions can be immeasurable, as the pair learns to share their hearts and shine their light with equal parts specialness and service.

VIRGO: Virgo-on-Virgo action is an intricate affair, as both signs' inner codes collide, and the universality of their respective standards is called into question. At its best and brightest, this partnership can bring each party into deeper communion with their value centers, helping these partners separate the wheat from the chaff and divine what truly matters. Together, they're developing integrity and learning to honor each other's distinctions, balancing acts of service with self-care. Allowing plenty of solo time allows these twin souls to flame on.

LIBRA: These two cultured cuties can find happiness through haute couture and sculpture wings, delighting in the potential to craft an increasingly perfect partnership. For Libra, growth lies in letting Virgo remind them that they are self-directed beings with natural urges that can't always be intellectualized. And by embracing some of Libra's devil's advocate ability to see both sides, Virgo can start to swap narrow critique for a 360 POV. Together, they're asked to balance perfect wedding visions with the willingness to do the dirty work.

SCORPIO: As the signs that connect us most explicitly to the genitals, there's an animalism in this partnership that hones each of their emotional instincts and heals fears of powerlessness. Virgo is here to help Scorpio learn greater trust and open to the naturalness of their urges with more ease. And Scorpio is here to challenge any last vestiges of Virgo's propriety, asking the Virgin to swap playing nice for following their own heat. Together, they can unleash each other's unapologetic wildness and awaken shame-free sensuality that soothes their very souls.

SAGITTARIUS: These two mutable sign magic makers find ecstasy by staying open to the experience. For Virgo, Sag wild ponies remind them that they can spread their light through excitement, breaking boundaries, and serving in a way that honors their very essence rather than simply toeing the line. And for Sag, Virgo reins in some of their tendencies toward excess, reminding the pony that an inner life is as vital as the outer party. Together, they're asked to upgrade tightly held beliefs, always ready to adjust their philosophies to follow the shifting winds.

CAPRICORN: These fellow earth signs collide around the concept of inner authority, here to teach each other about their respective rights to rule the castle. For the sometimes status conscious Cappy mountain climber, Virgo reminds them to take breaks in the ski lodges of humility while ascending to the peaks. And for Virgo, Capricorn awakens the witch's ambition, assuring them that their self-sovereignty is allowed a stronger seat at the table. Together, embracing shifting power dynamics reminds each of them that neither needs to struggle to stay on top.

AQUARIUS: Channeling the challenging inconjunct aspect in astrology, these lovers are learning to swap urges to analyze in favor of radical acceptance. For Aquarius, Virgo's conservation mode can help the sign bring their most eccentric gifts to the world, rendering Aquarian schemes useful for a greater audience. In turn, Aquarius reminds Virgo of their right to rebel against the straight lines and to question any acts of devotion that have become rote. Together, they're asked to bring the blood back to intellectualized systems, reminding each other of their respective humanity, and the personal needs that underlie their desire to serve.

PISCES: As opposite signs, Pisces and Virgo are here to make a tender exchange, each magnetized by the other's teachings. The answer lies in balancing between helpfulness and helplessness, softening savior complexes, and creating healthy boundaries to channel a love that heals their past lives. Virgo is here to embrace the sweet sense of allowing that Pisces embodies, relaxing any urges to "fix" Piscean emotion oceans while asserting their own needs. And Pisces is here to take greater responsibility for their permeability, letting Virgo's earthy pragmatism help awaken their own capacity to self-soothe.

VIRGO AT WORK

FOR A SIGN that is often thought of as synonymous with the word "work," Virgos are here to learn that they're far more than just human file folders, penned from as much stardust as Post-it® Notes. In the cycle of personal development, Virgo energy asks us to hone our craft, and this sign is invited to engage in complex forms of career witchery, ensuring that the tasks they're devoted to are best serving their whole body and soul. At the office, Virgo's very essence is on the line, and finding and cultivating their calling is a devotional practice that necessitates Virgo's full consciousness.

Associated with the astrological chart's sixth house, Virgo energy is sometimes pigeonholed into the mundane machinery of work life, associated with the 9-to-5 slog rather than evidence of our more philosophical higher purpose. In the sixth house, we learn to harness our fifth house Leo mojo and transform it into functional material, realistically assessing how we will actually paint that picture or write that hit song. But this realism is a necessary step in developing a soul-shaped destiny (which will reach its peak in the Capricorn-ruled tenth house). And as any Virgo will remind you, simply showing up is half the battle. Virgos are here to make every day count, apprenticing themselves to the professional process through practical assessment of their career capacities, and building greater intimacy with their art by staying close to the ground.

Their work lives are akin to elaborate gemstone mining missions, with Virgos extracting the raw materials of skills and opportunities and turning them into jewels, applying sweet sweat in an alchemical process that draws out what's already inherent. Yet if left completely unchecked, staying close to the ground can leave Virgos in the dirt, and the Virgo professional is asked to watch for tendencies to remain underutilized or unacknowledged. Tempering their urge for exhaustive performance reviews, Virgos can find contentment in the raw, uncut diamonds of their already worthiness, satisfied by shining their light, in whatever form. When they're careful not to equate their value with a list of completed tasks, Virgos find mastery in apprenticeship, unleashing their wild curiosity and compassionately partnering with whatever work weather is on hand.

Ultimately, Virgo's professional path is one best forged in solitude, as they learn to turn down the buzz of their so-called superiors and amplify their inner voice. While developing a craft necessitates careful honing and committed practice, in the end, Virgos are tasked with building faith in their own expertise, becoming self-sovereign sirens beckoning themselves toward callings that tailor-fit their own personal journey. The more time Virgos spend dipping

> **Ultimately, Virgo's professional path is one best forged in solitude, as they learn to turn down the buzz of their so-called superiors and amplify their inner voice.**

into their own process, taking walkabouts on long weekends away from the office, the more they can come back to the boardroom table ready to cast a spell that syncs their bodies with their bank accounts.

CASTING THE SPELL:
Discovering a Virgo's Calling

A creative tension lives inside every Virgo, borne from the contrast between the civilized, buttoned-up dress code and the wild undoing of nature. Before we enter the seventh sign of Libra, which is all sculptural ideals and potential perfection, Virgo leaves us to reckon with the reality of our urges, making peace with our natures so we can find the middle ground between fate and free will. This animal/mineral paradox often manifests at work, as Virgo struggles to reconcile their analytical ambition toward making good with a deeper call to just make something out of the beautiful mess, answering the hunger in their souls rather than the status quo. In order to avoid becoming the caged office bird, Virgos are asked to divine exactly how much of their effort is motivated by an abstract, anxiety-ridden "should," and how much is evidence of a deeply desirous decision-making that actually feels good in their bodies.

More than any other sign, Virgo thrives when given a proverbial "gap year" before plunging into professional pursuits, disappearing into the brush with a backpack, or simply spending a summer sitting on the dock of the bay. True contribution must spring from contemplation, and to avoid getting sucked into the rote mechanisms of day-to-day drudgery, Virgos are called to commune with this higher consciousness. No matter how much of a contraction it may initially feel like, waiting to sign on the dotted line or sleeping on it before taking the promotion is always in Virgo's best interest, as they develop a pacing and professionalism that is completely personal. Soliciting inner career advice in solitude, rather than asking around, ensures that these unwed warriors are answering first and foremost to their own calling.

In the professional diagram of potential pursuits, Virgos often gravitate toward their so-called "zone of competence" or "zone of excellence," exploiting what they've always been able to do well without questioning what they want, settling on any old job that will help the world benefit from their cleanup capacity. But the evolved Virgo worker lets themselves dance into their "zone of genius," beckoned toward what makes their pulse quicken. Virgos can easily do what the rest of us don't want to, scrubbing the dishes after the party rather than partying on. To find their true calling, Virgos must cultivate the courage to stick their hands into the cake instead of merely sweeping up the dry crumbs after the festivities are over.

Whatever field they choose to pursue, Virgos are invited to become experts, diving in and digging deep down the rabbit hole of their pursuit like perpetual PhD students. Finding their soul's purpose is a carnally led question of turf for this earth sign, and Virgos are asked to travel the land and discover the spot that is theirs and theirs alone, sometimes making complete career about-faces later in life. Their turf may prove to be an intensely specific, even quirky craft. No other sign has a greater capacity to become niche, whether creating bespoke bolo ties or acting as the world's foremost expert on a specific variety of beetle. In any field a Virgo follows, whether self-employed or tethered to a corporate ladder, they must carve out a kind of hermit cave, confident in a self-driven capacity for contribution that is irreplaceable. Following specificity rather than status markers, Virgos deepen their self-sovereignty, content to clock in by their own hand and burn the midnight oil at their own altar.

DEVOTIONAL DESKTOPS:
Virgo's Professional Style

Once they've taken a job, Virgos are quick to hunker down, dedicating themselves, sometimes blindly, to the day-to-day and disappearing behind paper trails. This sign can take great delight in the ritualized aspects of the office, finding comfort in the dry-erase boards of tasks to be done and tasks that are completed and carefully packing beloved Lunchables® for a long day at the office. This delight in the divinity of detail is never something to be written off as superficial, and Virgos are invited to embrace the aesthetics of their professional environment. Delicious mid-morning macchiatos, the most vibrant blooming desk plant, or the least scratchy suit fabric can all soothe their notorious physical sensitivities, helping Virgos build confidence in their actual ability to get the job done.

As the sign of personal assistants and backroom researchers, Virgos can sometimes become a kind of invisible, hotel-quality presence in the office, vacuuming the dust bunnies and keeping everything running smoothly after hours without a trace. And while there's certainly nothing wrong with taking on these necessary tasks, so long as they truly make Virgo's heart sing, this sign must consistently be willing to confront questions of ambition. When faced with the proposition of moving on up, some of these sign natives will say that such markers of achievement don't suit them, content to know their place and serve their purpose, no matter how small. And while this may sometimes be the case, in every Virgo there lurks a little leftover Leo energy waiting to be celebrated and integrated, even if it's just through a mention in the footnotes. Over the course of their professional lives, Virgos are asked to very carefully assess how much of their urge to avoid accolades is true dedication to the process, and how much stems from fear of exposure.

When Virgos do meet with professional success, there can be a kind of guilty feeling that creeps beneath the surface, as they're either convinced of their fundamental unworthiness or burdened by the sensation that they now have to forever secure their place in the sun. Virgos best mitigate this performance anxiety by adjusting their relationship to the concept of progress. In their most beautiful form, Virgo's workspaces are shop classes or chemistry labs, evidence of the sign's capacity to utilize and experiment with what's there, no matter the end game. Ensuring that a Virgo is delighting in each micro-moment during an unfolding project, mixing up the elements and carefully sanding the surfaces, is the key to developing a self-driven definition of success.

PERFORMANCE REVIEW:
The Virgo Coworker

Here to lend a hand or pick up an extra coffee, Virgo can easily become the living embodiment of an ideal coworker. This sign inherently sniffs out what must be done and gets to work doing it without extraneous pomp and circumstance, eager to be of immediate use rather than wait around for elaborate instruction. Often functioning behind the scenes, Virgos are the office fairy godparents, depositing little trails of professional gifts, picking up the undone odd tasks, and keeping the workplace bones in place, far beneath the surface.

> **Here to lend a hand or pick up an extra coffee, Virgo can easily become the living embodiment of an ideal coworker.**

Perpetually poised to extend praise to another, Virgo colleagues can be boundless cheerleaders for their fellow workers' capacities. Inherently blessed with the ability to separate the wheat from the chaff, Virgos see their coworkers as precious notes in an evolving symphony, acting as energetic sieves who draw what's best in each player to the surface. And as long as they remember the humanness of these constituent parts, Virgos can make excellent managers, matching each team member to their musical ability and celebrating slow and steady artistic evolution rather than forcing results. Like a perfumer, the Virgo boss must remember that their subordinates are delicately grown flowers to be sniffed and enjoyed as part of the mosaic of nature, rather than forcibly crushed in the name of production values.

In any collaboration, Virgo must balance some ingrained low-on-the-totem-pole tendencies with an increased capacity to claim the crown. After the explosive self-expression of Leo, Virgos check themselves, and this can often manifest through a kind of endless slog of self-imposed performance reviews, or an overattachment to external assessments. Developing an internal system of checks and balances is vital for this sign, as they learn to calibrate only in accordance with this inner code.

Easily absorbed into the office wallpaper, this sign's factory setting is often to keep their head down, following the predetermined course that was agreed upon and not asking too many questions. And all too easily, Virgos can take on more and more of the dirty work, potentially building resentment, to boot. In these cases, the Virgo worker is asked to consistently return to the question of turf, making sure that wherever they are placed within the office hierarchy, they have a highly personal field to tend. Whether it's identifying themselves as the office expert on a certain topic or pushing their edges by taking on even the tiniest task that's out of their comfort zone, this sign maps their domain through micromovements. Ensuring that they don't become mere prisoners on someone else's piece of professional land helps Virgos craft from a place of soul purpose instead of anxious compulsion.

THE COURAGE TO ENJOY IT:
Making Money

As an earth sign, Virgos are here to strengthen their relationship to the material world, embracing everything from tiny pebbles to cold hard diamonds. A sign of real world adjustment and learning, Virgos are in an active apprenticeship with earning, developing a highly personal money philosophy and learning to respond to inevitable ebbs and flows in their bank accounts. To maintain the money tree magic, they must connect to the roots, making sure that both the sources of earning and objects of spending are always in soul alignment.

For many Virgos, questions of "not enoughness" in other areas of their lives may manifest as scarcity mentality. The feeling of things never being quite right, or there always being more to do, can become a hunger for Virgo, showing up at both ends of the spectrum as either chronic underearning or a ravenous appetite for amassing more and more resources to weather the storm. But this sign doesn't have to suffer at the sacrificial altar of scarcity. Remembering that no one project or person is their "source" connects Virgo to wellsprings of abundance that go far beyond success and failure binaries. For this sign, money is truly energy, and in the face of a pay cut, client loss, or job change, they're asked to ungrip their palms and open the channel wide, letting new cash flow in from unexpected sources.

As with all things Virgoan, lasting security is found through the sensual rightness of the body. And whether they're paralyzed by the prospect of asking for a raise or stocking their cabinets with soup cans for the apocalypse, Virgos can turn fear to money medicine by remembering that they are absolutely allowed to just feel good. Following signals from the body lets Virgo read their environment, feeling rises and falls in the stock market like a storm-ready

animal. As the sign surrenders to the shifts, and starts to relinquish control over the bank balance bottom line, earning is somehow, mysteriously, upped. True money witches, Virgos are able to conjure something out of seeming nothingness, and when they feel full from the inside with worthiness, they can attune to even the smallest opportunities for greater earning.

For the aligned Virgos who know they are their own source and who surrender to seasonal financial shifts, heaven can become a place on earth. Able to amass stockpiles of delicious nuts over time, Virgos take powerful pride in saving, as they plan their seaside getaway or slowly accrue enough funds to purchase a piece of haute couture that's tailored and built to last. And as they attend to these long-term goals, Virgos are also asked to remember to savor the sweetness of spending, careful to balance their tendencies toward someday-sacrifice with relishing the ripeness of what's right here, right now.

CONCLUSION

Now that you've encountered the intricate inner workings of the zodiac's singularly sovereign witch, it's time to head out into the wondrous woods. Whether you're a Virgo Sun sign who's looking to re-up your commitment to your mission or a Virgoan aficionado building more trust in your integrity and personal process, consult the energy checklist that follows to tend your inner flame.

THE HOUSE RULED BY VIRGO

Check out the pie slices of your chart and look for the Virgo symbol. This is the arena of life in which you're invited to take a Virgoan approach, enacting deeper care, attention, and discernment, and living in alignment with your own code.

THE SIGN RULING THE SIXTH HOUSE

The sixth house is naturally ruled by Virgo and awakens the holistic connection between our bodies and our environments. The sign that rules this house in your chart reveals how to approach your daily routine and uncovers where you can apprentice yourself to the process, becoming an experiential learner without having to know it all.

YOUR MERCURY SIGN

This cosmic butterfly reveals how we assimilate information, perceive the world, attune our nervous systems to input/output, and relate to everyday change. Look to your Mercury sign to discover how you can more clearly communicate, find your love of learning and field of expertise, and adjust your approach, meeting transitions with more ease.

YOUR VESTA SIGN

This superspecial asteroid is the zodiac's internal, eternal flame keeper. In our charts, Vesta connects us to the territory that is ours and ours alone, showing us how we draw ourselves back to center, apply devotion, and tend our own creative and sensual fires.

> *During Virgo season, which signals the final throes of summertime in the Northern Hemisphere, we are starting to harvest the juicy fruits of our labors.*

VIRGO SEASON

As the sun travels through the entire zodiac, spending about a month in each astrological sign, we all have the opportunity to celebrate and integrate these twelve powerful archetypes. During Virgo season, which signals the final throes of summertime in the Northern Hemisphere, we are starting to harvest the juicy fruits of our labors. It's a time to right our internal rhythms, recommit to our distinctive contribution, and relish all of the untamable tasties we've grown with our own two gorgeous, perfectly imperfect, human hands.

VIRGO QUESTIONS

* **INTEGRITY.** Are my thoughts, words, and deeds consistent? Do I do one thing like I do everything? When do I come out of alignment with what I know to be true and why? What is my personal code of ethics, borne of my own experience?

* **DISCERNMENT.** Where is my energy leaking? In what situations and partnerships do I feel more drained than filled? Where do I want to say no, but keep saying yes? If I could curate my life exactly as I envision, what would it look like?

* **RHYTHM.** What "season" of my life am I in right now? How do I respond to change? What geographical place connects me to the feeling that I am part of the natural world? How can I respond to the rightness of timing, rather than just pushing my agenda?

* **RITUAL.** How does my daily routine support my wholeness? How do I care for my beautiful body? What alterations could I make, however small, to honor this life of mine? How does my personal environment (home, food, clothing, and so on) reflect my values?

* **WITCHERY.** What kind of magic am I capable of? How can I make something out of what's presenting itself in my life? What needs to be altered or shifted right now? How can I build faith in what I cannot see?

* **WILDNESS.** How do I honor my need for solitude? What area of my life or my self belongs to me and me alone? What parts of me will forever be untamable? How can I choose my wants over my shoulds? What would taste most delicious to do right now?

VIRGO IN YOUR BIRTH CHART

Whether or not you were honored to be born under the sign of the witch, Virgo's earth powers are for everyone. Here's how to connect to your turf, no matter your sign.

VIRGO PLANETS AND PLACEMENTS

When you look up your birth chart, you'll discover that you're not just your sun sign, but are composed of an array of celestial cuties, each symbolizing a different part of your life force and penning your personal cosmic story. Explore if you have any other planets or placements in the sign of Virgo.

* **VIRGO RISING:** The rising sign is the kind of packaging we arrive in. It indicates the energy of our approach (the lens we use to view the world) and calls on us to take this sign's principles to a deeper level. Virgo Rising babes naturally approach the world with a microscope in hand, carefully waiting on the sidelines before leaping in, eager to understand how they might better fit into the whole. Virgo Risings are asked to pay special attention to their inner code and outer world, making sure that they stay true to themselves on all levels.

* **MOON IN VIRGO:** The moon is a tucked-in shellabration of our inner worlds, symbolic of how we feel and what makes us secure. In Virgo, the moon carefully adjusts itself to every fluctuation of the environment, rendering these individuals highly attuned to emotional and physical feedback. Virgo Moons are invited to soften some of their analysis and practice simply feeling their feelings instead.

* **MERCURY IN VIRGO:** Quick-footed Mercury is the zodiac's butterfly, ruling perception, communication, and how we relate to everyday change. As one of the natural rulers of the sign, Mercury in Virgo delights in sorting and ordering, assimilating information rapidly and deciding what is most vital to the whole. Mercury in Virgos are asked to care delicately for their buzzy nervous systems and to notice when critique has trumped compassion.

* **VENUS IN VIRGO:** Pleasure-petaled Venus rules all kinds of receiving, from money to food to sex. It describes how we take in the world, content to magnetize rather than force our mojo. In Virgo, Venus bows down devotedly to pleasure, eager to bring breakfast in bed to their beloveds. Their growth lies in self-pleasuring, remembering that they have every right to relish the deliciousness of their own lives.

* **MARS IN VIRGO:** Mars is our red-hot muscle and mojo, the source of both our sexuality and success drive. Placed in Virgo, Mars is a carefully oiled ride, checking under the hood and tuning up before hitting the open road. Growth happens when this sign placement remembers that sometimes not everything has to be just right to be unleashed, and that they can step out from beyond the scenes to claim their place among the stars.

* **JUPITER IN VIRGO:** Jupiter is the planet that blows open our windows and doors, beckoning us to expand beyond our constrictive beliefs, and risk connecting to our wild natures. Placed in Virgo, Jupiter is expanding our

capacity to contribute in the world, asking us to raise our threshold for devotion and to see both the detailed dirt and the stars above. This sign placement gets lucky when they remember to attend to every last piece of the puzzle, leaving no stone unturned.

* **SATURN IN VIRGO:** Saturn is the planet of limits and laws, a sometimes hard-knocks school that paves the way toward lasting competence. Saturn placed in Virgo asks us to consider our relationship to effort and to check any urges to blindly keep "doing" when we're invited to just "be" instead. A serious sign placement that knows how to get the work done, growth comes from occasionally floating downstream.

* **URANUS IN VIRGO:** This rule breaker and change maker is here to shake it up, interrupting our usual societal programming and urging us to travel beyond the mapped roads. In Virgo, the revolution starts at home, and this placement is encouraged to adopt an innovative approach to caring for themselves and their bodies. Also here to interrupt rote status quo machinery, Uranus in Virgos must commit to finding their own distinctive cause rather than simply toeing the line.

* **NEPTUNE IN VIRGO:** A generational planet that shifts signs every fourteen years, Neptune is the zodiac's dream queen, an escape hatch that takes us into the mystical world and symbolizes where we crave transcendence. Bringing the heaven principle down into the dirt, this sign placement is here to connect us to the magic in every grain of sand. Neptune in Virgo is also encouraged to pay close attention to the direction of their devotion, making sure that where they place their faith and effort is loving them right back.

* **PLUTO IN VIRGO:** The outermost generational "planet," Pluto is ruler of the underworld, a jet-black metal detector of where we must enact karmic change. Pluto in Virgo's intensity is centered on the creative process, amplifying the sign's search for their specialness and expertise. Here to undo some of the expectations about what work looks like, Pluto in Virgos are here to respond to their own rhythms, unleashing the sign's lone wildness by reclaiming places where they've given away their power.

* **CHIRON IN VIRGO:** This touchy-feely planetoid is ready for healing, asking us to develop deep sensitivity and awareness in its sign placement, without expecting immediate fixes. Placed in the sign of the zodiac's notorious fixer, Chiron in Virgo is cultivating greater allowing in this lifetime, walking alongside their emotions and tempering any harsh urges to "move on" or "get better." Body consciousness is intensified, and healing happens when they explore their own right to humanness, diving into the beautiful mess.

* **THE NORTH OR SOUTH NODE IN VIRGO:** The Nodal axis connects us to past lives and future promises, as we're asked to integrate both our North and South Node signs to come closer to our soul's purpose. With one of the Nodes in Virgo and the other in Pisces, this placement is learning how to balance matter and spirit, blending the urge to merge into the mystically unseen world with the solitary work of incarnating in a body and acknowledging separation.

SEPT. 23–OCT. 22

text by Gabrielle Moritz

element — AIR

symbol — THE SCALES

modality — CARDINAL

house — SEVENTH

ruler — VENUS

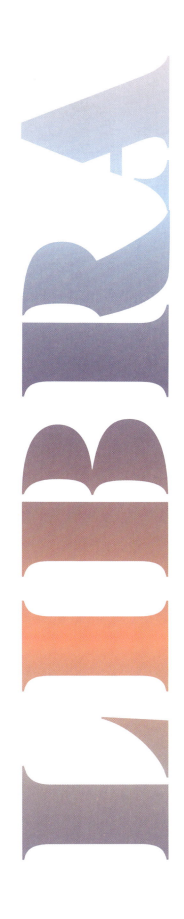

NIBR'A

INTRODUCTION

WHEN IT COMES to the zodiac, few signs have a sweeter reputation than Libra. And it's not by mistake. The sign of the scales is inherently charming, as Libra strives to be in meaningful connection with all of the world around them. They are the great balancers, easy lovers, and subtle reflectors. To be born as a Libra is to embody beauty, justice, and grace, in all forms. Through the wisdom of the Scales we are taught balance and shown what is fair. And they make it look easy, despite the many responsibilities the role can carry with it.

The world is often quick to oversimplify the nature of Libra, but there are many unseen complexities to this sign. Libras are so much more than pretty. They are so much more than a significant other. And they are so much more than "nice." Libra, like all signs, has layers. And to begin to illuminate and peel back some of these layers, we must look at the essential nature and fundamentals of this sign. Before we jump into the life and perspective of a Libra, we must know where they're coming from and why.

By examining Libra's specific set of rulerships and correspondences, we can uncover and define their specific nature. By thoroughly exploring these associations, we will come into a richer understanding at large. The laundry list to be looked at includes: the sign's symbol or archetype, ruling planet, element, modality, polarity, and corresponding tarot card. If any of that sounds too technical or confusing, you'll soon find it all to be rather intuitive and informative. So as we prepare to discuss Libra's fullness, let's first review their unique correspondences and build a foundational knowledge of what is to be woven throughout this chapter.

LIBRA'S CORRESPONDENCES

SYMBOL: The Scales—The first layer to explore, and probably the most well known, is the sign's symbol: the Scales. And just what do scales do? What is their function in the world? In the most basic of definitions, they are an inanimate object comparing the weight of two things. An impartial tool used to illuminate equality, or the lack thereof. It is from the Scales that we know Libra as the sign of balance. And it is worth noting that of all the zodiacal symbols, Libra is the only sign to be represented by an object rather than an animal or being. This is an important distinction to the singularity of Libra's character and deeper aims. The Scales provide a service, information, judgments, and evaluations. Functioning as a tool, they operate by and for others. Without others, they simply sit—balanced, still, and empty. With this, there is both a coolness and an eagerness in Libran interactions. On their own, Libras are able to rest and recalibrate, two very necessary things, especially for the Scales to function at their best. But it is not until they are engaged with other people and ideas that they come to life. And in coming to life, shifting and sharing with and for others, they learn the need for finesse in their relationships so as to preserve their own well-being. In speaking to the Libran experience, the symbol of the Scales will come up again and again as a critical reference point.

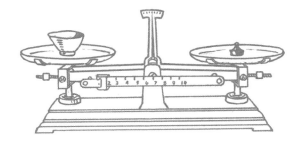

RULER: Venus—The next major player for the sign of Libra is the planet Venus. For Libra, it is their planetary ruler. Venus is the planet that governs their nature and essence, informing what they care about most. And Venus being the planet of beauty, sweetness, pleasure, and connection, Libras are naturally drawn to these things. It's thanks to this rulership that Libra has gained the reputation of being such a socialite, sweetheart, aesthete, and flirt. Working with this rulership, the placement of Venus in the birth charts of those born with significant Libra placements is incredibly important. Venus reveals specific depths and qualities for each Libra. Every Libra Sun would be wise to develop a deeper awareness to their natal Venus, as it profoundly influences their own unique expression of the sign. Due to this relationship, we will look at the nuances that different Venus placements cultivate for Libras in each section.

ELEMENT: Air—Of the four astrological elements—fire, earth, air, water—Libra is imbued with the element of air. Just like the signs of Gemini and Aquarius, Libra is gifted with a sharp and active mind. The air element holds the energy of communication, ideas, expression, reason. As an air sign, Libras have direct access to these powers via their wit, logic, language, and lightness. Their inherent airiness seeks to keep them afloat, allows them to think their way through (and out of) things, and keeps them well connected to the webs of community and information.

MODALITY: Cardinal—Another facet of the zodiac is modality, of which there are three: cardinal, fixed, and mutable. Libra—along with Aries, Cancer, and Capricorn—is a cardinal sign. This component of Libra's expression is one that is initiating and compels the sign to action and fresh starts. Each of the cardinal signs marks the turning of the seasons, the changing of the light. With Libra, we experience equinox energy, a point of balance between day and night, rest and activity—yet another reminder of the sign's affinity to symmetry. Libra encourages us to start again from a neutral point of view, and to initiate new connections that can keep us in balance, hold us in harmony. The spark of inspiration unique to Libra is one that prioritizes and celebrates equality, fairness, and shared resources.

POLARITY: Positive—The last astrological note we will speak to is polarity. The signs are equally divided between positive and negative polarities—alternating every other sign—with the odd-numbered signs expressing the positive polarity and the even-numbered expressing the negative polarity. As the seventh sign of the zodiac, Libra is one of the positive signs, carrying with it an active and expressive charge. They tend toward extroversion, engagement, and activity.

TAROT CARD: Justice XI—Beyond the astrological traits, Libra has ties to the tarot as well. Many connections have been made between

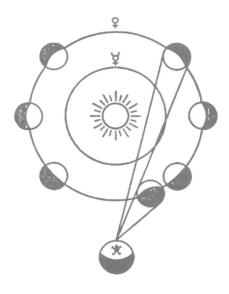

The phases of Venus

astrology and tarot, with each of the twelve signs being linked to a Major Arcana card. For Libra, their corresponding tarot card is that of Justice. Most commonly, its imagery depicts a courtly figure, seated between two pillars, holding an upright sword in one hand—the tool of air—and a scale in the other. It's a visual that epitomizes the values and strengths of Libra.

Hopefully this introduction to the fundamentals of the sign has already begun to deepen your understanding of Libra energy. Now we can move ahead to explore various facets of the Libra personality in life. Remember these threads as the foundation. These keys to the sign will be referenced both directly and indirectly going forward, and they provide the basis for understanding Libra at their core.

LIBRA AS A CHILD

AS WE ENTER the world—small, precious, and new—we each carry with us a particular energy. As children we hold a unique and yet untouched signature of being. We bring with us great potential and promise for who we are to become. And in these early days, we begin to know and to show what it is to be born under specific skies and the influence of the cosmos above.

A child with a Libra birthday is imbued with a light that is looking to spark balance. The rays that shine upon their emergence, that mark their becoming, are those of the Libra Sun—the season of harmony, togetherness, justice, and connection. Under these skies, the little Libran carries a pure and soft expression. They embody the energy of the scales in a fundamental way, as they are just beginning to become themselves.

There is a simple sweetness to the Libra child. With an eagerness to please and a contagious contentedness, they are likely to be smiling, observing, and engaging from a very early age. Their Venusian nature emits a warmth and kindness that pulls them into connection and teaches them to enjoy what is shared.

Employing the sacred tool of Venus—and the very image of the planet's glyph—Libras act as mirrors. And in their early days, their mirroring is pivotal in helping them learn how to be. Trying on the behaviors they see teaches them a great deal, and in this way, they are very attuned and responsive children. They pick up on surrounding energies—from parents, siblings, caretakers, pets—and they amplify their experience in their reflection of things.

When good things surround the Libra child, it feels lovely. They are able to magnify the warm energy they thrive in, as it lifts their energy and emanates outward. But when things are difficult, the young Libra can sometimes over-inflate perceived angst. When they cannot soothe a room or a problem, they are unsettled by the reality of their discomfort. These children often don't understand why they can't feel better or why someone can't be happier.

Sometimes this discomfort leads them to shut down emotionally or look for a place to project their experience. For this reason, it is vital that Libra children are taught early on to name and to know their emotional experience and how it is separate and different from those of the people they are in relationship with. It is easy for this child to prioritize others' feelings or to disassociate from their own. Their airy nature can quickly come in to sweep them off their feet when they don't like the way their lived reality feels.

Soothing a troubled young Libra is often as simple as sharing time with them and their imagination. Cultivate ease, play, and language around their fantasies, while also holding space for their felt experiences. Teach them that these experiences are just as valuable as their sweeter hopes and visions. And strive to keep their container as stable as possible. For these babes, it can be quite difficult to deal with erratic people or places. They don't yet have the ability or awareness to change or understand crunchy circumstances, so they look to the others in their lives to help ease the way.

And those others are their way! Friends, babysitters, coaches, relatives—as many bonds as they're open to. A diversity of relationships is important for expanding this child's understanding of themselves and who they can be. As they try on the traits of their partners, they are seeking out traits of their own. This is why a rich community is so important, so that they don't over-identify with behaviors that aren't true to them. It is natural for them to have an adaptable personality, but without early exposure to different types of people, it can be hard for a Libra to know what is unique and authentic about themselves in later years.

Even in stories, movies, and shows, presenting them with many characters, layered perspectives, and varied experiences will help to keep their minds open. And for the timid or shy Libra child, such exposure can help them learn about people in a manageable way. These kids should never be pushed into relationships or socializing that they are not wanting or ready for. Human connection is something they must be allowed to come to on their own terms, as it is so vital to their identity. It is important that relationships be something they are able to trust.

And beyond the social aspects, sometimes they simply need to witness other people to better note their own skills and persona. When they stand back and observe, they are able to collect valuable information that enhances their ability to decipher and discern the world around them. They are learning how people work to learn how life works, and they are developing a sensitivity to patterns and connections at large.

Finding these common threads often comes with ease for Libra kiddos, and it can be encouraged in fun and simple ways. Word games, puzzles, checkers, cards—play that encourages them to notice symmetries, similarities, and differences, and that asks for a strategy, will see them shine. And charades, dolls, figurines, and playtime are also realms in which these kids get to try on new personalities. They can provide opportunities for these kids to safely and gently process their experiences. A Libra child may feel better able to express their difficult or unpleasant emotions through the guise of a toy or a puppet, or maybe even an imaginary friend. What they may not be ready to identify as their own, or what

ADVANCED CONSIDERATIONS

To help clarify the specific nature of a young Libra, it helps to go beyond the sign of their sun and to look at a little bit more of their birth chart (the planetary snapshot from the minute they were born). As mentioned at the beginning of this chapter, Venus is a vital planet in determining how a Libra will evolve and show up in the world. It illuminates the driving force and deeper aims of a Libra individual. And what this looks like in a Libra Sun's birth chart is one of five potential Venus placements: Venus in Leo, Venus in Virgo, Venus in Libra, Venus in Scorpio, and Venus in Sagittarius. To further enrich your understanding of the sun in Libra, we will soon look at the different nuances each natal Venus sign brings. For those with significant Libra placements other than their sun, there are some notes sprinkled in for further chart insights as well.

they may find less than likable, they can release and witness through a projected self.

Additionally, this mirroring and reflecting can show up quite literally. There is a real fascination with seeing things another way. Water, mirrors, windows, glitter, photographs. Seeing and being seen from another perspective is really compelling for them. Things can be the same but different, viewing the experience of another, witnessing all of the many sides—along with just being able to see themselves in a new way.

Another layer of the mirror, of their Venusian way, is beauty. There is a real love and draw to images. Both images of self and images of the world, they all have the potential to be made beautiful, to radiate with pleasure and pleasantness. A Libra child will have an eye for such a glow. For some, it might result from watching a parent put on makeup and get ready in the morning, and then wanting to do the same for themselves or their favorite dolls. It might mean they want their room to look a certain way. Maybe they loved a specific coloring book and need their palette to fit a certain style. Aesthetics are inherently dear to them and can be expressed in any number of ways. Noting and indulging their interest will help them feel seen and appreciated, as well as calm and at peace, while immersed in an amusing and attractive space.

At this early stage of life, finding regularly peaceful environments helps Libras to feel steady and secure. And another way little Libras reach for this is in asking for fairness. These kids come here with a preexisting notion of equality and of what is right. Ultimately, they are working to cultivate justice in the world, but before they are able to navigate the full complexities of this, they start with naming what is fair.

There may be a fixation on what they believe fair is, freely proclaiming its virtues or questioning its presence in the actions of others. "That's not fair" can become a real catchphrase in the face of disappointments or disparity. Equal distribution of resources, the ability to share with others, and being courteous are early tenants and expectations for these kids. And when others don't agree, they can struggle. But they're unlikely to hold a grudge for too long, as they'd rather make nice and find common ground. In these moments, they learn to tap into their skills of persuasion, using sweetness to get what they want instead.

LIBRA AS AN ADULT

Entering adulthood, Libras have spent enough time mirroring and matching their environments. As they continue to individuate, they begin to care less about assimilating and more about discerning. In this phase of their lives, they are looking to reach mastery of right relations, refined taste, and rigorous kindness. In their expanding self-awareness there is a growing capacity for interdependence. They've learned the basics of how to be nice, how to fit in, and how to please, and now they are choosing when, where, and *why* they do these things.

Shifting their emphasis from connecting to the quality of their connections, Libra adults are learning to wield their sharp and perceptive minds just as much as their charm.

Not all associations are worthwhile ones, and connections that might have been superficial but fun in the past begin to sound less appealing over time. As their experiences accumulate, their values become more clear, and their scales become finetuned to these values so that their choices prioritize lasting harmony over short-term ease.

Understanding the weight of time, "easy" and "pleasant" begin to look a little different, too. Libras learn to weigh past, present, and future, maintaining a keen awareness of time in their decision making. Sometimes these layered considerations can delay action, leaving a Libra in a state of stagnation when stakes are high. But ultimately, they are calculating in their best interest, and that may mean that weeks of waiting are better for them than quick decisions they can't take back. Chaos and hurry are to be avoided as often as possible, as any Libra knows that such haste will rob them of their sharp perception and nuanced judgments.

A scale needs time to rebound and reset. If it is unstable or carrying too heavy of a load, it cannot accurately function. And so some Libras may avoid certain decisions or obligations entirely. When something comes up that they deem unwieldy, they can be prone to dodge any ties or responsibilities to it. They know their bandwidth (and the dangers of overloading it), and so they learn how to evade situations or sweetly say no. Whether through delegation, persuasion, or eluding a matter entirely, Libra adults are protective of their energy and intentional about what they take on.

Similarly, they are learning that they need to maintain adequate room for themselves in their connections with others. Once again, focusing on quality, a good companion will advance or reflect their principles and self-worth. As adults, Libras are increasingly learning the importance of their selfhood in how they are able to relate to the world. They are more than just agreeable, and their perspective has equal merit. Having spent a great deal of time studying and evaluating the opinions of others, they are now able to put more of a voice to their own thoughts, knowing their reflections are just as valid.

They also shift from an observer to a witness or an ally. The element of study, of self-reflection and vicarious experience, becomes more neutral as they grow into their own identity. And in that growth they are able to better show up for others. In their own self-rooting, they can see others as they are, with less bias and projection, and hold true space for them. They are able to see the greater web that they are a part of, and tend to it, thread by thread.

This is one of Libra's great gifts—to see each of us and keep us together—to link folks across perceived boundaries and divides. Libras unite disparate parts and create space for the spectrum that lies between two opposing points.

This vision carries with it a real idealism in seeking for honest ease and compromise. There's an air of innocence about them that may have been read early on as simply naivete, as they look for networks that don't yet exist and relations that seem too good to be true. In a world oft unsatisfied by and ill equipped for equity, kindness, and camaraderie, Libra serves as a beacon. They are advocates for advocates and take pride in their belief of human potential. Not only have they learned to look for the best in others, but they have learned that others' light helps to illuminate their own.

However, this truth is hard to carry at all times, and Libras are not immune to doubt and depression. They can become easily overwhelmed and disheartened by harsh realities. In their desire for fairness and grace, the absence of such dynamics can feel like a major burden or hurdle for these adults. And they may struggle to hold the fullness of this, trying to convince themselves of being fine or disassociating from what feels like too much. This is for their own coping needs and self-preservation, but it is also tied to their need to be nice—a need that is asked to evolve in adulthood.

What Libras begin to find is that being nice should never come at the cost of their own integrity. Their conception of kindness deepens over time to recognize that it is not always pleasant or easy. If their goal is to make meaningful relationships and live well, their personal needs have to factor into the equation alongside the needs of others. And once again, the short term must be considered against the long term. Some situations require sacrifices. Some need compromises. Some must be walked away from altogether. And some really are as simple as showing up sincerely. Whatever the situation, Libra needs to call upon their skills of discernment to judge in equal favor of self and other, knowing that the outcome of their actions is just as important as the intention.

This touches on their greater calling as well: justice. Recognizing the importance of their actions and impact, Libra carries the sword of justice throughout their life.

They know fairness from a very early age, but it's generally simplistic. Early on they can be more compromising and less nuanced in determining equality. But in adulthood, their understanding becomes enriched, and they can distinguish when what is deemed fair is not also just. Justice speaks when the scales are not enough. It cuts through appearances and weighs the intangible, the unspeakable. It is the

> Shifting their emphasis from connecting to the quality of their connections, Libra adults are learning to wield their sharp and perceptive minds just as much as their charm.

culmination of reason and wisdom. It is the gift of a Libra in alignment with their power.

And feeding this power is their eternal softness. Their sensitivity to beauty, pleasure, kindness. Tools that the world might see as luxuries, the Libra knows are birthrights. They seek out joy and indulgence in the everyday. They treasure their rest, belongings, style, and connections. They appreciate the sweetness of their bonds and the honey of time spent with others. Well-appointed rooms become sanctuaries. A good book can become simple medicine. Pleasure is pursued ardently because they know it is paramount. They know that ease is vital, achievable, and most likely to bring one into bloom.

Libra adults are the peacekeepers. They are persuasively passive and gently engaging. As eager accomplices, they are folks looking to lighten the load for all of us. They are giving and receiving, pausing and passing, negotiating at every turn so as to keep us comfortably afloat. Keepers of kind words, they encourage us to trust in grace and trust in each other. Libra reminds us that we are inextricably connected and that our bonds to each other are often our greatest teachers.

VENUS PLACEMENTS

SUN IN LIBRA AND VENUS IN LEO:

As adults, Libras with Venus in Leo are warm and gregarious creatures. They have a dramatic flair and unique charm. Their values are founded upon a strong sense of self, and they know that they have something special to offer others. Folks are drawn to their radiant energy and uplifted by their partnership. These Libras must be ever mindful of the balance between their own persistent desires and the wants and needs of those around them. While they are generally ones to share the wealth, sometimes their egos and grandiose nature can get the best of them, and they put their persuasive skills to work for their own ends rather than others' interests. A healthy ego keeps them in check about when to compromise and when to put on their crown instead.

SUN IN LIBRA AND VENUS IN VIRGO:

Adults with Venus in Virgo are greatly service oriented. They live very much in their heads, led by a distinctly practical nature and sense of reason. There may be a tendency toward anxiousness here, but there is also a highly refined capacity for discernment. These Libras make exacting critics, for better and for worse, often seeing themselves as their greatest work in progress. There is a constant striving and reaching for perfection made real here. And with their meticulous eye, these folks are able to cultivate and refine incredible systems in their lives and our world. They feel most at ease when they are serving a clear purpose or tangibly doing good. Sometimes this leads them to give to exhaustion, but being the efficient people they are, they know when and how to self-care themselves back to vibrant health.

SUN IN LIBRA AND VENUS IN LIBRA:

For Libra adults with Venus in their own sign, there is a natural grace and sensitivity to aesthetics. They are well-mannered and charming folks who have a strong sense of ethics. Their desire for balance sees them prioritizing leisure and simplicity, embodying an air of minimalism. But they also know how to show up meaningfully for others, with little tolerance for injustice in the world. They're quite equipped to "kill 'em with kindness," as they know that their greatest gift is connection. By modeling a gentle nature and devotion to harmony and ease, this Libra reflects to the world how smooth things could be with a little more care. These folks are also likely to hold a very wide perspective of the world and to be quite astute. Their minds are sensitive and sharp, looking for fairness wherever possible. Honey-tongued, they are often able to tip the scales in favor of their choosing.

SUN IN LIBRA AND VENUS IN SCORPIO:

The Libra with a Scorpio Venus grows up to be quite a force. They are unable to be as chill or complacent as some of their other Libra brethren can be. Rather than simple ease, they are also inclined to prioritize depth. They look for bonds that will be lasting and total,

ADVANCED CONSIDERATIONS

Having addressed the general temperament for Libra adults, it's time to get specific. Each Libra Sun has their own unique character, and Venus plays a big role in shaping that. Read all of the different solar blends here for more insight. And for folks with significant Libra placements other than their sun, research your own Venus sign to better understand who's influencing how you Libra. Those with Venus in Leo, Virgo, Libra, Scorpio, or Sagittarius can totally read these solar takes and still gain applicable insights. Readers with Venus in other signs, head to the Love and Work sections for some helpful key words.

commitments that are more than just pretty. This is the Libra with fierce loyalty and cunning charm. They are nice to a point, but they won't tolerate too many superficialities. There is a sense of longing in this Libra, a hunger that propels them and never quite goes away. And there is also a desire to be reborn and transformed through their relationship to the world and to others. This can show up through their appearance, taking on a new look with each phase they find themselves in. They are also a Libra who can alchemize and move through pain to inspire new and more authentic pleasures.

SUN IN LIBRA AND VENUS IN SAGITTARIUS:

As adults, Libras with Venus in Sagittarius pack an exuberant punch. They have both a liveliness and a depth that goes beyond Libra's general sociability. There's an urge for them to know and see more about their fellow man, looking for ties and similarities that cross boundaries and hold us all together. They are often idealists and driven by philosophy and myth. These Libras are able to use stories and experiences to bring people closer. Employing joy, vibrancy, and an inspired charm, they are able to cultivate many allies and a shared sense of hope and adventure. For this Libra, there may be more peace in movement than in being still. They are pulled by promise and potential and reach for that in their partnerships. And with their confidence and goofy grin, they're often able to bring out the brightest in folks.

LIBRA IN LOVE

LOVE. A TOPIC unique to every sign, but wildly dear to Libras. It is the driving force for many, as it is the gift of Venus. Goddess of Love, the planet of connection—Venus is always in love, and so, too, are the kin of Venus. For Libra, it is very much about being in love with the *idea* of love. Being in pursuit of love's essence and air. Getting lost in the motions of it and the pleasures they can bring.

It is also so much bigger than romantic love. Libras know this well. For the sign of the scales, all love is vital, and equal, and important. Friendships, family, self, partners—all relationships are to be held on sacred grounds, and all relationships have the potential to teem with love.

While not always so serious or dreamy in practice, these idealized notions are still at the core of any Libra. They never want to be in short supply of sweetness, and so they remain open to connection at every turn. Libras model grace and acceptance to others not only as a tool but as an offering. And it is for themselves just as much as anyone else.

In love, Libra is enlivened and soothed. It lights them up and helps them feel whole. The feeling also brings out their charm in full force. Their style is flirty, playful, alluring, and bright. Eager to connect, but just as happy to tease and taunt, they are quite social and amusing with their affection. Their airy nature enjoys lightheartedness, potential, and fantasy. They can be coy and subtle, looking to captivate and enchant rather than making any big moves. Libras in love long to be sought after and pursued, luring folks in like honey.

And however beguiling, it is also sincere. A Libra can truly be in love with anyone or anything. Maybe not for long, or with much depth, but as a concept, a state of mind, Libras drift into love often. And from this place, they are drawn to different types of love to meet their different needs. It is unlikely that a Libra would be satisfied by only one meaningful relationship in their life, however nice it may sound to some. They need diversity of attention and affection; they need the fresh and new. They need best friends as much as they need lovers or business partners or kids. Balance in love given and received is vital, and it comes from many sources.

This element of platonic love is woven throughout all of Libra's relationships. Again, love is very much an idea, and an ideal, for this sign. And it is Libra's work to make the ideal as

Venus, goddess of love, with Cupid

real as it can be. Kind natured, amiable, and attentive, they can reach others in such a tender and simple way. They make themselves approachable and easy to know, and they find common ground wherever possible. It is their gift to find the links between us, no matter how subtle or small. But that is also where they must be careful.

In bringing such ease into the lives of those they love, they sometimes lose sight of who they are in their own right. Libras can get lost in love, thinking that it exists outside of themselves or only when they behave some kind of way. They can so easily give away or subdue certain parts of themselves to make others more comfortable. In certain moments, this ability has its advantages, but ultimately, it keeps them from the love they need and deserve. Libras must learn to love themselves and to remember that love is shared. If they are not receiving as much as they give, they need to find another way to balance the scales.

It can be helpful for them to remember and call upon their element of air. Thanks to this element, Libras have the potential to merge love with reason, a capacity that keeps them impartial. And in the early stages of love, it is important that they keep their head. Their ability to be rational informs their ability to be kind, and when they lose sight of what's real, they can be caught making allowances that aren't fair to themselves. They are wise to lean on and love up their friends just as much as any new crush, as they might need other folks to help maintain their common sense when feelings get involved.

In general, Libra is not a sign that feels feelings so much as one that thinks about them. They can spin out and lose focus in the day to day, as too many emotions can start to cloud their thoughts. And this clouding doesn't help with their propensity for indecision. It can be hard for them to make major commitments, or at least to make the right commitments for themselves. Where love's concerned, some Libras struggle to remember that immediate gratification often comes at the cost of something more enduring, and vice versa. This dilemma brings up the issue of quality versus quantity for them, too.

> **A Libra can truly be in love with anyone or anything.**

Libras can get swept up in others' advances and say yes to every offer. They love the newness of puppy love and infatuation, and they feel good being so wanted. This can mean that some Libras look for all the relationships and flings that they can find. However, what they want to be able to receive and to give then comes into question. Quantity is great if it makes a Libra feel vibrant and loved. But when it's not great is when a Libra gets burnt out or is unable to connect to the degree they want. Libras need to practice discernment in their love lives in order to stay balanced and aligned with their personal values.

And despite certain opinions, Libras can date any other zodiac sign they want. In fact, all of the signs can date anyone they want, and Libra should know this best. There are many types of relationships that can be had and many types of people under every sun sign. Libras should let go of any idea that they should be with one over another. It's best they stay open to the reality of how others show up and make them feel in practice rather than on paper. Folks of any sign that celebrate, respect, and adore their Libra make a good match for the Scales.

RISING SIGNS

In addition to one's Venus placement, there are a number of factors that make each Libra unique. Another layer to the birth chart, a placement we all have, is the ascendant or rising sign. Based on when and where a Libra was born, their ascendant reflects the sign that was rising on the horizon, and it is tied to where the sun sat in the sky at the moment of their birth. This component of a birth chart is greatly important and informative, but for now, we will just be looking at how it influences a Libra in love. This is another layer that sits on top of the nuance that one's Venus placement provides.

* **ARIES RISING AND SUN IN LIBRA:** With Aries Rising, these Libras know how to go after what they want, and they enjoy a bit of chase and drama in love. They can also be quick to catch feelings and expect a relationship to help them stay balanced. They're drawn to folks who are well mannered and alluring, with social charm in spades.

* **TAURUS RISING AND SUN IN LIBRA:** For the Taurus Rising Libra, their love needs a little more intensity, with partners that aren't afraid to commit. They look for loves that are meaty and complex, allowing them to explore their hidden impulses. A fan of the slow burn, they're also willing to let love throw them a little off-balance if it means they get to share in another's depths.

* **GEMINI RISING AND SUN IN LIBRA:** As a Gemini Rising Libra, the emphasis is entirely on flirty fun and adventure. They are drawn to bold types, smooth talkers, and any cutie with enough charm. These Libras live for inspired romance and want to be swept off their feet. They're likely to date freely, always up for a good time.

* **CANCER RISING AND SUN IN LIBRA:** With Cancer Rising, Libras long for a little extra tenderness and want a love that is committed and stable. These Libras are more reserved and take relationships seriously, looking for mature partners that they can grow roots with. Love for this Libra looks like showing up on time, following through on promises, and having immense integrity.

* **LEO RISING AND SUN IN LIBRA:** Leo Rising Libras have a bright yet cool air in love. They want to be noticed for their charm, but they don't mind when somebody plays a little hard to get. They're drawn to confident types that have their own distinct style and can offer something unique. In relationships, they like somebody who's not intimidated by their vibrant glow.

* **VIRGO RISING AND SUN IN LIBRA:** With Virgo Rising, Libras long to be enchanted and transported by love. They can come off as a little reserved or straightlaced, but they're just waiting for the right lovers to unlock their dreamier side. These Libras are drawn to folks with deep compassion and big hearts, and they are impressed by partners that can bring their fantasies to life.

* **LIBRA RISING AND SUN IN LIBRA:** For the double Libra (with sun and rising) they like their loves with a little heat. As they are effortlessly considerate and always keeping things together, they're easily pulled in by the bold and brash. They like partners that take charge and bring out their fire. These Libras often look to their relationships to remind them of their own independence and unique spark.

* **SCORPIO RISING AND SUN IN LIBRA:** With Scorpio Rising, a Libra is looking for love to keep them grounded. They're drawn to slow and steady types that bring out their indulgent side and shower them in pleasure. These Libras are looking for love to bring release, to get them out of their heads, and root them more in their own bodies and hearts.

* **SAGITTARIUS RISING AND SUN IN LIBRA:** Sagittarius Rising Libras are likely to root their loves in friendship first. They like partners that feel light and easy and prioritize fun. This is a Libra that wants a dynamic, open, multifaceted love. They can bore easily, so they've got to be kept on their toes and well entertained. Confident, quirky, and delightfully quick-witted is the type to win over their hearts.

* **CAPRICORN RISING AND SUN IN LIBRA:** For the Libra with Capricorn Rising, love is meant to be lasting, tender, and true. Their relationships need a certain degree of grace and sensitivity and should feel secure, with sturdy roots. These Libras need lovers they can confide in and rest easy with. They might also seek connections that look good on paper, but if they don't feel good, too, they're not likely to last long.

* **AQUARIUS RISING AND SUN IN LIBRA:** With Aquarius Rising, these Libras are looking for lovers that indulge and inspire their ideals. They're rather friendly and open-minded and are in search of the connections that fill their hearts and make them feel special. Relationships bring out their dramatic side and see them enjoying bold declarations and sharing big gestures. In love they prioritize play, humor, and self-expression.

* **PISCES RISING AND SUN IN LIBRA:** Libras with Pisces Rising like a love that keeps things together. These Libras have a dreamy depth to them and look for partners that are attentive and kind. They are drawn to the smart, sensitive, and charitable. Love for these Libras is selfless, patient, considerate, and thoughtful—they long to feel safe and well cared for.

VENUS PLACEMENTS

SUN IN LIBRA AND VENUS IN LEO:

Venus in Leo is looking for a grand love. Big gestures, bright sparks, and total devotion. Love that is warm and inspired. They have excellent taste and like to share the wealth. Giving and receiving gifts is often a facet of their love language. They are also generous with their time for the ones they love. Their loyalty is lasting and bold, and they never forget a kind favor or brightened day. Compliments don't hurt either, as they love to feel celebrated and special. Their beloveds are expected to be demonstrative, and in return they get to share in the hearty glow of this Libra's affection. Being quite sovereign, they often need to feel that they are prominently seated on the throne of their lover's heart. Whether in love with one, with none, or with many, these Libras need to know that they are the most important person to any serious admirer.

SUN IN LIBRA AND VENUS IN VIRGO:

For Venus in Virgo, love is demonstrated through acts of service. Love is an action. A favor granted, a chore completed, an errand run. It is patient and pragmatic, grounded in true care. These Libras pay avid attention to their loved ones' needs, and they work hard to make sure they are met. They note nuances and preferences and get all the details just right, often an encyclopedia for the likes and dislikes of their beloveds. And in return, their heart sings upon acknowledgment of their diligence and service. Hearty thank-yous, naming, and witnessing how well they keep things together is often more than enough for their humble hearts. Affirming words can make them swoon. That and also tangible time, which can be spent talking or problem solving together, working on a shared project, or making a meal together. These Libras appreciate a simple moment shared. They can be nervous in love and hard to settle down, but underneath their busyness, they yearn to feel valued and adored for their virtue and versatility.

SUN IN LIBRA AND VENUS IN LIBRA:

With Venus in Libra, there is a desire for that first spark, for the newness that connection brings. These are the coy flirts and polished partners, emanating a cool grace in their every move. This Libra is looking for a fluid and easy exchange in their relationships. They are very accommodating and able to meet folks in the middle, especially in the name of love. And they're a sucker for sweet talk. A good conversation, a playful bout of banter, a letter from their admirer—they wanna *hear* the love as much as they feel it. Through charming appearances, these Libras look to entice others with their lively allure and have an earnest but measured approach. Often quick to bond, they are not necessarily quick to commit or get serious. While some enjoy a steady fling, plenty of these Libras like to date around just as much, basking in the glow of infatuation and new romance. And beyond the romance, these Libras are just as likely to be in love with their friends and community. With Venus in Libra, every relationship is an opportunity to share in loving affection and pleasant harmony.

SUN IN LIBRA AND VENUS IN SCORPIO:

For the Libra with Venus in Scorpio, love is eternal, powerful, moving. These Libras carry profound feelings and can get hooked on others. They want to be transformed by love, remade again and again in its image. They are also very loyal, with a fierce devotion to their beloved. Ease can feel a little difficult, or rather disinteresting for these Libras, as they tend to equate love with intensity. Ardent and passionate, they are often boiling underneath their cool exteriors. They may vacillate between playing hard

ADVANCED CONSIDERATIONS

Once again, Venus signs are paramount to understanding Libra in a chart—and doubly so for romance! Not only the ruler of the Scales, it's also the planet of love. Libra Suns can read their unique details here, and other Libras should use the rest of this book to further research and understand their own Venus sign. Some love style key words to get those folks started are: assertive and impulsive for Aries, grounded and sensual for Taurus, chatty and charismatic for Gemini, tender and nurturing for Cancer, enduring and elegant for Capricorn, cerebral and eccentric for Aquarius, and dreamy and ethereal for Pisces.

to get and then inundating their crushes with affection, sometimes struggling with knowing or trusting what they want. But when they do know, they allow their sweeties to become their world. These are the Libras who yearn for intimacy over flighty flirts and want love to claim them and reveal hidden worlds. Their brand of charm is synonymous with seduction and is infused with magnetism, charisma, and allure.

SUN IN LIBRA AND VENUS IN SAGITTARIUS:

Libras with Venus in Sagittarius prefer a grand and rowdy kind of love. Using their charm to sweep folks off their feet, these Libras steal hearts wherever they roam. They enjoy the pursuit and are after experiences more than maintenance, looking most for impulsive and wild fun. They find love in movement and adventure and share it best with the folks who can help them find such states. Unafraid to take a risk, these Libras are more likely to speak out and share their hearts, captivating others with their visions. They are lighthearted and inspirational, goofy and free. These Libras view love as a journey and look for those most willing to take the trip. It is important to them that love reflects their ideals and that their connections have a sense of purpose. They can be high-minded and philosophical, and they need bonds that are on the same page, looking to make meaning that is well beyond the here and now.

LIBRA AT WORK

For the sign of Libra, work needs to be sweeter than it is for most. In what is often a place of drudgery and stress, with either busyness or boredom dominating, Libra Suns look to shine a soothing light. These are the folks that keep people calm and connected, that put difficulties into perspective, and that find small ways to infuse their work with pleasure.

They note birthdays and plan coffee breaks. They listen and hold space. They make the mundane feel easy rather than stifling. These are the bright and attentive employees who aim to please as they keep the team on even keel. And thanks to their geniality, they find many opportunities and excel in a number of roles.

> Details like birthdays, anniversaries, and holiday planning are often opportunities for a Libra to do something nice at work.

Libras are natural negotiators for one. They know what's fair, and they know what others want. They can appeal to a wide range of people, and they gain favor with their cordial manner, softening folks into compromise. This also serves them well in a court and other facets of the legal system. Libras are well attuned to the law and skilled at enforcing it, as long as they deem it just. And when they find fault in the law, or in others, they advocate and work for change. They utilize their sharp minds to work to dismantle systems that they see failing.

Often seen in roles that connect them to people in need, their work tends to be quite relational, and they are most fulfilled by being in connection with others. So even if it's not in service or advocacy work, it may be that they deal with clients or have a business partner, or maybe they work as an assistant. It can also be that they relate to ideas. Libras with artistic leanings make excellent curators or designers. And others make for highly skilled writers. Whatever the role, the emphasis is on mental engagement, meaningful connections, and the ability to find joy in what they do.

Libras also have a very real need for balance in their work lives. What is an aspiration for some is more often a requirement for a Libra, at least if they want to sustain their efforts and commitment. Libras need to be careful not to overexert themselves. They have their own pace and will need to find work that is suited to it. They also need breaks spread throughout the day and the right mix of tasks. All day spent on one thing is likely to get old quick for a Libra. It's easier for them to divide their time, alternating between the more enjoyable tasks and the strenuous or menial.

They may also need an equal blend of time spent working with others and working alone. While their tendency might be to lean into more social engagement than less, too much (especially at work), can zap their energy or fog up their own sensibilities. They need enough windows throughout their day to return to themselves and clear their minds. Their ability to collaborate and merge into a project or partner can be very powerful, but it is just as liable to see them lose touch with their own needs and to burn out.

A daily errand that often keeps them in balance

is meals. Having good coffee or tea, stepping out to a favorite cafe, grabbing a snack—the little indulgences these moments provide help a Libra feel at ease. And they also allow for rebalancing. For the Libra that works alone, a simple outing allows for meeting a friend or flirting with a barista to get their social fix. And for those who need a break, it's an opportunity to slow down, find solitude, and recharge. Plus, the right treat can upgrade any moment.

And for the Libras less interested in indulgence via tangible treats, there's always the internet. Libras are pros at online shopping their way through a slow day or boring meeting. Scrolling through the news and social media helps to distract them from any unpleasant realities on the job and keeps their minds busy. As do chats and messages with coworkers or friends. For the Libra that doesn't like what they do, they find creative ways to look busy while keeping up to date on what they deem to be more interesting matters.

Similarly, Libras are pretty good at keeping up to date on office matters, too. Details like birthdays, anniversaries, and holiday planning are often opportunities for a Libra to do something nice at work. They're great at leaving notes or sending cards, and they're even better at planning an office party. Combining their refined style, love of leisure, abundant social graces, and a need to make our days more agreeable, they make work gatherings feel good. These folks are the champions of a mixer and are almost always thrilled to blend work and play. But if lines get crossed or work doesn't get finished, Libras can also flex their loyalty to all that is fair.

While they can be known to bend a rule or two in their own favor, generally their ethics are impartial and rules are rules. Libras will keep their clients and coworkers accountable and expect them to be just as honorable as they are. They also expect equal contributions. Few things irk them more than a peer that tries to ride on the coattails of another's hard work. Libras expect their associates to do their part and share in the labor.

When justice needs to be served, Libras are stern but kind. They know how to keep their cool with fussy clients and arrogant collaborators. And as much as they can, they seek to encourage and motivate. They rarely lead with a firm boundary and much prefer when they can incite folks to change through gentle words and thoughtful attention. But when their graciousness is not enough, they are able to cut through other's boorish behavior and lay out clear expectations in a cool and assured manner.

VENUS PLACEMENTS
SUN IN LIBRA AND VENUS IN LEO:
For the Libra with Venus in Leo, work is yet another place that they get to offer their shine. These Libras do well in charge and can lead by example, with a gentle confidence that others trust. They are likely to be rather creative, and many make great performers. Even if they're a little reserved, they have a need to be seen as gifted in the work that they do, and they respond well to praise for their efforts and offerings. A little prestige doesn't hurt either, so if they're not in a literal spotlight, it might be a title that they're after or an award of recognition. These Libras also make great coworkers, keeping the energy open and fun, with a slight taste for office gossip. Their easy charm brings out folk's gregariousness and can attract loyal clients. And while they're very generous in their work, they are not ones to go underpaid or overlooked. These Libras have no problem naming their needs and seeing that they are met.

SUN IN LIBRA AND VENUS IN VIRGO:
Libras with Venus in Virgo are skilled researchers and social servants. They are very adept at law

ADVANCED CONSIDERATIONS

Venus strikes again! Libra Suns—along with other Libra placements with Venus in Leo, Virgo, Libra, Scorpio, or Sagittarius—can read along here to learn more about their professional quirks. For Libra folks with Venus in another sign, here are a couple key words to kick off your own chart research: Venus in Aries craves leadership and action, Venus in Taurus wants stability and comfort, Venus in Gemini needs mental stimulation and variety, Venus in Cancer seeks sustenance and care, Venus in Capricorn wants integrity and prestige, Venus in Aquarius leans humanitarian and experimental, and Venus in Pisces dreams of glamour and compassion.

and legislation and have a penchant for tedious arts. Working with their hands can help offset their busy and restless minds, and it is likely to keep them grounded on the job. They may also have a penchant for working with nature, perhaps as gardeners or herbalists. These folks are able to retain an exhaustive amount of information about the topics that most interest them, and their eye for details helps them apply their insights in apt and meaningful ways. They are likely to be specialists in their field of work. Libras tend to keep the ship afloat when no one's looking. They keep tidy, run errands, send cards, fix the paper jam, and probably work longer hours than they're asked to.

SUN IN LIBRA AND VENUS IN LIBRA:

As a Libra with Venus in the same sign, there is a natural propensity for working with and for others. Be it advocacy work, social work, client management, or counseling, these folks need engagement with others in their jobs. They care about people deeply and are dedicated to cultivating harmony and equality for all. Especially in one-to-one settings. These Libras care about the connection and are most effective when they can work directly with another person. They are also quite skilled in law, with an acute sense of right and wrong, and the persuasive skills to gently win the nastiest of arguments. Serving as consultants or coordinators are intuitive roles for their skillset as well. They are able to keep folks connected and calm. And of course, any job imbued with beauty and keen on aesthetics suits them as well. They bring style to all that they do.

SUN IN LIBRA AND VENUS IN SCORPIO:

With Venus in Scorpio, Libras bring a real tenacity to their work. They are drawn to people and look to make a lasting impact more than superficial. They are often advocates for underdogs, outcasts, survivors, and the overlooked. They want their work to reach those who need it most, and they'll work tirelessly to do so. These Libras are highly motivated, looking for a calling more than just a job. They're the ones to fixate on a passion project or fiercely climb the ladder of success. It is important for them to feel that they have influence in their work and in the world. They need to feel that they are impactful. And they also provide a depth of care that not all Libras can. There is an innate awareness to others' wounding and a desire to help folks transform and overcome adversity. As a soft yet brutal force, they channel their intensity with charm and focus.

SUN IN LIBRA AND VENUS IN SAGITTARIUS:

Libras with Venus in Sagittarius bring with them a vivaciousness to work. These Libras are a little freer and wilder and are drawn to a higher calling. They want to feel that their work is meaningful and aligned with their vision of truth. Looking to inspire and be inspired, they are less bound by commitment and more bound by faith. They are also the storytellers and seekers, and may find success in entertainment, international relations, philosophy, and travel. Jobs that keep them on the road and meeting new people are well suited to their nature. They want some excitement and enjoy having a platform to speak about their beliefs. They're also likely to be improvisational and quite spirited in their work. Keeping the office lighthearted and energized is their specialty.

CONCLUSION

HAVING EXAMINED SOME essential life phases, we've come to know a thing or two about Libra. The details of childhood, adult years, love, and work have all been explored. Plenty of information has been shared to paint a lively portrait of Libra, and yet, no matter the nuance, the essence of the sign still remains simple and true. As stated in the introduction to this chapter, Libras are the sign of the Scales, they are of Venus, they are cardinal, and elementally, they are air.

While much can be said about Libra, these basics can tell you all that you really need to know. They are the bare bones of Libran spirit, informing a Libra's nature in any circumstance. They are how we know that Libras are balanced, charming, inviting, and bright. Those who carry the Scales are the ones to remind us of our sacred bonds and our ties to each other—of what meaningful relationships can help us become.

And every Libra has their own way. Venus has different directives for different Libras. Some are asked to partner with fairness, while others are asked to make peace with a little more grit. Those born at one hour may grow up timid and quiet, while those of another may be more outspoken and wild. There is a full and rich spectrum of Libras in the world, shaped by many different factors, both known and unknown. And there is also the factor of free will.

No matter the Libra, they have agency and they have say in who they become. What they do with their gifts and their fears and their hopes is entirely up to them. Libra placements imbue the beholder with distinct potentials, illuminating specific cosmic characteristics within them—but what they choose to do with their unique dispositions is open-ended. It is something they get to explore and engage in throughout their journey, that they will eventually come to know and embody in a singular way.

The astrology of Libra is a living, breathing thing. And it is an energy that longs to see us together, and to see us striving for justice. So Libra identified or not, know that the sign of the scales is a facet within all of us and that we are all heartened to share in its ease and love.

OCT. 23–NOV. 21

text by Danny Larkin

element — WATER

symbol — THE SCORPION

modality — FIXED

house — EIGHTH

ruler — PLUTO

ACOUSTIC

INTRODUCTION

I BEGAN THIS CHAPTER in Athens. I went to Greece in May 2019 to study the ancient mysteries of renewal and transformation with the astrologer Demetra George. She is truly a living legend. It was a mystical and transformative journey to several sacred ruins, concretizing the myths I've loved since I was a boy.

Astrology is an invitation into an ancient wisdom tradition. We all know that many people are born when the sun is in Scorpio, and that obviously they are different. This chapter is not going to try to prove the impossible—that somehow all Scorpios are the same. But it is the underlying principle of astrology that all Scorpios can become better versions of themselves by exploring the Scorpio symbols. And many Scorpios seem to resonate with these symbols and themes in such similar ways that we begin to see some common traits.

This chapter is first and foremost intended as a humorous and accessible initiation into this set of symbols and how they manifest in different spheres and phases of life.

The constellation Scorpius, from which Scorpio is derived, is itself a potent and venomous creature with much to teach everyone who is born under its sign. Seriously, watch some scorpion footage on YouTube tonight if you want to deepen your intuitive grasp of this sun sign. The way scorpions strut about with a menacing stinger in plain sight of any creature that may try to cross it is a metaphor for how many Scorpios often seek to solve life's problems with intimidation and aggression. Whether most problems are solved or exacerbated by such strategies is an open question.

If you are a Scorpio, you were born in the middle of autumn, so fall symbols also speak deeply to you. Because the Scorpio season coincides with the middle of fall, it was considered a "solid" sign by ancient astrologers. In modern parlance, we call this a *fixed* sign. It is not the beginning or the end of the fall, in which the weather is more transitional, this is the time of the year when the weather is mostly fixed as fall. Mirroring their season, Scorpios prize staying power and consistency, but they can sometimes cling too stubbornly, which is an emotional dynamic that we will explore later in this chapter.

Scorpio is a water sign, so Scorpios will have a deep, powerful, lifelong relationship with water. And the mythological meanings of the Western esoteric tradition offer much food for thought for Scorpio, which we will explore in section two.

And finally, we will meet again and again with the two gods that rule Scorpio—Pluto and Mars. In ancient texts, Mars is the boss of any planet in Scorpio. After careful observation in the twentieth century, many modern astrologers now see the planet Pluto directing the flow of Scorpio energy. The myths of the gods after which these planets are named offer a wellspring of inspiration to Scorpios. These two gods will be explored in each section as relevant to the subject at hand.

After beginning this chapter in Greece, I finished it in the parks of New York City while gazing at turtles swimming in the pools of Central Park. As a water sign, Scorpio can gain clarity by being close to bodies of water and it's my hope that Scorpios will experience this gift often as they turn this chapter's pages.

SCORPIO AS A CHILD

IT'S WITH A particular thrill that the Scorpio toddler discovers the word "No." It's good practice for any Scorpios reading this chapter to pause right now and reflect on their earliest memories of saying *no*. Perhaps these recollections are similar to the moment when a baby scorpion first realizes its stinger has grown large enough to successfully hunt and kill.

All children experience the terrible twos. However, each sun sign progresses through this stage of development in a profoundly different way. When Scorpio children discover aggression, they are deeply intrigued and fascinated by the apparent power they can wield over people. And of course, they become frightened of the harm older and bigger adults might inflict on them. They often become hyper-attuned to both ends of the spectrum: how to hurt and how they might be hurt. The anxiety that comes with this awareness means they'll want to know early on how to defend themselves. Other kids are more interested in toys; but threats, fighting, and protection come early to many Scorpios.

Some Scorpio children might experience brutal trauma as children. Others might witness a friend or parent suffer a vicious attack—either physically, emotionally, mentally, or spiritually. Many Scorpios learn too soon how vicious this world can be. Other signs have their fair share of trauma, but for Scorpios it's especially meaningful. Bad things don't happen to people because they are Scorpios. But what differs between signs is the response to the trauma.

LEARNING TO FIGHT

Whereas other signs decide the solution is to check out into fantasy land (Pisces), or to try to be smarter than everyone else (Aquarius) or prettier than everyone else (Libra), or to work harder than everyone else (Capricorn), many Scorpios conclude as children that the way to stay safe is to fight more cunningly than everyone else. And this is why the ancient symbol of the scorpion is so potent. Just as scorpions meander with a massive stinger in plain view, many children decide the way to survive is to have the equivalent of a stinger: they want everyone to know that if you mess with them, it will hurt.

There are many ways to fight. A young Scorpio's fascination with the so-called art of war is shared with the sign Aries. Both are ruled by Mars, the Roman god of war whose planet is red. Aries fights in an overt, hot, and loud way, which befits a fire sign. Scorpio fights in more subtle ways, because it's a water sign. Many Scorpios discover early on the potency of the silent treatment or how to get what they want in more nuanced ways. Some Scorpios may not even be known as aggressive, fighting types. But truth be told, they excel at subtle hints, manipulation, and persuasion to get what they want. Subterfuge comes so naturally to these children. They sometimes giggle when they watch Aries try to shout someone down. *That's not how to get through to them, but I'm not going to tell you that,* young Scorpios tell themselves.

But many nuanced ways of fighting aren't yet possible for toddlers to comprehend. As the terrible twos unfold, Scorpio children may choose to manipulate the intensity and drama they can create by refusing to go along with what adults want done. Again, there's nothing a Scorpio toddler enjoys more than declaring "No!" and daring their parents to duke it out with them. They find their parents' psychological buttons and don't hesitate to push them when they don't get their way. Scorpio children have a way with one-liners that hit below the belt. Many parents learn to think twice before disappointing their Scorpio child, because they know all hell will break loose. The metaphorical stinger hangs above these kids. Some parents might grow to resent how their Scorpio children have the guts to call them on the stuff other kids and even adults might not have the courage to talk about. Other parents tire of the equivalent of psychological warfare when, for example, it's time for bed.

> When Scorpio children discover aggression, they are deeply intrigued and fascinated by the apparent power they can wield over people.

Some Scorpio children may be more subtle. This is always the million-dollar question about Scorpios: How open is their zest for a fight? Or how subtle and under-the-radar do they act? Some quickly adapt to their parents' styles and figure out how to get what they want without making a stink or fuss. It's amazing how quickly puppy-face gets some parents to melt into honoring their kids' wishes or relaxing some limit. But other Scorpio kids might pick the weirdest and most unexpected fights and throw tantrums when parents set reasonable limits that are actually keeping them safe and healthy.

For many Scorpios, it is a challenge throughout childhood to know which hill to die on when instigating conflict—which fights are worth picking and which will only exacerbate their frustrations. Young and unformed Scorpio children—like baby scorpions—are almost in awe of their potential ability to sting, and they reflexively attack too often. What they are too young to understand is that sometimes we, as adults, grapple with paradoxes that can't be successfully conquered through brute force. Scorpio kids can scream, fight, groan, curse, and attack with all their might, but when the dust settles, there are always some problems that still can't be resolved. And this frustrates the Scorpio child immensely—they'll be frustrated all their lives by the idea that some issues in life are like beasts immune to their stingers' poison. And they are often too young to understand a paradox when they see one.

Scorpio children might delude themselves into thinking they can force a solution to any problem they face. They can be incredibly persuasive and perceptive, and they know it. But this talent can also backfire into an inferiority complex. These children may despise themselves for not being able to resolve some impossible Herculean problem. They are too young to understand that some problems can't be solved. It's helpful for parents to remind their Scorpio kids that they don't have to be superheroes to be special. Some problems are beyond the powers of both parent and child to fix. This is a bitter pill to swallow. But scorpions can't swim, and they can't fight an octopus. Learning to accept limits is key here.

PLAYING IN THE WATER

Scorpio is a water sign. Fighting with water is a potent metaphor for these children to unpack and explore. Parents should seriously consider buying their Scorpio kids a powerful water gun so that they can play out this symbolism in a fun way during the summer. Water parks are another winning summer activity. It will bring

Scorpio children immense joy to splash their friends and family—letting go of some of that aggression in a playful, non-harmful way.

Another clever way to galvanize a Scorpio child's development as a water sign is to take them to the aquarium. Underwater predators will fascinate these kids. They will love learning about all the ways the creatures of the sea protect themselves and hunt. Squids shoot ink. Electric eels shock. Jellyfish sting. Octopuses strangle. But equally important for them to learn about is how some fish evade instead of fighting. There are some very fast swimmers that simply outrun the sharks. These kids—and many Scorpio adults for that matter—would benefit from seeing how sometimes winning means *not* fighting. Sometimes the aquatic creature wins by not fighting, escaping danger for a nicer part of the sea with tasty food where it can just chill.

In nature, water has a way of seeking out the lowest possible ground. And part of the watery quality of Scorpio is a lifelong relationship with depth. Many little scorpions have far deeper and more mysterious thoughts than their peers. It can almost take parents aback, the way their young kids ask deep, emotional, probing questions about the human condition at such an early age. They are old souls in this way. It's crucial for parents to be prepared to answer the hard questions in age-appropriate ways. Little scorpions can push to learn and try to understand things that they may actually not be old enough or emotionally ready to integrate. And this frustrates them to no end. It's crucial for parents to seek guidance and counsel about how and when to answer these questions in ways that are honest but also appropriate for kids.

Parents need to be incredibly mindful of discretion. Scorpio children might eavesdrop on their parents' conversations, later weaponizing what they've overheard. It can be a bit surprising, what comes out of a Scorpio child's mouth, and what they remember, or what they caught wind of one night when you thought they were sleeping.

Parenting a Scorpio child is not for the faint of heart. It requires iron tolerance and forbearance, particularly when baby Scorpios overreact to things that ultimately don't matter. These children are quick to retaliate, hit below the belt, play mind games, and push buttons, and often there's no reason for the fuss. Little Scorpios aren't old enough yet to know the wisdom of sparing themselves the pain of making mountains out of molehills. They must learn the hard way to pick their battles, and when the strongest thing they can do is to let it go. Why freak out and panic and lose the day to some-

> **Scorpio children might eavesdrop on their parents' conversations, later weaponizing what they've overheard.**

thing that doesn't really matter? Or, as Cher puts in her own special way in capital letters on her Twitter Bio page, "DOESNT MATTER in 5 yrs IT DOESNT MATTER THERE'S ONLY LOVE&FEAR." Hopefully, Scorpio children can come to this realization before they are as old as Cher.

Scorpio is ruled by two different planets in astrology. When the sun shines in the sign of Scorpio, these ruling planets are like celestial bosses that order the sun around and tell it how to shine its light. In ancient astrology, the war god's planet Mars rules Scorpio. This augurs how Scorpios can be quick to believe that the only way to get what they want is to wage war against someone else.

However, in modern astrology, Scorpio is ruled and ordered around by the remote planet Pluto. This dwarf planet's discovery corresponds with the atom bomb as well as the emergence and popularization of psychology. And in many young Scorpios, there is a tendency both to go nuclear and to try to engage in intense psychological warfare. What these kids don't always get is that sometimes a subtle, polite request works better.

Many parents struggle to persuade their Scorpio children that gentler and softer ways may be better in terms of achieving their agendas. But it is the recurring perception of Scorpios in both childhood and adulthood that the only way to win is to fight dirty, leverage secrets, and get inside other people's heads—to frighten and to raise hell. What many Scorpios fail to see is that they often up the ante with a mean comment or a probing question. This perception of a world that feels out to get them is actually, in truth, a series of retaliations for when Scorpio crossed the line, and other people pushed back. "You didn't need to get that nasty" is a piece of feedback Scorpio kids often receive, but struggle to heed and integrate.

LEARNING TO DISGUISE

Halloween fascinates Scorpio children. Many of them have significant experiences in Halloween costumes. Of course, the sun is in Scorpio on October 31. The Scorpio child appreciates the theatrical opportunity to portray a mythological character and explore the more gruesome themes it may represent. It's amazing how Halloween is often the first conduit for children to learn about death, magic, and the occult. But just as importantly, the young Scorpio is fascinated by the costumes that other children select. The costume selections of their friends and family can be quite revealing of inner psychological issues. Ruled by Pluto, many young Scorpios have a knack for psychology, for picking up on the subtle nuances of personality that other people might miss. And so when Halloween comes around, they often can see the deeper meanings in why certain classmates picked certain outfits.

Discussing Halloween costumes is an excellent way for parents to explore psychology in a developmentally appropriate way with their Scorpio child, although it may be surprising for parents to hear what their child reveals. For Scorpios reading this chapter, it may well be useful to pause for a moment and recall some of your most significant childhood memories of becoming something else and transforming on Halloween.

In addition to Halloween, Scorpio children connect energetically with autumn. The sun is in the sign of Scorpio between October 23 and November 21, though dates may differ from year to year. It's the time of year when the leaves turn crimson and yellow and all the plants begin to die. Autumn festivals create a safe container for Scorpios to understand nature's cycle of life which resonates with them deeply.

HADES AND PERSEPHONE

Pondering the Ancient Greek myth that explains the first fall, and the cycle of seasons, can give us some further insights into the intense experiences that Scorpios have as children. Here's the condensed version: Earth was once always bountiful and perpetually in harvest. This abundance was presided over by Demeter, the goddess of agriculture. Demeter had a daughter, Persephone. One

Perſephone und Hades (Relief im Vatikan zu Rom).

day, Persephone wandered away from her mother and picked the powerful and aromatic narcissus flower. Upon plucking the flower, the ground beneath her opened up and out sprang Hades, the lord of the underworld, in a chariot pulled by his dark horses. He abducted Persephone, put her in his chariot, took her down to the underworld, stole her virginity, and made her his bride and queen.

Poor Demeter didn't know where Persephone had gone. She searched and searched but couldn't find her daughter anywhere on earth. Finally, she talked with the sun god Helios, who could see everything, and he revealed to her that Hades had taken Persephone to the underworld. She then went straight to the king of the gods, her brother Zeus, and told him to order Hades to return her daughter. She was dismayed to discover that Zeus actually approved of Hades and Persephone marrying and wasn't going to interfere. In Greek mythology, an uncle and niece marrying in the family of gods wasn't a big deal. But Demeter was livid because her brothers hadn't consulted her.

Demeter retaliated against Zeus and Hades for scheming to take away her daughter by inflicting a massive famine upon the earth. The eternal spring ended, and the first fall and winter descended upon the earth. Human beings began to suffer and die from starvation. Zeus soon realized that all humans would die, which consequently meant no one would make offerings to him or honor him. And so out of vanity and so that he would continue to be honored, he sought to find a way to make peace with his sister and brother over Persephone's fate. That way, humans would continue to live, prosper, and worship him.

A truce was negotiated so that Persephone would spend six months of the year on the earth with her mother, Demeter, and six months of the year with her husband, Hades. Originally,

Demeter had hoped that the marriage could be annulled and that Persephone could return to the earth full-time. However, once humans died and ate the food of the underworld, they entered into Hades's jurisdiction. The same was true for Persephone, who had eaten six pomegranate arils while underground. Therefore, Hades insisted she had to spend some time there. This compromise was agreed upon by all the gods. But, to keep score and to get back at her brothers, Demeter decided that when Persephone was gone from her side and with Hades, it would be autumn and winter. And when Persephone came back to her side, the earth would become fruitful again, and it would be spring and summer.

This is one of the most intense and powerful stories in Greek mythology, and it holds some keys to unlocking Scorpios' childhoods. Many Scorpios, no matter where they fall on the gender spectrum, have experiences that allow them to identify strongly with Persephone's loss of innocence. So often there is a ripping away of the naïvety of childhood. Many take a journey into the underworld that leaves them forever changed. But they also grow up too soon, and the feeling of having innocence ripped away can be very painful.

There is also a push and pull between Scorpio children and their mother, which can be compared to the Persephone-Demeter dynamic. Like all children, there is a yearning to be close and get the special chemical releases in the brain that only mother can unlock. But there is also a conflicting desire to pull away and discover the corners of the world that mother would fear our visiting. Of course, mother's fear of these places is what makes them irresistibly intriguing to explore. This makes for some theatrical episodes of teenage rebellion. But some Scorpios struggle to outgrow this dynamic. As they step into maturity, it will be a major test whether they spend their adult lives trying to prove a point to their moms, or if they focus instead on becoming their authentic selves—regardless of the responses their choices would provoke.

SCORPIO AS AN ADULT

AS ADULTS, SCORPIOS keep getting the same feedback: *You are too intense.* But the meaning of the phrase rarely registers. They just don't get it.

"Why are you saying 'too intense' like it's a bad thing?" a Scorpio wonders.

"And plus, I was actually holding back," a Scorpio tells herself, patting herself on the back.

So what was supposed to be criticism ends up being taken as a compliment. The reaction their intensity tends to provoke actually reads as success to Scorpios—they see an offended person as someone they have successfully gotten through to. Is it really Scorpios' problem that other people can't handle the bitter truth?

What does "intense" really mean, anyway? Is intensity like beauty: in the eye of the beholder? Yes and no. It behooves all Scorpio adults to ponder the etymology of this word "intense," which is so often thrown at them. The English took the word from the French. And to be in Paris, where criticizing others is a kind of high art, gives you a taste of the French usage of this word. Scorpio adults, like the French often are, can be hard on other people, and will sting like a scorpion when they see something that needs to be corrected.

But we can glean more insights, moving beyond the quirks of French culture, when we look back at the Latin roots of the French word: *intentus* and *intensus*. These are the roots of "intent" and "intense," and they are closely linked. Both spring from the older Latin root: *tensus*. This root word *tensus* means to stretch and strain. And this meaning is still salient in our modern English word "tension." But whereas *tensus* in Latin is a physical tension, *intentus* and *intensus* developed as variants to express a kind of mental pull. This etymological bond reflects how a major aspect of intensity is a clear and strong intention to make a stretch toward a certain goal dominate the moment.

> And a lot of Scorpios' problems as adults seem to start when they fall out of alignment with their partner, friends, family, or colleagues who just want to chill for a moment.

Often there is an agenda and an intention that Scorpios are trying to enact. Now, in a Scorpio's mind, everyone has an agenda and intention like Scorpios do all the time. It seems foreign to them that people sometimes might just want to let their hair down and relax. And it seems like a ruse: there must be something hidden. In fact, the more the moment is about "chillaxing," the more Scorpio's spidey sense gets tripped up and the more suspicious they grow of everyone else's hidden agenda. And a lot of Scorpios' problems as adults seem to start when they fall out of alignment with their partner, friends, family, or colleagues who just want to chill for a moment. Meanwhile, Scorpio goes against the moment with their *Intentions* with a capital I, deciding that now is the time. And everyone else is like, "Actually, now is *not* the time, we are all trying to relax here." And Scorpio is like, "Liars—no one is ever just relaxing." And everyone else responds: ". . . you need to relax."

There is one more insight about intensity that we can glean from the old utterances of the Roman Empire, by expanding on the idea of stretching inherent in *tensus*. There is an eagerness in Scorpio to stretch and push forward with intention against any resistance. In this sense, it can be revealing to think about the variant spelling of intention as "intension." Sticking with an intention often puts us into a state of tension, and intensity sometimes results in enforcing an intention and insisting on a mental and emotional stretch.

Scorpios, as adults, get frustrated with most human beings. When they look at their partners, their friends, their colleagues, and their families, they keep seeing the same thing: people who could be pushing themselves more but aren't. Scorpios don't perceive such mediocrity from the position of the lazy armchair critic—they observe as people who have challenged themselves very hard to become better versions of themselves. It's almost like Scorpios want to scream at everyone: "I walked to school barefoot in the winter through six inches of snow, and so can you. I walked over coals barefoot, and so can you!" But actually, what most Scorpios don't fully understand is that they possess a unique gift to be able to tolerate a higher level of mental and emotional anguish than most other individuals which helps them manifest an intention they prize.

Scorpios have a potent relationship with the vow. They make these powerful promises to themselves and others, and they stick to them with tenacity. To fully understand this resonance, it would be helpful to dive into some of the water mythology that underlies astrology.

In modern times, many astrologers see the planet Pluto as the ruler of Scorpio. This means that the King of the Underworld, known as Pluto to the Romans and Hades to the Greeks, is like the boss of the sun to Scorpios. In astrological doctrine, Pluto orders the sun around and tells it how to shine. The sun corresponds to the mind, soul, and judgment of the individual. Thus, the god Hades energetically commands the mind and soul. Deep within the psyche of Scorpios, there is an unconscious drive to honor Hades and to connect with underworld energies to enact agendas and achieve goals. Now, at first, this might sound a little silly. Most Scorpios don't fancy themselves Neo-pagans who yearn to make offerings to an old Pagan god of the subterranean realm of the dead, or pause for a moment to wonder "What would Pluto do?". What rulership really means is that Scorpios are more attuned to the psychological forces that Ancient Greeks associated with Hades and his realm of the underworld. And by exploring some of the mythological stories associated with Hades, Scorpios can gain keys to how to unlock their own inner doors and become better versions of themselves.

Scorpios are not all carbon copies of one another. But the premise of astrology is that there is something in these symbols and stories that will fire Scorpios' imaginations more profoundly than other signs, and will galvanize their individuation, to use the term C. G. Jung coined to express embracing the unique process it takes to fully become our singular selves.

RIVERS OF THE UNDERWORLD

The ancient Greek underworld was completely different from the Christian conception of hell. And so we need to begin by disentangling the two. Dante Alighieri was an incredible writer who mixed Christian and Pagan elements to create a fascinating piece of literature about hell, purgatory, and paradise. His *Divine Comedy* (1320) is one of the great masterpieces of late Medieval literature. However, the collateral damage of his explosive popularity is that we often project Dante onto our mental images of the underworld. And, truth be told, a different underworld emerges when we go to the older texts of the Greeks and Romans. The fire of Medieval hell is nowhere to be found; instead, we meet a cooler watery realm with numerous rivers flowing through it. These rivers each possessed a magical power.

Scorpio is a water sign. As Scorpios move through adulthood, the symbolism of these underworld rivers can help us understand the potency they bring to every interaction. To compare signs, Scorpio wades through water in a profoundly different way than Cancer or Pisces, which are the other two water signs of the zodiac. It is this underworld element that differentiates them. There is something darker and more mysterious about how Scorpio travels through the world. These rivers that the ancients perceived to be flowing deep underneath the earth in the underworld tell us much about what lies in the emotional depths of many Scorpios.

Before continuing with our exploration of this line of thinking, I wish to acknowledge Liz Greene. She is one of the most influential astrologers of the twentieth and twenty-first centuries. She pioneered a new synthesis of astrology and depth psychology with Howard Sasportas. We lost Howard too soon to AIDS. Liz Greene's

exploration of underworld rivers forms one strand of her influential work on Pluto. I traveled to Cornwall in England to study with Liz in person in 2017. I also participated in her online Pluto seminars in 2016. Liz outlined this approach to Pluto in her book *The Astrology of Fate* (1984), which is a dense but excellent read. It is hard to say that astrological doctrines and ideas belong to any single person. But I do wish to acknowledge the tremendous inspiration I have drawn from Liz Greene which informs the following accessible primer on how the rivers of the underworld flow and ripple through Scorpios' minds.

ACHERON

And so we begin, as the old stories often did, with the river Acheron, which means "River of Woe." Now, that not might sound very uplifting; but let's face it, many Scorpios battle with intense feelings of melancholia as adults. And as astrologers, we want to inspire and teach Scorpios how to better handle this river within and transmute this melancholia that often hangs over them like a dark cloud.

In ancient Greece, when a person died, the living relatives left a coin under the dead person's tongue. The deceased would then use this coin to pay Charon, the ferryman, who would take the newly dead across the river Acheron to the underworld. So the Acheron was the first river of the underworld that newly dead souls would encounter. Many Scorpios have powerful experiences with death. Some have near-death experiences. Other Scorpios are called upon to serve the dying. Other Scorpios are deeply touched by the death of a parent, family member, or friend.

This is a hard point to explore, because death touches all of us. All of us must bear the weight articulated so pithily by that old Latin aphorism *Ars longa, Vita brevis*. Art is long, Life is brief. But different sun signs experience the inevitability of death and its ever-present specter in profoundly different ways. Most signs just shut down. Gemini tells a funny story but buries its feelings. Aries avoids it and finds something else that doesn't actually matter to be angry about and yells and screams. Pisces drinks its feelings away or finds another way to escape. But Scorpio seems more receptive to death and to the deep and the rewarding, albeit frightening, insights that can come from contemplating the brevity of life. In this there is melancholia, but there is also much richness.

But from this awareness also stems much of the way Scorpio resents others. Don't these people realize how short life is? Why are they wasting their time "under-being"? Who knows how long they have? Such morbid thoughts are mostly thought by Scorpio but often held in and left unexpressed. Finding a healthy outlet for these stirrings is of utmost importance. I hate how the standard advice for Scorpios is to seek out therapy. All signs benefit from exploring their own psyches more. However, what many Scorpios really need is a friend they can "go there" with—a friend who can go to the underworld with them and talk about the dirty, scary, frightening truths that bubble beneath the surface but that Scorpios fear being open about.

Scorpios can feel an incredible attraction toward stepping into the role of Charon. They may feel a yearning to care for other souls. But the key is to balance this motivation with their own inner work. Only a divine being could ferry the dead in perpetuity. The rest of us mere mortals need a break. Some Scorpios might arrogantly think they can be Charon, overburdening themselves with relationships in which they are the caretaker of someone else's deepest, darkest secrets. It will be a lifelong challenge to understand how to balance their talent for this role with other aspects of their lives.

STYX

Let's move on to the next river, the Styx. Styx is an intriguing chthonic deity whose story is seldom told. Styx was originally a water nymph. She was one of many sisters, who were collectively known as the Oceanides. Styx was the daughter of Titan Okeanos, the original ruler of the sea before the Titans were defeated and the sea was given to Poseidon. Now Styx was actually present at the abduction of Persephone by Hades; she was one of the nymphs attending to her. But Styx's story does not end here. During the epic war between Zeus and Saturn and their respective allies, Zeus called all immortals to Mount Olympus and promised any deity that took his side enduring power and respect if they swore an oath to him. Most Titans sided with Saturn and lost. But upon the advice of her father, Styx bucked the trend and came with her children to pledge loyalty to Zeus. Her children were quite powerful—Nike (victory), Zelus (rivalry), Cratus (strength), and Bia (Force), and they helped Zeus win.

Zeus elevated Styx into the powerful underworld river of oaths. Oaths would be sworn upon her—by both mortals and immortals—and if you broke your oath, you would incur her wrath. In ancient art, we see images of Iris, the rainbow messenger goddess, who would bring a jug of water from the Styx in the underworld to the gods on Mount Olympus for them to use to make promises, which the Styx would then enforce.

The oath is a potent and sacred concept for many Scorpios. Everyone makes promises. And many of us break promises to others and to ourselves. And while many of us seem to have accepted long ago that this is part and parcel of this comedy of errors known as the human condition, many Scorpios can't get on board with this. There is something deep within many Scorpios that cries out to honor the Styx and the sanctity of certain vows. And Scorpios may well have a point. Recovering alcoholics take a vow to never drink again and count their days of sobriety. Sticking to that vow is the bedrock foundation of that program of recovery. There is great wisdom here that healing entails drawing certain red lines that we never cross again no matter what. Those of us who aren't alcoholics may well suffer from other destructive compulsive behaviors. And we may benefit from discerning and respecting certain bottom lines. This process comes easier to Scorpios than to other signs. So Scorpios often find themselves in the position of the Styx, holding people accountable to the importance of keeping a promise—but also staring at the world in bewilderment as a diet gets broken yet again, or a gym membership goes unused, or agreements struck at an annual performance review go unimplemented. Scorpios are sometimes accused of being angry. But when they work so hard at holding themselves to certain vows, it can become enraging when others don't.

The Styx was also the river that Thetis dipped her son Achilles in to make him nearly invincible—save for the notorious heel by which she dangled him. Scorpios need to be very careful of falling into the delusion that they are invincible, because everyone has an Achilles heel. Most Scorpios don't think they are literally invincible. But driven as they are to stick to their vows, they can become self-righteous as they watch other people stumble as they stay the course. But while Scorpios may stay the course on many things, they can't remain completely consistent on all things. They have their own places where they stumble again and again. In this way, some Scorpios may have a fundamental weakness that they are incredibly ashamed about and which they seek to hide. The problem with this concealment and Scorpio's desire to avoid talking about it is that they often deny themselves the emotional support that they need the most.

LETHE

Next, let's look at the river Lethe. Lethe was the river of forgetfulness, concealment, and oblivion. Souls would drink from this river to forget their past lives and prepare to return to earth in a new incarnation. It was also understood to be the river of letting go. Within each Scorpio there is a latent ability to master the art of letting go. But while many of us can appreciate the letting go as an ideal, we struggle to release anguish and pain about the past in practice. It is easier said than done. Carl Jung comes to mind with an insight about how to get better at letting go. Jung once said, "I am not what happened to me . . . I am what I choose to become." It's intriguing how Jung connects letting go with ushering in a new future, just as in ancient mythology the purpose of the Lethe waters was letting go in order to prepare for a new life.

In Scorpios, there is an avid hunger to better understand the process of letting go and to transform. It can lead them to various occult, spiritual, and psychological interests that deepen the soul. But all this knowledge can backfire. Scorpios can appoint themselves other people's shamans, convinced they can use all their knowledge to force an issue with someone. But they do so at their own peril. And they may need to hold back on their desire to tell someone to get over it already or get off their pity pot and get to work. If only shaming people really worked. It would do well for Scorpios to remember the fall season into which they were born. It would be silly to expect the leaves of an autumn tree to

> **In Scorpios, there is an avid hunger to better understand the process of letting go and to transform.**

turn yellow, orange, or crimson in August. Just as you can't force a tree to prematurely let go of its leaves, we can't force humans to go against their own wishes or speed up their inner processes. Scorpios can delude themselves into thinking their "Jedi mind tricks" are causing someone to change faster. But often the person is just telling lies to appease the scorpion in their lives. What Scorpios really need to do is focus more on the things they are struggling to let go of and to get to work on envisioning and imagining what they actually want to be, and on supporting other people in what they wish to become in their own terms, ways, and time.

This Lethe energy is one of the greatest blessings for Scorpios in the unique way they experience Scorpio as a water sign. If properly understood, the Lethe's flow can be channeled into healing and releasing the deepest emotional challenges that face Scorpios. The overuse of the word "transformation" has emptied it of most of its meaning. In the esoteric tradition, we revere the ancient stories of the underworld journey as an archetype for the transformation and healing we seek here on earth. The deep wisdom within many Scorpios is an appreciation for the patience it takes to go on an underworld journey to reach the Lethe. Just as the Lethe was not the first river shore that souls encountered, Scorpios show that tenacity is toughing out the required journey along the Acheron first. So often, implementing a new pattern requires a period of difficult adjustment that can cause some of us to break under emotional pressure and revert back to the undesired pattern. Scorpios can stick with it even when it gets tough, and they won't give up too soon. "Don't quit five minutes before the miracle" is advice this sign should keep in mind. This tenacity means that Scorpios might be more successful at transformation than other signs.

COCYTUS AND PHLEGETHON

Two other underworld rivers we also see mentioned in ancient sources are the river of wailing—the Cocytus—and the river of fire, the Phlegethon. It is ironic that the Christian imagination became stuck on the fire of the Phlegethon and the wailing conveyed by the Cocytus. In ancient mythology, the Acheron, the Styx, and the Lethe had more stories of interacting with both gods and humans. But the insight here is that many Scorpios struggle with intense anguish that burns inside of them. Or they can turn on the people close to them when they miss the mark and unleash rivers of fire and wailing. Everyone makes mistakes, and whether fire and brimstone works to resolve this is dubious. Part of the work for Scorpios, ruled by Mars and Pluto, is to understand how to hold their fire, lest they burn bridges among friends, family, and colleagues.

Scorpios have a lifelong relationship with the symbols and rivers of the underworld as adults. When Carl Jung coined individuation, his point was that each adult goes on a journey to discover symbols that speak to their subconscious which galvanizes their inner healing. This section—Scorpio as an Adult—has been intended as an introduction to the rich symbols of the underworld. They are like keys. With further work and exploration of these themes, Scorpios can glean the insights into the underworld transformation they are craving.

SCORPIO IN LOVE

WITH SCORPIOS, IT always starts with that intense look in the eyes. They're immediately drawn to any person who can meet and match their piercing gaze. They find it very alluring when someone can flash an amorous look that speaks words the tongue cannot utter. And Scorpios may well make a beeline across an entire room at a party to open a conversation if someone's gaze feels strong, deep, and intense enough. When glancing at online profile photos, they feel a similar thrill when there is something (even if it's Photoshopped) about the eyes. Scorpios are such suckers for eyes that they may not even care that the sparkle they see is actually a Snapchat filter.

The trouble for Scorpios can start as soon as they open their mouth to begin a conversation with the individual who has caught their eye. Flirting is supposed to be light, carefree, easy, and fun. But Scorpios like substance, shattering insights, darkness, and secrecy. They feel irresistibly drawn toward redirecting the conversation from small talk to deep talk. "Oh, wow, you want to take the conversation there," the targets of Scorpio's advances often remark to themselves. It seems lost on Scorpio that speaking lightly with an "I want to have sex and love you for the rest of my life" look in their eyes is intense and charged enough.

Scorpios need to work on not getting carried away into darker and weirder topics. That tendency is why so many Scorpios get turned down for a second date. In this sense, Scorpios might benefit from having a best friend with whom they can explore all this material that fascinates them. When it comes to the opening moves with a new potential lover, they will have an easier time holding back and not overwhelming their sweetheart, knowing they can just text their best friend with that weird thought instead.

SCORPIO IN LOVE

When Scorpios become infatuated, it can be hard for them to distinguish whether something is first-date or tenth-date material. They're prone to thinking a date's curiosity and admiration is carte blanche to hold a microphone to their internal monologue and share everything. Scorpios may think they know this, but in the heat of the moment, they're prone to excitedly overshare. It's not that certain topics like politics, sex, religion, or our pasts (and all of our exes) are off limits on early dates; it's just that it may be better for developing relationships if we tread carefully. Scorpio's way of broaching these topics—that is, with way too much intensity and detail—is problematic. Perhaps it's analogous to light levels. A light in darkness is desirable, but don't shine it so brightly that it blinds the other person.

Let's bring this down to the practical level. When someone vents about the sad state of

> Scorpios are such suckers for eyes that they may not even care that the sparkle they see is actually a filter.

politics on a date, the right move is generally to make a light-hearted joke and then listen to the response to see how much that person really wants to talk about it. Were they just venting for a moment or do they want to dive into this subject? Their response will tell you how to steer the conversation going forward. When someone brings up an ex, the key is to validate their feelings but not to draw the discussion out or ask a lot of follow-up questions, and then perhaps crack a joke to pivot to something lighter. Successful dating escalates intensity mutually, with conversation partners embracing their roles as copilots.

Scorpios can be so enthusiastic with what they want to share that they forget to check the temperature when a new topic comes up. A long diatribe sharing numerous insights without pause might well be one of Scorpio's most irritating traits early on in dating. The poor person across the table might feel like they just opened up Pandora's box. If the topic is intellectual, they might feel condescended to, because half the things Scorpio lectures them about, they already know. It can get too professorial, as over-enthused Scorpio tries to get to the bottom of things and reveal the ultimate truth that the other person didn't even ask for. If the topic is emotional, the other person can quickly get overwhelmed. "I actually wasn't really ready to talk about this heavy stuff with you yet, because I am still getting to know you," the dates say to themselves. They conclude that Scorpio sucks at reading them and feel uneasy. Scorpio thinks they are doing this person a favor by enlightening them, but are actually just turning the other person off.

Scorpios might also need to work on keeping their love of psychology in check. As the date unfolds, the apple of their eye is going to drop hints and reveal certain parts of their story. Scorpios will get to work on trying to figure them out. Don't jump to premature conclusions when you don't have all the pieces of the puzzle, Scorpio. It takes a long time interacting with a person before you get what makes them tick. Refrain from sharing these psychological observations early on. No one likes it when a date degenerates into an attempted free psychotherapy session offered by someone who barely knows them—and who ends up being wrong most of the time. Keep things light in the beginning and trust that the depth you love will form in time if it's meant to.

Scorpios also need to guard against turning their date into a corporate pressure interview. Look, none of us wants to waste each other's time. But sometimes Scorpios can get impatient and ask hard and intense questions way too early about money, kids, marriage, converting religions, family, relocating, etc. What they seem to miss is how the most important question is right in front of them: Can you relax, giggle, and kick back with this person? None of the other stuff matters if that foundation isn't there. There are many people who look good on paper and check all our boxes that we can't even fathom coming home to at the end of the day.

It would be better for Scorpios to ask light questions like "What kind of restaurants do you like?" and "What kinds of activities do you enjoy?" Use the information you gather and do your homework. Circle back and pitch a place for the next date that the food critics are raving about that serves the food they crave. Scorpios possess amazing research skills with a passion for getting to the bottom of things. It's really alluring when Scorpio finds that hidden gem that makes for a lovely evening. And it's a much better outlet for their research skills than amateur psychoanalysis.

SCORPIO LOVERS

It may seem like we've devoted a lot of time to the mistakes that Scorpios make early on in dating, but the truth is that the most common reason Scorpios are single is because they come on too strong too early in dating. But Scorpio's dogged fierceness makes them incredible as long-term partners. They can take the heat that comes with intimacy.

Few signs are better with sex than Scorpio. Everyone enjoys sex. But Scorpios often get it better and more profoundly.

Some Scorpios may experience sexual trauma and feel blocked, but they actually have an incredible capacity to unblock and enjoy sex as adulthood unfolds. This sign responds well to sex therapy, which taps into the flow of the Lethe that we explored in section two.

Scorpios will meticulously research the person's body to figure out just what gets them off. And while other folks can get lazy, Scorpios view it as their solemn responsibility to do right by their lover and go full-throttle between the sheets. And not just at the beginning, but throughout the relationship—even after the honeymoon period ends. Scorpios are also masters at make-up sex. They love to show their lover that they still care after a spat by going down on them like there is no tomorrow.

One of the most amazing parts of being truly intimate with a Scorpio is that no story and no subject is off-limits. The way their intensity can be a net negative in early dating turns into a net positive as true intimacy begins to unfold. Other sun signs can subtly discourage the open sharing that makes bonding possible. Scorpios know just what to say after their lover shares a hard part of their story and knows just what to say to remind that person that they don't need to be perfect to make Scorpio happy.

Nothing turns a Scorpio on more than when their partner asks for some help in exorcising their inner demons. All of us have unresolved psychological issues. Whereas other signs get intimidated when things get complex, Scorpios get even more into it and are all-in. Just as we all have our sexual spots that get us off, we also have our emotional sweet spots. Scorpios delight in using all their depth and intensity to craft the most incredible pep talk. They love to inspire their partners to take the next step or the next leap of faith.

Nevertheless, it's important that Scorpios allow their partners to initiate and say, "This is where I need some support." Or, if the partner is not forthcoming, a gentle "How can I support you this week?" can be helpful. The danger for Scorpios is when they start deciding that their close bond means they get to tell someone else how to live their life. Unsolicited feedback is rarely well received, especially when one partner goes for the other's jugular, which Scorpions can do when they sense someone is blocked.

Scorpios need to work with their anger as they endure the humanity of their partners. We are *all* works in progress. And it is human to miss the mark when we aim high. But Scorpio needs to pause and reflect on why their partner doesn't hit the bull's-eye every time. They may jump to the conclusion that their partner is being a wimp and needs to man up (or woman up). But the truth is more complex. We all wake up in the morning and aspire to be successful, sane, sociable, and loving. What brings us down is our unresolved emotional issues. We err again because there is a hard feeling we are bearing, and what we often need is more support.

> **Nothing turns a Scorpio on more than when their partner asks for some help in exorcising their inner demons.**

Saint Francis de Sales once observed: "Nothing is so strong as gentleness, nothing so gentle as real strength." Now, this paradoxical aphorism may well seem like outdated nonsense to a Scorpio. Don't underestimate the power of the gentle question, and tenderness after a setback. In dentistry, it takes gentleness to remove a cavity. And so, when it comes to helping our partners face the music of their unresolved issues, a soft, light touch can go a long way. Ultimately, Scorpio has to decide whether they care more about dramatic means or dramatic results. If you want to lose your shit on someone, inflict a shame spiral, and watch nothing change, go ahead. Often, gentler, softer dialogues can produce the deeper shifts Scorpio craves.

ORION THE HUNTER

The ancient myth of the giant scorpion constellation in the sky is actually a love story. And it offers several lessons for Scorpios as they embrace the dance of love. There are many variants but let's tell the story this way:

> There was once a good-looking, but conceited hunter named Orion. One day, while wandering through the woods, Orion came upon a naked woman bathing. He immediately turned away out of respect and humility. What he did not realize is that this was not a human woman, but actually the goddess Artemis. Impressed by his respect for her modesty and captivated with his fine skills and good looks, the goddess decided to take Orion as her hunting companion. The two went hunting every day. But Orion eventually made the grave mistake of bragging that he surpassed Artemis's prowess as a hunter. Enraged that a mere mortal would claim greater power than a goddess, Mother Earth decided that Orion had to be punished for his hubris so she sent a giant scorpion, Scorpio, to kill Orion. Skilled as he was, Orion was no match for Scorpio. The gods then placed Orion and the scorpion as a constellation in the night sky to warn humans of the dangers of big egos.

Scorpios—whatever their gender expression or sexual preference—can often step into the role of Orion in a relationship. They bring much strength, intensity, skill, and sexual desire. What's really key for the success of the relationship is to have a light touch. Looking away from the bathing Artemis is a metaphor for the reward that comes from holding back. The image of two hunters out on a hunting trip together with a bit of friendly competition but always having each other's back might be a powerful archetype for Scorpios to explore. And think of date night as two hunters sitting by the fire, swapping stories and getting ready for their next adventure. Be forewarned: it can all go to hell when Scorpios start acting like they are better than their other half. Don't underestimate how attractive and powerful humility and grace can be!

SCORPIO AT WORK

SCORPIO CAN QUICKLY take to the dog-eat-dog environment of the corporate workplace. Many Scorpios have what it takes to fight for their success and climb the ladder. But the challenges come fast as well.

The trouble is that Scorpios can get bogged down in pointless power struggles. They can waste precious time duking it out with another professional when instead they could be pouring all their energy into the next project that will make them a success. If you're a Scorpio and you are reading this advice, this probably isn't the first time you've heard this: Pick your battles and keep your eye on the prize. With that in mind, let's go through the different bombs that can blow up in Scorpio's face and explore how to better maneuver around these mines in the workplace.

SCORPIO VS. EMAIL

For many Scorpios, the inbox can be excruciatingly frustrating. Now, let's be honest—the twenty-first century is rife with folks writing terse words in emails that they wouldn't have the guts to say in person. And there are many little twists of phrase people put in emails that smack of immature passive-aggressive nonsense. Such tactics can drive those born under the sign of the scorpion bonkers. At least once every workday, Scorpios receive an email that completely infuriates them. It takes a bit of work for them to calm themselves down, avoid overreacting, and write poised and professional responses.

Scorpio's colleagues might pick up on their tendency to go ballistic when they get triggered by an email. Scorpio needs to be vigilant and careful about how a nemesis in the workplace may intentionally push their buttons to provoke a reaction and make poor Scorpio look like a maniac. Scorpio, please don't take the bait when you get a message that is clearly "off." Yes, it's hard for you not to respond with something even more vicious when you feel like you've been slighted, and it feels like the aggressor is getting away with it if you don't answer back with force and bravado. But sadly, sometimes these messages are actually cleverly laid traps. Most Scorpios early on in their career learn the hard way that whatever you write in an email

At least once every workday, Scorpios receive an email that completely infuriates them.

is just one Forward to your boss away. And their enemies at work might try and use mind games via email to get Scorpios to crack and write something they will regret. When Scorpio claims that the initial email was inflammatory, the boss says that a terse email doesn't warrant that kind of overkill response.

SCORPIO VS. COWORKERS

When a colleague gets under Scorpio's skin, they're often told to "calm down." Scorpio has heard this piece of advice numerous times. But Scorpio misinterprets this to mean "stop fighting." And for a sun sign ruled by Mars, fighting is a big part of life. So let's explore it in a different way. There are many ways to fight back. Let's take a proverb from Sun Tzu's *The Art of War*: "The Supreme Art of War is to subdue the enemy without fighting." What if you forwarded the initial aggravating email to your boss and asked for advice on how to respond? What if you ignored it? There are so many other ways to win without fighting. So instead of telling yourself to calm down, ask yourself: How can I be more strategic? Is there a way to lose the battle but win the war?

Most Scorpios hate meetings with a burning passion. They loathe sitting there and listening to people brainstorm stupid ideas. They despise watching the boss make a fake smile and avoid telling people to their face how silly that idea was. They also hate when people give rationalizations for their mediocrity when pressed on why a project has fallen behind. They resent what they interpret to be the boss giving their colleagues a free pass for missing a target. In truth, the boss is just trying to be diplomatic and regain some momentum. Sometimes, Scorpio can lose their cool at a meeting and launch into a harsh and mean diatribe, creating a super-uncomfortable silence. Bear in mind that if someone else looks bad at a meeting, it is really their problem and their raise that's on the chopping block. But while this may seem logical, Scorpio can struggle to hold back, especially when they feel like the boss is cutting everyone too much slack. And other colleagues start to resent how Scorpio keeps trying to bust their chops with feisty looks or pointed comments. Just remember: you aren't the boss.

SCORPIO VS. DIPLOMACY

Scorpios also have a way of naming the elephant in the room that the boss is diplomatically trying to avoid. Sometimes your boss is going to call a meeting to try to offer the person they are gently calling out a way to save face and get back on track. As Sun Tzu wrote in *The Art of War*, "Build your opponent a golden bridge to retreat across." And Scorpio blows it all up by saying, "Well, we all know that we wouldn't be in this situation if this person hadn't screwed up." When this happens, your coworkers will probably say something like, "You just had to say that, didn't you?" It's true, and everyone was thinking it. But was it necessary? And shouldn't the focus be on moving forward? Scorpios would do well to ponder the words of Winston Churchill, who said: "Diplomacy is the art of telling people to go to hell in such a way that they ask for directions."

Scorpios get way too psychological and intense with their bosses. There is a school of thought out there that believes the way to achieve success is to get inside your boss's head, figure out what makes them tick, and then to ingratiate yourself to him or her as much as possible. And this appeals to the little Freud inside of every Scorpio way too much. But they can get carried away with inventing elaborate fantasies that the little thing they said in the elevator, or that extra line in the email they spent fifteen minutes sweating over, will somehow be the key to the kingdom. And they're just plain wrong when they get carried away with these ideas.

The truth is that most bosses care about results. In most places, there are bottom lines that are as clear as crystal. Are you making money for the company? Are you meeting deadlines? Are you creating excellent work products? Do you keep making the same mistakes or are you adjusting based on the feedback you're getting? Do you arrive to work on time? Do you play games when it comes to vacation time? Sometimes Scorpios can delude themselves into thinking that they don't have to meet these basic targets because they have their boss "figured out" and therefore they can cut corners. But bosses can pick up on this pretty quickly, and they actually hate it when Scorpios try to play them for fools.

SCORPIO VS. DRAMA

Scorpio can be a big gossip at work. Well, maybe "gossip" isn't exactly the right term, since they play detective to try to get everyone else to spill the beans but seldom share much themselves. Similar to their boss dynamics, Scorpios can convince themselves that the workplace is a mystery novel. And that if they learn every colleague's backstory, and read in between all the lines, they will discover the mystical key to success that will catapult them beyond their wildest dreams. This is where Pluto, lord of the underworld, ruling Scorpio can really cause problems. Scorpios can get carried away and invasive with their coworkers, when what they really need to do is just work hard and get the next task at hand done efficiently. Now, of course, many workplaces have interpersonal dimensions, but Scorpio can get way too caught up in the drama. Meanwhile, it's really amazing how many workers in the twenty-first century struggle with

basic issues of focus and concentration. It's not as exciting as attempting to manipulate the palace intrigue of your workplace; but if your goal is to set yourself apart, nothing shines brighter than being the hardest worker who knows how to put their nose to the grindstone, avoid getting sidetracked by the drama, and just focus on meeting deadlines and getting projects to the finish line.

Now, all this fascination with secrets and psychology has another very strange effect on Scorpio. They are very aware of just how screwed up everyone is at their job. They can't hold back from prying into their coworkers' life stories and getting involved in the drama. And this means they often know why someone keeps making the same mistake over and over again, and they can become really frustrated and enraged with that colleague. There may be some point to the aphorism that ignorance is bliss—it probably would be better for Scorpio not to know these things about the people they work with. Most Scorpios need to just let other people dig their own graves. How much is that other person's mediocrity affecting you? Do you really need to spend so much time thinking about and analyzing it?

If someone you work with keeps screwing up consistently, and is endangering your shot at success, don't appoint yourself her fixer. Speak to that person's supervisor, because ultimately it's the company's product and reputation that's on the line. Scorpios often don't like to bring things to their boss's attention. They may fear being called a snitch. Or, more likely, it's because they don't know how to broach the conversation without ripping their colleague a new one and coming off too harsh. The key to this is to use soft language that sounds like you are drinking the Kool-Aid. Here's a script: "Shirley, I want to be successful and get these projects completed. I am wondering if you have any feedback on how I could work with Jim more effectively. I've noticed a pattern and I'm curious if you have any advice on how we can resolve this and be more successful." Scorpios find such sugarcoating to be annoying. But the point is to send a subtle hint at the actual issue while simultaneously conveying that you are committed to keeping things positive, professional, and humble. If Scorpios show their stingers too much and come down on a colleague too hard behind their back, even if the observations are true, the supervisor will suspect that Scorpio has personal animus and may discount what's been said, even though it is actually the bitter truth.

Scorpios may resent their bosses for not having "fixed" everyone—although hopefully Scorpio is wise enough to understand that bosses seldom are able to hire the perfect employee. Nor do most people actually seriously listen to the feedback their bosses give them and make changes. People try for a little bit and then slip back into certain patterns. Most bosses are busy trying to put out

> **Most Scorpios need to just let other people dig their own graves. How much is that other person's mediocrity affecting you? Do you really need to spend so much time thinking about and analyzing it?**

the biggest fire of the moment, trying to find a way to move the ball forward as human beings make mistakes they have already been gently told about, to keep the peace when folks start to bicker.

THE SCORPIO BOSS

The day that Scorpio starts to supervise people is a rude awakening for all involved. Scorpio discovers just how stubborn most adults are and how all the deep insights that they share can end up feeling like pearls thrown before swine. Scorpios as supervisors can give some of the most intense and powerful performance reviews. They really want to help all their employees become better. But it can be really hard to watch so many employees be unable or unwilling to integrate the feedback they get and put it to work. Scorpios need to remind themselves that not everyone gets promoted for a reason, to stick with the winners, and to reassign or fire someone that isn't working out after they've blown their chances to adjust. The workplace is not the place for taking on people as special charity projects. Save that energy for your family and for when your good friends have bad things happen to them and ask for support and help.

As bosses, Scorpios can, at times, be too hard on the people they supervise. And when you are mean to people, they usually start to be mean right back and resent you. As supervisors, Scorpios need to be able to do the professional equivalent of "kiss and make up." But they can be reluctant to be affectionate toward subordinates until they see the changes they want. The problem is that when you feel like your boss viscerally hates you, it's hard to feel motivated to make the hard changes they've asked you to implement. Instead, you start looking for another job while you are at work and begin to cut corners. Once again, this is another place where a light touch can work wonders.

Overall, Scorpio's formula for success in the workplace boils down to some simple slogans: Don't set off fireworks. Keep the drama to a minimum. Stay laser-focused on the tasks at hand. Don't get bogged down in all the "he-said, she-said" that doesn't matter. Be kind. And remember, we work to live, we don't live to work. Keep your team focused on being successful so that you all can enjoy the abundance you're earning with the people you truly care about.

CONCLUSION

THE CONCLUSION TO this chapter is not going to be some longwinded riff on being less intense. Because no matter what happens, individuals born under the sign of the scorpion are going to be intense.

My parting words to Scorpio are this—cultivate a wicked sense of humor.

Laugh at the wild adventures of your childhood and your school years. Don't be too hard on yourself. You were still discovering that special spark inside of you. And growing into your scorpion energy is a contact sport.

As adulthood unfolds, find ways to broach the difficult subjects that keep coming up with wit, warmth, and goodhearted humor. Warmth can be very underestimated, but with a bit of kindness it will serve you well when you have to wade into the chilly waters of underworld rivers as often as you do in your life. And when you do have to, as much as possible steer toward Lethe and the art of letting go.

If you're a parent, and your child is pushing at your limits to the point where you know you have to say something, why not crack a joke as the first warning shot? Sometimes kids learn more when they giggle, but they'll still know you mean business.

In love, use everything your deep Scorpio mind can discover about your date to make them laugh. It will make the romance more fun. And as you lean into commitment, remember—doesn't everyone want to be with someone who can make them laugh? Laughter helps to balance out the moments of inevitable tension.

At work, look at a comic or a political cartoon every day. Delight in knowing what kinds of jokes your colleagues will enjoy around the watercooler. Use your Scorpio intuition to divine what will amuse your coworkers as opposed to what will destroy them. And above all, focus on just doing the best work you can do. Laugh off most of the drama instead of getting sucked into it.

In daily routines, giggle at how attached you can become to stuff that's no longer serving you. Isn't it ironic that you often call out other people on their bad habits while you persist with your own? When you're implementing and integrating a new routine and feeling sort of crazy, watch some funny clips on YouTube. Stepping back from your current obsessions works wonders.

In love, use everything your deep Scorpio mind can discover about your date to make them laugh.

As you look out at the world, don't waste your time comparing yourself to the rich and famous. Focus on being completely *you*. Or, as Oscar Wilde once quipped, "Be yourself; everyone else is already taken." Party with your friends late and laugh heartily. Work hard on your projects and then crack some jokes and let go. Giggle at yourself as if you wish you had rich-and-famous-people problems. Money, success, fame, and glamour don't count for much if you don't understand the flow of your own underworld rivers.

Why get bogged down in the drama of life when it could be a comedy instead?

NOV. 22–DEC. 21

text by Nathaniel Craddock

element — FIRE

symbol — THE ARCHER

modality — MUTABLE

house — NINTH

ruler — JUPITER

SYLLABUS

INTRODUCTION

IN 1934, THE American songwriter Cole Porter penned the national anthem of the Sagittarius, which includes these lines:

Just give me land, lots of land, full of starry skies above,

But don't fence me in! . . .
I want to ride to the ridge where the west commences,
And gaze at the moon till I lose my senses,
And I can't look at hobbles and I can't stand fences—

Don't fence me in![1]

This Sagittarian song gives voice to the juicy center of this sign's essential style and identity: fences are your Kryptonite. Limits are your Achilles heel. The word "impossible!" never entered your vocabulary. The insatiable longing for the view of unfolding, unlimited terrain takes up residence in your heart from the very beginning, and there is nothing you would love more than to continue forward to endless horizons.

Sagittarius, this is your MO: *when God closes a door, throw a chair through the window.*

The Sagittarius style is that of a teacher, a sage, a wizard, someone who has *learned* their way through life in a perpetual cycle of experiment, experience, and explanation. Everything in your world has a story as to why it became just so. Knowing and telling those stories is how you weave the net that holds your world together.

You've been gifted with an insatiable spirit of optimism, adventure, enervation, and expansion. Because of the core motivation of your life being focused on ever-higher, ever-farther goals, part of what you've been given to do in this lifetime is to perfect the art of aim. Just as an archer must aim above their target to correct for gravity, so must we, who would dream of a world that is more just, more peaceful, and more abundant, learn how to aim higher than we think we can possibly hit with our goals and actions.[2]

You, dear friend, have been called to this world for such a time as this: by being true to who you are, you have the blessed opportunity to teach the rest of us how to do the same. By helping us to keep our eyes fixed on the imagined targets that help us achieve our goals more accurately and authentically, you can lead us into the uncharted territory of hope.

I'm so pleased to be taking this journey with you, because wanderlust courses through your veins. Heroism burns like a fire in your bones. A desire for truth, for perspective, for justice, and for a way to tell the stories of *why* things came to be is the engine that drives you forward through this life. Together we're going to spread out our wings and catch this jovial updraft to see what uncharted territory we can explore.

As we do so, we'll come to understand more deeply what it means to be under the patronage of Sagittarius's ruling planet, Jupiter. Jupiter's children have their unique mission in this world just the same as the children of any of the other planets do, but to be a Sagittarius means that you have a special tie to everyone's favorite Sky Zaddy, and your motivations and gifts are aligned with all the best—and sometimes the less-than-best—characteristics of uplifting, enervating Jupiter.

As we examine different slices of life from the perspective of Sagittarius, we'll explore how learning to mature and train the wild energy of this celestial boon can lead to a life of imagining better futures for ourselves and others, sharing an endless supply of generosity with everyone we encounter, and healing the world through healing ourselves.

BEFORE WE BEGIN, A NOTE:

I practice astrology from the classical Western tradition, and throughout this chapter I plan to use that tradition as a backdrop to tell your story. My goal is for you to be able to take this information and utilize it to take inspired action throughout all areas of your life.

If you are reading this and you are a Sun Sagittarius, I want you to be thinking about how what I describe in this chapter is related to your conscious motivation, the factor that pulls you out of bed in the morning and into action throughout your daily life.[3] The sun represents the single-pointed *desire* that drives all of existence in the astrological imagination, and we can use the sun to cast a golden thread around all the stories and details of our lives to craft a cohesive narrative.

However, I would highly recommend that you consider reading the chapter that matches your **rising sign**, also called the ascendant. If that's Sagittarius, too, great! If not, be sure to check out that chapter, too. You'll be reading your **rising sign** chapter from the perspective of your **baseline operating personality**, the "way you are" in the world. It describes the routes we take and choices we make to achieve our core motivations and impacts our appearance and personality in significant ways. If what you're reading in this chapter doesn't land with you and you're a Sun Sagittarius, you'll want to check out the chapter for your rising sign.

If you don't know your rising sign, you can find that out very easily by going to an astrology site like astro.com and entering your birth data, if you know it. If you *don't* know your birth data (date, location, and exact clock time), feel free to ignore this suggestion.

One more note: if you were born during the night, the moon plays a more important role in your chart than the sun does. That's simple enough to figure out: had the sun set by the time you were born? If so, then you have a nighttime chart, and you'll want to check out the chapter that matches your moon, too. The moon describes our "juicy center," our emotional security patterns, our coping skills, and the way our solar identity plays out in our day-to-day lives through our habits and unconscious actions.

UNDERSTANDING HOW SAGITTARIUS WORKS

I have a lot of Sagittarius in my chart (both my moon and my ascendant ruler, Saturn, are there), and I'll *happily* take the opportunity to share things with you that you might find interesting or compelling. Of course, I think you'll find them interesting or compelling because *I* do, but that's fine. (Was your life changed when you discovered Wikipedia? If so, you understand *exactly* what I mean.)

When we say, "I'm a Sagittarius," there's a risk of identifying with the sign itself, and that tendency is helped by pop astrology. In the classical astrological model, we talk about signs not as being distinct persons, because *planets* are the ones who are the agents or actors in astrology. Instead, we talk about signs as being the style in which planets are acting.

Think of it this way: if you wolf down your dinner in a split second and get stuck waiting around idly for everyone else at the table to finish their meal, do you identify as a "Quick Eater"? I mean, you *could*, but there's so much more to you than the style in which you eat. But what happens if more of your life is baked into the Quick Eater style? What if you make your livelihood by competing in eating contests? What if you have a corporate sponsorship from Nathan's® hot dogs?

The more of your life that expresses itself in the qualities of a given way of being, the more you're prone to identify as that *way* instead of you, your unique individual self, as a person for whom a lot of your life expresses itself through a given style.

With each sign we're talking about a particular *style*, right? So what defines the Sagittarius style? This is going to be crucial to our understanding of all the other slices of life that we'll explore throughout the rest of this chapter, so keep this in your back pocket. If you're a Sagittarius Sun, Moon, or Rising, *big* parts of your life express themselves in the Sagittarius style, and so will any other planet in this sign.

First, each of the planets in astrology rules at least one sign. We might think of the sign a planet rules as that planet's "home base." Because it's their home, they've got it decorated in the precise way that they like it, their favorite food is in the fridge, their favorite shows are on the DVR, and their favorite spot on the couch has a butt print that fits them like a glove. When a planet is in its own sign, it wants for nothing, and any other planets that come into that sign are obligated to use the resources they can find there to execute their unique mission in the *style* of that sign. Some planets have an easier time of this than others.

When it comes to Sagittarius, the first thing to keep in mind is that it is a sign ruled by Jupiter.

Everybody likes Jupiter, honestly. A couple of pages ago I called him "Sky Zaddy," and I did so for good reason. The astrological Jupiter is what you would get if you put Zeus, Dumbledore, and Pope Francis into a blender and poured the results into a mold shaped like *Game of Thrones*'s Tormund Giantsbane (played by Kristofer Hivju).

Throughout astrological history people have referred to him as "the greater benefic"; he has rulership over life, over luck, over philosophy and wisdom, wealth and status. He has, along with Venus, a share in fertility and the generation of new life. He's the one everybody wants

Jupiter

on their team. He does yeoman's work to make things better for the people under his care, and all he needs to hear is that something delightful is *possible* to shoot off in that direction, moving heaven and earth to bring it into fruition as best he can. He also has rulership over wisdom, philosophy, spirituality, religion, fidelity, and teaching; in fact, in the Indian astrological system, he is known as *Guru*. He knows the names of every plant, animal, person, and place in the universe, and he also knows the stories behind how those names came to be, and he'll happily share them with you.

But, of course, Jupiter is not without his share of vice. As much as we characterize him as generous, benevolent, and of great fidelity, he can also slide into extravagance, wastefulness, and fundamentalism, convinced that *his* way is the right way. He can doggedly believe that his vision of the world is the only right one, and if everyone would just trust him they'd eventually come to see it that way, too. This being the case, he might react poorly when he's told that his way isn't, in fact, the right way for everyone.

If we're imagining Sagittarius as a *style* that fashions us into the likeness of Jupiter, we might think of how such a character would decorate and arrange his abode. I'm thinking of the soaring archways and spires of a Gothic cathedral perched on the top of a mountain on the western coast of Spain, overlooking an unobstructed view of hills that tumble down to beaches on the uncharted waters of the Atlantic. There's no roof on the cathedral so that the clouds of incense and song can spiral joyfully straight up to the firmament. While services are going on attended by swaths of the faithful, there's a wild festival happening in the forecourt; it's Carnival all year round here.

The image in my mind is a fantasy version of the church of Santiago de Compostela in Spain, which, for Europeans, was about as far west as you could go, *period,* until the discovery of the Americas. Today people still go on pilgrimage to this sacred place on an ancient road that starts in southern France, crosses the ridge "where the west commences" in the Pyrenees, and follows the northern coast of Spain. Pilgrims have trod this sacred way for millennia, even well before the advent of Christianity, as they sought broken-open horizons and an unobstructed view of the limitless world that lies beyond the setting sun. *That's* Jupiter's kind of place.

One thing you'll want to keep in mind is that cultivating a relationship to Jupiterian places—whether that's going on a pilgrimage halfway across the world or taking a pilgrimage to a favorite quiet spot in your neighborhood park—is essential for your well-being.

Besides their ruling planet, the style of individual signs coalesces around their elemental nature, as well as their modality.

We can think of each of the four astrological elements (fire, earth, air, and water) as relating to one of four essential security processes that being fully and authentically human requires of us: in other words, our identity security and drive (fire), physical security (earth), intellectual-social security (air), and our emotional security (water) can be explored astrologically. Classically, these four elements also serve as the basis of *temperament,* which impacts personality as well as health and vitality.

Meanwhile, when we're talking about modality, we're talking about which *phase* of the elemental security cycle we're looking at: cardinal signs initiate, fixed signs maintain, and mutable signs adapt and transform. Each of the four elements has one sign of each modality.

Sagittarius is the mutable fire sign. Being a fire sign, Sagittarius is one of the signs that is involved in our human process of identity, self-esteem, and self-expression. Its style invites any planets placed there to take their part in helping you to understand yourself better and to engage in an ever-unfolding process of deepening that same self-understanding through learning, both through experience and through imagination.

The fire triplicity is described by astrologers Demetra George and Robert Schmidt as being associated with the *imperative* mood in grammar, the kind of language we use to issue commands.[4] "Go! Do! Be!" are all fire ways of speaking. Sagittarius's style is to issue commands—but remember, they're Jupiter-flavored commands, since Jupiter rules it: "Grow! Learn! Change! Explore!" Fire signs aren't especially given to subtlety, but unlike fire peers Aries and Leo, Sagittarius's style has the benefit of having Jupiter as its ruling planet to soften some of the harsher edges. It's easier for people to obey you if they like you, anyway.

The notion of "drive" is especially important for fire signs, too. It's important for fiery people to understand the factors that push us forward in life. Sagittarius wants to know *why* those factors came to be, since knowing those stories can help us course-correct and keep our trajectory true. Remember the archer aiming above her target.

Sagittarius's need to utilize these narrative factors as a means of improvement is because Sagittarius is also a *mutable* sign, its style is oriented toward adapting and improving based on incoming information related to self-understanding and the process of learning who you are. The Sagittarius style understands that self-concept is always on the table for revision, amendment, and adjustment based on the lessons we take in from our experiences in this world.

To be sure, everyone has moments in their life that expand who they know themselves to be, but for Sagittarius, having these experiences and milking the last drop out of each of them is a lifelong habit, even a compulsion. Because this phase of the identity security process is under Jupiter's patronage, that process becomes an upward spiral, and anything that would stand in the way—a fence, perhaps—will be consumed in the fire of purpose-bent desire. As one matures, a Sagittarian recognizes that their identity is caught up in this process itself, and it never ends—the process of improving identity *is* an identity.

PROBLEMS TO SOLVE, GIFTS TO SHARE

One of the most important ways for you to understand how your Sagittarian story is at work in your life is to look at the sign through which your ruling planet, Jupiter, was traveling on the date of your birth.[5] This is easy enough to do if you know how to calculate your chart using a free online chart calculating service. The reason you'll want to do this is because you'll want to understand whether Jupiter is able to express his priorities and principles easily or whether he's having a rougher go of it.

When Jupiter is in one of the signs he prefers most to be in (namely Sagittarius, of course, but also Pisces and Cancer), everything he touches turns to gold. He can make incredible things happen for those who cultivate a relationship with him, and they come easily to him because he has everything he needs at his disposal and is no slouch when it comes to lavishing gifts and grace on those who seek his favor. But remember King Midas, whose golden touch became a curse in its own right.[6]

If your Jupiter is in Sagittarius, Pisces, or Cancer, one of the most important lessons for you to keep in your back pocket is to understand the right use of the gifts you've been given. Leaning into the Sagittarius style, for you, looks like cultivating the Santa Claus side of Jupiter: learning to share your gifts freely, abundantly, wildly, and utilizing what you have to generate even more abundance in the world—abundance of money, love, friendship, resources, and peace, all those conditions essential to human thriving.

When Jupiter is in a sign that he has a rougher time in, namely Gemini, Virgo, or Capricorn, he maintains all his power and majesty, but he's in an environment where the game has changed. What's needed in those settings is not festal extravagance but rather inspired vision among the ordinary and the mundane. Remember the divine strangers who, in disguise, visited mortals to offer wisdom and boons in uncanny ways: this is Jupiter in disguise, ready to bring a bit of magic and mirth to a world that has lost its way.

When he is in these signs, Jupiter has been given a problem to solve, and understanding how that problem manifests in your life will require you to both cultivate and maintain an expansive vision of the possible amid the minutiae and containers of daily living. Not everything will come as naturally or as easily to this Jupiter, or to you, but when breakthroughs come they will do so with tremendous power. This Jupiter is the one who has learned the secrets of turning poison into medicine, and so must you learn and teach others how to do the same.

If, dear Sagittarian, your Jupiter is not in one of the six signs I mentioned already, your story straddles both worlds. By turn, life will ask you to be the master of ceremonies at a celestial feast or to don the disguise of mortals and offer wisdom to those who don't know they need it. You will have to learn how to strike the balance between the two and be ready to change from one to the other at a moment's notice.

In all cases, the experiences you have as you walk through life in different Jupiterian avatars will add to your bank of narrative information which will help you tell the story of who you are, where you've come from, and whom you're becoming.

SAGITTARIUS AS A CHILD

CHURCH RUMMAGE SALES are often the final resting place for junk we've accumulated over the course of our lives that is too nice to throw out but too chintzy to keep around. My dad, who, besides being a Methodist pastor, is also a relentless nostalgia junkie, lived for it. Mercifully, I very narrowly missed having hoarder parents (likely because my Sagittarius mother kept home like Sherman marching on Atlanta), but Dad still found ways to bring home treasures from time to time. It was a regular occurrence for him to salvage odds and ends of interest and stash them away to surprise my sisters and me—with varying success, usually, but occasionally he hit the jackpot.

One autumn afternoon when I was five or six, my dad came home from the annual rummage sale at the church he served at the time. Tucked under his arm was a musty, cloth-bound book the size of a single volume from an encyclopedia; the dust jacket was missing, and one could make out where the cloth binding had been exposed to the elements, just on the spine. The rest of the cover was pristine. Beaming but with very little ceremony, my dad pulled me away from the TV to present the book to me. It was big, too big to be something for kids, and I tentatively cracked it open. The spine was still stiff, and it smelled of the 1980s, of wood paneling and neglect. The book fell open to something majestic, the likes of which I had never seen: one of the Voyager II photographs of the planet Saturn.[7]

This book owned me now. It became, to me, a sacred text, a grimoire: it opened the heavens to me and served as a touchstone for imagination,

SAGITTARIUS IN SUMMARY

Let's recap: Sagittarius is a **mutable fire sign** ruled by **Jupiter**. Sagittarian priorities are focused on the adjustment and improvement of one's self-concept and sense of desire by adapting to incoming narrative information gained through experiential learning, heightened perspectives, and crossing of thresholds and boundaries.

When your jovial Sagittarian story is moving toward integration or harmony, your personal style embodies these key words[1]:

* Sagacious, moral, truth-telling and truth-seeking, open-minded, ethical, philosophical, aspiring

* Hopeful, jovial, expansive, philanthropic, merciful, generous, optimistic, benevolent

* Authentic, speculative, outspoken, freedom-loving, frank, wondering, adventurous

When your jovial Sagittarian story is moving toward disintegration, stress, or unhealth, your presentation will skew more toward these key words:

* Opinionated, zealous, ungrounded, baseless, condescending, self-righteous, fundamentalist

* Extravagant, risky, prodigal, false, bloviating, delusional

* Excessive, scattered, restless, tactless, insensitive, irresponsible, a moocher

If Jupiter is in Sagittarius, Pisces, or Cancer, your Sagittarian story is focused on gifts to share out of your abundance of wealth and jollity.

If Jupiter is in Gemini, Virgo, or Capricorn, your Sagittarian story is focused on problems to solve with your inborn wisdom and far-reaching vision.

You'll also want to keep these planets in mind, because each of them rules a different slice of life for you, and we'll consider them in the relevant sections later in the chapter.[2]

* Your money is ruled by **Saturn**.

* Your neighborhood, siblings, and daily environment are also ruled by **Saturn**.

* Your home life and family relationships are ruled by **Jupiter**.

* Your tastes, creative work, and sexuality are ruled by **Mars**.

* Your responsibilities, labors, and illnesses are ruled by **Venus**.

* Your relationships are ruled by **Mercury**.

* Your relationship with life's unavoidables (death and taxes!) is ruled by the **moon**.

* Your spirituality, education, and travel are ruled by the **sun**.

* Your career is ruled by **Mercury**.

* Your friends and groups are ruled by **Venus**.

* Your search for transcendence and unconscious limits is ruled by **Mars**.

---

1 These lists of key words are an adaptation & reimagining of similar lists offered by Douglas Bloch and Demetra George in *Astrology for Yourself*, revised edition (Lake Worth, Ibis, 2006) p. 217ff.

2 These planets are derived from projecting houses out from Sagittarius as the first house. For example, if Sagittarius falls in the first house, Capricorn falls in the second and is ruled by Saturn, Aquarius in the third, and so forth. This presumes whole sign or equal sign houses, which is a helpful shorthand technique.

myth, magic, and meditation for years to come. It was a comforter, a companion, and an inspiration, something I had never experienced before as a child. My dad's gift of this book is one of the reasons that I'm writing this chapter today: my Sagittarian fire was given something to catch on and sink its blaze into. Flame becomes drive. Drive becomes action.

To the Sagittarian child, these kinds of touchstones are like catnip. They serve to spark the imagination and to fan the spark of hope, magic, and imagination into flame like none other, because they provide a view of the unbounded futures that are possible. Remember, all that a Sagittarian person needs to hear is that something is possible before they race off and strive to make it so. This is as true for children as it is adults. Cultivating the imagination and keeping the magic alive becomes, for the Sagittarian child, as essential to life as breath, water, and food.

BEFORE THE FIRST JUPITER RETURN
Zero to Twelve Years Old

The Sagittarian child before the first Jupiter return (from birth to about twelve years old) embodies all the youthful, effulgent, and effervescent qualities of Jupiter, qualities that make them a delight just as much as they can also make them a jovial pain in the butt. Consider the Sagittarian child to be like a tomato plant. They hold the promise of so much fruit within each of their leaves, but if left untrained, they'll grow sideways—they'll invest their energies in expanding their reach instead of bringing anything to solid fruition, and at the end of the day they'll have achieved a spate of sound and fury without anything solid to show for it.

The Sagittarius child requires loving structure, discipline, and training to grow into their best possibilities, as does every child. The difference is this: what you are working with in this instance is a child whose basic way of being in the world is to hop over fences and throw chairs through windows when they encounter limitations and obstacles in their life.

A Sagittarian child needs latitude to live. They need to explore, to play outside unsupervised, to make collections of bugs and rocks and leaves, to check out twenty books from the library, to live life to the absolute fullest. To chain a Sagittarian child to a strict schedule or to restrict their freedom for exploration, play, and experimentation either will backfire with explosive results or will slowly stifle their inborn soulfulness until there's nothing left but a smoldering ember of their innate excitement for the expansive joy of living. If you watched *The Magic School Bus* as a kid, remember Sagittarian Ms. Frizzle's mantra: "It's time to take chances, make mistakes, and get messy!"

Throughout their early childhood, you can expect the Sagittarian child to go through phases of intense, focused interest in whichever topics and activities catch their fancy.

Chances are they'll have several loves at once, too. The Sagittarian child is one that forms obsessions, squeezing as much as they can out of anything they find interesting, until they master it: they will cultivate an encyclopedic knowledge of their favorite video game characters, or they will memorize all the tales in their favorite books and repeat those stories to their friends with bravado on the playground. Even at this age they have begun to manifest Jupiter's sagacious and seeking principles.

Because of the breadth of a Sagittarius child's interests, there will inevitably come a time when they have bitten off more than they can chew. They will need to drop out of something because it's not working for them. If you are the parent of a Sagittarian child, your role is twofold here: you must cultivate their impulse to try new things and experiment while teaching them the virtue of following through on their commitment, but even more so you must teach them the ability to quit *well*. If quitting well is a skill that you never developed in your own life, your Sagittarian child will be taking *you* to school.

An additional caveat: the Sagittarian child will also tell you *exactly* like it is, being a fire sign. Their bluntness can be softened by Jupiter's influence, but that's not a guarantee. Get ready to be eviscerated by a fifth grader.

Speaking of which, when I was in fifth grade, I was a member of my elementary school's Student Council Association (a natural expression of the Sagittarian must-be-in-front tendency). At our monthly meeting in the fall the question of the SCA's participation in the town Christmas parade came up; the guidance counselor in charge of the SCA suggested, foolishly, that we could dress as elves, because it would be "cute."

"I'm not dressing up like an elf," I bleated, cutting her off. I was already one of the largest, loudest kids in my class, and I wasn't about to let a parade costume paint another ring around the target on my back for my peers' malice. She asked to see me after the meeting in her office.

Dutifully, I went to her office after school dismissed for the day, and I simply said, "You wanted to see me?"

"'*I'm not dressing up like an elf,*'" she said, repeating to me what I said as though there was a problem with it.

"That's right," I stated, deadpan. "I'm not dressing up like an elf."

"Excuse me?"

"I'm not going to embarrass myself in front of the whole town because you think it's cute." I turned and walked out of her office and walked home. Nothing was ever mentioned of it again.

Prepare for such moments to be part and parcel of your life with a Sagittarian child. Of course, I could have done well with a conversation about, you know, decorum or something like that. But I disagreed with both the plan and the principle behind it, and I would not be sold on it. If you want a Sagittarian child to go along with a plan, you need to be ready to sell them on the plan itself, and you need to have a good *reason* for the plan. Remember that the Sagittarian's favorite question is "why?"

If you can't answer that question to their satisfaction, they'll be sure to let you know.

BETWEEN THE FIRST AND SECOND JUPITER RETURNS
Twelve to Twenty-Four Years Old

The Jupiter return occurs around the time that many of the world's religious traditions begin to mark a child's transition into adulthood. In Judaism this is marked with B'nai Mitzvot; in many streams of Christianity this takes the form of Confirmation. Initiations take other forms throughout the world, and the Jupiter return marks this time for children across the globe, whether they take part in a formal initiation or not. That said, the teenage experience in the West suffers from a dearth of initiatory experiences. As more and more families move away from formalized religious traditions that have coming-of-age rituals programmed into their communal structure, teens, and especially wanderlust-addled Sagittarian teens, look to other forms of communal validation of their growing wisdom, strength, and power.

Because of Jupiter's rulership of the Sagittarian soul, marking this initiatory passage formally and honoring the wisdom of your Sagittarian child are particularly important for their development. Because the Sagittarian child has a direct line to the wisdom of Jupiter, it becomes vital that this principle has an avenue of expression, giving the child ample opportunity to share their wisdom and far-sighted leadership skills with their peers and, by turn, ever-larger communities of adults who are invested in their best intentions.

This might take the form of a leadership role within a school or extracurricular setting. It may look like having opportunities to speak publicly in front of an audience on a topic that is of great import. It may also take the form of achievement within organized athletic competitions (a great fit for the natural Sagittarian athleticism). These avenues serve as additional stakes to help train and focus the growth of the upward- and outward-spiraling Sagittarian spirit.

> **Yes, it's vital for the Sagittarian teen to learn how to honor their agreements and responsibilities.**

To put it another way, the Sagittarian child knows that they have wisdom to share and they will find places to share it, whether their parents "approve" of it or not. A Sagittarian child whose family environment is deeply restrictive will retreat into the inner realms of their imagination and allow their voice to come to its fullness there, or their need for the validation of their wisdom and self-expression might turn into outright rebellion as their desire for an unfiltered experience of all that life has to offer is suppressed.

They will try, they will fail, they will get back up again and try again. They will test any limits set before them simply to see how far they can go before sailing off the cliff. Sagittarian teens need a curfew, yes, but they also need wiggle room. They need to be allowed to let their burgeoning sexualities blossom as they approach adulthood and the second Jupiter return, but it's crucial to teach them the principles of consent and safer sex.

During the teen years, the need to develop the art of quitting well becomes even more crucial for the Sagittarian child as competing priorities begin to occupy more and more of their time. Homework, extracurriculars, parttime jobs, and high school drama turn from snowball to avalanche at an alarming pace, and the Sagittarian teen will need an exit route at some point. Parents and adult mentors of Sagittarian teens can aid in this process by allowing them the flexibility to bail when it becomes clear that following through on every commitment they've undertaken will spread them too thin.

Yes, it's vital for the Sagittarian teen to learn how to honor their agreements and responsibilities. Remember the tomato stakes: the places where the Sagittarian teen is exercising leadership and cultivating further wisdom are the areas where their energies are best invested. But all the same, knowing adults understand that there is no shame in retreating from a battle that can't be won.

The last thing that the Sagittarius adolescent must do, and *will* do if not shamed for it, is to maintain their connection to the subtle and deep magic of experience that initially drew their hearts into wide-eyed wonder. Whatever their interests are at this moment or have been in the past, they need the freedom to continue to pursue them, and at the same time, they will do well with some guardrails to keep them from flying off the freeway as they pursue them at full tilt.

SAGITTARIUS AS AN ADULT

THE TRANSITION TO adulthood is a long road for Sagittarians. Children of Jupiter spend so much time as youth with an uncanny level of insight and wisdom locked down in restlessly scattered packaging. They may spend years always wanting to know, be, do, and see more of the world than their experiences can provide for them—even more of a challenge if the Sagittarian child is part of a family without access to the financial means to slake their child's thirst for new experiences. In Western culture, the legal transition into adulthood begins at eighteen, but unless circumstance has forced a child to mature early, eighteen-year-olds are hardly ready to have the full breadth of adulthood laid on their shoulders, and Sagittarius is no exception.

Even the most well-traveled Sagittarian adolescents will take the newfound freedom that comes with being of majority age and rocket off into space as though they're making up for lost time. The first few years of adulthood between eighteen and twenty-four become a limitless playground that can set the Sagittarian up for success: these years are prime time for undergraduate education, discerning a career path, and discovering the ways in which one is uniquely gifted to make an impact on one's world. That said, there's always the chance that they, like Icarus, will fly too high and wind up crashing back down to earth, discovering the hard way that they're not as ready as they think they are to handle life in its unfiltered reality.

This peculiar challenge emerges from the confluence of Jupiter's spiraling updrafts of idealism and prodigality, the newfound freedom of being of majority age, and the not-insignificant hobble of one's brain not being fully formed until twenty-five years of age. Common wisdom tells us that if you give a Ferrari to a teenager, you shouldn't be surprised when you see it in a ditch later that day. In like fashion, if you give a Sagittarian adolescent unlimited rein and resources, don't be surprised when they wind up back on your doorstep without two dimes to rub together as they tell you exactly how they lost all the money. Studied, careful, and responsible decision making doesn't happen until the transition into adulthood has occurred in earnest.

Sagittarian adolescents shouldn't be expected to socket themselves into a predictable career, or even standard educational experiences during this time of their life. Remember that the patterns that have begun in childhood haven't gone away at all; they're simply unfolding in the body and actions of a larger human being who can now vote and open a bank account. The unfettered freedom to travel, explore, and experiment in new ways is something to which the Sagittarian adolescent should pay close attention, especially during the early twenties, because there is a solid chance that the variety of opportunities for study abroad programs, elective courses, and even the rich possibilities of a gap year won't be as feasible when the cool shock of adult responsibilities set in later in life.

Maintaining the freedom to expand one's horizons with new experiences will come to depend on the Sagittarian's ability to attend to their own needs and to not take what they have for granted. Jupiter allows tomorrow's troubles to worry about themselves, so while it's unnatural for the Sagittarian adolescent to spend too much time fretting over how they'll continue to bankroll an all-you-can-eat buffet of life experience, they'll do well to figure out the mechanics of a budget and set limits for themselves that they choose. There's no sense in trying to impose arbitrary limits, and sometimes allowing the Sagittarian adolescent to mess up provides them with a lesson from Experience, the most venerable of teachers in a Sagittarian's world.

Once the second Jupiter return comes around at the age of twenty-four, however, the transition to adulthood has begun in earnest. Biologically, of course, an adolescent's brain is fully formed by twenty-five, and they now can use the full breadth of mature cognitive capabilities. This is true for everyone, not just for Sagittarius. The point to keep in mind here, however, is that, as children of Jupiter, Sagittarians are especially keyed into the Jupiter return cycle.

This second return, which marks the transition to astrological adulthood for all people, serves as an opportunity for Sagittarians to reconnect with their essential purpose and understanding in life. At this juncture, they are being asked by their ruling planet to draw together all of the experiential learning of the last twelve years into a cohesive narrative that describes *why* they have come to be who they are, and *how* it is that they will share the wisdom that they have gained with the broader world, either as a benevolent gift (if Jupiter is in Sagittarius, Pisces, or Cancer) or as a life-saving balm (if Jupiter is in Gemini, Virgo, or Capricorn)—or somewhere in between. The question that Sagittarian adults are introduced to at this point, and that shapes their life to come, is this: "What is the grander story in which I am playing a part?"

Imagine the blacksmith hammering away at a new tool or weapon in his forge. If the Sagittarian is like the glowing steel itself, each strike of the hammer that shapes the metal is like another experience, episode, conversation, or passing vision that brings the Sagittarian into closer awareness of the way that their role as a sage and adventurer in the world is intended to function. The artisan masterfully hammers us Sagittarians into shape as exemplars and then plunges us into cold water, quenching us, so that we hold our shape and may be further honed into excellence. The Jupiter return *quenches* us. It solidifies the lessons that we have gained over the past twelve years and turns them into something that can be finely honed and used in generous service to the world. In so doing, it draws a golden thread of meaning around these lessons and helps the Sagittarian connect more deeply to the basic question that drives them: "Who am I supposed to become?"

However, the adult Sagittarian might encounter another challenge at the second Jupiter return: what happens if the narratives that we've been handed about the way that the world works no longer square with the narratives that we've discovered and learned to tell for ourselves? Sagittarian wisdom is not the kind of wisdom that accepts anything blindly or blithely on faith simply because "that's the way it is." The transition into adulthood for Sagittarians often coincides with a crisis of deconstruction, where the belief structures that had contained and given shape to experience throughout the teen and adolescent years are suddenly shown to be woefully inadequate for containing the reality of all of life's infinite complexities. The old stories don't *work* anymore. They're less true than they used to be. And so, the Sagittarian, facing this crisis, does what Sagittarians do: they strap on their boots, grab their walking stick, and head out in search of deeper truths.

There is a shift in terrain that each Sagittarian will encounter sometime before they turn thirty—the closer you were born to the winter solstice, the earlier it happens in your life.[8] As this landscape changes, your Sagittarian

SAGITTARIUS: TENDERS OF THE FLAME

A First Nations friend of mine recently introduced me to the Hopi people's way of making decisions.[9] According to him, when it comes time to make a decision that impacts the entire community, the eldest man and woman in the tribe sit in the middle of a circle of leaders, tradespeople, elders, and influencers as different courses of action are discussed. Each person has an opportunity to share their insight into ways to handle any given situation, representing their own interests and the interests of their intimates.

But the eldest man and woman, seated in the middle of the circle, have but one job: what will the impact of this decision be on the children, those too young to have a voice among the adults, those who have yet to burst into existence? How will the community's action leave the world better for them? These two revered elders are called the "tenders of the children's flame."

If these two, eldest and world-wizened, discern in their wisdom and far-reaching vision that the choices of the community under discussion will create problems for their children, grandchildren, and generations not yet imagined, that action is vetoed. Their job is to hold vision for the future that will be, a vision that requires sight beyond the present, faith beyond the everyday, and fidelity to the entire community.

The ultimate calling of the Sagittarian adult is to be a tender of the children's flame.

energy shines through a Capricorn-flavored Instagram filter, joining your expansive vision to a desire for material security and achievement that encourages you to begin setting your *own* boundaries and limits.

By the time diligent Saturn returns to his natal position around your twenty-ninth birthday, you'll have ample opportunity to unite a sky's-worth of dreams and visions to conscious, practical efforts that begin to bring those dreams into reality. At the end of the day, the adult Sagittarian must learn that, as nice as dreams are, they linger and languish in the realm of the imagination until put into action in the physical world. You'll come to realize that the higher perspective and deeper truths that pull you forward into life do, to your chagrin, require sacrifice to attain.

As Sagittarians mature, their ground-floor question of "who am I supposed to become?" changes course. Even though in their younger years, Sagittarians often think that there's supposed to be an endgame, maturity foists new challenges on them that cause them to recognize that there's not an endgame at all. The journey itself *is* the endgame. If a Sagittarian doesn't learn this at the second Jupiter return, each subsequent Jupiter return after that—every twelve years—will conspire with circumstance to offer them a chance to reassess their relationship with that basic question of living. Better to learn it the first time around than to be forced into it repeatedly.

In working with this question, the Sagittarian adult can take their wildly galloping life by the mane and nudge it, ever so slightly, into alignment with the deeper magic of living. Heartbreaks, defeats, and loss will all come at some point in life. Accept this now. Lay aside your escape plans and understand this: maturity requires that you allow your search to carry you through deathly valleys, for there is wisdom to be gained there, too. The Sagittarian who has learned how to manage their search for *becoming* will be able to meet all such tragedies as revered sages.

As much as a Sagittarian's hope-addled vision can be a boon for those who need a vision of a better future to hold their course steady, this Jovian optimism can quickly turn into the blinders of privilege if the Sagittarian refuses to acknowledge the lessons that only such forces as great love and great suffering can share. Sometimes, life in this world sucks and there's nothing we can do about it. As much as the Sagittarian would like to try, there are moments that simply can't be avoided. They must turn and face their fear.

And yet, pain does not mean the end. The Sagittarian who humbly welcomes this truth can transmute pain into meaning for themselves and for multitudes. With each revolution of your ruling planet Jupiter, the heavens invite you to step even further into maturity, wisdom, and grace. Maturity and wisdom do not, however, mean that you are meant to forget the magic of the possible, nor are you meant to stifle the flames of adventure.

The people who look to you for well-intended insight throughout your life do not do so because they view you as a "responsible adult." Rid yourself of the need to embody any such trope; that's not your calling. Your responsibility is to the *deep meaning* with which your limitless sight lines can imbue all facets of life. Each experience, each encounter, each triumph, and each tragedy serve as more raw material for the grand work of the story with which you've been entrusted.

SAGITTARIUS IN LOVE

CHILDREN OF THE '90s likely remember the 1992 Disney film *Aladdin*. Midway through the second act, the eponymous hero, a child of the streets, has enlisted the supernatural aid of a genie to fashion himself into a globetrotting prince to win the affections of the sultan's daughter. Under the light of a full moon, Aladdin beckons Princess Jasmine onto a magic carpet, on which they sail through the skies of the Near East, taking in the feast of sights while Aladdin croons, "I can show you the world!" They share a quiet kiss before the scene ends; all seems to be well. Sagittarian Aladdin has become, in his estimation, the person he needed to be to win Jasmine's affection.

But as successful as this initial encounter is, Jasmine eventually sees through Aladdin's performance, which falls apart with the slightest scrutinizing nudge. Jasmine has spent her entire life being subjected to the advances of noble suitors from the world over, and, as the rest of the film unfolds, we see that she can only be won over after Aladdin accepts his own limitations and is able to show up to the relationship as himself. Such is the challenge of the Sagittarian in romance: they would offer everything to change themselves into the imagined person who can win the affections of their intended. Their hearts are set on the ideal of love and so they launch into Jovian rhapsody, not realizing that their partners often want nothing more—and nothing less—than for them to be as they are in this moment, all bravado and extravagance laid aside.

In love, Sagittarians ask themselves a variation on their never-ending question, "Who am I becoming?" Just as Aladdin makes the ill-informed assumption that he must become someone else to win the affections of Jasmine, the lovestruck Sagittarian asks him- or herself, "Who must I become to win you?" Once love has pulled them into its snare, this question entrances them, and they begin to put all their Jovian energies into becoming more expansive, generous, and optimistic than perhaps they ever have before. No adventure is quite like the journey deep into the heart of one's beloved, and the Sagittarian wants to amplify each indolent moment as they stride hand in hand with their lover into the imagined forms that their relationship *could* take. If they can believe it, they can achieve it, in their minds.

A Sagittarian wants to *win* the hearts of their beloved, but it's not a conquering or domineering sort of victory. Rather, the ultimate Sagittarian prize is the validation of their perspective, wisdom, and experience from the person who has captured their attention. They want to be able to know and to trust that the one they love values what they have to offer, and that this person appreciates the fruit of the Sagittarian's life work of *becoming*. When their beloved acknowledges that their Sagittarian lover's efforts to become lovable have had their intended effect, it's as though they are festooning their lover's crown with a wreath of laurels.

Once the Sagittarian has someone in their sights, the person on the other end of their affections will know it. A Sagittarian in love benefits from all their mutable flexibility and Jovian uplift to speed them into learning about their beloved's interests to the point of obsession. They think nothing of getting a tattoo to impress a potential suitor (I may or may not have done this myself). Ready to step into the next adventure? Sagittarians take next steps hastily in a series of constantly escalating dares. Once they know what they want, nothing will prevent them from arranging their experiences in such a way to make it happen. Sagittarians are the type who date for three months and then elope. Everything is up for reevaluation as they seek to adapt their way of being in the world to suit the needs of the person they love, and the more adventure, the better.

The prize, for the Sagittarian, is not their beloved themselves but the *experience* of their beloved. The more this experience maps with their lovesick reveries, the better. In their imagination they have concocted an idealized version of a romantic partnership, one in which they are able to take their beloved on a magic carpet ride, showing them everything that they have learned and experienced, inviting their partner into an ever-grander adventure through their life. Once their beloved consents to love them, they ask, "Who shall we become together?"

Even if the Sagittarian and their beloved arrive at this coveted point, there's a small difficulty: due to the Sagittarian's need for freedom and, shall we say, continued stimulation, they've often got one foot pointed toward the door—sometimes without realizing it. The second the relationship becomes stagnant, they'll start to get antsy. "Why aren't we growing?" they'll ask themselves in moments of quiet doubt. "What happened to the fire we once had? Where did the adventure go?" Without realizing it, they'll have taken that initial step out of the relationship because they no longer have anyone to *become*. Jove forbid that their beloved tries to lock them down in a predictable routine, or worse, that their partner want them to *settle down*. Sagittarians settle down when they're dead—or more accurately, settling down might kill them.

That said, *all* relationships go through seasons of stagnation. They *all* go through the ebb and flow of passion's tide; even the most exciting, adventurous partnerships will have moments when a pair of knit-together souls enters the stable adult routine of wake, work, dinner, Netflix, sleep, repeat. *And that is okay.* Any sign can form commitments. Any sign can be *stable*. But for Sagittarians, the challenge is to keep their eternal quest for the truth of who they are becoming on the table. What quenches a Sagittarian's flame in a relationship is any pattern that suggests that "this is all you'll ever be." For a Sagittarian is made to believe that to be in a relationship is to kill an essential part of themselves.

For a Sagittarian to continue steadily in love once they have established a partnership with their beloved requires continued attention to the fires of their search for truth. It's essential that they have a shared, deep interest with their partner, preferably one that gets deeper over time. They need something into which they can grow together with their beloved. This shared interest serves as life-giving warmth that allows the living container of their relationship to grow, stretch, and change as the individual occupants do so as well.

For some couples, this looks like a shared commitment to an academic discipline; for others, a shared artistic endeavor or recreational practice. For my beloved and me, this is our shared love of music and personality theory. Elsewhere you might see the stereotypical Sagittarius "adventure couple" as a great example: jet setting all over the world to take in the sights, sounds, smells, and sensations of distant lands and legends. The more that the Sagittarian in a relationship can experience all that life has to offer with their partner, the stronger their ties to that beloved person will become.

The challenge of the Sagittarian in love is to show up for the here and now, which isn't as hard as it would initially seem. It simply requires that the Sagittarian develop a modicum of discipline. What is interesting for Sagittarians, however, is that, in their natal charts, their beloved is usually signified by the planet Mercury, the ruler of the Sagittarian's seventh house of relationships. This is true regardless of whichever sign the Sagittarian's lover represents; we're talking about the Sagittarian's perspective here.

Mercury's character is the opposite of the Sagittarian's planetary patron, Jupiter: where Jupiter is tremendous, expansive, generous, trusting, and laissez-faire in his approach to life, Mercury is small, fleet of foot, exacting, precise, and scrutinizing. Mercury *is* the here and now, the day-to-day details, the still, small voice that insistently begs, "What? Who? When? Where? How?" in response to Jupiter's resonant "Why?" If a Sagittarian is not used to being held accountable, their lover will gladly fill that role for them. Where Jupiter trusts, Mercury frets. Where Jupiter blithely assumes details will work themselves out, Mercury dives in and *makes* the details work out. Crucially, while the Sagittarian partner believes that they must become something that they're not to win the affections of their beloved, their partner often sees straight through this posturing. Their loving, exacting gaze sees the Sagittarian exactly as they are, in this moment, right here, and loves them for it. For the Sagittarian to recognize this gift can be liberating in ways they had never imagined.

It's a power pairing when it's working well. Jupiter dreams, Mercury schemes, and together their forces can bring dreams out of the realm of the imagination into the here and now, both within their day-to-day life together and in the thrust of the grand narrative that the Sagittarian will lead them on into the future. The Sagittarian is the *ideas* person, their partner the *details* person. Every Sagittarian who accepts the grounding influence of their partner and capitalizes on it can find both their relationship and their adventuresome endeavors sailing to new heights, as though they're working alongside a master navigator.

But if the relational dynamic is not healthy, or if a relationship is a fundamental mismatch, the Sagittarian will feel needlessly scrutinized and nitpicked into submission. Such is a recipe for heartbreak. Their partner's Mercurial navigation assistance morphs into tethers and leashes to try to keep the Sagittarian in one place. Often this is the case with especially scattered or prodigal Sagittarians, or Sagittarians whose itch for adventure and excitement isn't being scratched within the context of their established partnership.

When this happens, the Sagittarian's generosity can express itself sideways. Their habit of lavishing attention and affection in the direction of everyone they meet can quickly cause their Mercurial partner to feel insecure. Often this isn't without good reason, as a Sagittarian may sometimes find that a little bad behavior outside the consensual bounds of their relationship reignites their desire for adventure. Of course, this will make the Mercury partner double down on their insecurity. A badly-behaved Sagittarian proves them right. When the Mercury partner feels insecure, they turn their shifting wiles toward examining their Sagittarian lover from all possible angles, scrutinizing them to death, and ensuring that every word and every promise is notarized and filed in triplicate.

If a Sagittarian is not used to being shown receipts for their actions, their partner will often be happy to point out exactly when and where the Sagittarian did something out of line, made a promise they neglected to keep, or failed to show up when they were needed. A healthy Sagittarius will have already learned to accept the critique and to course correct while maintaining a reasonable hold on the truth of the situation.

When tempers run hot, the Sagittarian has Jupiter's natural forbearance helping them to keep a clear head. If they can stay present to the conflict and allow the Mercurial process of examining intentions and details to play out as intended, the Sagittarian will easily find themselves not only in a position to forgive and move onward in partnership, but also to welcome conflict as an opportunity to expand their perspective on themselves and on their relationship. Conflict in love, for the healthy Sagittarian, becomes one more field of new experience. That said, the immature Sagittarian can too easily slide into the position of self-effacing martyr, tearing their own hearts out for having failed their beloved. That, or they may simply pack their bag and hit the road without a second thought. Ghosting your spouse isn't an option.

Well, it *is*, but I recommend against it.

For a Sagittarian to cultivate lasting love they must acknowledge that their natural posture is to have one foot out the door. This is true no matter how sincerely devoted the Sagittarian is to their beloved; there's always a nuclear option. Simply to acknowledge that fact reduces its power in the relationship, and crucially, it invites the Sagittarian's partner into considering the ways in which they must show up for the adventure, too, just as much as the Sagittarian must show up for the workaday world of relationships. If the Sagittarian and their partner consciously work against stagnation and allow the shape of their relationship to be vibrant and flexible, there's no stopping the magic carpet ride.

SAGITTARIUS AT WORK

A **BAKED-IN NEED FOR** flexibility, expansion, and rampant idealism isn't normally the character trait that leads to steady, forty-year careers tethered to a series of ever-larger cubicles. Not only that, but a Sagittarian's idealism makes them ever-ready to speak truth to power, to critique the systems that no longer serve a company's mission, and to break open painted-shut windows to let in fresh, revivifying air. A Sagittarian can't be fenced in. It's not natural to expect a Sagittarian to be able to rise to the upper echelon of corporate status through dutiful obedience to their superiors, keeping their head down, and laboring away in silence. To wit, Sagittarians aren't "company men."

Except, of course, when they *are*.

This happens most often when the company loses its way. Take, for example, two twentieth-century popes of the Roman Catholic Church: Pope St. John XXIII and Pope Francis. John XXIII famously convened the Second Vatican Council and initiated a series of reforms that the Roman Catholic Church is still figuring out how to handle, most notably the move to the celebration of the Mass in vernacular language and a renewed dialogue between Catholics and other faith traditions. To paraphrase his rationale for convening Vatican II, John XXIII reported that it was time to "throw open the windows of the Church so that we can see out and the people can see in." Traditionalists continue to balk at the impact of his call for reform to this day; Pope Francis has made him a saint of the Church.

Francis himself, meanwhile, has become the icon of a left-leaning Catholicism that privileges the marginalized and prioritizes the ethical teaching of Catholicism, rather than focusing on the maintenance of doctrinal purity and preservation of the institution's status quo. We'd expect nothing less from the first pope to take "Francis" as his regnal name: Francis of Assisi, of course, was one of the great reformers of the Church, himself poor and a champion *of* the poor. Both men transgressed boundaries, ruffled feathers, and ignited no small amount of consternation among their more conservative contemporaries. (Francis of Assisi's birthdate is unknown, but it's highly likely that he was either a Sun Sagittarius or a Capricorn, being born either late in 1181 or early 1182 CE.)

Both Pope St. John XXIII and Pope Francis have their sun in Sagittarius, and both became the leader and figurehead of one of the world's major religions. One does not get to be the pope by refusing to play the company game; one becomes the pope by keeping one's aim squarely fixed on the field beyond the target. Their concern has demonstrably been less with the maintenance of any kind of institutional status quo. Of course, both men had to "play the game" to a certain extent to become *papabile*. Nevertheless, their commitment to the putative ideals on which the Catholic Church was founded—justice, mercy, grace—allowed them to temper a Sagittarian need to hop fences and burn bridges under the guise of "saying it like it is." This, in turn, allowed them to enter into positions of power where their commitment to the vision of a world made whole in justice, mercy, and grace could have the most impact.

The Sagittarian's career is ruled by Mercury, specifically through Mercury's earthy domain of Virgo. This is because Virgo is the tenth sign counting forward from Sagittarius; note that this is *especially* true for people with Sagittarius Rising. Career, as in "what you do for a paycheck," is but one facet of this domain of life, but we'll start there at the very least.

Mercury's processes of data collection and application shine most brightly in Virgo, where Mercury channels all the data that he's cataloged through experiment and experience into real-world applications. These applications, in turn, improve physical circumstances for those on the receiving end. Consider Mercury's archetypes: the magician, the alchemist, the trickster. Now, consider what it might mean for such a character to have at its disposal all the wisdom, vision, foresight, and generosity of Jupiter bankrolling their attempts to apply all the world's knowledge to improving it. The Sagittarian at work is the magician who knows what they're conjuring, the alchemist who knows exactly how to dissolve and reconstitute their materials into life-giving elixirs. More importantly, the integrated Sagittarian is the magus who knows exactly what must, and must *not*, be done.

I'm reminded of the wizard Gandalf's line to his friend Frodo near the beginning of *The Fellowship of the Ring:* "A wizard is never late, nor is he early; he arrives precisely when he means to." The Sagittarian at work brings a precision and focus to institutional vision from which their peers, subordinates, and superiors all benefit. That focus is, of course, centered on the mission; for the Sagittarian, the most satisfying work is a means to an end, and that end is improving the world in accordance with the hope-addled vision that possesses them. If the mission of the company is in alignment with the Sagittarian's sense of idealistic purpose, then they will happily become a "company person."

SAGITTARIUS AS A SUBORDINATE

The Sagittarian privileges their ideal over any human authority. Should we be surprised? To ask a Sagittarian to be blindly obedient to their boss's say-so is like asking water to flow upstream. Sure, you can get water to move up a hill, but the machinery and energy it requires often makes it not worth the effort. Crucial to remember here is that, for the Sagittarian, work is a *means* to an end. It's never going to be their ultimate priority except in the rare cases where a Sagittarian's goal of becoming lines up with the priorities of their employers.

Take, for example, a Sagittarian social worker who went hungry often as a child and who has taken it upon themselves to improve experiences for kids in the same situation. Say this person works for an agency that has as its vision the end of food insecurity for children. All other factors being equal, that Sagittarian will probably see their work for that agency as a means to make manifest their inborn sense of purpose. They'll give it their all, readily contributing as much time and intention as they can muster to the goal.

On the other hand, take that same Sagittarian social worker and place them in a role where they're determining eligibility for assistance services, and we've got another story. If that same Sagittarian social worker is asked, instead of being a Jupiterian provider, to be a Saturnine gatekeeper, they'll fizzle and balk. In this sort of situation, where purpose and profession are misaligned, the Sagittarian might be tempted to self-sabotage. They'll get it in their head that they're not meant to work in a given industry at all, they'll have one foot out the door, and they'll readily burn bridges in order to give themselves an excuse to leave it all behind.

Where the Sagittarian subordinate might run into trouble in their professional development is the fact that a Sagittarian is no respecter of persons. Simply because their boss has organizational authority over them does not mean that the Sagittarian's boss has earned their respect. They will be the first to tell their supervisor that their plans are stupid. I'm reminded of the time as an impetuous twenty-one-year-old that I told my boss, "I don't respect people who aren't respectable." (I didn't last very long in that job.)

Beyond workplace politicking, the Sagittarian subordinate will have no trouble telling their superiors that the way they have been asked to accomplish a task doesn't make sense. Balking at procedure and norms is simply the Sagittarian way, and the best superiors will take a beat to explain to their Sagittarian employees the precise reason as to why a given procedure exists or why a task is intended to be accomplished in the way it is.

The Sagittarian is best as a subordinate when their superiors make the expected result abundantly clear but give their reports full freedom to carry out their tasks in whichever way they see fit. Paint a target on the wall and let the Sagittarian figure out how to hit it; easy enough. If the Sagittarian has latitude to expand, bend, and become within the confines of the job description, they'll be able to cultivate loyalty (so long as their personal purpose and the company's are in alignment). If not, look out. Procrastination, daydreaming, and lagging performance are obvious tells that there's a mismatch between the Sagittarian and their employer's priorities.

SAGITTARIUS AS A SUPERIOR

The benefit of not being a respecter of persons for the Sagittarius is that they do not allow their title to go to their heads when they enter senior leadership at work. They'll value the input of their subordinates; they're apt to be generous, forgiving, and allow their team plenty of space for their individual processes and working styles. So long as the team hits the target, they'll be happy.

Moreover, Sagittarians readily assume a natural leadership posture of joining with their teams to explore uncharted territory. They'll get right in the thick of the daily work with their direct reports, and they'll have skin in the game. No other sign's style is so ready to give their team this degree of freedom (except, perhaps, Pisces). Nor is any other sign's style so ready to serve as a motivator and inspirer to their subordinates. They're ultimately concerned with who each of their employees is becoming.

Sagittarians in leadership would do well to learn some basic project management practices, particularly Agile, a model used in the software world. This practice can be applied to any industry, but the essential principle at work is the idea that the desired result of a team's work can be a moving target. (Sagittarians love moving targets.) Such an approach imports a degree of flexibility and expansion into the work that Sagittarians will find refreshing, even exhilarating. This allows for the Sagittarian leader's sense of personal purpose and their team's vision to operate in a synchronistic dance.

Every boss has growing edges, however, and Sagittarian bosses are no different. The leadership posture of a Sagittarian is often so forward-looking and ideal-driven that they may say to their reports, either aloud or implicitly, "Come with me or get left behind." It might be difficult for the Sagittarian leader to focus on celebrating their team's accomplishments here and now. They're so driven to continue their upward journey that they may inadvertently damage their employees' morale by failing to recognize how far they've come. It's almost as though the Sagittarians in leadership have committed themselves to a series of escalating dares: constantly one-upping their own performances to drive them further toward their idealized goals.

It's crucial for the Sagittarian superior to recognize that not everyone under their command works or even thinks the same way that they do about their team's vision or the ways in which it can be accomplished. It's even more crucial for the Sagittarian superior to recognize when their subordinates require clear direction and firm guidelines for performance. That said, the Sagittarian is also at risk of unintentionally withering their reports with frank feedback. Involving subordinates in problem solving and empowering them to participate in rectifying performance concerns is one of the most crucial gifts a Sagittarian in leadership can offer their people.

The Sagittarian boss will always be willing to step in and offer what they can to employees when they're struggling, but they must recognize that not every person works as well within the fuzzy field of possibility in which a Sagittarian exists. Their peculiar leadership finesse comes from their ability to impart to their employees the experiential wisdom they need in order to navigate daily challenges *on their own*.

CHOOSING A CAREER PATH

Remember: the Sagittarian's career unfolds best when it is in alignment with their own sense of "who am I becoming?" Of all the signs, it is the most difficult to separate vocation and profession for the Sagittarian, because of their need to aim their entire life toward an expanded experience of reality.

I don't like saying things like, "Sagittarians make good scholars, clergy, or travel agents." Any sign can do any of those. When selecting a career direction, the Sagittarian needs to hold in mind their answer to these questions: "What is my ultimate concern in life? What occupies my daydreams, my hobbies, my mental bandwidth?" If the Sagittarian can answer those questions honestly, then it follows that they'd do well to orient their career decisions in that direction. For instance, if a Sagittarian's answer is "understanding how the world works," then they could make a fabulous scientist or scholar.

Meanwhile if their answer is, "alleviating people's suffering," then they could, of course, go in the direction of social worker, medical professional, or philanthropic investor, just to name a few. Whatever the case, the benefit of being a Sagittarian is having a wealth of lived experience and wisdom out of which they can draw; indeed, some Sagittarians might even consider an entrepreneurial career where they are sharing their collected wisdom with the world in any number of ways.

Remember that the Sagittarian at work is the wizened alchemist, set on changing the world by applying their collected experience to the realities that surround them. To change the world, they will need to seek work that changes them. If they're able to see the way in which their work fits into a grander narrative of the world's becoming that is in accordance with their vision, they'll become an unstoppable force.

CONCLUSION

WHERE WILL YOU GO NOW?

Astrology is a tremendous gift, but at times it can feel like attempting to assemble IKEA furniture without instructions. If this has been your first tentative adventure into the wild and wooly world of astrology, I congratulate you on taking it. The journey we've been on in this chapter is the first step of an endless apprenticeship. There are any number of directions in which you can go now, but I have no doubts that your Sagittarian desire for adventure will carry you far in whichever direction you feel right for you.

If you've been kicking around the idea of astrology for some time and dabbling with different approaches to understanding yourself in the world, I'll offer this suggestion: go whole hog. Allow your Sagittarian interest engine to turn over and set you buzzing toward something you don't know about. Astrology invites us into thinking about time in cycles and patterns that can't be contained to the flavor of a single day.

> **Our world needs Sagittarians, just as it needs the gifts and graces of each of the other signs.**

These cycles span decades, centuries, even millennia. And the Sagittarian who has learned to think of time in such scale is a Sagittarian whose perspective will be uniquely valuable to the work of healing the world.

In either case, I highly, *highly* recommend that you consult a professional astrologer to get deeper insight into the way that the world of your chart works. The insight you will get from a specific, detailed look at your unique interior landscape will outmatch anything you can gather from reading a book about your sign.

My hope is that this short chapter has served as a foretaste of the adventure that can unfold before you as you encounter the Sagittarian story that plays itself out in your life. Our world needs Sagittarians, just as it needs the gifts and graces of each of the other signs. *Your* gifts and graces, dear Sagittarius, are critical, however: you offer us the ability to see into the realm of the unbounded future. You have the ability not only to imagine the world as it *could* be, but you also have the energy, drive, and infectious *joie de vivre* to help us get there without losing our hope.

Your spirit of optimism, enervation, adventure, and expansion can carry us to heights we never thought possible. What we need from you is for you to maintain your holy discontent with the boxes in which society would trap you. We need your fire, your passion, your joy. Indeed, by helping us to keep our sights fixed on the distant goals that lie beyond the horizon, you can lead us into the undiscovered realities of hope.

NOTES

1. Cole Porter, "Don't Fence Me In," Warner/Chappell, Inc. 1934.
2. I am indebted to astrologer Austin Coppock for bringing this powerful image to my attention.
3. See Demetra George, *Astrology and the Authentic Self* (Lake Worth, Ibis, 2008), p. 100ff.
4. Demetra George, *Ancient Astrology in Theory and Practice, vol. 1* (Auckland, Rubedo, 2019), 163–164.
5. I am indebted to astrologer Kelly Surtees for the "gift to share/ problem to solve" language to describe these placements, which she introduced in a presentation at the State-of-the-Art Astrology Conference in Buffalo, NY, in October 2018.
6. See Ovid, *Metamorphoses*, XI.85 and following.
7. I would cite the book, if I remembered what its title was. Unfortunately, the book was a casualty of moving house several years ago, and I've never been able to find another copy.
8. This is the result of a gradual development of the natal chart known as "secondary progression," in which the movements of the planets for each day after birth are stretched out to represent symbolically one year of life. For more information, consult a professional astrologer, or see episode 144 of *The Astrology Podcast:* http://theastrologypodcast.com/2018/02/22/secondary-progressions/.
9. This was shared with me in a personal conversation. I cannot vouch for its factual accuracy, but the image remains powerful.

DEC. 22–JAN. 19

text by Kelsey Wilpone

element — EARTH

symbol — THE SEA GOAT

modality — CARDINAL

house — TENTH

ruler — SATURN

СЪЫВСОЫ

INTRODUCTION

ASTROLOGY IS A symbol-based language of cycles and time. It is the study of how celestial bodies, such as planets and asteroids, and their motion through the twelve signs of the zodiac influence life on planet Earth. Dating back thousands of years, astrology spans many different cultures and geographic regions. Nearly every human culture has, at one time, looked up and told stories about what they saw in the night sky above them. Western astrology as we know it now is an amalgamation of 2,400 years of symbolic language that speaks of gods and goddesses, mythical creatures, and archetypical wisdom.

The language of astrology can be interpreted differently, depending on cultural values, since mores affect how we choose to apply astrological insights. We can look at agriculture (based in the northern hemisphere) through the lens of astrology to see cycles of light and plant life. We can look at traditional medical practices through the lens of astrology to better understand how the planets function in the human body in health and also at the onset of disease. Using astrology, we can weave our human stories to understand change over time, for one individual or for an entire generation. We can look at the current astrological weather and how it impacts life on planet Earth. We can use astrology in conjunction with spirituality and religious philosophy to peer deep into our inner knowing and cycles of personal unfolding, yet the atheist and agnostic may also study astrology for a practical understanding of ancient archetypical language. There should be no conversation about whether or not astrology "exists": it certainly does exist—as a tool of human creation that either works for you or doesn't.

As is true for many languages, the interpretation of astrology has been influenced by colonialism and oppression. Western astrology exists today primarily because of Roman conquests influencing common language in what are now parts of Europe, Asia, Africa, and the Middle East. Many ancient texts were destroyed as Roman and British colonizers used brute force to erase the indigenous cultures of their rivals. Astrology is a language developed by

> **We can use astrology in conjunction with spirituality and religious philosophy to peer deep into our inner knowing and cycles of personal unfolding.**

and for the ruling class, and was available only by consulting skilled astrologers. It is only in recent years that laypeople have had access to software that will instantly calculate their own natal or birth chart, providing a map of where the planets were at the time of birth. Now more than ever, people can view their natal charts, which means that taking time and care to translate accurately is important. Unskilled translation of astrology means that unfortunately the internet is rife with astrology blogs and memes that reinforce narrowly defined and sometimes racist or sexist stereotypes that say less about astrology and more about the culture we live in.

Memes are fun, but usually present simple, boring, rigid interpretations of a deeply complex language. Astrology is meant to be multifaceted and ever changing, so it is especially important to know who is behind the translation.

MYTHOLOGY:
The Birth of Capricorn

Capricorn is one of the oldest myths, dating back to ancient Babylonian culture as the deity Ea, who was described as the "antelope of the sea." Ea is related to Enki in Sumerian mythology, the trickster god of fresh water, culture, fertility, wisdom, healing, creation, and art. Enki was one of the three major deities in Mesopotamian mythology, as well as one of the seven earliest Sumerian gods. He was portrayed with the upper body of a goat and the tail of a fish; both fish and goats were common symbols of fertility. He was also shown as an old man wearing a horned cap, climbing mountains, with water streaming down his body. Myths featuring Enki told stories about the corruption of power, sexuality and life-giving water (semen), creation and birth. Many stories of Enki are about how he brings positive change to humankind, though humans misunderstand his intentions.

CAPRICORN'S BUILDING BLOCKS:
Element, Modality, and Polarity

Each of the twelve members of the zodiac can be described by their element, modality, and polarity. While planets are the actors of the story, the zodiac tells us what those characters are wearing, how they are behaving, and what motivates them. Capricorn is the only member of the zodiac that is two distinct animals fused together, which suggests a complex relationship or hidden knowledge in the human psyche.

Capricorn's catchphrase is "I utilize." Capricorn's temperament is cold and dry, perhaps bitter and old but softening with old age. Capricorn is associated with the colors black, dark gray, drab browns, and muted greens.

If we let go of the idea of Capricorn as a person with a Capricorn Sun, we can see the Capricorn archetype in everyday life. Capricorn shows up synonymous with many familiar archetypes: the hermit, the devil, the governor, the executive, the father, the boss, the daddy, the workaholic, the mentor, the go-getter, the mountain goat, the patriarch, and the wise elder crone.

MODALITY: CARDINAL

Cardinal signs of Aries, Cancer, Libra, and Capricorn are initiators. The cardinal signs initiate the beginning of each season, as the sun moves into these signs at the spring/fall equinoxes and summer/winter solstices. When harnessed with skill, cardinal signs start new projects, begin new relationships, and bring an entrepreneurial spirit to everything they do. Planets in these signs have the energetic power to push us out of our comfort zone and into new, scary, exciting pursuits. When unskillfully expressed, cardinal signs may be rushed, overcommitted to every new thing, and overly forceful with their energies. Cardinal signs can get so excited to embark on a new journey that they neglect to finish anything. Earthly Capricorn is capable of moving literal and metaphorical mountains. Capricorn's cardinal energy comes out in the form of building a reputation, starting a new career or business, and the commitment to patiently climb up any winding path that leads to their goal.

ELEMENT: EARTH

Earth signs of Taurus, Virgo, and Capricorn are grounded in practical, tactile reality. Earth rules the physical realm and operates through tangible form. Planets in earth signs are dependable and grounded, persevering and enduring in order to achieve. Yet, like all aspects of astrology, the earth element has negative expressions; earth can be conservative and unimaginative, rigid and possessive, unable to change directions once a goal is identified. Capricorn manifests earth power through a drive to create structure and organization, as well as a desire for public recognition and tangible rewards.

POLARITY: YIN

Polarity is sometimes called "gender" in astrology texts. All fire and air zodiac signs are classified as yang, which is masculine and active, while all water and earth signs of the zodiac are yin, or feminine and receptive. Though we may interpret this polarity in a similar way to other rigid binaries, such as gender (male-female), brightness (light-dark), or even the general good-bad or right-wrong binary, the implication is more about expression as introvert or extrovert. Yin signs are internal and receptive in their expression. Water and earth hold and contain; they are introverts connected to night time, mystery, and darkness. Western society, influenced by the brute power of colonialism, highly prefers and prioritizes the external, active expressions of yang energy. Capricorn's yin qualities are often overlooked in astrology texts. The sea goat is seen as masculine, even gendered as male, due to patriarchal values and misogyny. We see rigid, emotionally controlled, responsible, mature, teacher Capricorn and assume that this archetype must be male. We even assign Capricorn as the father of the zodiac. Yet the archetype of Capricorn speaks to the power of earth and water, the powerful receptive elements that support and respond to, rather than express and assert.

PLANETARY FOCUS:
The Sun

The sun is not classified as a planet, but instead as our solar system's star and one of the two luminaries that light up the sky. For the purpose of this chapter, we will discuss the sun as a planet, because it functions like other planets. The sun is certainly the best-known and most misunderstood celestial body in the current landscape of pop astrology. When someone asks, "What's your sign?" you will respond with the zodiac sign where your sun is located; if you're reading this chapter, you will probably say, "I'm a Capricorn!" But you are so much more complex and dynamic than just your sun sign. Sun sign astrology, that is, the idea that you "are" your sun, is less than 100 years old, while the language of astrology has thousands of years of history. The natal or birth chart contains all twelve signs of the zodiac

> *The archetype of Capricorn speaks to the power of earth and water, the powerful receptive elements that support and respond to, rather than express and assert.*

and ten planets, along with thousands of mathematical points and asteroids you may choose to include or exclude. Though your sun is centrally important, your entire chart can tell a more accurate, complex narrative of your lived experience here on planet Earth.

The sun is the giver of light, the luminary of the day. Humans and many other animals are awake, alert, and active when the sun rises, and they retire to a resting place when the light shifts below the horizon. The sun's light creates the possibility for all life on planet Earth. In modern psychological astrology, the sun is our identity and how we perceive ourselves. The glyph or symbol for the sun is a circle with a dot in the middle, which is also the alchemical sign for gold. This astrological symbol has remained unchanged for thousands of years; the ancient solar glyph dates back to ancient cultures in what is now Greece, Egypt, and China. It is also the primary astronomical symbol for the sun, as astrology and astronomy were the same practice until astrology was dismissed by seventeenth-century philosophers. The circle, unbroken and without a distinguishable beginning or end, is a human-created representation of the infinite universe, and the dot in the middle represents the internal light of potential, unmanifested energy. In essence, the sun represents all possibilities and potential. In astrology, the circle represents life force, spirit, soul, or vitality.

The sun plays the role of the shining star: the center of action, self-development, and the way our self-image operates in the world. Individuals spend their lives with a particular focus on themes related to their sun signs, especially if other planets reside in the same sign. The sun helps us focus our willpower for action and change. When the sun is visible in the sky, we cannot see other stars or planets. We feel the warmth of the sun, asking us to stand tall and grow toward our goals.

In ancient astrology, the sun represents who you are becoming during your lifetime. Capricorn Suns, therefore, are *becoming* Capricorns. They are not necessarily born with inherent tenacity and stamina—usually these qualities are earned during their lifespan and become emphasized due to the events and circumstances of life as it progresses over time. Though you are your Capricorn Sun, you are also your moon, your rising, your Mercury, and so forth. You are not defined only by your hand, or your left eye, or your genitals. You are the entirety of your body and how those parts intersect and interact with one another, now and over the course of your life.

HOW TO READ THIS CHAPTER

This chapter draws on both classical ancient astrology techniques, as well as more modern psychological interpretations of the planets and zodiac signs. While Capricorn (and particularly the Capricorn Sun's experience) will remain at the center of this chapter, the writing is intended to be applicable to anyone who is curious about what the archetype of Capricorn has to say. Believe it or not, we all have Capricorn in our chart! Whether or not you have natal planets in Capricorn, or a strong Capricorn influence, you can learn more about yourself through the sign of the sea goat.

Each section begins with an overview of the Capricorn archetype: What is the flavor, temperature, and texture that Capricorn brings to childhood or daily adult life? How would the pure archetype of Capricorn function in work or in love? Then, we dive into what motivates the Capricorn Sun or Capricorn-dominant person to act, and how they may act in different areas of life. Special attention is paid to how a Capricorn may find balance, because Capricorn energies can be utilized for growth and integrity, but shadow Capricorns can also be extremely selfish in their pursuits. Each section ends with some practical advice and/or affirmations for the Capricorn.

Please note that while this chapter focuses on the Capricorn's experience, numerous factors influence how Capricorn energy is expressed. Some Capricorn Sun people will exhibit more traits of the moon or rising sign than their stern, achievement-oriented sun sign. Alternatively, some Capricorn Moon or Capricorn Rising folks might find they identify more with the sea goat than their sun sign. Each section includes a special planetary focus to tease out some details about variety in Capricornian expression. We will explore the variation in moon, Mercury, Venus, and Mars for Capricorns. These planetary variations strongly impact a person's individual expression. If you don't know what sign your natal planets are located in, you can easily look it up with your birth time and an internet connection, or you can work with a professional astrologer. Astrology is complex and complicated, and the way we express our natal planets changes throughout our lifetime. There is not one universal Capricorn experience. If the descriptions don't resonate with you, trust yourself and don't despair! As an astrologer, I expect practical Capricorns to be critical thinkers, so take what works and leave the rest.

A note about Capricorn and gender: though earthly Capricorn is a feminine sign, many astrology texts gender Capricorn as male. The pronouns "he" and "him" are used to describe Capricorn in his quest for achievement, as he expresses exquisite self-control. This chapter uses they/them pronouns exclusively when describing the generic Capricorn expression. Using "they" instead of "he," "she," or "he/she" is a way to include folks of all genders and keep the focus on the Capricorn's behavior. In shifting away from using gendered pronouns, I hope this chapter will provide more universal descriptions of the archetype in action.

CAPRICORN AS A CHILD

EACH YEAR IN mid-December, the sun's movement into the tenth zodiac sign of Capricorn marks the winter solstice in the northern hemisphere. Declaring the beginning of winter, the sun in Capricorn is a cold and dry light, noticeably dimmer and drearier than the sun's light in Cancer or Leo in the sweltering heat of July. Though Capricorn season begins with the shortest day of the year, the winter solstice is when the days begin to grow longer and is thus also seen as a rebirth of the light. As the sun moves through Capricorn, our access to sunlight on Earth slowly begins to increase.

We in the United States celebrate holidays that mark the passing of time as the sun moves through Capricorn. Christmas celebrations have roots in the Roman pagan holiday Saturnalia, where gifts and sacrifices were offered to agricultural god Saturn. In addition, new year festivities are based on the Roman tradition of giving offerings to the deity Janus, the god of change and beginnings. Marking the passage of time with rituals is an important, often undervalued, human experience, especially in the darkness of winter.

Capricorn is ruled by Saturn, known as the Greek Kronos, god of time and cycles. Saturn brings to mind hardship, limits, blockages, delays, and responsibility. Saturn is a feared planet and perhaps for good reason. Saturn does not discipline randomly and without reason. Saturn wants us to understand the rules, structures, and boundaries, and when we disregard them we must face the Saturnian consequences.

In winter, plants die back to the ground, purging every part of their body they don't need to survive. Annual plants produce seeds during the heat and abundance of summer, and these seeds are the only part of the plant that will bring life into the next cycle. The seed is the DNA, the genetic code that determines how, where, and when this plant will come back to life. Winter is not usually a time for growth and unfurling, which require warmth and wetness; it's a time of crushing darkness, cold, and a desire to stay inside and rest. This lack of light asks us to turn inward and contemplate our relationship with shadow.

The Capricorn child is born into darkness, something feared and demonized by Western culture. But there is truth in the dark, and there is beauty in the shadows. Darkness is necessary to rest the tired soul and connect with the mystery behind what is illuminated. The child born during Capricorn season contains a seed of Capricorn's grit and determination, the bare necessities required for survival. Perseverance and commitment to follow through in spite of hardship are in the Capricorn DNA.

BORN RESPONSIBLE

The Capricorn child is motivated to create, enforce, and follow the rules and laws of society. Cardinal signs desire movement forward, growth, and initiation of something new. With an incredible drive and energy, the Capricorn Sun person wants to pursue a path of growth and purpose.

There is no peak high enough to deter the Capricorn. And yet, children do not have the kind of decision-making authority that they will obtain in later life. Childhood comes with necessary limits and rules, which can either be comforting or restrictive, but the process of gaining freedom through fulfillment of responsibilities can be very satisfying for the Capricorn kid.

Capricorn is nothing if not responsible. Who or what Capricorn Sun kids are responsible to and for may depend on any number of things, such as the placement of Saturn in the natal chart and the parenting style or environment where the child is raised. Positive attachment in early life helps the Capricorn child develop a healthy sense of ego, purpose, drive, and autonomy. However, many Capricorn children feel the influence of Saturn during childhood and experience loss, trauma, and wounding that in turn emphasize the need for structure, rules, and independence in later life.

Capricorn children may be incredibly goal-oriented, serious, and focused on achievement in academics, sports, or other areas where a linear and progressive success is the goal. Capricorn children often identify goals early in life. The serious sea-goat child wishes to spend their life on a pragmatic and deliberate path to their dreams. The goals and desires may change over time, or they may identify their lifelong career by age five, but Capricorn will always be able to identify something they want and work toward it with awe-inspiring determination.

Take the singer Jordin Sparks, for example: her sun, Mercury, Saturn, Uranus, and Neptune all in the sign of Capricorn give her a natal gift for focused achievement. Sparks participated in and won many singing competitions as a child and became the youngest person to ever win the title of American Idol in 2007. This single-minded focus on getting to be the best of the best fuels many young Capricorns.

Capricorn children thrive on a steady routine from which to grow. Methodical and practical, Capricorn enjoys predictable boundaries. The

CELEBRITY FOCUS

James Earl Jones

To better demonstrate the Capricorn child and the emphasis of a strong Saturn, let's take a look at the iconic actor James Earl Jones. Born in Mississippi in 1931 during America's Great Depression, Jones is a triple Capricorn: Capricorn Sun, Capricorn Moon, and Capricorn Rising, with additional planets Mercury and Saturn in the sign of the sea goat. At age five, he was sent to Michigan to be raised by his maternal grandparents. He developed a severe stutter as a result of the stress and trauma of moving, and as a child refused to speak. He was essentially mute for eight to ten years, not speaking to anyone other than close family. As a teenager, he had a teacher who helped him develop his voice through writing, poetry, and acting. In college he studied acting and went on to become one of the greatest actors in American history. Jones transformed his greatest weakness into his greatest strength, winning many awards during his six-decade career, though he is best known for his iconic voice.

Capricorn child is one who would appreciate a strict schedule; knowing that bedtime is at the exact same time each night or that pizza is served for dinner each and every Friday gives these tykes a predictable structure to lean against.

To be fair, the Capricorn Sun will spend an entire lifetime trying to relax enough to play, have childlike wonder, and have some humor about life's sour taste. Push and push and push some more is the Capricorn Sun's natural state, but life doesn't always have to be a struggle. The Capricorn child should be instructed to pursue achievement and accolade, but also take time to smell the proverbial roses. Capricorn children should be encouraged to play, rest, and experience the pleasure of being a child. To avoid loneliness, sea-goat children need to make friends their own age and participate in groups and associations, where they can better learn about interdependence and collaboration.

A natural part of human life on Earth, especially during childhood, is relying on others for care, connection, nourishment, and protection. The Capricorn child may fear vulnerability; the instinct to get everything right the first time and achieve all goals can be extremely harsh for a young being. And though the Capricorn child may have strong opinions that they proclaim loudly, their feelings are hurt when someone disagrees or challenges their authority. Once hurt, the Capricorn child will retreat into solitude. Security is a huge driving force in everything they do.

Capricorns are process-oriented and fixed on the outcome but also determined to find the most productive, efficient way of being. There is a cardinal drive for constant improvement. While Capricorn kids of all ages might behave like mini adults, American culture may be more willing to accept the Capricorn boy, as accomplishments, strength, and seriousness are attributes we tend to assign to the male sex. However, Capricorn girls may find that their desire to build and achieve is not supported by caregivers as much as adults encourage them to be emotional, relational, and sensitive creatures.

CAPRICORN CHILD IN BALANCE

At their best, Capricorn children are curious, independent, serious, and mature. They are self-sufficient, but they seek guidance from elders; they are self-directed, but they allow input from others. They take time for themselves to play and grow.

At their worst, Capricorn children are rigid, isolated, bitter, and prone to taking on other people's responsibilities. They resent those who shirk responsibility. They are critical, fixated on winning, overly serious, and dominating.

Capricorn children are mature for their age. You may find Capricorn Suns voluntarily taking up a parental role with peers and younger siblings, or they might even parent their own parents. The Capricorn child is captivated by power and might be especially motivated by financial rewards and trophies that demonstrate their worth. Even as a youth, the Capricorn has a healthy appreciation of duty, responsibility, and work. As Capricorn children sometimes seem wise beyond their years, adults in the child's life may treat them as a peer instead of as a developing young person.

While most children are engaged in fantasy, play, and self-expression, Capricorn Sun children have interests much older than their chronological age. The Capricorn child is perhaps the most stern, pragmatic child you've ever met. Saturn-influenced Capricorn children have a reputation for being rule-followers and old souls. We may even think of Capricorn as the Benjamin Button of the zodiac; born old and serious, with increased ability to frolic and enjoy leisure time in later life. Capricorn children may prefer the company of adults, engaging in conversations about practical matters that are years beyond their age.

PLANETARY FOCUS:
The Moon

The sun is the bright, forward-moving, conscious, and active luminary of the day; by contrast, the moon is quiet, receptive, reflective, and focused on the felt experience. Mother Moon represents a divine, nighttime goddess in every culture, whether she is called Yemaya in Santeria tradition, Selene to the ancient Greeks, Ishtar to the Babylonians, Isis to the Egyptians, Ixchel to the Mayas, or Hina to those of Polynesian descent. The glyph or symbol for the moon is a crescent moon, instantly recognizable and familiar. The moon is the fastest moving astrological body, circling the entire zodiac every twenty-eight days. The astrological moon speaks to our dreams, cyclical time (such as tides and menstruation), and emotional experience. The moon is a soft, internal creature, influenced by the ever-fluctuating pace of daily life.

Children tend to embody qualities of their natal moon sign more than their sun sign. The moon placement can point to how the child experiences protection and love. The moon's sign indicates how we like to be nourished, nurtured, and held. Qualities of the natal Capricorn Sun sign might be visible or may remain hidden until adulthood.

Because the moon sign and element are so important to how the Capricorn child expresses themselves, what follows is a brief description of how the moon, by sign, element, and moon phase, will alter the classic Capricorn demeanor. Read your moon sign or look up the phase of the moon you were born under to add depth and nuance to your understanding.

FIRE MOON
(Aries, Leo, Sagittarius)

Fire Moons are bright, energetic, impatient, fun, and creative. Beware of impulsive and destructive tendencies, or volcanic temper tantrums when things don't go their way.

CAPRICORN CHILD WITH AN ARIES MOON
(First Quarter Moon Phase)

The child whose moon is in the first sign of the zodiac is an adventurous, spontaneous firecracker! Impulsive and dominant, the Aries Moon child may speak out of turn, because they must emote immediately rather than sit with their feelings. Aries and Capricorn both initiate action, so this sun/moon combination will seek out opportunities to create and take action. Energy is abundant, but fire can also bring explosive heat and inflammation. **Celebrity example:** Canadian prime minister, Justin Trudeau (Capricorn Sun, Aries Moon, Virgo Rising).

CAPRICORN CHILD WITH A LEO MOON
(Disseminating Moon Phase)

Leo Moons are flamboyant, heart-forward, self-centered children. Combined with the Capricorn Sun, the Leo Moon child has incredible leadership potential, especially if they learn to share the stage. The child with this combination should be encouraged to find an outlet for artistic self-expression. A growing edge for this placement is to learn how to access unconditional self-love and self-worth without relying on external approval. **Celebrity example:** Actress Marlene Dietrich (Capricorn Sun/Mercury/Saturn/Jupiter/Mars, Leo Moon, Virgo Rising).

CAPRICORN CHILD WITH A SAGITTARIUS MOON
(Balsamic Moon Phase)

The Sagittarius Moon kiddo wants comfort and connection through finding a truth to rely on. Truths may be sought through exploration of religious texts or esoteric ritual. Individuals with this sun and moon combination may seem especially wise, with a desire to distill wisdom with others. **Celebrity example:** Actor Anthony Hopkins (Capricorn Sun/Mercury, Sagittarius Moon, Capricorn Rising).

EARTH MOON
(Taurus, Virgo, Capricorn)

Earth Moons are grounded, practical, responsible, and predictable. Beware of stubborn, overly slow, and critical tendencies.

CAPRICORN CHILD WITH A TAURUS MOON
(Waxing Gibbous Moon Phase)

The moon is exalted in Taurus, meaning that the individual is able to touch into emotional desires, find pleasure in the body, and express needs in order to get them met. Capricorns with a Taurus Moon might be a bit rigid or stuck trying to do everything right. Individuals with this combination should release perfectionistic tendencies and embrace the process. **Celebrity example:** American folk musician Odetta Holmes (Capricorn Sun/Saturn/Mercury, Taurus Moon, Aquarius Rising).

CAPRICORN CHILD WITH A VIRGO MOON
(Disseminating Moon Phase)

This combination produces a child who is intelligent and practical, yet a fussy perfectionist. Capricorn Sun and Virgo Moon children may find themselves with a strong desire to teach and lead others, convinced that their earthly reality is better than others'. Meticulous and a bit fearful, the service-oriented moon in Virgo shows up with a grounded temperament, a cautious, stable approach, and a strong desire for synthesis. **Celebrity example:** Actress Aja Naomi King (Capricorn Sun/Jupiter, Virgo Moon)

CAPRICORN CHILD WITH A CAPRICORN MOON
(New Moon Phase)

The Capricorn Moon child may be unable to fully embrace the softness of childhood. A Capricorn Moon is motivated to build and sustain real human connection but may feel extremely uncomfortable with vulnerability. Those with Capricorn Sun and Moon may feel that they must be autonomous as they make their way through life, and that they cannot or should not rely on others for their survival. The Capricorn New Moon person may experience obstacles to securing their emotional needs, making them close off even more. But the Capricorn Moon child should be encouraged to feel the feelings, acknowledge the empathy that is born from scarcity, and continue forward. **Celebrity example:** Composer Lin-Manuel Miranda (Capricorn Sun/Mercury, Capricorn Moon, Aries Rising)

WATER MOON
(Cancer, Scorpio, Pisces)

Water Moons are sensitive, fluid, compassionate, and deep. Beware of emotional reactivity, grudges, and overly fearful tendencies.

CAPRICORN CHILD WITH A CANCER MOON
(Full Moon Phase)

The Capricorn Sun born with a Cancer Moon was born within a day or two of the full moon in Cancer. The child with these placements will spend their lifetime trying to manifest tangible, external results of their labor while also tending to their desire to create a vibrant, fulfilling home and family life. Moon is at home in the sign of Cancer; Cancer Moons are incredibly perceptive though perhaps a bit moody. The Cancer Moon child can attune easily to others and may have a desire to nurture or take care of others. The child with these placements is driven to nurture the growth of others. **Celebrity example:** Singer Mary J. Blige (Capricorn Sun, Cancer Moon)

CAPRICORN CHILD WITH A SCORPIO MOON
(Last Quarter or Balsamic Moon Phase)

This combination brings out a secretive nature and a compulsion toward privacy. The Scorpio Moon child is intuitive but more likely to share their magic with one or two close confidants than a gaggle of pals. Scorpio Moon is both gifted and cursed with the ability to see what lurks below the surface, and Capricorn Sun is insistent on doing something about it. With both these internal signs, this child will thrive with more solo activities rather than team sports. **Celebrity example:** Author David Sedaris (Capricorn Sun/Mercury, Scorpio Moon/Neptune)

CAPRICORN CHILD WITH A PISCES MOON
(Crescent or First Quarter Moon Phase)

Pisces Moon is incredibly sensitive, and almost psychic, with one foot in on this plane of reality and one foot firmly planted in another realm. Capricorn will want to shut down the emotional self, but Pisces won't allow that to happen. Intuition, dream life, and spiritual growth may be a motivation for the fishy water moon child. Though the Pisces Moon is incredibly skilled at

PRACTICAL ADVICE
for the Capricorn Child

Play! You have your whole life to be the responsible adult. Spend some time enjoying simple pleasures and being alive. Put your hands in the dirt, make up a silly joke, and let go of control. Feel into your body and your emotions. Don't bottle it all up inside—make sure you share your internal world with others. Don't be afraid of the darkness that is within you. Darkness is healing, generative, and sacred. Honor the mystery of the unknown within yourself.

absorbing and transmuting other people's pain, they can use Capricorn Sun's focus to learn better boundaries and self-discipline. **Celebrity example:** Singer Patti Smith (Capricorn Sun/Mars, Pisces Moon, Sagittarius Rising)

AIR MOON
(Gemini, Libra, Aquarius)

Air Moons are alert, pragmatic, and have a strong capacity for critical thinking. Beware of flightiness, indecision, or "know-it-all" tendencies.

CAPRICORN CHILD WITH A GEMINI MOON
(Waxing Gibbous Moon Phase)

Writers Junot Diaz, Haruki Murakami, and Rudyard Kipling all share this placement. Lighthearted and mutable, the Gemini Moon sea goat makes an excellent teacher, instructor, and facilitator. Capricorn grounds some of the flighty qualities of the twins, while Gemini Moon gets emotional needs met through connection. Silly humor and word play bring out the softer, playful side of this combination. **Celebrity example:** Comedian Jim Carrey (Capricorn Sun/Venus/Mars, Gemini Moon, Scorpio Rising)

CAPRICORN CHILD WITH A LIBRA MOON
(Last Quarter Moon Phase)

The Libra Moon just wants everyone to be kind and beautiful. Motivated to keep the peace, Libra Moon kids might be fond of white lies to spare the feelings of those around them. Then again, Libra can be the sign of justice and liberation. Adjustment and balance are the keys to happiness and success. **Celebrity example:** French singer Francoise Hardy (Capricorn Sun/Mercury, Libra Moon, Virgo Rising)

CAPRICORN CHILD WITH AN AQUARIUS MOON
(Crescent Moon Phase)

The birth of new ideals, visions, and eccentric style, the Aquarius Moon brings some futuristic magic to the sea goat. This combination wants to start something new, build new technologies or systems of power that better serve the people. Witty and hard-working, the Capricorn-Aquarius can be overly serious at times and has a hard time knowing what to do with emotions. Beware of the "my way or the highway" rigidity. **Celebrity example:** Professional boxer and activist Muhammad Ali (Capricorn Sun, Aquarius Moon/Mercury/Venus, Leo Rising)

CAPRICORN AS AN ADULT

ADULTHOOD HAS NO standard definition. In the biological definition, a human or other creature reaches adulthood when sexual maturity has taken place and reproduction is possible. In the United States, eighteen is the age that a person becomes a legal adult. This is true for the majority of the world, but some countries declare a person an adult as early as fifteen or the onset of puberty and as late as twenty. The human brain does not completely develop its capacity for rational decision-making until about twenty-five years of age. Some ancient peoples whose cultural values included astrological information believed that a person didn't become a true adult until the completion of the first Saturn return, around age twenty-eight to thirty. The Western colonizer culture associates adulthood with specific activities, such as leaving the family home to pursue education and work opportunities, or perhaps entering into marriage and having children. These definitions are flawed; cultural and economic differences mean that adult life at eighteen and beyond is extremely varied.

The very notion of "adulting" was invented by and for millennials, particularly the Capricorn stellium generation. The concept of adult as a verb, a thing to be done rather than an age, is just as preposterous as assuming every eighteen-year-old has the ability to manage their own life that they did not have at age seventeen. Adulting is a way to describe the boring, mundane tasks associated with being responsible, such as grocery shopping or getting a routine oil change for your car. But things that involve bearing responsibility for a person or thing present a unique perspective. Responsibility is necessary for growth and development.

Adulthood is the time of life when one becomes responsible for their own choices, and thus the consequences of those choices. Don't want to wash your laundry? You certainly don't have to, but you will either have to pay someone else to do the work or you may lose friends and employment because you smell terrible. Social norms influence what is considered "adult" and what is not; Capricorn should be sure to understand their internal values before they blindly try to follow what others expect of them.

The limitations that the Capricorn often experiences in childhood are transformed into a healthy respect for time and duty in adulthood. Ruling planet Saturn is associated with old age and the end of life, so adulthood is more productive, satisfying, and fruitful than childhood. Saturn rules death, disease, and maturation. Though Saturn is often gendered as male, the archetype of the wrinkled crone is appropriate here, the ancient wise woman who is secure in her inner power though the outer power of beauty has diminished.

Because of the connection with Saturn, Capricorn is solid. In medical astrology traditions, the sign of Capricorn rules the skeletal system, the spine, and connective tissues; in effect, everything that holds us together. Capricorn is also said to have a special affinity for the knees "which must bend in humility" according to medical astrology texts. Preventive care for the knees, bones, teeth, and joints should be a special focus for the Capricorn adult.

CELEBRITY FOCUS

Michelle Obama

Michelle Obama has her natal sun/Mercury in Capricorn, ruled by her natal Saturn in Aquarius. Born and raised on Chicago's South Side, she traced both her maternal and paternal lineage back to enslaved African Americans in the pre-Civil War American South. Bright and steady in her achievements, she graduated cum laude from Princeton University in 1985 and received her J.D. from Harvard Law School in 1988. Though she achieved the ambitious goal of becoming a lawyer, she soon realized that corporate law was not the place for her and left to pursue a career in public service. As the First Lady of the United States, she grounded her Leo Sun husband with her traditional values. Michelle Obama was praised for her classic, traditionally elegant Capricornian fashion sense, while she also faced racist attacks on her looks and critique for being too rigid or unfeminine. Her motto "When they go low, we go high" speaks to her reliable moral compass. Capricorn's influence is noticeable in her focus on individual upward mobility and respect for the political establishment.

PLANETARY FOCUS:
Saturn

The myth of Kronos (the Greek name for Saturn) begins with Kronos castrating his father, Uranus, and taking his place as ruler of the universe. When Kronos hears that his destiny is to be usurped by his own son, he eats his first five children with Rhea (Demeter, Hades, Hera, Hestia, and Poseidon) so he will maintain his rulership. Rhea secretly gives birth to his sixth child, Jupiter or Zeus, in a cave and leaves infant Zeus to be cared for by the nymph Amalthaea. Zeus goes on to kill his father Kronos, free his siblings, and reign as king of the gods.

Saturn is the greater malefic, the planet that is known for bringing hardship. Ancient astrologers linked Saturn with experiences of misery, pain, sorrow, grief, punishment, solitude, and loss. Saturn is associated with the Devil card in the tarot; indeed the planet of discipline is sometimes called Satan. Saturn presides over the end of December and the months of January and February, the cold, dry winter when little can grow in the northern hemisphere. Saturn is associated with destructive and constricting qualities of life, especially in terms of agriculture and growth. A Saturn-dominant person was characterized as dark, wearing black, silent, unable to express emotion, and serious. People and things connected in some way to long-lasting perseverance were thought to be ruled by Saturn: elders, ancient practices, and long-standing cultural norms. Because of Saturn's position as an agricultural god, those who worked the land as farmers, rented or earned money from leasing land, and individuals living in bondage or slavery were associated with the rigid and unforgiving Saturn. Saturnian expressions of human illness include depression and gloom, diseases of the bones, and hardening or crystallization within the body. Conditions such as heart disease (hardening of the arteries), cysts, arthritis, and rheumatic pain are considered under Saturn's rulership. Saturn rules most trees, and so we may think of Saturn-dominant people as the trees of their community: pillars of strength, solid and rooted in the ground, a dedicated home to other creatures and plant life.

In the modern psychological astrology tradition, Saturn is seen as a part of the human psyche. Here, Saturn represents our self-discipline, self-sufficiency, and self-respect. Saturn-dominant people may have the gift and burden of seeing the dark and painful side of life. Saturn has long been associated with darkness; there are modern astrology texts that state that Saturn is associated with those who have dark skin. This is simply racism; the idea that whiteness and lighter complexions are pure and worthy while darkness is evil is based in the history of European colonialism, which created a system of racial prejudice in order to dominate, conquer, dehumanize, and murder indigenous people.

The glyph or symbol for Saturn is the cross (representing matter) over the half circle (representing receptivity). The glyph is also associated with a sickle, which speaks to Saturn's place in ancient Roman culture as an agricultural god. We can also think of Saturn's sickle and Saturn in our charts as a force that helps us harvest the fruit of our labor. Fruit is not harvested the same day the tree is planted, so Saturn also represents patience, time, and an ability to put in the work before expecting rewards.

Saturn is a somewhat slow-moving planet, circling the entire zodiac approximately every thirty years. Saturn cycles can illuminate the themes or topics that are pertinent to self-development and growth, bringing about opportunities to manifest, act, and define the self. Saturn cycles can also bring depression and pain, as Saturn often asks us to take responsibility in various aspects of life.

Saturn cycles are especially significant to the Capricorn Suns. Generally, astrologers study these cycles by looking at how current astrological movement interacts with an individual's natal or birth chart. For example, when Saturn in the sky circles the entire zodiac and returns to the place it was when you were born, you experience what is called the first Saturn return, around age twenty-eight to thirty. Saturn will circle the zodiac again, and around age fifty-eight to sixty, you experience the second Saturn return. The Saturn return is a period of time that will bring opportunities to wield your power and steer your life in deeply satisfying, and/or deeply frustrating, ways. These moments in the cycle help define maturity and adulthood. Life is spent integrating and learning Saturn's lessons, which are not for the faint of heart. The Capricorn Sun will find that either they work their Saturn cycles, or the Saturn cycles will work them.

SELF-IMPROVEMENT

Adult Capricorn is motivated by improvement. They want to mature, to grow into their own power, and to cultivate self-awareness through self-control. Adult Capricorn seeks wisdom that is the result of deep inner self-knowing. Self-awareness and self-control are motivational forces in the Capricorn's daily life. The Capricorn adult spends their life cultivating wisdom via self-reflection; looking backward to make sense of how to move forward.

Self-improvement and self-mastery are important tools of growth for the Capricorn archetype. Activities such as competitive sports, cross-training or other disciplined exercise regimens, and running races can be excellent outlets for measured self-improvement. Capricorn Sun thrives on any activities that reward the individual for creative strategies at pushing ever forward just a bit faster or writing a few more words. Unlike fire sign companions Aries and Leo, Capricorn is not interested in being the team captain. Instead, cool and measured Capricorn is the coach. Capricorn adults (unless fire-dominant or with a natal chart that says otherwise) enjoy behind-the-scenes, or shall we say pulling-the-strings, activities. The director of the play and conductor of the orchestra, Capricorn sits back and observes. When in balance, the Capricorn Sun adult encourages others to achieve their personal best and leaves no one behind.

ADULT CAPRICORN IN BALANCE

At their best, Capricorns are responsible, kind, ambitious, and able to balance when to be generous and when to be stingy.

At their worst, they are conservative, power-hoarding, emotionless robots. They may lack empathy and they may take their bitterness out on others.

Adult humans whose natal sun is in Capricorn probably enjoy the second half of life much more than the first. Unlike most other sun signs, Capricorns look better with age—more distinguished, self-assured, and regal. It's hard to say whether they have relaxed into a more comfortable, confident self or whether vanity has driven them to the dermatologist. In any case, Capricorns might find retirement and/or elderhood to be the best time of life.

Pessimism and mental anguish are not uncommon for the sea goat. The Capricorn adult might be prone to bouts of depression, either in a cyclical manner or in an Eeyore-esque way that permeates everyday life. Grief, depression, trauma, and loss can rule the Capricorn's world well into adulthood, especially as Capricorn encounters setbacks, limitations, and the pain of failure. The Capricorn Sun is learning to wield their own inner power. Experiences of suffering and powerlessness inform the way the Capricorn Sun continues to develop during adulthood. Some Capricorn Suns may use their pain to cultivate more empathy; others may sharpen their own power in order to hurt others before they are hurt.

Capricorn symbolizes the nonstop quest for power, such as worldly power. Sea-goat Capricorns can move effortlessly up cliffs and swim with ease to the ocean floor. They cultivate the power of self-control. Capricorn is not necessarily after money or fame, but these external displays of power serve to elevate status in a capitalist society. Capricorn seeks power as freedom, not power as glory. Integrity is the ultimate endpoint for the Capricorn archetype—merging public reputation with the inner self-image, to project only ideals and realities that are true, rather than projecting false self-confidence.

> The Capricorn Sun is conservative—not necessarily politically conservative but conservative with their money, time, resources, and emotions.

The Capricorn adult can get a reputation for being uncaring and unemotional, but many Capricorn adults simply struggle to express authentic emotions. Though they feel deeply, showing true softness or rage on the outside can present a challenge—especially if they have been taught that emotions are weak and unproductive. They project a beautiful picture of a well-curated lifestyle on social media, but behind the scenes can lurk trauma, abuse, chaos, and addiction. Projecting a self-sufficient and false sense of

PRACTICAL ADVICE
for the Capricorn Adult

Capricorn adults won't be instantly good at everything you try, but you can achieve greatness at anything with enough time, practice, energy, and commitment. Instead of becoming a teacher or mentor prematurely, you Capricorns would do well to spend your twenties, thirties, and maybe even forties learning from teachers and mentors who inspire you. Focus on your aspirations first, not just what is easy and desirable for others (i.e., parents, friends, colleagues). If you fail, you should get up and try again. You cannot predict every twist and turn of life. Stop trying so hard and simply enjoy the ride of life. Find safe paths and places to rest.

self can be a coping mechanism for soothing the inner critic. Capricorn adults are more likely to offer help than receive it, even when they are in pain. Though a Capricorn is a yin, internal, receptive, nonlinear sign, it is ruled by Saturn and may thus be cold and dry, a place where emotions cannot thrive. This is the place of wisdom and death, not birth and growth.

Capricorn is cautious, unlikely to risk money or use all of their vacation time in one go. The Capricorn Sun is conservative—not necessarily politically conservative but conservative with their money, time, resources, and emotions. This may seem at cross-purposes with Capricorn's desire to be the provider, the one that the entire family can lean on. Yet it is Capricorn's self-development of the ego, of being of service, and finding confidence to facilitate rather than dominate or control that is at the root of many behaviors. Capricorn differentiates power between, power over, and power within. Capricorn Suns may wield their power for social justice or they may wield power in more self-serving ways. Capricorns may have a personality based solely on what is owned or conquered. The phrase "absolute power corrupts absolutely" brings the Capricorn archetype to mind. They may be overly ambitious and opportunistic and may be impatient in early adulthood, thinking they have earned the status of mentor and elder before it is appropriate.

Individualism is an easy trap; Capricorn-dominant folks are strong believers in individualism, and want to believe that they have the self-determination to manifest their own destiny; however, positive thinking and individual behavior cannot undo external forces of social, political, and economic oppression. The very notion that someone is solely responsible for their own successes and failures, that one should have a linear path toward greatness and achievement, is enmeshed within our current sociopolitical framework. Though Capricorn adults have a lot of choice about how they respond to their lives and can create their own realities in that sense, systems of institutional power are always operating in the background. The Capricorn adult who is born into a body that is assigned less value in our culture (that is, non-white, Indigenous, disabled, female, trans/gender nonconforming, and so forth) will struggle to assert their worth within a world that has been socialized to dehumanize them and devalue their gifts.

CAPRICORN IN LOVE

THE CAPRICORN ARCHETYPE takes love seriously. In all areas of life, romance included, Capricorn is pragmatic and practical. Because of Capricorn's desire for improvement and success, matters of the heart can be viewed as a task to be accomplished, almost the same as pursuing a job or a degree. If love, relationships, or marriage are identified as a goal, Capricorn will use their dedication and perseverance to obtain that goal. But to love and to allow others to love you is a vulnerable process, one that requires letting down the walls of pretense and the appearance of perfection. Capricorn may feel unsafe or exposed while letting their guard down.

Capricorn wants to know your five-year plan before they swipe right. On the first date, Capricorn might prefer to stick to serious or traditional subjects rather than make surface connections. Their mature, sophisticated style and cool attitude can make them seem much older than their actual age, but don't be fooled, as there is always something to be improved hiding behind the sleek exterior. You may expect Capricorn to take the role of the dominant or assertive partner because they seem so confident, but they love to be pursued and fawned over as much as the next sign. The goat-fish prefers to show affection in sensible and unsentimental ways, but don't think that Capricorns are as stone cold as their outer appearance may convey. Capricorns need tenderness and a shoulder to cry on just as much as the next person. Ancient astrology gives us the god Pan as the Capricorn archetype: sexual, horny (literally and figuratively), and playful.

BALANCED CAPRICORN IN LOVE

At Capricorn's best, they are strong, capable, trustworthy, and dependable. Their outward confidence matches their inner strength. They allow people to make their own mistakes and take responsibility for their own actions, without unnecessary power dynamics. They hold on to mutually beneficial relationships, lovingly keep others accountable for their mistakes, and release relationships that aren't working.

At their worst, they are controlling, mean, selfish, and judgmental. They might think they know better than everyone else, and ego prevents them from making meaningful connections. They either crave constant validation, or they are hermits who pretend to need no one. Their jealousy makes intimacy difficult, even on a platonic level.

While the pure expression of the Capricorn archetype has a difficult time with vulnerability and love, keep in mind that Capricorn Sun people contain the entire zodiac and other planetary bodies that contribute to a person's experience of love and relationships. But Capricorn Suns must also remember that love and romance are not linear, goal-oriented

> *If love, relationships, or marriage are identified as a goal, Capricorn will use their dedication and perseverance to obtain that goal.*

practices. Romance and interpersonal relationships are more than just the identification and pursuit of a goal. Capricorn folks might have an extremely hard time with the emotions that come with breakups, betrayal, and jealousy.

As an earth sign, Capricorns may find it difficult to emote and may prefer to perform acts of love through practical service and gifts. To be loved by a Capricorn partner is to always have clean, laundered sheets, a packed lunch, and both necessities and creature comforts. Or perhaps the earthy Capricorn wants to receive acts of service as a tangible, practical expression of love. Capricorn can love and be loved without any difficulty or drama, but Capricorn does not want to rely on others. Part of Capricorn's growth edge is to allow vulnerability without tipping into codependence, and to allow for solitude without becoming isolated. Alone time is necessary for the Capricorn to integrate and grow. Capricorns may be more comfortable alone, or with one or two trusted comrades. Anyone romantically or intimately connected to the Capricorn Sun must be willing to let their sweet sea goat withdraw to process their deep emotions at their own pace. The sea goat is half fish, after all, and needs solitude and time with their dreams as much as any water sign.

Loneliness may be a plague of the Capricorn. Sometimes it's much easier for the Capricorn to project an aloof, detached, almost cold energy than to warm up and attempt connection and vulnerability. Others who are seeking a non-committal or unattached relationship might be drawn to Capricorn's steely demeanor, but they will be surprised to see how much tender emotion is lurking just below the surface. As much as they have a reputation for being a boring stick-in-the-mud with a 9 p.m. bedtime, Capricorn is drawn to intimacy, safety, and loving security. They just want you to know they don't need a partner. Living unattached can bring much self-actualization and growth, but it's important for Capricorns to bond and form reliable emotional connections with others.

Capricorn has high standards; they are prone to self-protection by setting their standards so high that no one could ever attain them. But Capricorn will also try to live up to their own high standards and will aim for perfection in the dating relationship.

FAMILIAL LOVE

People love to use astrology as a tool to determine the outcomes of romance and love. The answer is always more complex than matching sun signs. Love and compatibility extend far beyond the bonds of sexual and romantic love. Humans are social, interconnected animals who feel strong attachment to friends, immediate and extended family, coworkers, and community. Our culture values the heteronormative bond of two opposite-sex people in a monogamous relationship, living together but separate from other adults. Perhaps those two marry and have children. This is the acceptable path for some, but not for others. Capricorn is one sign that may find satisfying relationships full of pleasure, joy, and connection in platonic relationships outside of their spouse. Chosen family may be part of Capricorn's support system. Because of Capricorn's need for integrity and strong internal values that lead to certain external behaviors, it may be difficult for the Capricorn to maintain authentic vulnerability with family and friends who do not behave with integrity.

RELATIONSHIPS AS WORK

Capricorn is a natural worker and will put in the work to form a healthy relationship. Self-discipline is a much-admired and respected quality, but Capricorn may expect partners to exude

CELEBRITY FOCUS

Dolly Parton

Dolly Parton was born in 1946 with the sun, Venus, and Mercury all in Capricorn, ruled by her Saturn and Mars in Cancer. The fourth of twelve children, she describes her upbringing as "dirt poor." Parton began singing and performing as a child, especially in the Pentecostal church, and moved from rural Tennessee to Nashville the day after she graduated high school. She met Carl Thomas Dean almost immediately upon arriving in Nashville; they were married a few years later in 1966. Originally breaking into the public eye as a country singer and songwriter, she has become an actor, music producer, business entrepreneur, author, and advocate for causes such as childhood literacy and HIV/AIDS. Parton has remained in the public eye since the 1960s. She is not your typical Capricorn Sun; her public persona is warm and bubbly, but she is intensely private and shrewd in business. Parton never received a formal education beyond high school, yet she is smart and wildly successful. She never had children of her own, but helped raise some of her younger siblings, and her nieces and nephews call her "Aunt Granny." Parton's relationship to her Cancer Sun husband may seem unconventional to some, but has lasted throughout her expansive career. Though her husband avoids the spotlight and prefers to stay at home while she tours the country solo, it seems to work well for her independent and driven Venus in Capricorn. In 2016, the couple renewed their marriage vows to honor their fiftieth anniversary.

the same willingness to forgo rest and relaxation for accomplishments. For example, the Capricorn Sun or Moon person might opt for a longer workday to make that overtime money or a daily exercise regimen that begins at 5 a.m. and then judge others who prioritize rest. The Capricorn's romantic partnership provides opportunities for compromise. Capricorn is prone to thinking their way is the best way, so therapy or other opportunities to reflect on and define values can help the Capricorn person feel confident and grounded.

DADDY CAPRICORN

As a Saturn-ruled sign, Capricorn has Daddy issues. In queer and kink communities, Daddies come in all genders, shapes, and sizes, but Daddy is always in charge. Daddy is the archetype of the older, wiser partner, perhaps the primary earner, and the one who sets the limits and discipline for those who aren't following the rules.

As a relational species that needs boundaries in order to thrive, humans like to have limits set for them. Domination and submission within the sexual relationship is charged with arousal, and once Capricorn lets their guard down a bit, they can enjoy exploring the limitations and boundaries of the sensual and sexual experience, especially with a trusted partner. They may find satisfaction in edgeplay and challenging sexual boundaries, choosing to integrate experiences of pleasure-pain.

Of course, kink is not inherent in any planet, sign, or placement. Romantic and sexual expression are varied and diverse in ways we cannot even imagine, and the zodiac has a lot to say about the many flavors of human desire. So while some Capricorns may enjoy playing the Daddy in romantic and sexual endeavors, other Capricorns will tap into power dynamics with a dominant partner.

Power dynamics aside, Capricorn Suns have a reputation for being a bit prudish and traditional when it comes to sex and relationships. Many Capricorns prefer a more standard, normative approach to relationships and can be found in long-term monogamous relationships. Capricorn-dominant people may be driven to marry early and solidify their relationship as part of an old-fashioned, religion-based institution, making a relationship into a concrete, tangible contract. Getting their affairs in order and proceeding the traditional way, instead of "shacking up" as an unmarried person, might be important for them; what would their elders and ancestors say about their relationship?

Capricorns are also likely to enjoy an unattached single life where they can pursue their dreams freely, so long as they can find connection and platonic intimacy among friends and family.

PLANETARY FOCUS:
Venus

Venus is the planet of relating. A person's natal Venus speaks to what they value and don't value, what they find beautiful and pleasurable, as well as what they find repulsive. In ancient astrology, Venus (or Aphrodite) is the goddess of pleasure, love, desire, connection, beauty, and fertility. Venus wants us to experience decadence, luxury, and beauty. Venus has something to say about how we decorate our homes (or leave them bare), what our favorite foods are, and our styles of dress. Venus is far above and beyond just a planet of romantic love.

The glyph or symbol for Venus is the circle with the cross of matter below it, familiarly known as the female symbol. Sun and Venus are only ever forty-eight degrees apart, meaning Venus is never more than two signs away from the sun. Venus spends about twelve months circling the sun and making its way across the entire zodiac. Each year you have a Venus return, meaning Venus in the sky returns to the place it was the moment you were born.

When we think about love, desire, relationships, and connection to others, we inevitably think about Venus. Of course, all planets (including sun, moon, Mercury, and Mars) have something to say about love and relationships. The following details about Venus in different signs can illuminate the wide diversity of experiences for Capricorns in loving relationships with others.

VENUS IN SCORPIO

Venus has a natural affinity for water, where emotions can run free and deep. However, Venus in Scorpio is motivated to pursue the deepest, most intense relationships possible. Capricorn with Venus in Scorpio may be more likely to play with power dynamics in relationships, exploring the taboos of society through their private sex lives. Outlets of personal expression, like art, cooking, or other ways of transforming items to release inner feelings, are healthy for folks with this placement. Addiction, secrecy, and repressed emotions can be a problem. **Celebrity examples with sun in Capricorn and Venus in Scorpio:** Actor Denzel Washington, Republican politician Ted Cruz, fashion designer Kate Spade

VENUS IN SAGITTARIUS

Fire signs are the least able to maintain Venusian balance and harmony. Connection can be singularly focused, and egoistic individualism can run amok. Capricorn with Venus in Sagittarius will be more spontaneous, charismatic, and freedom-seeking than your average Capricorn. This combination may be more likely to want alone time or long-distance relationships. **Celebrity examples with sun in Capricorn and Venus in Sagittarius:** Professional wrestler Chyna, American jazz trumpeter Chet Baker, American soul and gospel singer Merry Clayton, actor Jude Law

PRACTICAL ADVICE
for Capricorn in Love

Listen: Capricorns don't have to be so hard. You don't have to try so hard. You can soften by slathering moisturizer and fragrant oils onto your skin and wrapping yourself in silk. Self-soothing and sweetness are as easy as drinking tea from flowers and taking baths with the crystals and rocks that you already have easy access to. And you can have a wild orgasm alone and/or with others. Earth signs find a great deal of pleasure located in the body. Find partners who value your secret softness as much as they value your public displays of strength and capability. Find friends who love you deeply and allow them to see your messy humanness.

VENUS IN CAPRICORN

Capricorn Sun with Capricorn Venus will be slow-moving with emotions, reliable, and practical. This sun-Venus is the picture of beautiful perfection. Love is hands-on, material, and brings sustenance. Traditions must be examined and respected. This placement loves money and power and, when balanced, can put it to good use. **Celebrity examples with sun in Capricorn and Venus in Capricorn:** singer Elvis Presley, actress Diane Keaton, American polymath Benjamin Franklin, writer Susan Sontag, visual artist Kiki Smith

VENUS IN AQUARIUS

Venus in air sign Aquarius can connect and move about with ease. However, Venus needs to find an ability to act in loving connection, not just talk endlessly about the idea of connecting. Venus in Aquarius may like the concept or theory of love, but putting love into action may be a challenge. Besides, Aquarian Venus has higher visions to implement before settling into a monotonous relationship. **Celebrity examples with sun in Capricorn and Venus in Aquarius:** Actor and musician Jared Leto, songwriter and producer Phil Spector, Blue Ivy Carter (daughter of Beyoncé and Jay-Z), singer/musician Joanna Newsom

VENUS IN PISCES

Venus in Pisces softens the edges of rigid Capricorn Sun. By loving through merging, this combination is a softer, gentler version of Capricorn. Venus is especially strong in Pisces; those with this placement have an easier time connecting to the idea of universal love, forgiveness, and emotional connection. There may still be the desire to disassociate away from the feelings, so Capricorn Sun should focus on emotional responsibility. **Celebrity examples with sun in Capricorn and Venus in Pisces:** British singer-songwriter Rod Stewart, singer Pat Benatar, writer and poet Edgar Allan Poe.

CAPRICORN AT WORK

CAPRICORN THRIVES AT work. Old-fashioned, orderly, and prone to making and following the rules, Capricorns may be the best capitalists you know. The Capricorn archetype is a workaholic, bound to the rules and methodology of the system where they support implementation. Measured input of effort that results in external reward in the form of money, awards, or promotions thrills the Capricorn archetype. There is always room for improvement in the Capricorn's world, and it is no different in their work. Capricorn strives for achievement and accomplishment, and thrives in later life as a teacher, mentor, or CEO. There is no room for emotions or weakness in the Capricorn's work life.

If there is one aspect of life where Capricorn thrives in the struggles, accomplishments, and achievements most, it's at work. Capricorn loves to work. The Capricorn archetype is practically synonymous with work. Capricorn puts in the time and effort required to succeed. They commit to the hard work, whether or not they receive any recognition. Capricorn must be thoughtful about becoming too attached to their work and becoming a workaholic. Capricorn can envision the outcome, then perfectly execute their plans and pursue the goal at a slow, steady pace. They are truly able to accomplish whatever they put their minds to. They know about perfectionism, but they also need to learn about interdependence.

It's easy to see Saturn's influence in the Capricorn archetype in mainstream corporate culture; you must stay within certain boundaries and follow Saturn's rules. You must limit your clothing choices, your language, your behavior, and be willing to pay close attention to time. As the god of time, Saturn (Kronos) seeks to praise those who follow the laws of the land. In our system, money is the reward for obeying and worshiping orderly, chronological time. If you disrespect Saturn by running late or something about you falls outside of the limits, punishment and boundary setting take over.

BALANCED CAPRICORN AT WORK

At their best, Capricorn is a leader, mentor, and honored elder. They wield power over self to set high standards, and their work's quality and integrity speak for themselves. Their self-discipline serves to keep them in line with their goals. At their worst, they are individualistic workaholics who wield power over others through fear and domination. They can be materialistic, never satisfied, and always hungry for the next prize. Their self-discipline hurts them and those around them as they neglect relationships and prioritize profits over people.

Capricorn creates tangible results. The sign of utilization and public reputation is slow and steady, bound to the earth realm, and oriented toward what is real and practical. Capricorn is the dependable taskmaster, though perhaps at times pessimistic, depressed, and gloomy, but one who can fulfill their responsibilities. The sea goat must persevere through tedious to-do lists in order to get clarity around their sense of purpose and capability. Capricorn's journey through the work life and career will be filled with challenges, and the Capricorn's unique need is to pursue their goals even though they feel fear and insecurity. The person with a Capricorn Sun spends their life learning the lesson of dedication and follow-through—a lesson filled with dead ends, missteps, and hardship.

CELEBRITY FOCUS

Jeff Bezos

Jeff Bezos, CEO and founder of Amazon, has Capricorn Sun, Mercury, and Mars, with moon in either Sagittarius or Capricorn. He also has Saturn/Venus in Aquarius.

Bezos certainly exhibits the traits of a well-oiled Saturn machine: calculating, exacting, and driven to achieve. He embodies the Capricornian traits of self-control and shrewd decision-making, but he also seems to show the shadow side of Capricorn, which can be cruel, ruthless, and power hungry.

Bezos may be seen as a hero to some—a self-made billionaire who sits in a position of extreme wealth and power. The CEO of Amazon is one of the richest people in the world, and Amazon is slated to become the first company worth a trillion dollars in the coming years. He projects a steely, controlled exterior; he even sculpted his body from scrawny and bookish to bulked-up and buff as his company became more powerful.

Bezos is also loathed by some people and can be viewed as a villain: a rich white man hoarding wealth and power, causing mass devastation in pursuit of financial gain. The workplace environment at Amazon has been reported to be brutal and dehumanizing, especially for lower-level employees. Bezos is known to have made cruel remarks toward his staff, calling them stupid and lazy. And yet there are working-class Amazon employees who rely on food stamps and federal aid because wages are so low, job security is nonexistent, and work conditions are inhumane. Journalists have shed light on policies that discourage warehouse employees from bathroom breaks and moving slowly, as slacking off will get you fired. Yet even the success of Amazon has not been enough to quench his thirst for power—he has acquired Whole Foods, the *Washington Post*, and Blue Origin, his private "space tourism" company. Though he has caused suffering in the name of profit, in some corners he continues to be seen as a success story and continues to find new ways to dominate, colonize and "pioneer."

However, the Capricorn Sun at work is pursuing the soul's path through determination, patience, discernment, and ambition. Capricorn sees no way around the hard work and instead plunges into the task with incredibly focused self-discipline. Perhaps it seems to the outsider that the Capricorn employee or boss always takes the long way; Capricorns may find themselves annoyed with coworkers who take shortcuts or fail to meet a deadline. Once a goal is reached, another goal is soon identified.

Though the archetype of Capricorn fits perfectly into corporate culture, the Capricorn Sun person might not. Many actors, singers, entertainers, and pop culture icons have their sun in the sign of the sea goat. Depending on many other factors in the chart, the Capricorn Sun may pursue accomplishments in many different fields. Capricorn finds purpose and structure within institutions, such as academia, government, or in the political/public service realm. Systems of government and businesses might be places where Capricorns flourish. But given their ability to take responsibility and build an external structure of power and influence, Capricorn Sun people can also be successful business owners and entrepreneurs. Yet Capricorn must be aware of how they wield their own power over others; be aware of corrupt behavior and hoarding of resources that often accompany access to power. Capricorn individuals should focus on wielding power over their own behavior and using self-discipline for personal development rather than meddling in the lives of others.

David Allen, a Capricorn Sun with a strong Libra influence, is an author and productivity coach who is known for creating a time management method called Getting Things Done. He is quoted as saying, "You can do anything, but not everything," which should be the mantra for Capricorn Suns all over the planet. There are limitations to our achievements, and we are more than the sum of what we achieve. Capricorns must exercise patience and focus on their goals. While the Capricorn person is incredibly determined, they must be willing to stay with their ideas for the long haul, rather than immediately discarding the dreams that don't bring instant satisfaction.

Archetypical Capricorn wants to influence the systems that govern the world and help influence those systems of power whenever possible. Though extremely capable, Capricorn should beware of shadow expressions at work. Astrologer Steven Forrest calls Capricorn "ambitious, materialistic, power hungry...calculating, manipulative, quick to exploit any weakness." Indeed, when defining self-worth based solely on achievement and accomplishment, the Capricorn archetype becomes a Scrooge, capable of hurting others to achieve success. A challenge for the Capricorn at work is to deconstruct the myth of individualism. Capricorn believes that if they just try hard enough, they can accomplish any task. However, life on planet Earth is connected, collaborative, and interdependent. Though Capricorn may believe that they don't need anyone to reach great heights, and perhaps that is true, the Capricorn's life will be much less satisfying without community and relationships. Instead of sitting on a pile of hard-earned resources and money, the Capricorn person can focus on community wellness and redistribute some of their wealth.

PLANETARY FOCUS:
Mars

Mars is the planet of assertion, courage, aggression, impulse, and rage. The ancient planetary force known as Mars to the Romans (and Ares to the Greeks) was a destructive and destabilizing god who ruled agriculture, military, and war. Mars in the natal chart points to our inner warrior; it speaks to how we protect ourselves when threatened. Mars needs conflict and tension, something to fight for or fight against. Mars can also be experienced as a gut reaction of desire or repulsion.

Mars takes approximately two years to travel around the entire zodiac, staying in each sign for approximately one and a half months. The glyph for Mars is the circle of spirit with an outward-focused arrow, also representing the shield and sword of the Martian warrior. This symbol is also used as the male symbol, though every person has a natal Mars that influences anger and enthusiasm. The element and sign Mars is located in can add nuance to the questions: What is work? How and why do I engage with work? What is satisfying about my actions and how do I assert myself out in the world?

MARS IN CAPRICORN

When a person has Mars is in Capricorn, fiery hot Mars is exacting, powerful, and able to bravely pursue what they desire. However, Capricorn Mars-Sun individuals may find a need to control their anger and beware of

affirmations for
CAPRICORN AT WORK

* I don't have to do everything by myself. Yes, I am strong and capable, but I am so much more than what I can produce.

* I am worthy, even when I am broke and unemployed. I am worthy, even when I am just starting out on a new path.

* I connect with others in the workplace and practice reciprocity.

an overinflated, power-seeking ego. Mars is exalted, or supremely powerful, in the sign of Capricorn, where the planet of war is strong, capable of assertion, and gets things done. The cold/dark influence when Mars is located in Saturnian Capricorn means that the internal fire of the individual burns a little less brightly, but it gains extreme self-control and a cardinal urge for power, or the exploration of power dynamics. Mars in Capricorn emphasizes the relationship between Mars and Saturn, the two planets that bring us face-to-face with hardships, limitations, and challenges. Aquarius Sun artist Barbara Kruger has natal Mars/Mercury in Capricorn; her work primarily consists of messages critiquing cultural constructs of power and sexual politics.

MARS IN AN EARTH SIGN

In receptive signs of earth and water, Mars has a hard time acting with impulsive courage. This can be a good thing, as is cools the temper and slows things down, but it can also bring indecisiveness. Earth Mars has their feet planted firmly in reality. Mars wants to know: What are the real opportunities and limitations? How do we best proceed with what is here? This Mars is not interested in fantasy and play as much as completing the tasks at hand. Earth Mars can bring patience and focus to the planet of war but can also get stuck or too detail-oriented to act.

MARS IN A WATER SIGN

Like Mars in Earth, the watery Mars is more introverted and passive. Water's sensitivity and depth can support Mars in behaving with more compassion, but it can also lead to passive-aggressive actions. Water Mars gives an intuitive and empathetic edge to the god of rage. Mars wants to assert the individual needs, yet water signs are extremely aware of the impact they have on others and the consequences of their behavior. Mars's energy can be unfocused and more internal than external. Art and spiritual practice may be positive outlets for those with this placement.

MARS IN A FIRE SIGN

Mars is a hot, dry planet, and when located in the hot and dry element of fire, Mars is competitive, aggressive, and powerful. Fiery Mars is strong, yet a strong Mars is often a destructive force in a person's life. A hot Mars is great for getting personal needs met, but more likely to cause ego issues and an inflamed temper. Physical activity and an outlet for healthy competition are great ways to focus this placement.

MARS IN AN AIR SIGN

Air signs deal with connection, fluidity, and duality, which is difficult for the planet of assertion. Air Mars wants to take action, whether it be fight or flight, and does not want to have to weigh multiple options or see both sides. Mars can get stuck trying to accommodate the changeable nature of air; it may be difficult to figure out which battles to fight and which battles to walk away from. People with Air Mars may have many interests; they may waffle back and forth about an important decision.

CONCLUSION

Capricorn deserves the freedom to pursue their own path. The path that works for the Capricorn may not be what works for their friends and siblings or their parents and mentors. Defining the self is a lifelong process, so Capricorns shouldn't be discouraged if they are still stumbling around in the dark. They should tend to their future ancestor selves, the part of themselves that will be humble and humorous, a grandparent type, the wise and knowing elder.

Capricorn has so many ways of expressing and wants so badly to be seen as capable. The most difficult part of the Capricorn archetype is the capacity for pain, depression, suffering, and anguish; these are the sea goat teachers, directing them toward what is important and away from what is frivolous. Lessons about when and how to follow the rules will always be difficult, but many Capricorns look backward through the ups and downs of life and see the important lessons in the hard times. A devastating breakup can be a chance at freedom. The loss of a job gives opportunity for travel and a new career trajectory. Illness can help us slow down. No one makes it through human life unscarred, but the Capricorn can seek to find the wisdom buried in hardship.

An individual's natal chart is a complex and beautiful thing. Looking to the natal chart gives more depth and understanding than a book about all the ways archetypes could possibly express in a person's life. Working with a professional astrologer can shed light on how individual strengths and weaknesses show up over time. As was mentioned earlier, the natal chart is somewhat static but is also moving and shifting, influenced by planetary cycles. Astrologers have different ways of interpreting the same information, so interested Capricorns should find one whose voice resonates with them. They should beware of interpretations that are actually just vaguely masked sexism, or more specifically, the idea that Capricorn men are strong and Capricorn women are bitter. Or better than seeing an astrologer for a reading, Capricorns can study astrology and learn the language themselves!

Everyone can benefit from astrology. Benjamin Franklin, J.P. Morgan, and Nancy Reagan were some unlikely advocates for astrology. Astrology can be helpful for those with a strong spiritual belief system (including mainstream religion) as well as those who are non-religious or who find a spiritual connection in nature.

A WORD ABOUT FATE VERSUS FREE WILL

Do we have control of our lives, or are our lives destined by the stars? Astrologers always want to talk about fate versus free will, whether the unfolding of human life is predetermined by outside forces or within our control, whether we should view the planets as actual forces of a higher power, and so on. I prefer analogies: astrology is the weather, and when you can predict the weather, you might be able to find out if you'll need to carry an umbrella or wear shorts. Why can't we see these outside forces as energies to work collaboratively with, instead of bending them to our will? Perhaps that's the wrong question for a chapter on Capricorn.

Maybe there are fated fates. Planetary condition can be determined, though modern astrologers prefer to give things a positive twist. We always have some ability to act, the capacity to make decisions that either reinforce our own worldview or dismantle it. Even within the notion of fate exists some variation. Astrologers may be able to read the general vibe, but they cannot predict with certainty the outcome of a situation. While it may be tempting to view astrology as a predictive tool, or astrologers as magical psychics who can peer into the future, it's always most helpful to pay special attention to the environment and social constructs around us. What are the planets telling us about our conditioning and our world? What can we learn by viewing things a slightly different way? Are there opportunities to see an obstacle as a gift from a place beyond our control? As a scientist, I see astrology as data collection. While the data is flawed, just like all data, it can tell us something important. And just like scientific data, astrological interpretation is somewhat subjective and influenced by sociopolitical context. Astrology as a language has survived and is now flourishing among younger generations. This is a connection back to source, back to the misunderstood and mysterious parts of human life on planet Earth.

JAN. 20–FEB. 18

text by Taylor Moon

element — AIR

symbol — THE WATER-BEARER

modality — FIXED

house — ELEVENTH

ruler — URANUS

SAMPLING

INTRODUCTION

I REMEMBER THE FIRST time I looked at my horoscope in the local newspaper. I was around eight years old sitting with my grandma at her kitchen table while she was drinking her coffee and reading the front page. Though I usually grabbed the comic strip section, I also liked reading the advice section where people would write in and get advice from the columnist.

Right below this section was labeled "Your Daily Horoscope." Intrigued, I looked a little closer. Each horoscope seemed to predict how your day would go based on your zodiac sign, and according to my birthday I was apparently an Aquarius. It gave a basic prediction that I would have a great conversation with a friend that day, and my young mind was shocked that someone had the ability to predict how my day could go. This was my introduction to learning about the zodiac signs, and I've been hooked ever since!

From that day forward, I would read my horoscope in my small town's newspaper almost daily. I also discovered that my mother had a few astrology books on her bookshelf, so one day I decided to look up "Aquarius" in one of the books. As I read, descriptions such as "aloof," "detached," and "unemotional" seemed to be a theme. "This doesn't sound much like me..." I thought, but also being the Aquarius I am I tried to keep an open mind about it.

All of these years later, I realized that even those of us who call ourselves astrologers have a difficult time describing Aquarians. Often called the "aliens" of the zodiac, they possess a certain quirkiness, but also a groundedness that makes it difficult for people to put their finger on them. All at once, the Aquarius personality can be active, expressive, interesting, and inspirational, yet at other times moody, indifferent, and apathetic due to their sometimes serious way of thinking. Because they have a coolheaded demeanor and tend to keep emotions somewhat under lock and key, people can't easily point Aquarius out like they can a passionate fire or sensitive water sign. And if they are more of a Saturnian Aquarius, they may be mistaken for a responsible and stable earth sign.

So what exactly does it mean to be an Aquarius? First, let's discuss a little astronomy. From our viewpoint on Earth, the sun travels around the Earth once per year. Over the course of that year, the sun seems to appear "in front of" or "in" different constellations for about a month, and the dates often listed for horoscopes are when the sun appears in that specific astrological sign. The passage of the sun through a particular zodiac assisted ancient cultures in knowing what time of year it was. The sun is our most powerful planet. Without it, the Earth would cease to exist. Just like the sun gives light, food, life, and warmth to the planet, in astrology, your sun sign is the essence of your personality. Your sun sign is your identity, your energy source, ego, and the true you. If you were born between January 20 and February 18, you were born when the sun was in the constellation Aquarius. So congratulations, you are an AQUARIUS! Dates may differ from year to year, though.

Aquarius, the eleventh sign of the zodiac, is typically depicted as the water-bearer and is symbolized by a glyph that looks like water or electric waves. Because of these two symbols, people mistakenly think that Aquarius is a water sign, but that's not the case. Aquarius is one of three air signs, and is represented by a human figure pouring water from an urn (i.e., the water carrier), eternally ready to pour forth spiritual knowledge to the people. The water does not represent emotion, it represents wisdom and truth.

According to the book *Archetypes of the Zodiac* by Kathleen Burt, Aquarius is "artistically depicted as an angel, an immortal messenger to mankind from the gods, a perfected being who has liberated himself from the limitations of time and space so that he can fly between heaven and Earth with his lofty concepts. Angels inspire, guide, instruct, guard, protect, and sometimes struggle with us to do the right thing. Superior beings, intermediaries between God and man.

"Some Aquarians have the gentle and generous disposition of the (Buddhist) Bodhisattva, others are fiercer angels who fight for principle (which displays the courageous nature of the Leo polarity). Like all signs, it depends on the energies in the individual horoscope."

Embracing their angel-like gifts and truth-telling natures, most Aquarius are born to give back to humanity by spreading truth and knowledge to everyone around them. The dominant key phrase of Aquarius is "I KNOW." And Aquarius does know, to an extent. Even an Aquarius child seems to be wise beyond their years, but the true wisdom of an Aquarius is developed through their life experiences and personal quest for knowledge, in which bits and pieces of valuable information are obtained throughout the years. Their keen powers of observation (scientific mind) allow them to move through life noting important details while engaging their power of analysis, synthesis, and classification rather quickly. Aquarians also have an amazing imagination (artistic mind) and are able to use it to visualize the creation of new things essential to their progress and the progression of humanity. Their imagination allows them to reflect on the past with clarity and help them form ideas and a practical vision for the future.

As the eleventh sign of the zodiac, Aquarius is considered the visionary sign of the future. The ruling planet of Aquarius is Uranus, which means that an Aquarius will embody many of the characteristics that Uranus represents. Uranus rules innovation, sudden change, and revelation. It also governs the future and new technology, including all that is newly invented, newly designed, and yet to be perceived. Innovative, unpredictable, determined, imaginative, quirky, and willing to do what has never been done before, Uranus also rules creativity and scientific genius. Uranus is considered

> Aquarians also have an amazing imagination (artistic mind) and are able to use it to visualize the creation of new things essential to their progress and the progression of humanity.

to be revolutionary—ready to break rules and demolish established patterns or structures, creating sudden and radical change. Uranus's movement through the Universe usually creates great change here on Earth. Uranus gives a strong impulse for rebellion, independence, and upheaval. Wave-maker and reforming Uranus will overturn anything traditional, conventional, or orthodox that it believes has outworn its usefulness.

Uranus produces the most liberating results as quickly as possible, and blends fact with intuition on its journey to uncover universal truths. Uranus is considered the perceptive and intellectual companion of the planet Mercury (Mercury represents our communication style and mental processes), and is strongly objective, brainy, and eager to share. People with strong Uranian influences (like Aquarians) in their charts are trailblazers and trendsetters in their communities.

With revolutionary and avant-garde Uranus ruling Aquarius, it is understandable that Aquarians are unique, individualistic, and unconventional people who refuse to follow the crowd and insist on following their own path. Aquarius revels in nonconformity and demands freedom and independence for themselves and for others, which is why you will find many Aquarians who are activists and working in the social justice and human rights fields. Their personalities are progressive, liberal, and inventive, and they have both an objective and creative mind. People view Aquarius as slightly eccentric—not necessarily weird in a "bad way" (because people love to be around them), but definitely a character that marches to the beat of their own drum with an unusual way of viewing the world. Sometimes a bit of a daredevil, most Aquarians have a hilarious sense of humor with an ability to shock and amuse at the same time (for example, there are many famous comedians that are Aquarians!). Most people know that Aquarians are open to new concepts and the discussion of radical ideas (an Aquarius loves a good conspiracy theory and isn't afraid to share their opinion!).

"Uranian Aquarians look skyward and tend to be utopian souls unless they have many planets in Earth, Capricorn Rising, or strong Saturn in their [birth] chart. They want to live spontaneously in the here and now, and they usually express disdain for the mundane routines of the work world with its balanced budgets and pension plans. Uranian Aquarians ask questions like 'why is it necessary to hold down a dull job? To get married and take on all that responsibility—mortgages, kids' orthodontal bills, tuition fees—Why go through all of that? What is the purpose of it?'" says Kathleen Burt in her book *Archetypes of the Zodiac*.

The quote above doesn't mean that an Aquarius won't decide to settle down or have children (because many do), it's just that as an air sign, Aquarius's perspective is intellectual rather than emotional. They are willing to weigh the pros and cons of every option before making a decision. Most Aquarians also take a lot of pride in their expression of freedom and individuality. They refuse to be boxed in, and usually encourage others to rock the boat and go against societal norms too! They may be your neighborhood "purple-haired weirdo" and express their uniqueness through their choice of fashion (e.g., tattoos, bold clothing choices, fun hair styles, or bohemian flair), their strange and interesting set of friends and associates (has your Aquarius friend invited another eccentric stranger to dinner?), or their varying hobbies and interests (an Aquarius may be at a real estate conference one day, and the next day they could be speaking on a panel about paranormal activity in old homes—you never know!).

The complexity of Aquarius may be explained by Aquarius not only being ruled by Uranus, but also being traditionally ruled by the planet Saturn. Before Uranus was discovered in 1781 by Sir William Herschel, Aquarius used to be considered governed by Saturn for centuries, which some astrologers still reference (though it's not clear exactly what date Uranus became the modern ruler of Aquarius). It is a bit easier to understand an Aquarius once we understand the integration of the different energies of both planets within them—Uranus with its need for freedom and the destruction of systems and structures that are old and in need of replacement, and Saturn with its restricting, structured, and disciplined method of operation.

Saturn is a planet that is always building toward the future. Saturn brings structure and meaning to our world, and knows the limits of time and matter. It reminds us of our boundaries, our responsibilities, and the commitments that we make. Saturn makes us aware of the need for self-control and discipline as a means for greater consciousness and fulfillment. Saturn is often associated with our fathers or authority figures. In childhood, the discipline, rules, and regulations imposed on us by our authority figures—from parents, teachers, and the like—were not always pleasant, but they actually helped us to understand the world around us. Similarly, Saturn's lessons actually help us to grow.

People are surprised to learn that Aquarius is one of the zodiac's four fixed signs, which means that although they love to live life unrestricted by society and want everyone to experience their own liberation, there is a stubbornness and judgmental aspect to an Aquarian that may be explained by Saturn's influence. As much as Aquarius loves to tear down systems that are outdated and no longer serve the people, they still believe in stability, structure, and order. They prefer to set a goal and then begin building toward that future and, strangely enough, can be resistant to changes if they believe things were working just fine the way they were. So as radical and eccentric as they can be, Aquarius, being the sign of the scientist or inventor, insists on maintaining order and strict procedures so they can obtain the most accurate results. This fixed aspect is especially apparent in Aquarius friendships. There is no sign that is as loyal as an Aquarius to their friends—they are ready to defend and care for their friends for a lifetime.

Due to Saturn's influence, Aquarius may need to learn to compromise their rebellious nature somewhat in order to function and have some level of success on Earth. Unless they are able to do this, they may have a hard time embodying the water-bearer quality of pouring spiritual wisdom into others. Saturn takes responsibility very seriously, and this works well with the independent and freedom-loving nature of Aquarius by giving them time to live life and ask the appropriate questions along the way.

Even the most radical Aquarius—you know, the one who had a blue mohawk as a teenager, dabbled in recreational drugs, and bucked against the system—begins to feel the pull of Saturn as they get older, especially around the ages of twenty-seven to thirty when Saturn returns to the position it was at their birth. At this point, called the Saturn Return, the rebellious Aquarian will become a bit more serious. They may begin to think about settling down, asking questions like "what is my purpose in life?" and considering the opinions people have of them. This doesn't mean that a free and easy Aquarian will all of a sudden don a suit instead of leather pants, but they do begin to consider their impact on the world and what kind of person they want to be.

On the flip side, the Aquarius that was always a bit more focused and serious—you know, the one

> There is no sign that is as loyal as an Aquarius to their friends—they are ready to defend and care for their friends for a lifetime.

who excelled in school, is loved and adored by friends and family, and is known to be responsible and wise—may begin to go through a shift of energies when approaching their Saturn Return.

During this time, friends and family may witness the usually logical and thoughtful Aquarius give up their long-term career and begin to hang out with some new and unusual friends, rebel against traditional religion, and unabashedly try new experiences and hobbies that peak their interest.

Like all of the signs, Aquarius is beautiful, complex, and inspirational, yet sometimes confusing—which is typical of the human experience! The following pages will discuss how an Aquarius engages with the world and operates in different areas of life. My hope is that after reading this chapter you have a better understanding of what it means to be an Aquarius or of the awesome and unique Aquarians in your life. Of course, studying your sun sign is just the beginning of understanding your unique nature as you have many planets in your birth chart that make up the totality of your personality. We are all complex humans, but at the minimum, understanding your sun sign gives you an amazing advantage and a pathway to self-awareness and self-determination, and a deep understanding of your personality.

AQUARIUS AS A CHILD

EVERY CHILD BORN comes into this life with their own unique personality and life purpose. The adults in that child's life are their teachers and guides, helping them to navigate through life and learn lessons necessary for their growth.

Aquarian children are bursting with energy, feeling, and a touch of genius, and parents should be prepared to raise a visionary soul filled with curiosity. Since they are often marching to the beat of their own drum, from an early age you will notice that your little water-bearer is an independent thinker and wise beyond their years. As their teacher and guide, be prepared to answer a ton of questions, as an Aquarian child is always trying to understand life through their personal experiences and the experiences of others.

Aquarius is ruled by the rebellious and freedom-loving Uranus, which means your little water-bearer will definitely keep you on your toes! You may notice your Aquarius baby taking in the world around them with wide-eyed wonderment. As they grow and develop, Aquarius babies will fixate on anything that captures their attention, and once they are able to crawl, they will explore to their heart's content, usually bypassing the awesome toys you bought them to experiment with household items that aren't meant for play (such as houseplants, cabinets, and furniture). Make sure to keep an eye on your Aqua-babe, but also understand that they are invoking their scientific natural gifts by engaging the five senses.

As an intellectual air sign, Aquarius children tend to have a calm and inquisitive personality, mostly because they are busy taking in the world around them. However, Aquarians are known to be the rebels of the zodiac, so you may be caught off guard when their calm and cool attitude suddenly turns into an emotional tug-of-war! As the last of the zodiac's fixed signs, Aquarians can be quite stubborn, especially when something

AQUARIUS CHILD MOMENTS

Unexpected sweet moments like the example below are not uncommon to the experience of an Aquarius child:

ADULT: (sits down and sighs heavily)

AQUARIUS CHILD: "Are you okay?"

ADULT: "Yes, I'm okay, just stressed out about a few grownup things. I'll be okay though."

AQUARIUS CHILD: "It will be okay! Sometimes things are bad and then they get good again. Maybe you can ask someone to help you!"

ADULT: "That's actually a good idea. And you are right, things always get good again. Maybe I can ask my daughter for help."

AQUARIUS CHILD: "You have a daughter? What's her name?"

ADULT: "Her name is Amy, she's twenty-two."

AQUARIUS CHILD: "Wow, twenty-two! She can definitely help! She's a grown-up!"

ADULT: "Yeah, but her brother is twenty-six and does not act like a grown-up at all. That's actually what I'm a little upset about. I wish he would get himself together. I—(pauses when they realize they are talking to an eight-year-old). He will be okay though. Thanks for your help! You are such a kind and wise young person!"

happens that they don't like or didn't expect to happen. Though your little water-bearer may insist that things go their way, it is important for them to learn the difference between freedom and rebelliousness.

The cosmic key phrase of Aquarius is "I KNOW" and as symbolized by the image of the water-bearer, Aquarians are here to pour their water of knowledge into the souls and spirits of humanity. There is a wisdom, kindness, and compassion that is apparent in Aquarian children from the start. Once these children are old enough to start communicating and exchanging ideas, adults may find themselves accidentally wrapped in mature conversation with an Aquarius child without meaning to. There's something about an Aquarius child that screams "old soul." In the African American community, there is a saying that "he/she has been here before," and this is definitely applicable to Aquarian children. They are born with a wisdom and understanding that is sometimes seen as otherworldly. This is why other people tend to label Aquarians as being aloof, detached, or unemotional. Their ability to put logic over emotion is a bit unorthodox. Sometimes referred to as the "aliens" of the zodiac, it can be difficult to put your finger on an Aquarian child. But according to ancient Greek mythology, Aquarians are often depicted as angels, immortal messengers from the gods here to inspire, guide, protect, and sometimes struggle to help humanity do the right thing.

You may notice that they are a bit eccentric or a tad different from other children. As an air sign, Aquarius has a mental approach to life and often approaches situations from a scientific point of view. They may surprise you with occasional weird statements or odd behavior, but it's best to just let them be themselves and absorb the world in a way that works best for them. Aquarius is the rebel of the zodiac, and if you begin to try to control their behavior, they will surely rebel!

According to Shefali Tsabary, author of *The Conscious Parent*, "Children learn who they are and what they really enjoy if they are allowed to sit with themselves." Inundated with activity and subjected to lesson upon lesson, how can they hope to recognize their authentic voice amid the din of all this "doing"? Your Aqua-child needs freedom and room to think, to explore, and to just be. They may be more interested in the world of thoughts and ideas rather than physical activity, but what's most important is to nurture the things that they find interesting. Some Aquarians have a competitive spirit and love sports; others may have a creative streak and like to act or paint. Anything technical will typically catch their eye and anything having to do with electronics, space travel, computers, or the esoteric will peak their interest. Most likely your Aquarian child will dabble in a bit of everything!

One of the key characteristics of all Aquarians is their need for freedom. Your little Aquarius needs to be out and about. Set them free in outdoor spaces! Allow them to run, jump, scream, laugh, dig in the mud, climb trees, and play with neighborhood children. It is also great to introduce your Aquarian child to travel early in life. It doesn't have to be another country; even the next town over will invoke their curiosity and they will drink in each moment. They will love learning about new places, people, and cultures and will carry those experiences with them forever.

An Aquarius child can either be a popular socialite (as Aquarius rules groups and friendships) or they may be a bit of an intellectual oddball. It's important to cultivate and nurture an Aquarius child's natural way of being. If they are more of a socialite, get them involved with clubs, activities, and sports at an early age to encourage their Aquarian sense of humanitarianism, tolerance, and team spirit! Aquarius rules teamwork, so getting them involved in sports early on (even if they aren't the greatest athlete) will be a great benefit. Team-focused sports like basketball, softball, dance, or even bowling will be great for their competitive spirits and need to socialize with others. America's favorite NBA player Michael Jordan is an Aquarius, so don't be surprised if your little Aquarian makes the all-star team!

If the Aquarius child is more eccentric and off-beat, sign them up for activities that nurture their intelligence and passions and allow them to interact and form friendships with children similar to them! Is your child more interested in naming the different galaxies in the Universe than playing on the playground? Nurture their expansive mind by taking them to the bookstore and signing them up for a class at your local planetarium! It may even be a good idea to look into alternative educational settings so they can be stimulated by a curriculum that supports their interests and be surrounded by other children who share their intellect. This will prevent them from feeling like an outcast by providing that sense of belonging we all desire.

The scientists Charles Darwin, Thomas Edison, and Galileo were all Aquarians, and it is likely that your child will display some of their own traits of being a scientist, no matter what. Aquarians love science, magic, and mysteries. Your little genius will love any activity that stretches their mind and allows them to experiment. Get them a chemistry set or a magic trick kit and give them a tablet with scientific computer games/puzzles and watch them soar to new intellectual heights! Get ready—your baby genius will want to show you all of the cool things they are learning!

Aquarius children with siblings are great role models. As young children, they are the best to create fun games and activities with, and they are leaders who will make sure to look after their siblings when out and about. Aquarius is known as the defender of the underdog, so trust and believe that no one will be messing with their brother or sister when their Aquarius sibling is around! This type of loyalty and care also extends to good friends. If you mess with a loved one of an Aquarius, you better be ready for a fight!

Aquarians are the rebels of the zodiac, and this will be apparent in an Aquarius child from an early age. As a fixed sign, they are convicted in their beliefs and ideals, and it can be difficult to change their minds once they are made up. Be mindful of not talking down to your Aquarius child or treating them like a baby. It's best to approach Aquarius children with logical and sensible rules and expectations; otherwise, they will turn into little activists and protest against your authority. Again, this is when you will see that Aquarius is a fixed sign because they will dig their heels in and not budge until a compromise is made. It is important to make sure expectations are clear, because if you do not follow through with a consequence or punishment, your Aquarius child may begin to lose respect for your authority and begin to walk all over you. It's important to stress that true freedom comes with responsibility, and they should know the difference between freedom and rebellion.

Aquarius children may also express their daredevil spirit and need for freedom in the way they dress. Born with a unique sense of fashion, they will prefer to choose their own outfits to wear for the day, and will often have a few favorites that they always wear. You may also have a few of your own forehead-slapping moments when your little Aquarius attempts to leave the house in an outfit that doesn't particularly match or even a costume when it's way past Halloween. If you can bear it, let them wear it. Otherwise, you may find yourself having a debate that you didn't sign up for!

This sign loves to have a goal to pursue or something to look forward to. Guide them through life by helping them analyze their decisions and answering questions they may have. Oftentimes, Aquarius children are very observant of the people closest to them and will ask questions to gain a deep understanding to apply lessons to their own life.

As they get older, parents of more eccentric Aquarians may wonder when their child will find their niche in life. (When will he stop rebelling and join the rest of us here on Earth? Why is he so rebellious? Will they always be a bachelor? Will I ever have grandchildren? I'm okay with them finding themselves, but can they find a job or profession in the meantime? Why are they so restless? Why are they always asking "why"? Why are they running away from responsibility?) Parents may also be concerned because as the sign representing groups and friendships, an Aquarius tends to have friends from all walks of life. However, it is important for an Aquarius to choose the right friends and companions for their journey through life, and it's important for parents of Aquarius teens to carefully monitor who their child is allowing into their circle.

Raising a child is the highest assignment from the universe, no matter their sign. And with an Aquarius as a child, know that you are not only their greatest teacher, but also that you are meant to learn many lessons from them.

AQUARIUS AS AN ADULT

ADULTING ISN'T EASY, but when a person understands the qualities and characteristics of their zodiac sign it can help them navigate life with more confidence. A person's zodiac sign is actually their sun sign. When the sun sign is assigned at birth by the cosmos, the qualities of that sign are what a person is in the process of becoming. While the moon sign represents a person's instincts and who they already are, their sun sign is their birthright—the personality and qualities that make them uniquely them, which they will learn to develop over their lifetime. As they express the full characteristics of this sign, they will become more confident and experience greater fulfillment.

Aquarius is the eleventh sign of the zodiac and is typically depicted as the water-bearer: a human figure pouring water from an urn or container, symbolically ready to pour forth spiritual wisdom to the people. Aquarius is also symbolized by a glyph that looks like water or electric waves. Because of these two symbols, people mistakenly think that Aquarius is a water sign, but this isn't the case—Aquarius is actually an air sign, one of three zodiac air signs representing mental processing and communication. The water pouring from the urn does not represent emotion as it would for zodiac water signs, it represents wisdom and truth. As an air sign, Aquarius is curious, observant, and social, and loves to share ideas with others. Air signs are thinkers, and it is typical to find Aquarius in their own head processing their experiences as well as figuring out next steps for the future.

An adult Aquarius is unique, people-oriented, and diverse in their way of thinking and behaving in the world. Always thinking in large terms and creating plans that cover a large number of people, Aquarius governs friendship, community, groups, and technology. Because of this, you will find Aquarians participating in all areas of society—politics, entertainment and media, education, art, technology, and more! No matter what area they find their purpose in, Aquarius is always on the search for truth that leaves no room for intolerance or conformity to out-of-date ideas. An Aquarius's vision is broad, and they value intellectual viewpoints rather than emotional ones because they believe emotional confusion can cloud judgment. This is why they weigh the pros and cons of every theory before coming to a final conclusion—not to prove or disprove, but to uncover the truth and the best possible path.

Some of the words used to describe Aquarians include philanthropic, innovative, avant-garde, strange, community oriented, fair, open-minded, original, connecting, inviting, rational reasoning, coolheaded logic, objective, and visionary. Using these descriptive skills and personality traits, Aquarians love to collaborate with others to improve the lives of the people who need it most and are not afraid to buck tradition to make the world a better place for everyone.

Speaking of bucking tradition, Aquarius is known as the rebel of the zodiac—ready to reject societal norms and refusing to conform to a singular way of thinking or being in the world. Being the forward-thinking visionaries that they are, Aquarians are known for reaching into the future to discover new technologies and new concepts for tomorrow, while also tearing down outmoded structures and systems of the past. Aquarians question everything, especially those systems and rules that do not serve people in a way that works well. They are also known as the zodiac's conspiracy

AQUARIUS IN SUMMARY

Apparent Sense of Humor

Most Aquarians have a quirky personality and a hilarious sense of humor. This quick-witted air sign loves to dish out a joke or two, though usually not at the expense of anyone in particular. Friendly and social overall, their attitude toward others is kind, friendly, and tolerant. They are usually out and about and can be found as a participant in many community events, groups, and social organizations. They also like to hit the town and attend beautiful events like art gallery openings, panel discussions, or a nice dinner with friends—anything that stimulates their minds and gives them a new experience to look forward to!

Great Conversationalists

Air signs love to have conversations and bounce ideas off of others. When you're having a conversation with an Aquarius in particular, all topics are on the table. As they are natural humanitarians with a wide variety of interests, talk to them about books, art, social issues, culture, and scientific matters. Feel free to bring up philosophy, aliens, politics, cloning, racial injustice, etc.; no matter the subject, an Aquarius is always ready to dive into the discussion. Though they may not remember the names of the people they were talking to later on, they will be able to remember details about what they talked about in their conversation as well as particular phrases used. Aquarius has the ability to catalogue and file away all kinds of relevant and irrelevant data—like what color the person was wearing or the fact that someone they were talking to loves sushi—but later the Aquarius may realize they don't remember that person's name!

Coolheaded and Emotionally Detached

Aquarians aren't big on displaying their deepest feelings, especially when asked to share their vulnerabilities or acknowledge someone's hurt feelings. This gives them the reputation of being aloof. However, this doesn't mean they don't care! Aquarians have feelings just like everyone else, of course, but prefer to process their emotions internally rather than openly or with another person. While this doesn't help in intimate relationships, this coolheadedness is great for leadership positions as Aquarians will be able to make levelheaded decisions that work for everyone. People can't "get" to an Aquarius because Aquarius can see what the agenda of the other person is. Even if they are upset, an Aquarius will hold it in so those people won't get the satisfaction of seeing them unhinged.

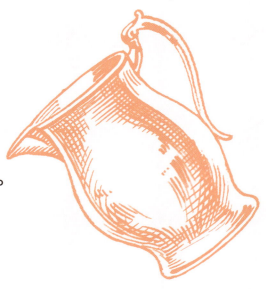

Awesome Eye for Design and Style

Uranus-ruled Aquarius is also known for having an artistic eye. This is apparent in the way that they dress to the way they design their home. Many Aquarians are fashion forward—no matter the style they choose (whether it's bohemian or more conservative), an Aquarius likes to express their uniqueness in the way they choose to dress (even if that uniqueness is refusing to wear anything that isn't comfortable!). They also like to have a well-designed home filled with trinkets from their travels and adventures based on their preferred choice of style. Aquarians can also be found in many artistic and design fields such as entertainment and media, acting, start-ups, human-centered design, and interior decorating.

theorists—they are not afraid to question the things that everyone else takes as truth—especially if all the facts aren't adding up! But Aquarians should also be mindful of maintaining a healthy rebellious balance as this sign can produce militant radicals, extremists, and "rebels without a cause" when led with misinformation or connected to the wrong people. But this group has also produced some of the most famous and effective humanitarians and thought leaders in history—including Angela Davis, Susan B. Anthony, Charles Darwin, and Fredrick Douglass.

Some Aquarians may feel out of sync with their time because not many people their age seem to "get them" or be in sync with their way of thinking. This is why many Aquarians are friends with people older than them, even if they do have a peer group that they connect with. Aquarius is a sign of rational thinking, clear logic, and philanthropic concerns. They are not a fan of open and public displays of emotion and tend to process their thoughts and feelings internally in order to approach situations in the most sensible way. Their preferred way of dealing with problems is to approach them from an open-minded perspective by stepping back to understand the issue from a human-centered point of view. This is why Aquarians get the reputation of being so tolerant of others—even when a person does something upsetting to the Aquarius, they will usually be able to take a step back to understand where that person is coming from and why they took the action they did. But don't take their tolerance for weakness—an Aquarius will only let a person get away with hurtful behavior for so long before they speak up for themselves. This clear and direct way of communicating the way they feel may be surprising for the person on the receiving end who is used to the Aquarian's usually unbothered and cool as a cucumber attitude!

Because they are so unconventional and unique, it can be hard for anyone to pinpoint an Aquarius. However, there are a few key signs that a person is in the presence of an Aquarius. Whether a person is hanging out with an awkward Aquarian artist or an Aquarian social justice warrior—here are a few traits to look out for:

An Aquarius adult is a walking paradox. They love being with people, but are also happy to be alone. They love to travel and hit the town to see new things, but also love being at home. They can be the life of the party but want to go home alone so their minds can wander freely. They can be very friendly and outgoing, but also moody and reserved. People find it hard to put their finger on an Aquarius, but an unconventional Aquarius kind of prefers it this way. They like to do things their own way on their own terms. Physical and mental freedom are important to Aquarians, but sometimes their nomadic lifestyle can leave them feeling lonely and disconnected because their friends aren't sure when the Aquarius will be feeling like hanging out or when they might be feeling like secluding themselves.

There is a level of distance that an Aquarius likes to keep between themselves and others. While they tend to have many friends who love them dearly (and vice versa!), close relationships are reserved only for the few people who have proven their loyalty and devotion. Intimate relationships require a level of commitment and emotional vulnerability that isn't the most comfortable for an Aquarius, so the number of people they allow to tap into that part of them is very limited. They prefer intellectual sharing—they will let someone else probe their mind as they will be probing the other person's, but an Aquarius would rather people keep their emotions and physical touch to themselves!

When going through an emotionally tough time, Aquarius will often withdraw to process what they are feeling. This may include not answering phone calls or responding to text messages. And when really stressed out, an Aquarius may be annoyed that people are even contacting them because they need the time and space to analyze and work through their feelings. This is usually an indication that the Aquarius needs to reset and take time to refill their "urn" because they have been pouring into others more than they have been pouring into themselves. As an information gatherer, an Aquarius loves connecting with others, but when it's time for them to go internal and process their emotions, they need to shut everyone out. This may leave close friends and family confused, especially when Aquarius pops back up after some time like nothing ever happened. This is why people consider them aloof or unfeeling, though this isn't the case. To honor their intimate relationships and avoid upsetting the people who love them most, it's important that Aquarius communicates their need for space and share some of their internal process with loved ones once they are ready.

An adult Aquarius is fun, responsible, and avant-garde, with a smidge of mystery. If a person is lucky enough to have an Aquarius in their life, they will have a companion who not only is a good listener, but also a person who has a wealth of knowledge and advice. Not only that, their wide variety of interests will ensure that the relationship will be fun and gives everyone who comes in touch with them a sense of fulfillment.

AQUARIUS IN LOVE

THERE'S NO QUESTION about it—Aquarians are different from other people. The silly concerns and emotional outbursts that consume the minds of others are beneath their cool and controlled way of handling daily issues. Their approach to life is more open-minded, and their point of view is more intellectual than emotional. Aquarians are alluring, funny, charming, quirky, and intelligent. Because of this they usually don't have a problem with attracting the attention of potential admirers from all walks of life. Aquarians are very friendly and outgoing, and have a special glow that sparks the interest of those who come around them. It's that hint of mystery underneath their warm personality that draws in the curiosity of potential partners who hope to stir up their hidden emotions and capture their heart.

Aquarius is the sign of friendship and community and their loyalty for the people they consider friends and loved ones runs deep. However, the time and emotional commitment that intimate relationships require put a demand on them that their intense need for independence and fear of restriction would rather avoid at times. Despite their love for exchanging ideas, socializing, and communicating with others, Aquarians can actually be introverted at times. As air signs, Aquarians are big thinkers and like to spend time in their own heads contemplating their own life experiences and daydreaming about the latest conspiracy theory or scientific experiment. While they are just as emotional as any other zodiac sign, Aquarians can find emotions to be somewhat unnerving because they prefer to be rational and logical in the way they approach their feelings and the feelings of others.

Love requires a commitment and dedication from partners that sometimes makes Aquarians feel as though they will have to let go of their fierce need for independence. Loving someone and being vulnerable with them also means that Aquarius will have to make room for them in their own life, and as a fixed sign they do not easily adapt to other people. Partners who love an Aquarius must understand that to love an Aquarius means giving them room to spread their wings and express themselves freely. For example, Aquarius Oprah Winfrey has been with her partner, Stedman Graham, for many years. People have tried to convince them that they should be married at this point, but they have chosen to continue their relationship in a way that works best for them. Oprah is quoted as saying, "I happen to be with a man who has always appreciated the fact that I was . . . considered a powerful person. . . . [He's] not trying to crowd in on it, not competing with it. He knows how to hold his own." Her partner understands her mission in life and continuously gives her the space and freedom her Aquarian humanitarian and independent spirit needs to be the best version of herself that she can be.

For an Aquarius, love and romance is an ideal or model to achieve—and not necessarily just about passion and lovey-dovey feelings. Falling in love and loving mean two different things for them. They are in search of truth, and their potential partners must be able to answer deeper questions about life and complement their quest to deliver knowledge to all of humanity. There are many astrology books and horoscopes that say Aquarians don't want to settle down and should never get married. Though this is not exactly accurate, there is some truth in Aquarius not wanting to be with someone just to say they are in a relationship.

They enjoy their independence and freedom and require both in intimate relationships. They can spend time with someone special and have a great time and good conversation, but not necessarily want to dive into the level of commitment and engagement that it takes to maintain an intimate relationship. They tend to think in larger terms and make plans that cover a larger number of people. This attitude is great for platonic friendships, humanitarian pursuits, and politicians, but not so great for individual relationships.

"You can never love anyone to your own detriment. That is not love, that is possession, control, fear, or a combination of them all."

—IYANLA VANZANT

This quote is a great representation of an Aquarian's approach to love and partnerships. Anyone who attempts to box them in or press relationship status (especially too early) is guaranteed to be disappointed. As a matter of fact, the fastest way to ruin a bond with an Aquarius is for their partner to attempt to limit their freedom or give ultimatums to maintain control over the relationship. Being with a jealous or possessive person would be a huge mistake for an Aquarius as they typically have a lot of friends who they will refuse to let go of just because they are in a new relationship. A potential partner must be secure enough to understand this about them and be willing to become part of the group. An Aquarius can easily be in a "friends with benefits" situation because relationships can take a bit more emotional bonding and commitment than they are willing to give. As air signs, they live in their heads and it can be more difficult for them to open up and share their deepest thoughts and feelings in intimate relationships unless there are other factors in their birth chart that help with this. Sometimes emotions and feelings can be a little too much for Aquarius, and they would rather deal rationally with the ups and downs that come with relating to others.

Aquarius has friends from all walks of life. They love to talk to anyone and everyone and ask deep personal questions about many different subjects, and other people may take those personal and penetrating questions as romantic interest. This is an easy mistake to make due to the easy flow of communication and slight flirtation from the Aquarius, but an Aquarius will usually (and very bluntly) let them know that they are not interested in anything but friendship. This confusion is also quickly cleared up upon meeting the Aquarius as they have a multitude of male and female friends and may have some crazy stories about their past.

Admirers of an Aquarius should expect to build a friendship of trust and appreciation before they will consider moving them from the friend zone into something more. Aquarius makes friends easily and is the best person to engage in conversation with. Like a typical air sign, Aquarians have a wide variety of interests. Potential partners should be interested in the Aquarius's hobbies and leisurely pursuits and share their own. Talk to Aquarians about books, art, social issues, aliens, culture, and scientific matters. Show them something different—on a first date, don't stick to a dinner and movie—do a unique dating experience such as a panel discussion on a social justice issue or a cute sushi restaurant in a part of town they've never been to. Give them time to get to know you, build a friendship, and trust you. Aquarians are likely to RUN when they begin to feel tied down, controlled, or like their choices are very limited. Aquarians look for loyalty in potential partners, and can be equally as loyal in relationships, but it may take a while for trust to be established between partners. They need to be constantly stimulated by their minds and can sometimes get wrapped up in their latest project, hobby, social gathering, degree, or friendship—and neglect their partners and lovers. Communication is THE MOST important factor for Aquarians, and romantic admirers must stimulate their minds before an Aquarius begins to feel a sexual attraction to them. When it comes to sex, Aquarians unleash their imaginations and can be creative and a little unpredictable. They prefer some variety and novelty rather just hard pumping and heavy breathing. But keep the hands-on action behind

> An Aquarius can easily be in a "friends with benefits" situation because relationships can take a bit more emotional bonding and commitment than they are willing to give.

closed doors—Aquarians do not like emotional displays of affection and are not a big fan of butt grabs, hand-holding, and other PDA. And don't even think about arguing in public—an Aquarius would NEVER. They cannot take jealous responses and looking out of control and will walk away from emotional scenes.

It is well known that some Aquarians would prefer not to be in a committed relationship or may choose to be a bachelor or bachelorette forever. But what is most important, attached or not, is their independence and the freedom to live their lives the way they want. Within the boundaries of an exclusive relationship, an Aquarius must have the freedom to be unapologetically themselves. The biggest mistake a partner can make when loving an Aquarius is trying to tie them down. This is why some Aquarians are more likely to choose alternative relationship styles such as non-monogamy, polyamory, long-term relationships without marriage, or even have a few people that they can trust and gain a sense of companionship with. Friendship and true companionship are just as important as having an ideal love and partnership. Although Aquarians need freedom, they may choose a partner they can control somewhat. While friendship comes first, as a fixed sign, Aquarians need to know that they will always have that person and companion to come home to at the end of the day. So although they give the same type of freedom that they require to stay in the relationship, don't be surprised if your Aquarius partner gets a bit bossy from time to time.

Although an Aquarius may be wary about relationships, like a typical fixed sign they are extremely loyal and devoted once their heart is involved. People in successful love relationships with Aquarians say they can be the best partner ever because they are tolerant, not easily offended, trusting, kindhearted, and not overly needy or clingy. All an Aquarius usually wants in return is a loyal partner who respects their privacy and won't get in the way of their spontaneous lifestyle and interests. The quickest way to lose them is to try to hold them down or put "rules" or restrictions on them. There is too much in the world to be discovered and their goal is to get out into the world to see it all. A potential love interest has to share their love of a challenge and learning, otherwise, they will get left behind.

Once they decide to be in a relationship, an Aquarius is very loyal. But when an Aquarian is ready to leave a situation, they will leave without a backward glance. This may take their partner by surprise as it will seem out of the blue due to their internalized way of processing their feelings. Aquarius won't leave out of heightened emotions—usually the decision to leave is something they have been considering and mulling over internally for months and after trying a multitude of ways to make the situation work. But once an Aquarius has made the decision that they are done, there is no going back. An Aquarius is pretty optimistic about love and sees it like a train on a track—another relationship is always on its way. But don't mistake this way of thinking as them being players or cheaters—they value truth and honesty and are usually exclusive in their relationships and aren't necessarily trying to have a lot of lovers around at once (if they do have more than one partner, they are pretty honest about it). Some Aquarians will be monogamous and loyal to one person, some will be loyal to one person—until the relationship has lost its appeal and it's time to move on. They do not consider the relationship to be set in stone—when they are ready to move on, they will.

The twelve zodiac signs are arranged into four elements—fire, earth, air, and water. Each of the elements represents a part of a person's personality type, and each one of us has a different mix of each element. Here is a short description of a love relationship with Aquarius and each element:

AQUARIUS IN LOVE WITH AIR SIGNS
(Gemini, Libra, Aquarius)

Air signs are entertaining, curious, chatty, and observant, and when two air signs are in a relationship, ideas flow freely and relating happens on an intellectual level rather than an overly emotional one. When an Aquarius is in a relationship with a fellow air sign, they have met their intellectual equal—the partnership will be filled with great conversation, debates, and creative pursuits. Air signs are a great companion for Aquarius as they understand each other's way of thinking and behaving. However, because air signs are not the greatest at expressing their emotions, an Aquarius in a relationship with another air sign may have a hard time putting their true feelings on display. Communication is key in this love match—as long as Aquarius and their air sign partner continue to talk to each other through the inevitable ups and downs of the relationship, they will be just fine!

AQUARIUS IN LOVE WITH WATER SIGNS
(Cancer, Scorpio, Pisces)

Water signs have feelings that run deeply, and a sensitivity and softness that is represented in their kind and beautiful souls. An Aquarius in a relationship with a water sign can be a dynamic duo—utilizing the combination of Aquarius's logic and visionary insight and a water sign's emotional strength and sensitivity to heal the world. While Aquarius is understanding and tolerant of everyone, they may find that water signs require more emotional commitment than they are comfortable with. Aquarius's detached and laid-back attitude when it comes to expressing their feelings or considering the feelings of others may leave their water sign partner confused and questioning Aquarius's true intentions. If both parties are willing to compromise by meeting in the middle—by Aquarius being willing to listen to their water sign partner's concerns and respond with empathy and the water sign partner willing to try to communicate their emotions in a more logical way—anything is possible!

AQUARIUS IN LOVE WITH EARTH SIGNS
(Taurus, Virgo, Capricorn)

Earth signs are stable, gentle, and hardworking souls who value routine and security. Earth signs are deeply loyal and have a desire to hold on to their partners—which may cause an Aquarius to feel a bit tied down. Aquarians are free-spirited and independent, and though they are very loyal when in a committed relationship, their earth sign partners must be willing to give them space to be their own person—which may be very hard for them to do. Aquarius is a fixed sign with strong opinions and practical decision-making skills that could work well in an Aquarius/earth sign match, or they could find that their mutual stubbornness gets the best of both of them! Aquarius and their earth sign partner can build a stable long-term relationship if it is built on support and trust and allows for the space and freedom to be themselves.

AQUARIUS IN LOVE WITH FIRE SIGNS
(Aries, Leo, Sagittarius)

Fire signs are enthusiastic and driven, and speak and act passionately from the heart. Aquarius gives air to the fire sign's flame, while fire signs will take assertive action toward Aquarius's dreams and wishes for humanity. Aquarius holds the vision, while fire signs have the drive and passion to make that vision a reality. Aquarius and their fire sign partner live by their own rules and will have a good time hanging with friends and attending fun events. However, Aquarius's need for freedom and tendency to internally manage their emotions may make attention-needing fire signs unsure of where they stand in their Aquarius partner's life or even breed feelings of jealousy. For this union to work, Aquarius must remember that no one is a mind reader and it's important that they let their fire sign partner know how madly in love they are with them. It's also important for the fire sign partner to give Aquarius the space they need to express themselves and occasionally get lost in their thoughts.

If a person is lucky enough to capture the heart of an Aquarius, they will be gifted with fierce loyalty and access to a wealth of knowledge that isn't accessible to just anyone. Aquarius is not compatible with any particular zodiac sign—all signs have the capacity to be the perfect partner to an Aquarius if they are willing to love with trust, honesty, openness, and independence. The following quote sums up the key to an Aquarian heart:

"A loving relationship is one in which the loved one is free to be himself—to laugh with me, but never at me; to cry with me, but never because of me; to love life, to love himself, to love being loved. Such a relationship is based upon freedom and can never grow in a jealous heart."

—LEO F. BUSCAGLIA

AQUARIUS AT WORK

AQUARIANS ARE HARDWORKING, deep-thinking, and extremely socially conscious, and they can be found in careers that nurture the goodness of society and help people to become the best version of themselves. Their genuine spirits and charitable attitudes allow them to have a positive relationship with the people around them.

Embracing their angel-like gifts and truth-telling natures, most Aquarians are born to give back to humanity by spreading truth and knowledge to everyone around them. Wise beyond their years, the true insight of an Aquarius is developed through their life experiences and personal quest for knowledge, in which bits and pieces of valuable information are obtained throughout the years. Their keen powers of observation and scientific way of thinking allow them to move through life noting important details while engaging their power of analysis, synthesis, and classification rather quickly. Aquarius also has a creative mind with an amazing imagination and is able to use it to visualize the creation of new things essential to their progress and the progression of humanity. Their imagination allows them to reflect on the past with clarity and help them form ideas and a practical vision for the future.

As the eleventh sign of the zodiac, Aquarius is considered the visionary sign of the future. The ruling planet of Aquarius is Uranus, which means that an Aquarius will embody many of the characteristics that Uranus represents. Uranus rules innovation, progression, and revolution. It also governs the future and new technology, including all that is newly invented, newly designed, and yet to be perceived. Unpredictable, determined, imaginative, quirky, and willing to do what has never been done before, Uranus also rules creativity and scientific genius. Uranus is considered to be rebellious—ready to break rules and demolish established patterns or structures, creating sudden and radical change. Uranus's movement through the Universe usually creates great change here on Earth. Uranus gives a strong impulse for rebellion, independence, and upheaval. Wave-maker and reforming Uranus will overturn anything traditional, conventional, or orthodox that it believes has outworn its usefulness.

Because of Uranus's influence, Aquarians are sometimes considered mysterious, eccentric, and maybe even a little strange. There is a duality about them that stands out from the crowd. While they can be friendly, a team player, and can love being around people, Aquarians can also be moody, like doing things their way, and like being alone. The duality also allows the sign to be both an artist and a scientist, so it is common for them to have multiple areas of work they are involved in. For example, an Aquarian engineer may also be a drummer in a band in the evenings and an educator may also be an activist marching for human rights on the weekend. Being untethered and independent is very important to an Aquarius, so a typical nine-to-five career may not be the best option for them. Aquarians respond best to unconventional careers, especially ones that are in the public eye and get a lot of attention. Most importantly, a potential career cannot be boring or mundane as the routine will get old for Aquarius quickly and they'll be looking to move on to work that is more in alignment with their natural desires.

As one of the zodiac's fixed signs, Aquarius does prefer financial stability (though it's not their first priority). When it comes to money, this sign really has a knack for keeping a healthy balance between having the things that they need and putting money away. So, when searching for a career, Aquarius should make sure prospective employers are progressive and allow their employees a bit of freedom and welcome new ways of thinking. The best work environment is one that gives them the freedom to perform tasks without someone standing over their shoulder. Aquarius is unconventional, and given the opportunity to show their true talents, they can perform amazing deeds.

Professions such as writing or journalism, human-centered design, multimedia, teaching, or entertainment would be good options for this sign, as they allow Aquarius to express ideas and provide the world with knowledge. The desire to move freely and maintain their own independence can complement the entrepreneur within every Aquarius—so starting their own business can bring much success to an Aquarius who is brave enough to take the entrepreneurial route. Aquarius is on the search for the meaning of life and many Aquarians often have a belief in a higher power or force. This can lead to careers in esoteric, religious, and spiritual communities. These careers bridge the gap between "out-there" concepts and humankind, which is an Aquarius specialty. Professions such as tarot reader, astrologer, life coach, or counselor allow Aquarians to explore their creative and expansive imaginations and connect with people without deep personal commitments.

One of an Aquarius's strongest features is their ambition. They have a deep-set desire to succeed, which creates an endless drive in pursuit of knowledge. For this reason, it is common for Aquarians to hold multiple degrees and certifications. Not only do Aquarians dream of making it big in the world, they are drawn to what will assist in making the world a better place. It is pretty easy to find Aquarians doing awesome things in the world currently and in the past, from the famous African American activist and author Frederick Douglass (born February 14, 1818) to the thirty-second US president, Franklin D. Roosevelt (born January 30, 1882), and ranging from actors like Kerry Washington (born January 31, 1977) to musician Bob Marley (born February 6, 1945).

AQUARIUS CAREERS

Teacher

As the zodiac's water-bearer that is here to deliver knowledge to the people, being a teacher is a natural fit!

Researcher

It would be hard-pressed to find an Aquarius who does not conduct their own research in some way—whether by reading or watching documentaries. Being a researcher invokes their talent for analysis and intellectual pursuit of truth.

Comedian

Aquarians are hilarious. As an air sign they are quick-witted and able to pull from their vast pool of life experiences and keen observation skills to come up with awesome punch lines.

Artist

Painter, musician, dancer—whatever medium naturally creative Aquarius chooses will lead them on a path to success. Their ability to connect to a higher force will help them create beautiful art to share with the world.

Tarot Reader/Astrologer

Known as the zodiac's messenger from the gods to humanity, Aquarius is used to receiving messages from beyond. Exploring alternative belief systems and their tools is right up Aquarius's alley, and they will be able to connect with like-minded people who share their point of view.

Activist

No one can point out a possible conspiracy theory like an Aquarius. But is it a conspiracy theory or a pattern that Aquarius has put together faster than everyone else? That's why when an Aquarius chooses to stand up for a certain cause, it's important for everyone to listen and follow.

Writer

Aquarius is filled with knowledge and experience, and as the water-bearer of the zodiac they have a responsibility to spread that information to the masses. What better way than becoming a writer? Whether for a blog or a national magazine—writing is a great fit!

Following their true nature, Aquarians make their mark by doing amazing work in the areas of social justice, spirituality, activism, art, education, comedy, entertainment, politics, and science. For each characteristic of Aquarius, there is an occupation that aligns closely with it. For example, occupations in social work allow them to help people, education gives Aquarians the opportunities to pour the wisdom they have gained into the minds of their students, and a career in politics allows for the formation and implementation of new ideas. Word on the street is that Aquarians are destined for greatness, and they tend to achieve at very high levels. Independent, grounded, and nonconforming, no obstacle is too big for them to handle.

As a matter of fact, Aquarians also dominate the entertainment field and many of our favorite celebrities are Aquarians! Comedian Ellen DeGeneres (born January 26, 1958), music producer and rapper Dr. Dre (born February 18, 1965), and actor John Travolta (born February 18, 1954) are all talented water-bearers! And for the record, many of the US presidents have been Aquarians, which is more common than any other zodiac sign! This includes presidents Abraham Lincoln (born February 12), Franklin D. Roosevelt (born January 30), Ronald Reagan (born February 6), William McKinley (born January 29), and William Henry Harrison (born February 9).

> *"The price of success is hard work, dedication to the job at hand, and the determination that whether we win or lose, we have applied the best of ourselves to the task at hand."*
>
> —VINCE LOMBARDI

While in the workplace, Aquarius tends to be a favorite of their fellow colleagues. With their humorous, visionary, and trustworthy way of communicating, they can easily keep people interested in what they have to say. Both intelligent and appealing, an Aquarius is well suited for both staff and leadership roles. In leadership roles, an Aquarius's rational and logical approach to solving issues and their dislike of conflict work together to solve any tension that may exist among coworkers, while their detached approach to emotional contention generally works well when managing others. The only downside they must look out for is that an Aquarius in a management position should be mindful of not appearing too aloof and emotionally detached from their team members and make sure to invest in their colleagues' morale to ensure that they feel heard when emotional conflicts arise. Being the team player of the zodiac, both Aquarius the leader and/or the Aquarius staff members are always willing to work together to resolve any issues in the workplace. As a staff member, they enjoy being responsible for various tasks or projects. They will be driven and thrive on being the best in their field. Coworkers tend to enjoy Aquarius's thought-provoking conversation and original ideas.

While the relentless ambition and drive an Aquarian possesses can be a good thing, it can also become an obsession if they are not careful. When truly interested and invested in a career that they love, the drive to be the best can cause them to work tirelessly, and not surprisingly the likelihood of this increases in humanitarian occupations like social work, education, or psychology. As one of the zodiac's fixed signs, Aquarians can be set on their own ideas, making them stubborn and inflexible to others' opinions and impatient with people who don't share their vision of what needs to be done. While Aquarius is tolerable and overall accepting of people's personalities, eventually they can become irritable with certain traits. In return, an Aquarius may fire back with sarcastic humor and crack the occasional joke on someone. Although Aquarians typically work well with everyone, there are some signs that have stronger and weaker connections. Aquarians work well with fire signs because of their excitement and the direct action they bring to an Aquarius's visionary ideas. They work well with other air signs because their intellect mirrors their own, and this is especially the case with other Aquarians. They are least compatible in the workplace with water signs because of their emotional sensitivity (although Aquarius and water signs will often have the same goal of helping and healing others), and earth signs because of their resistance to change and strong opinions (though they will get the job done and have the capability to bring Aquarius's lofty ideas down to Earth).

Overall, Aquarius can be a great addition to any team. Ideally, they would like to do something to leave their imprint on the world; they aren't motivated by money and material things but by improving the human condition. Their intelligent, logical nature allows them to excel in most work environments. Because they are unique and intellectual individuals, they are best suited for work that allows expression of creativity and wisdom. Their hunger for knowledge makes them interested in almost anything, which allows them to learn their jobs quickly. Whether in the role of a leader or an employee, Aquarius gets along well with most and enjoys working as a team when necessary. Their ideas for new things and world change can be viewed as idealistic, and they will never back away from intellectual challenge.

When actively on the job hunt, an Aquarius will excel at any job they are passionate about. You can find a few career paths that naturally fit their innovative, visionary, and humanitarian natures on page 290.

CONCLUSION

BEING A HUMAN being and navigating life can be complex, but learning more about your sun sign allows you to understand yourself better and gives you the advantage of navigating life with more confidence. Your sun sign is your essence and the core of your personality, and learning more about your sun sign is the beginning of your pathway to self-awareness and self-actualization. An Aquarius is beautiful, complex, inspirational, and visionary. The water-bearer is the eleventh sign of the zodiac and governs friends, groups, and community, which means you'll find Aquarius working with others, participating in various groups and activities, and doing humanitarian work at all levels. If you are lucky enough to have an Aquarius in your life, you have a person who is wise, friendly, with a unique perspective of the world on your team. While an Aquarius needs freedom and space in their intimate relationships, once they are hooked you have a loyal partner for life!

Due to the influence of Uranus and Saturn, Aquarians are often called the "aliens" of the zodiac because they are both multifaceted and grounded, which makes it harder for people to figure them out. All at once, the Aquarius personality can be active, expressive, interesting, and attractive, yet at other times moody, indifferent, and apathetic due to their sometimes serious way of thinking. While the fluctuation in mood may be a little confusing to the people who love them, with a little understanding it will become obvious that an Aquarius's sulky periods don't last long and they'll be back to their fun and adventurous selves rather quickly.

Aquarius is typically depicted as the water-bearer and is symbolized by a glyph that looks like water or electric waves. Because of these two symbols, people mistakenly think that Aquarius is a water sign, but this isn't the case. Aquarius is one of the three air signs, and the water-bearer symbol is represented by a human figure pouring water from an urn or container (i.e., the water carrier), symbolically and eternally ready to pour forth spiritual waters to the people. Because their life purpose is to spread their wisdom to humanity, Aquarians usually begin their personal evolution and quest for knowledge in their early years. Even Aquarian children are curious little rebels who march to the beat of their own drum. Some Aquarians are high achievers and use their logical and analytical mind to excel in their studies, whereas some Aquarians may use that same energy to begin to challenge the authority of their textbooks and beliefs of their teachers and peers. Either way, Aquarius believes life is our greatest teacher, and believes every experience helps us become the greatest version of ourselves.

Aquarians are funny, stylish, coolheaded, and great conversationalists. They can be found achieving at all levels, and some of the most famous Aquarians, like Oprah, Bob Marley, Dr. Dre, and Ellen DeGeneres have made a huge impact on society and culture as a whole. Aquarius can detach themselves emotionally to preserve their own peace of mind, but they are also the most loyal friends and lovers once they have committed.

We can all learn a lot from an Aquarius, including keeping a cool head and approaching situations from a rational and logical perspective, rather than getting overwhelmed by our feelings and making rash decisions. We can also learn to socialize with friends more often and be down for fun experiences that will teach us more about ourselves. Lastly, Aquarius can teach us to dive into subjects that peak our interest and share what we learn with others.

Learning about the Sun Aquarius is just the beginning of understanding your unique personality and character, as you have many planets in your birth chart that make up the totality of your personality. This chapter describes the Sun Aquarius, but to discover the true scope of your birth chart you should reach out to a professional astrologer (like me!) for a birth chart reading to help you dive deeper into your strengths and weaknesses, your purpose, opportunities for growth, and the best times to make business and personal moves. Whether you choose to look deeper into your chart or not, astrology can be a fun tool for learning more about your personality and the characteristics of others.

PISCES

FEB. 19 – MAR. 20

text by Shakirah Tabourn

element — WATER

symbol — THE FISH

modality — MUTABLE

house — TWELFTH

ruler — NEPTUNE

Pieces

INTRODUCTION

To understand Pisces, the twelfth sign of the zodiac, you must first understand the eleven signs that precede it. The zodiac itself is a literal expanse of constellations that form a belt around our cosmos. It can be imagined as the backdrop of the story that the celestial bodies play out before us. The zodiac is also a spectrum, symbolic of our life cycle, with energy that pervades everything we know.

> *In Pisces, we encounter an energy that can be described as compassionate and empathetic, sincere and heartfelt.*

Aries, the sign that begins the zodiac (in most traditions), represents the beginning of life—birth, the moment we actualize as human beings separate from the womb. This fiery sign is therefore associated with the separation of the self from others. Its phrase is "I am," and its energy is forward moving, in a straight direction, like a newborn emerging from the womb. Through the next ten signs of the zodiac, we see the development of values in Taurus, communication in Gemini, comfort and security in Cancer, creativity in Leo, service in Virgo, partnership in Libra, loss in Scorpio, belief in Sagittarius, purpose in Capricorn, and community in Aquarius. In Pisces, we encounter an energy that can be described as compassionate and empathetic, sincere and heartfelt. Its presence as the final sign of the zodiac belt—the one that comes after life, but before (re)birth—is somewhat mysterious and often misunderstood. There are good reasons for this! As the final sign, Pisces holds some of life's deepest mysteries—the realm of illusion and delusion, faeries, mystical beings, spirits, and angels. Pisces is a world of universal love that exists between Earth and spirit at all times, and those born under this sign have the ability to tap into its energy whenever they need to.

Pisces is a sign frequently associated with Jesus Christ through the symbols of the fish and the feet. The symbol of Pisces is two fish swimming in opposite directions, representing the different currents that Pisces are pulled toward at any given time, as well as the inherent duality in the sign. Jesus is also often associated with fish for many reasons, one being that he is said to have fed five thousand people with two fish and five loaves of bread. Feet are the body part ruled by Pisces. In the Bible, Jesus washes the feet of his disciples, showing his dedication to a life of service. Pisces are often said to have Christlike spirits, and the souls of the people born under this sign seem to gravitate toward service and compassion. Pisces tend to operate from a fundamental sense of empathy. It's not uncommon for Pisces to believe that they've already lived many lives. Perhaps this is why Pisces can empathize so well with other people and why they often give the impression that they've walked many miles in other people's shoes. Indeed, this empathy is a strong argument in favor of reincarnation. The basic idea here is that, because Pisces have experienced so many different lives through reincarnation, their souls possess an expanded view of what life on Earth is all about.

Their deep understanding and acceptance of others often leads people to describe them as "old souls," even when they are young.

Pisces possess deep emotional knowledge and strong intuition, as their sensitive bodies and souls can pick up on subtleties in the air and people around them that others simply don't recognize. Pisces can look at people on the street and sense their stresses, problems, and sufferings, though they can't explain this phenomenon. They may not know specific details about others, but they have general intuitive hunches. Through simple interactions, Pisces who have honed their intuitive skills can often pinpoint specific locations in the body experiencing pain or uncover the emotional troubles someone is dealing with. This doesn't necessarily mean they're all psychic (although many are), but they all have the ability to use their intuitive energy in this way. Intuition is the bedrock of Pisces's ability to move through the world. They must learn that their intuition is like a muscle; continuous practice is the only way to strengthen it. This can lead to a lot of pain and confusion during the teenage and young adult years. As their brains develop during this critical time, it can be difficult to discern truth from deception, love from infatuation, or intuition from intrusive thoughts. The earlier they are taught to honor their intuitive hunches and trust themselves, the better off they'll be. Of course, this isn't foolproof! There will be plenty of mistakes made, tears shed, and hearts broken throughout Pisces's lifetime. Despite all this, they cannot abandon their intuition—it's their greatest strength and their secret weapon. They are here to experience all of life—the highs and the lows—and they ride through these changes like the waves of the ocean.

And just like the ocean, Pisces are known for their immense depth and expansive nature. Their strength is in their watery essence—their ability to transcend earthly boundaries through deep emotional knowledge and a spiritual mindset. Their moods wax and wane continuously each day, changing like the ocean's tides. The truth is that they can experience an influx of emotions at any given time, from any number of random stimuli. This is a result of their immense sensitivity. They're often referred to as sponges, as they tend to soak up the memories, words, and energies of the people and places they associate with on a daily basis. A Pisces might hear a song playing in the grocery store and become overwhelmed with emotion. This can happen if the song brings them back to a tender memory from childhood. Or perhaps they go out with a friend who can't stop complaining about their significant other. Pisces might return home feeling extremely tired, as if they've spent all their energy. Even if they've had a relaxing day otherwise, the mere act of sharing space with a person in turmoil can bring their energy down. Pisces learn the effects of taking on other people's energies throughout their lives, and it's a constant struggle for them to maintain personal boundaries. Pisces are inherently boundless. They need to be free to ride the waves of the ocean of life.

MUTABLE SIGNS

Also like the ocean, Pisces is a mutable sign, meaning its energy is changeable, adaptable, flowing, and fluctuating. Mutability is a characteristic of Pisces's modality—the quality of energy by which a sign operates. There are three other mutable signs: Gemini, Virgo, and Sagittarius. A helpful way to categorize the modality of a sign is to take note of the quality of the weather during the thirty days that the sun is in one of the signs mentioned above. They share a number of inconsistencies. During Gemini season, spring changes to summer (in the Northern Hemisphere). There are cold days, hot days, and in-between days. The weather can't be properly categorized as either spring or summer quite yet. In Virgo season, a similar transition happens, this time from summer to fall. The weather begins to cool down, but exceptionally warm days are still interspersed throughout the season. In Sagittarius season, the shift is from autumn to winter. The final leaves begin to fall off the trees, animals begin to slow down and move into hibernation, and humans begin to switch from light jackets to winter coats. When the sun is in Pisces, the season begins to change from winter to spring. A thawing occurs. The weather moves back and forth between sunshine and windy, wintry days.

Pisces, like the other mutable signs, ushers in the changing of the seasons. These signs always precede an equinox or solstice. They therefore help prepare us for the major turning points of the year. Pisces gets us ready for the spring equinox—the moment when the sun moves across the equator, marked by a day in which the daytime is equal to the night. The spring equinox can be seen as a rebirth of sorts, as it takes place when the sun leaves Pisces and enters Aries, the beginning of the zodiac. Pisces therefore possesses energy that spurs growth. It is the space between thresholds, suspended between endings and beginnings. It can be thought of as the chrysalis of a butterfly, meaning the time just before the butterfly emerges from its cocoon. Pisces holds space for transformations to occur, providing a safe container to completely dissolve into nothingness and reemerge as something brand new.

NEPTUNE ENERGY

It is worth mentioning that Neptune, a far-out planet often associated with Pisces, has been moving through the sign since April of 2011. It will remain there until late January of 2026. Neptune's influence in Pisces cannot be overlooked. It heightens and intensifies the significations of the sign as it slowly makes its way to the end of the zodiac. Piscean children born under this influence will have heightened sensitivities and intuitive powers, as well as a greater propensity toward Neptunian delusions. Neptune acts to spiritualize the sign it is moving through, dissolving boundaries and creating illusions, fantasies, and out-of-this-world experiences. It shows us that separation is the biggest illusion there is, that everything that ever was is one, and that we are all connected, always. Neptunian energy means universal love consciousness. The wavelength that it vibrates on connects the hearts of all living beings.

But it doesn't always emit love and good vibes! Neptunian energy can be quite destructive, and not all structures should be destroyed. Neptune has the potential to leave us completely blinded toward the truths dangling right in front of our faces. There are deeper lessons to this planet, but they usually aren't revealed until long after its effects have worn off. Neptune in Pisces has affected our culture at large in many ways, some good, some harmful. One aspect of Neptune in Pisces is the continued growth in popularity of spiritual practices and traditions. People around the world are beginning to search for deeper connections to a force larger than themselves outside of traditional religions. A downside of Neptune's influence has been the rise in addiction to pharmaceuticals and opioids. With Neptune in Pisces, the propensity to "check out" from life is strong, as both Neptune and Pisces significations allude to the need to remove oneself from the harshness of reality. A whole generation of children has been born to addicted parents, and we've yet to see the long-term effects this will have on their psyches.

PISCES SUN AND MOON

Many of you reading this chapter are Pisces Suns, but some may be Pisces Moons or Risings! Here's an explanation of all three and the differences between them:

Sun Sign

The sun illuminates wherever it shines its rays. You are the sun in your life, casting rays synonymous with the particular unique shade of your sun sign. The sun represents your essential self, your central personality, your vitality, who you came here to be, how you shine, your self-expression, and the energy you need to recharge with.

If you were born while the sun was in Pisces, your primary mode of being is compassionate and creative. You are someone whose self-expression is based on feeling and tuning into your intuition to navigate the world around you. You came here to help people, to guide people toward self-healing, and to use your creativity to share your elaborate fantasies with others. Emotional connections fuel your soul, and creativity and world-building come easy to you. You are gifted with the ability to see through the lines and tap into other realms of existence through just being you! Rest and regeneration are wildly important for Pisces Suns, as your energy is often scattered in many directions. Rest will refuel you so that you can shine brightly once again.

Moon Sign

The moon is our constant reminder of the past; a piece of the Earth that long, long ago detached and became flung into orbit around our Earth. The moon, therefore, represents where you come from, your roots, home, and family, as well as your internal and emotional self. It's your intuition and instincts, what you need to feel nurtured and cared for, and how you do the same for yourself and others. The moon also represents what feels comfortable, safe, and natural for you.

If you were born while the moon was in Pisces, you are a sweet and sensitive soul. Your emotional currents run deep, and you may have a hard time differentiating between your emotions and others'. Your instinctual reactions tend to be deeply felt within your psyche, which means it can often take a while to fully process what's happening. In order to feel safe and comfortable, you need to be able to feel like you can escape the intensity of the world around you. You may decorate your home or room so that it feels like a space to retreat to within your environment. Escapes of some sort are necessary for Pisces of all types, but especially Pisces Moons! Making art, watching movies, reading stories, exploring nature, and meditation are some examples of healthy ways to retreat from the world around you.

Rising Sign

Also known as the Ascendant, the rising sign is the sign that was rising on the eastern horizon at the time of birth. To figure out your rising sign, you have to know the time, place, and location of birth. The eastern horizon represents the point where the sky meets the earth, or where spirit meets matter, and represents the energy that a person's life begins with. Your rising sign is the general vibe that you give out to the world. It's the energy you move about the world with, and it's how others perceive you, as it's the first layer of the personality that people encounter in others. The rising sign will point to what you look like, how you dress, and how you show up in the world. It represents you at your highest and best self. It's your temperament and outward personality.

If you have a Pisces Rising, you'll find that people of all types are drawn to you like magnets! This is because Pisces Rising people appear to be so open and empathetic to others. Because Pisces is a water sign, you might give off an energy that shows others that you are caring and compassionate, which is super alluring to most people! As a Pisces Rising, you may also give off an

elusive and mystical vibe, seeming to embody out-of- this-world energy to those that meet them. This can be seen in the way you dress and interact with people. You may be described as "Zen," "chill," or "so sweet!" by others. There is an air of mystery, glamor, and fantasy about you that others find intriguing. You may find that you're extremely sensitive to the people around you and the environments you inhabit, as your outer layer (rising sign) is so elusive and boundless. Be sure to find ample time to retreat, re-center, and ground your energy when you're feeling tired and worn out.

This chapter is suitable for Pisces Suns, Moons, and Risings, as it will give you a helpful perspective about the energy you inhabit every day, and useful tips on how to work with it instead of against it.

BEFORE YOU BEGIN

As you dive into this chapter, keep in mind that there is so much more to astrology than your sun sign! If you've ever had the magical experience of seeing your birth chart—or even better, of receiving a reading from a professional astrologer—you probably already have an idea of how vast the subject matter is. A birth chart is a two-dimensional map of the heavens at the time of your birth. In other words, it acts as a roadmap, guide, or blueprint for your life. It shows the entire zodiac belt and the location of each of the planets at the given time of birth, and each planet holds its own special meaning! Additionally, it describes the conversations taking place among the planets through the geometric angles they make in relation to each other. These angles are called aspects. The birth chart shows the sign and planets that were rising in the East and setting in the West at the time of birth, and which signs and planets were high above you in the sky or below the Earth when you came into this world. Yes, all of this has meaning! You'll be able to learn about your rising sign, your moon sign, your Mercury and Venus signs, and so much more!

The good news is, you can see your entire chart for free online, and it's even possible to research a few simple delineations. A great place to start is astro.com; however, it is best to consult a professional astrologer if possible to help give context to the information you find on the internet. Visit your local metaphysical store for a selection of books and reading materials to get you started if you're really interested in learning more! Astrology is an invaluable tool that can help you in myriad ways, some of which include learning self-acceptance, getting in tune with the timing of your life, and being able to better understand others.

This chapter will resonate with you if your sun sign, moon sign, or rising sign is Pisces. After reading this, you may also want to read the chapters that correlate with your other signs. That way you'll develop a fuller picture of your specific attunements!

PISCES AS A CHILD

PISCES CHILDREN CONTAIN the purest forms of energy—imagination, creativity, and especially sensitivity. Pisces children born between April 2011 and January 2026 also have the addition of Neptune in their sign, which means they have an especially sensitive disposition. Neptune's influence is similar to Pisces's nature in that it sensitizes, spiritualizes, and dissolves boundaries. These children will find Piscean themes to be especially potent in their personalities.

All Pisces possess a necessary need for escape. This need stems directly from their immense sensitivity! The world is perceived as entirely too harsh for the sensitive Piscean soul. Therefore, retreat of some sort is necessary in order to cope with the reality of incarnation. In Piscean children, this often looks like long periods of play in fantasy worlds, watching movies, or getting lost in artistic activities such as drawing or painting. You'll find a Pisces child engaging in these activities as a form of play, but they also serve as ways to cope with the complexities they might face at home, such as arguing or upset parents. These children are so sensitive that they can pick up on the energies of others regardless of how hard they may try to hide them. Actually, it's best not to try and hide feelings and emotions from Pisces. This only results in mixed signals, which can lead to confusion. The Pisces child will think, *I know Daddy is upset about this, but he keeps telling me everything is okay.* These children can easily internalize passive-aggressive behavior and interpret it as being their fault. Instead, a simple explanation is much easier for them to process. *Mommy is upset because of x, y, z, but I want you to know that none of that is your fault or for you to worry about. You're so sweet for being concerned about me, and I appreciate it.* These children react very poorly to angry and aggressive communication and tend to shut down and retreat further into their preferred methods of escape when confronted in this way.

In addition to the need for regular escape, the need for a protected physical space to express themselves in is just as important. This cannot be stressed enough! The Piscean child needs space within their home to feel safe, held, and contained. Without this, they will most likely be unable to fully and freely express themselves. This sacred space should be their own, free from the rest of the family's clutter. Even if it is only a small closet or a corner of a room, it should be their private area, safe and secure enough for them to slip into their own world. They will probably find this place by themselves, through their own explorations around the home. Wherever they end up, be sure that they feel no shame about their choice. This is their area of safety, where they'll continuously retreat to throughout their childhood (and possibly beyond). Everyone deserves such a space, no matter their age.

Additionally, Pisces needs a steady connection to nature. If this isn't available at home, then make sure they have ample time and opportunities to play in parks, explore the woods, or lie next to bodies of water. Pisces are connected to the subtler energies around us, and nature helps ground what may be excesses in our energy fields. This is essential for any Pisces, but especially for children, who are so open and impressionable. Ample time in nature is also an important part of Pisces's learning process. They learn best through direct experience, through their senses, and with their hands. They will most likely enjoy learning about nature—trees, the four elements, gardening, animals, etc. They usually prefer to have direct, hands-on experiences with that they're learning. If you're teaching them about the cycle of seed to plant, you better have a seed ready for them to plant and watch grow! Piscean children take their time when learning a subject. They'll do it at their own pace and can't be rushed toward a quick understanding. Again, this is why direct experience with the given subject is helpful, as it allows them to absorb the information easier. The Pisces child wants to learn all the time, as they enjoy the process of collecting information from everything around them. This is comforting and safe for Pisces, who loves to be curious, ask questions, and learn. Because their subtle bodies are always picking up information from what's around them, speaking their curiosities out loud helps them build new neural pathways. So, there should be plenty of books and educational tools at home. They learn more at home than at school most of the time, as their home space is where they integrate what they've learned in the classroom. They read through books in a breeze, so frequent trips to the local public library are also very helpful! They feel a special kind of safety and comfort surrounded by books. They love becoming lost in the fantasy that books provide, and they can easily become emotionally attached to the characters they read about, even going as far as to embody their personalities while steeped in their world. In addition to books, TV shows and movies are other comfortable sources of escape for Pisces of all ages.

The Pisces child will have a special relationship with the family pet, whether it's a fish, a cat, a dog, or a lizard. Pets are connected to Virgo in astrology, the sign opposite of Pisces. Therefore, Piscean children feel a particular affinity for and magnetism toward animals. They're sympathetic to animals of all kinds, communicating with them almost telepathically. Tarot enthusiasts might look toward the Page of Cups, often depicted as a young person communicating with a fish. It's almost as though little Pisces can tap into another realm that contains the thoughts and feelings of their animal friends. A pet allows a young Pisces to learn responsibility early on, as they are already empathetic to the basic needs of animals. The daily routine of feeding, walking, or caring for a pet is helpful and healing to Pisces's soul, as being grounded in routine helps balance out the propensity for too much escape. Their pet will be their very best friend, and it will bring out their capacity for love and compassion early on in life. Pisces has the unique ability to love everyone and everything on a soul level, and this trait will manifest in how the Pisces child acts toward their pet.

It isn't uncommon for Pisces children to have food sensitivities, which are often caused by their sensitive bodies. Whether this means a serious allergy, stomachaches, hives, or just a strong distaste for particular foods, it's important to honor the given sensitivity. The worst thing for a Pisces child to hear is that they're crazy or that their intuitions about their own body are wrong. This can lead to an eventual distrust of the self and their decision-making capabilities. Instead, work with them in concert with their doctor(s) to learn more about their sensitivities. It is highly important that a young Pisces is given a healthy diet with low amounts of added sugars and caffeine, as these can prove to be overly stimulating for such sensitive kiddos. It's also important that they aren't criticized for their eating habits or food intake. A young Pisces will internalize any negative talk about food or their body, and as a result, they could learn to be uncomfortable with their body early on. This can lead to Pisces disassociating from their body at a young age, potentially causing depression or disordered eating practices that can take a lot of effort, therapy, and time to heal.

A Pisces child is similar to a Pisces adult—they just want to love and be loved! That is the core of their needs. Lead with your heart with these children, as they need to be in tune with emotions. Their parents are the mirrors by which they learn emotional intelligence. There is no such thing as a perfect parent, but the Pisces child will see and recognize efforts made on their behalf. What these kids need most of all, besides displays of unconditional love, is structure. Their parents need to be able to provide a strong, reliable foundation rooted in compassion rather than punishment. If this is created, the young Pisces will grow to maintain their empathy and loving spirit while also developing balance and maturity.

PISCES AS AN ADULT

AN ADULT PISCES might find that they move through life aimlessly and without direction until their Saturn Return hits, which is usually between the ages of twenty-eight and thirty. The Saturn Return is when the planet Saturn makes its way back to where it was initially when a person was born. This period, lasting about three years, marks a time of major maturity and growth. We are forced to make decisions and lay the groundwork of our adult lives. Before this time, Pisces can be found holding onto lofty ideals, unsure of where life is taking them. They tend to shuttle from job to job and relationship to relationship, with no real direction or sense of purpose. The Saturn Return forces them to become aware of the reality of their situation and life path and makes them realize that it is time to solidify plans for the future. A major part of learning life's lessons is facing the reality of incarnating into the physical body. This is rough for everyone, but especially for Pisces, who has a difficult time facing reality. Pisces is a rather ethereal sign, one that can easily disengage with reality and live in a fantasy world. It prefers that world to real-life horrors and responsibilities. During the Saturn Return, Pisces is forced to face the realities of being in a physical body on this earthly plane! There is no real way to escape other than death.

Pisces's opposite sign, Virgo, puts this in perspective. Virgo, a mutable Earth sign, is all about physical incarnation, work, health, and learning to live in the body. Virgo rules routines and physicality, lifestyle development, and everything we do to function on a day-to-day basis. Pisces can often deny these parts of life, preferring fantasy and illusion to the mundanity of everyday living. The Saturn Return forces Pisces to accept this reality one way or another. There needs to be room for both the mystical and the mundane! When Pisces is finally able to realize this, they can truly begin to create magic in their everyday life. The Saturn Return humbles and humanizes Pisces in a very real way. Looking at the full birth chart is necessary to paint a more accurate picture of the areas of life the Saturn Return will affect the most, but in general it usually touches every aspect of a person's life. The sobering part of this time is most noteworthy, as Pisces aren't typically known for being sober!

Pisces experience deep pain when they sit with reality for too long. They tend to view it as too limiting and harsh, and they can be rather fatalistic in their views of life on Earth. To cope with this pain, Pisces pursues escape by any means necessary. As a child, escape might look like extended periods of play, becoming lost in the fantasies provided by movies and books, spending a long time outdoors, or engaging with nature. However, the pressures of adulthood make these types of escape seem out of reach, especially for Pisces with demanding day jobs, unsatisfying personal relationships, or feelings of uncertainty and hopelessness. Many turn to other forms of escape, such as drinking, recreational drug use, retail therapy, endless social media scrolling, or mindless internet surfing. Often these things go hand in hand. Numbing the pain of incarnation is both necessary and destructive. The truth is, there is no hiding from reality no matter how hard one tries. Alcohol, drugs, and other forms of temporary escape are just that—temporary. The high never lasts, and Pisces are left in a cycle of numbing pain, dissociation, guilt, regret, and repetition. It becomes less about facing the reality of incarnation and more about hiding from the self. Addiction of one sort or another is common among Pisces. The same is also true for people with Pisces Moons, as their instinctual reaction when faced with any kind of discomfort is to find escape.

The Saturn Return shatters the illusions of addiction and substance abuse in major ways. This period of time takes place over a few years, so its full story is bound to be a long one. It is likely that Pisces will first begin to notice ways in which their life can no longer continue in the direction it's headed. However, they will likely be in denial about it. A Pisces has incredible intuition, but they very often doubt it! They know what needs to change, but they won't be able to acknowledge it head-on for some time.

As the Saturn Return progresses, what they've realized will become more and more difficult to ignore. Loved ones will begin to notice, too, likely because whatever they're denying has by this time become a more obvious problem pushed to the forefront of the psyche. As time progresses, it is very likely that Pisces will continue to try to ignore or push back on this core issue, preferring to remain in denial until they absolutely can't any longer. The best way to handle this time in their lives is by being brave enough to face the realities of growing up in a physical body. They must attempt to live life within certain structures and boundaries. Once Pisces comes to understand that boundaries can be loving containers of growth and experience, they begin to experience a sense of freedom that they never knew existed!

Suffering is a real part of incarnation, and it is something Pisces in particular must reckon with in this lifetime. To be a Pisces is to know suffering, to witness the abuses and sorrows of the world, to feel the aching Earth within the self, and to somehow choose to continue to see the divine in everything. That optimistic view is the ultimate life purpose for Pisces! The Saturn Return shows them the importance of embracing this reality. They have the ability to truly help others with their suffering, but to do so they must acknowledge its existence and its potential to be changed. Through this process, Pisces has to reckon with the choices they've made so far in life and decide if the road they're on is leading them toward the life they want. If not, how can this be addressed? Should Pisces pivot in another direction entirely or wander off course slightly and explore until they find their way back to the main road? The process of undoing can be heartbreaking and difficult to move through, as it involves a breakdown of previous ways of living. It is one thing to quit drinking, for example, but it's another to let go of the weekly hangouts at the bar with coworkers on Friday nights, or to have to isolate oneself from certain friends and situations to stay sober. A total recalibration must take place once Pisces is ready to commit to changing their lifestyle, and suffering comes into play once again. They may have a breakdown when they realize how boring life becomes once their everyday escape has been removed, as this forces them to find meaning in the mundane. The best remedy for this is nature. Returning back to the Earth always stabilizes an otherwise restless Pisces. Meditation is also essential. This is true for life in general, but it's particularly true for troubling and confusing periods like the Saturn Return. It is way too easy for Pisces to get stuck in their heads, running through feedback loops of despair. Worry constantly plagues the Piscean mind, which leads them to self-medication and escapist behaviors. They want to avoid the reality of a potentially meaningless life. To move through this is notably difficult, as the Saturn Return is often the undoing of the spirit in order to reach new depths of understanding about the meaning of life. Hopefully, after the Saturn Return, Pisces is able to find meaning and a newfound understanding of what it means to live in a human body on this Earth. Yes, suffering is inevitable, but so is beauty, love, magic, and connection. The Saturn Return shows Pisces how necessary their contribution to the world around them is. This period helps Pisces understand that every part of life is necessary to make the whole, including the ugly, dark parts and the beautiful, uplifting ones. They begin to understand that suffering can be recategorized as tolerance.

Pisces in Love

Piscean lovers tend to be idealistic, romantic, and very much invested in the idea of love. Pisces wants to be seen completely and fully by their beloved. They search for a love that defies the boundaries of space and time. They want themselves to be seen and accepted by their lover on a soul level. This aspect of life might prove to be one of the most difficult for Pisces, as their relationships are everything to them. They dream of the perfect partner and marriage from a very young age—someone who understands them from the inside out and who is just as devoted to love as they are. In short, they want a romantic type with whom they can create a beautiful life.

Unfortunately, it usually takes a series of disappointing love affairs before Pisces realizes what they really want and need in relationships. Pisces fall in love hard and fast; when they find someone who seems to meet their standards (which can seem low to others), they often fall into a dream state, putting their beloved on a pedestal while falling into patterns of devotion and idolization. Because of their fast descent into love-land, they can be seen as gullible and easy to deceive. This is especially difficult for younger Pisces, as they can easily fall into toxic or abusive relationships with people they feel they have a deep connection with. They enter relationships wearing thick rose-colored glasses, happy to have found someone who seemingly fulfills their fantasies.

Pisces must learn that a soul or fated connection doesn't necessarily mean everlasting love! They often attract other hopeless romantics and people with visible mortal wounds, as they tend to believe that they can fix anyone with love and affection! There's real danger in attracting people in need of fixing or healing. Pisces are so sensitive and absorbent they can easily become confused, not knowing if the feelings and emotions they are experiencing at any given time are theirs or their partner's. This can be truly detrimental to Pisces, who need to learn how to maintain clear boundaries between themselves and others to avoid both physical and mental sickness. They are subject to taking on the experiences of others because of their emotional vulnerability, their extreme sensitivity, and their transparency. There is no telling where Pisces ends and their partner begins. When their partner is sick or in pain, Pisces will subliminally take that on themselves as they try their best to heal the other person, often neglecting to take precautionary measures to protect themselves. The same goes for emotions. If their partner is angry or upset, Pisces may find themselves taking on those same feelings, most of the time without even noticing it's happening.

Because of their tendency to attract lovers who end up draining them of their magic and vitality, cycles of shame often manifest in their relationships. Their partner can make them feel ashamed for the loss of spark or fantasy that occurs when Pisces is worn down and drained of energy. This, in turn, can make Pisces even more cold and withdrawn, which means they'll be less willing to share themselves with their partner.

Pisces must learn that they can have soul-altering experiences with people who might not be "the one." Just because they have incredible sex or feel seen on an entirely different level doesn't necessarily mean that they're meant to stay with this person forever. It can be challenging for them to accept that they'll have many different types of lovers and varying types of experiences with love and relationships throughout their lives.

BEST SIGNS FOR PISCES

In terms of the type of person that's best suited for Pisces, they should look toward their opposite sign, Virgo, for some clues, as well as to their fellow Water signs, Cancer and Scorpio. Virgo is a mutable Earth sign, so, like Pisces, it is changeable and in concert with the flux of life. Because Virgo is an Earth sign, it can act as a container and help ground others in the reality of everyday life. Pisces need this balance in relationships—someone who can hold space for them, act as a counter to their ever-flowing, sensitive nature, and help keep them grounded on the material plane. Virgo also rules the process of critique and refined selection, something that Pisces often lacks when in search of a mate, since Pisces are very open and welcoming to almost anyone they feel a soul connection with. This isn't to say that every Pisces should be with a Virgo, but they should look for similar traits to help balance out their watery natures.

The other two Earth signs, Taurus and Capricorn, can be great matches for Pisces.

> *Pisces must learn that a soul or fated connection doesn't necessarily mean everlasting love!*

They too can provide an earthy, stable, and comforting container for their water. Pisces, in turn, acts to nourish the Earth, adding magic, mysteriousness, and creativity to otherwise dry or stagnant earth. Together, water and earth make fertile ground, where creation and growth can occur. Being with an Earth sign allows Pisces to feel held and contained, which is comforting for a sign with emotions that change depending on who they're with or where they happen to be. The downside of Pisces dating an Earth sign is the potential for stagnation, as well as a lack of depth. Earth can be stable and secure, but will the relationship bore Pisces? For Pisces, the possibility of stability leading to limitations, boredom, or restriction is a constant fear. This can make them swim away quickly from relationships, often without much of a warning.

The strong, reliable container of Taurus can soothe Pisces's anxieties and fears of being left behind, but their slow-moving nature and inability to change might drive Pisces crazy after a while. Tauruses move at their own pace, which is often quite slow and steady. They don't like to be pushed or prodded (think of a bull), and they will stay in one home, job, or relationship for decades out of comfort and fear of change. They're known for being stubborn, which Pisces quickly rejects. Their mutable nature can't fathom why someone would want to stay put for so long, especially when they aren't happy with where they are! Taurus's unwillingness to change, even when presented with ultimatums, can eventually be a deal-breaker for Pisces. However, if these two can find the right balance, a long-term union is easily possible. They'll enjoy spending time in nature together more than anything, perhaps growing their own food, cooking delicious meals, and building a fruitful life together.

Capricorns are alluring for their go-getter attitude toward life and career, which is particularly sexy to Pisces. Capricorn has the energy of a caretaker—someone who can provide material comfort and security for their partner. Capricorn and Pisces can create a meaningful life together, with Capricorn providing the material needs and Pisces bringing the warmth, creativity, and caretaking to the home and family. However, will Capricorn's focus on career and financial stability prove to be too cold and hollow for Pisces? Pisces need to be able to share themselves fully with their partners, so plenty of quality time is necessary. Capricorn might not always be able to provide that for Pisces as they focus on building and maintaining their career status. Plus, Capricorns aren't exactly known for warmth and softness—quite the opposite actually! It isn't that Capricorns aren't emotional people. They just don't express it as much! Instead, it's usually kept inside, as their purpose is to build reliable structures to support their families and communities. This pair can last if Capricorn devotes enough time and energy to Pisces and makes them feel deeply noticed and understood. Pisces must also take care that they're aloofness doesn't throw off the otherwise grounded Capricorn.

With Virgo, opposites can definitely attract! The mutable natures of these two signs work well with each other because they're able to bend and change to adapt to new circumstances. Pisces's natural inclination toward dreaming and fantasy definitely contrasts with Virgo's connection to the everyday hustle and bustle of life. Virgo stays tethered to the earthly plane through their work, which is seen as service in their eyes. The daily give-and-take with the world around them keeps them grounded and sane. Pisces, on the other hand, also lead lives of service, but these are centered in connection, healing, and empathy. In fact, both signs hold natural healing abilities. Virgo is best equipped to work with the physical body, offering healing herbs and movement therapies for folks. They are gifted in paying attention to minute details and understanding the complexities of the human body in ways few others can. They are in tune with the body, whereas Pisces often strives to find release from the burdens of the body. Pisces are gifted in the art of healing what is unseen. This includes energy work, psychic abilities, empathy, and heart-centered connection. Both can heal, and together they can be an unstoppable duo! However, opposite signs are opposite for a reason! Although they can be categorized as two sides of the same coin, there is a tension between the two. Pisces can be exhausted by Virgo's relentless scrutiny and criticism. Virgo can easily become aggravated by Pisces's lack of boundaries and direction; they tend to drift through life, going wherever the wind takes them. This tension can lead to struggles and arguments in which the two find it impossible to see eye to eye.

It is, however, truly magical when two Water signs fall in love. Pisces can find a sense of connectedness with Cancer, Scorpio, or another Pisces that is hard to find with any other sign. In this combination, the two allow each other to feel noticed, held, and accepted on a deep soul level. Water signs just *get* each other, as they all hold the depth, psychic ability, and sensitivity of the element. They are able to nourish each other and understand the same fears, anxieties, and weird, mysterious abilities. They are all deep healers by nature and can offer this to each other. However, there is a danger of falling into toxic cycles, which is true in all relationships. Water signs share depth, which means that they can easily get lost in each other's issues. When Water meets Water, it is difficult to tell where one ends and the other begins. Serious boundaries have to be established early on, and both parties must make their intentions clear to the other so that a healthy relationship can develop.

When Pisces pairs with Cancer, sparks immediately fly. Both signs have a deep love for love itself, and they will probably find that their romance easily blossoms. Cancer makes Pisces feel held, soft, and surrounded by warmth and compassion. Pisces feeds off of Cancer's nurturing energy, which quenches Pisces's thirst for true love and connection. When Pisces feel the safety and comfort Cancers provide, they easily open up romantically and sexually. They feed off of each other's open-hearted energy. These two can have a world of fun together, often preferring to stay inside to cook delicious meals, have sex, eat again, and binge-watch their favorite movies together. Conflict begins when Pisces's capricious nature becomes too much for Cancer to contain. Cancers rely on emotional security. If Pisces appears too difficult to pin down or too much in flux, Cancer may give up on trying to secure a long-term relationship. Pisces, on the other hand, may find Cancer to be a little too nurturing and sensitive—yes, even for Pisces! Cancer is connected to the mother archetype, which may turn Pisces off if it becomes too overbearing.

Pisces and Scorpio are a truly mystical pairing—one that neither of them will ever forget. Pisces and Scorpios tend to have instant and penetrating connections. Often, they are immediately attracted to each other's deepest (some might say *baddest*) desires. Pisces mystifies and allures Scorpio with their big eyes and open aura, while Scorpio's mysterious vibe easily captures Pisces's attention. When they pair up, it's usually intense, as both signs have a deep urge to be understood on a soul level, and both are usually happy to form an intense bond when they find someone else willing to be with them. As with other Water signs, this pair can quickly become lost in each other's psyches and emotions, often seeming to communicate telepathically or through subtle gazes. Their sexual chemistry tends to be a major driving factor in the union, and they can both become insatiable for each other's deep love. This pair finds trouble when Scorpio becomes too intense for Pisces's mutable nature or when Scorpio, who can be a somewhat jealous and controlling sign, can't fully trust Pisces's staying power. If Scorpio can trust Pisces, and if Pisces can understand Scorpio's heavy and intense moods, they can find lasting happiness together.

When a Pisces meets another Pisces, the two fish are able to create magic that is truly out of this world! They are able to see each other as mirror images, seamlessly merging into each other's lives, like the blending of two oceans. Pisces may be taken aback by the effortlessness of the connection between the two, as they'll probably be able to understand each other instantly. Their fears, joys, and even senses of humor easily coalesce, and they quickly realize they've found something special in each other. The beauty and danger of this paring is the possibility of becoming lost in a shared fantasy. When this happens, neither one wants to come down from the high of deep, passionate, and endless love. Their connection can last if both parties have stable foundations to continue to grow from, and of course if they can maintain a level of separation between each other. It's all too easy for them to become lost in one another. The only way this couple can last long-term is if they both maintain a degree of independence. Certain parts of their lives must remain disentangled. The love and compassion these two signs can hold for each other is next-level, and it can be fostered through their shared ideals.

Pisces finds Fire signs to be exciting and alluring. Who doesn't want to stand next to a warm fire? Although Fire and Water don't typically mix well, there are always exceptions to the rule. Chances are good that Pisces will date at least one Fire sign in their lifetime. Water and fire can be hot and exciting, like boiling water! However, water and fire tend to lead to hot steam, meaning arguments will erupt and fizzle into nothing. This isn't to say that Pisces can't find love with a Fire sign! Pisces has a special connection with Aries; Pisces represents the end of a cycle, the last sign of the zodiac, and Aries represents the beginning, being the first sign. These two signs hold the energies of death and birth, last and first—the major threshold of endings and beginnings. Pisces finds Aries exciting and thrilling, like a shiny new car! Aries's energy and enthusiasm light something up inside Pisces that wants them to take risks, be bold, and follow their Aries into the sun. Aries quickly relates to Pisces's mystical and mysterious energy, as Pisces makes them feel seen and understood. And indeed, Pisces does hold deep knowledge about Aries. The symbol of an ending must understand the magic of its beginning. Things may begin to fall apart when Aries becomes enamored with something (or someone) new. These Fire signs tend to have short attention spans when it comes to love, especially in their younger years. Pisces may eventually tire of having to tiptoe around Aries's ego. However, because these signs are right next to each other on the zodiac wheel, it's possible for them to share planets in each other's signs. For example, Pisces might have Venus in Aries, and Aries might have Mercury and Venus in Pisces; they share more of each other's traits than previously thought when one considers the sun signs. A further analysis of both birth charts is always needed to determine true compatibility. If compatibility is possible, they should be able to build a lasting relationship together and have a ton of fun while they're at it.

Pisces and Leo have a unique connection with each other in that they share a love for fantasy, love, and beauty. Like Pisces, Leos love to love, and they also lead life from the heart space.

Both signs are highly creative and can bond over their obsessions with certain movies, artists, style trends, or celebrities. Pisces is enamored with Leo's playfulness, and Leo can't get enough of Pisces's eclectic, mystical energy. Their similar love for aesthetics and cuddling can take them far; however, a more substantive love will have to be the foundation of their relationship, or else it will become old pretty quickly. Although Pisces is able to give Leo the consistent love and validation they crave, Pisces can easily dull Leo's flame if they become far too depressing or sad for Leo's solar fire. Similarly, Pisces may grow tired of Leo's constant focus on themselves and how others perceive them. Pisces's caring and empathetic nature doesn't take well to people who are self-absorbed, and Leo simply can't stand anyone who may be blocking their light in any way. If their connection is rooted in something deeper and more substantial than aesthetics or sex, they can certainly have a long-lasting, happy relationship.

Pisces and Sagittarius have the ruling planet of Jupiter in common, which is present in both of their expansive and belief-oriented natures. They both have strong morals and ethics that they live by. Pisces may be more humanitarian, whereas Sagittarius is often more philosophical. These two can talk for hours at a time, ruminating on the meaning of life, social and political issues, history, or just about anything! They both have boundless natures that are difficult to contain. Pisces wholeheartedly looks up to Sagittarius for their incredible mind. To Pisces, Sagittarius can seem like the smartest person they've ever met! Sagittarius enjoys Pisces's sensitivity and openness. Sagittarius knows that Pisces won't hold them back from their adventures but will rather nurture, support, and accompany them wherever they go. Where these two falter is when Sagittarius fears commitment or can't see themselves with a long-term partner that is so sensitive to their brash quips. Pisces may eventually find Sagittarius too pompous or dogmatic for their taste. However, if both signs maintain a sense of security and stability with one another and understand that they don't want to hold each other back, then they can often find a lasting harmony that includes tons of laughs and fun experiences.

Pisces finds most Air signs especially exhilarating, intellectual, and hilarious. However, Air tends to lack depth, which is one of Pisces's biggest cravings. The air element rules communication of all forms, including speech, writing, and even thinking. Air signs inherently need verbal back-and-forth in order to process the thoughts that travel continuously through their minds. Pisces communicate through symbols, signals, art, music, and body language, while Air signs communicate through spoken and written language, equations and arithmetic, and facts and figures. However, this is by no means saying that Pisces can't end up with an Air sign. They have a lot in common with each of them. Pisces finds Gemini quite clever, funny, sociable, and entertaining. Gemini is a curious sign constantly mentally processing everything around them. Gemini's main concerns while going about their life are to gather information and make connections between these bits of information. Pisces is also constantly communicating, but usually subconsciously! While Gemini speaks as they think, Pisces generally doesn't have much to say, as they're always processing how they feel! These two can end up having a lot of fun together, staying up and chatting through the night or lightly debating topics of all types. Pisces enjoy the mental stimulation to a point, but this bubbly energy can quickly wear them out! Pisces really need to connect on a deep level, and this can be difficult with Geminis, who tend to hover around the surface. In addition, Gemini gets bored easily, and Pisces can't really be bothered to try and keep up. These two can last if they share common interests or if Gemini can get used to Pisces's sensitivities. Pisces must also get used to Gemini's restlessness!

Pisces has an affinity for Libra, a sign associated with partnership and union. Pisces finds Libra's beauty and sense of style especially attractive, and Libra is equally allured by Pisces's mysterious sensuality. Libra is ruled by Venus, a planet that thoroughly enjoys Pisces, and these two definitely share a keen interest in love, aesthetics, and fantasy. They both appreciate each other's impeccable taste and propensity to beautify everything they come into contact with. Libra's willingness to partner pairs well with Pisces's open heart, which is ready to give and receive love. Conflicts arise when Pisces feels that some of Libra's behaviors cause them to feel personal shame. Libra's often wishy-washy nature doesn't always mix well with Pisces's strong morals. Libra tries to argue both sides of a conflict, which can confuse Pisces and send them into a tailspin. Libra can also quickly tire of Pisces's constant confusion over problems and solutions that seem simple to them. However, there's a lot of potential here for long-lasting love if Libra possesses meaningful depth and if Pisces expresses their wants and needs clearly.

Aquarius comes right before Pisces, so they are next-door neighbors on the zodiac belt. They have a lot in common, notably their propensity to experience life from the margins of society. Both signs tend to have underlying feelings of being alone or of not fitting in with society at large, which includes their families and peers. They both long for human connection and acceptance of their true selves. Pisces and Aquarius have the potential to provide that for one another. Pisces finds Aquarius's oddities quirky and attractive, and Aquarius easily falls for Pisces's open and accepting nature. Aquarius can teach Pisces how to emotionally detach from situations in order to gain a broader perspective. Pisces can teach Aquarius the power of embracing feelings and diving into the full experience of emotions. Such developments are of course extremely difficult for these signs to imagine! Still, they can learn a lot from each other by exploring their differences. This partnership can start to go downhill if Pisces tires of Aquarius's rebellious nature. Pisces may find themselves thinking: "Aquarius seems to have an opinion about everything, and it's usually filled with disdain!" Aquarius may eventually become fed up with Pisces's constant fear and anxiety, in which case they'll have thoughts such as: "Just grow up already!" These two can make it work if Pisces maintains a degree of detachment and logic and if Aquarius learns to lead with love instead of criticism.

Whatever sun sign Pisces ultimately ends up with, it's important that they see themselves as separate from their relationships and partners. This is the only way for them to have a truly satisfying union. Compromise is a given, but as long as Pisces is willing to stick with it for

the long-term, beautiful relationships can be formed with any partner. Hopefully the firm embrace of Saturn's Return teaches them the importance of boundaries, that boundaries are in fact love, and that structure does not have to mean limitations. Pisces must remember to only take on what is theirs, meaning that their partner's issues aren't theirs to deal with, worry about, or hurt from. They can empathize without embodying!

PISCES AT WORK

PISCES ARE A true powerhouse when it comes to work and careers. Their inner fire begins to roar when they see the fruits of their labors. Pisces are hard workers unafraid to put in longer hours, and the results are usually bountiful! However, their true potentials are only realized when they're working toward something they actually care about. A Pisces will have many different passions over the course of their lifetime and will try many different jobs as they search for their purpose. Ultimately, Pisces yearns to alleviate the suffering of others, so they often seek out careers that allow them to feel as though they are achieving that purpose. Working with children, the elderly, the sick, the impoverished, or the disabled, and counseling are great places to start. They are not always the best at organizing or managing others, as their empathy can prevent them from becoming impartial and objective managers. However, they do excellent work behind the scenes, organizing stockrooms or tending to customer needs. Because of their mutable natures, Pisces often hold many different jobs at once, likely one that pays the bills and another that fulfills a certain passion or purpose. They can be quite adept at juggling multiple responsibilities as long as they remain organized and don't become too overwhelmed.

Pisces do really well when they are self-employed, as they like making their own money and being responsible for their own work. They are very self-sufficient in that way. However, this is only if they are able to develop a steady and reliable routine. Pisces, a mutable Water sign, isn't well-known for its self-starter energy. They can definitely be that way when they have an initial passion for a particular idea, but this can easily wane once they realize the hard work required to achieve their goals. It's not that Pisces is averse to hard work, it's that they often have a difficult time sticking it out for the long haul. New, exciting goals or distractions can pull them away from their original objectives. Because of this, having multiple jobs suits them well. They get the steady structure of a regularly paying job and the opportunity to explore other interests. For Pisces to be happy, this regular job should align with Piscean principles. Firstly, the people they work with must be openhearted and kind. Pisces should do their best not to subject themselves to toxic work environments, especially if they have to work in these environments most days of the week. They are simply too sensitive to be immersed in environments that are too harsh or whose employees lack empathy for others. Usually, if the people they work with are "chill" and get along with them, Pisces will stay with the job for a while. However, they do get bored easily! The Piscean mind must be constantly stimulated, otherwise it will resort to lofty daydreaming and escapism to help the hours pass. This can lead to depression and feelings of worthlessness, and Pisces would much rather keep busy with tasks that are helpful and necessary to the business rather than wander without direction or focus. Pisces need structure, consistency, and a healthy work-life balance in order to thrive in any position. Because of their extreme willingness to help others, they can easily fall victim to work situations in which the work becomes endless and their selflessness is taken advantage of. Pisces can easily feel as though they're becoming slaves to their jobs, especially when they lack proper boundaries at work. This is why being upfront with themselves (first and foremost) about what they will and will not tolerate in the workspace is important before beginning any job search. Of course, these critical-thinking skills probably won't appear until later in life, after some trial and error at different places of employment.

Pisces must be able to acknowledge the work they do and their value to their team or company in order to properly advocate for themselves. This includes asking for promotions and raises. These forms of direct confrontation with authority figures might be terrifying to Pisces, but they are necessary to prevent getting stuck in assistant or associate positions. Pisces needs to learn that they too deserve to be acknowledged for their work and fairly compensated. They may fear being seen as "rocking the boat" or disturbing the order of things, but it's crucial that they realize they're only doing a disservice to themselves by remaining in positions that don't allow them to grow. As stated earlier, it's important that Pisces is recognized for their work, otherwise they can grow bitter and resentful, which can lead to a lack of passion and desire to do good work. This can become a vicious cycle—Pisces starts to do less work to compensate for a lack of acknowledgment from their higher-ups.

In turn their falling productivity keeps them from receiving praise or promotions.

Their main drive is to help others in some way. An adult Pisces has seen the world in all its beauty and horror. They've learned first-hand the power of love and compassion, and this is what they crave most. Above all, they have a deep understanding of equality. They believe we are all connected at the heart level and that human beings want love more than anything else. Pisces will feel unfulfilled in life if they are not working toward a cause larger than themselves. So, a mundane day job will likely have to involve helping people because Pisces has a hard time working for something they aren't

> *Pisces need structure, consistency, and a healthy work-life balance in order to thrive in any position.*

passionate about. The pathway toward Pisces's ideal career can often be quite long and aimless, though some learn early on what they're meant to do. This really depends on the individual. Pisces are very powerful manifestors, so when they make their minds up about what they want to pursue, they usually have no trouble finding opportunities. Pisces's ability to manifest is often taken for granted or left unrealized. Once they recognize their power to almost seamlessly create the life they desire, they can start taking advantage of it. The main issue is settling on a path! Pisces are so mutable that their minds change easily, which can make them feel incapable of following through with their decisions. This can stem from a fear of failure or a lack of self-confidence in their ability to see their plans through. They know themselves better than anyone else, meaning they understand their propensity toward change. They often quit when challenges seem too difficult or "impossible" to solve. The thing is, Pisces should understand that choosing a direction is essential to their growth. This decision doesn't have to mean they'll be restrained in any way! The ability to manifest means that Pisces can create the life they want—the life that makes the most sense for them! In order to do that, it's important that they get specific. They have to take the time to acknowledge their present circumstances. They won't be able to manifest anything if they are in denial about their current state of being. For example, let's

> Wishing will only get Pisces so far, but taking meaningful steps toward manifestation actually works!

say Pisces is at a career crossroads. They're stuck in an office job they hate, but they have an idea for a coaching business. The first step toward manifesting their dream is to recognize where they're standing. They'll need to continue working another job in order to make ends meet while they build their coaching business. So, if they want to quit their current job, they'll need to manifest one that's in proper alignment to serve as a bridge for the next step. A Pisces acting too hastily might believe that manifestation involves simply asking for enough clients to go full time and then quitting the job they hate. A Pisces in tune with the power of manifestation would first ask for a job that fits their current needs in order to get them to where they ultimately want to go. For instance, they might have worked service jobs when they were a bit younger. Such jobs can provide the fulfillment and money needed to help bridge them to the next opportunity. As an adult, they have a clearer idea of the type of restaurant environment that suits their needs, so they can be even more specific in what they're asking the universe for. To get even more detailed, they can ask for the specific amount of money they'll need and the number of clients they can realistically expect to pick up as they're starting out. Specificity is the key to manifestation. Once the universe knows exactly what's desired, it can act accordingly to make it happen. Compare this to someone who simply "wishes" things would go their way. They say things like "I hate this job. I wish I could just quit and do my own thing." Wishing will only get Pisces so far, but taking meaningful steps toward manifestation actually works! After the specifics are figured out and a plan is developed, the next step is to let the universe know. Writing plans down on paper allows desires to be grounded in the physical realm, and saying them out loud helps speak them into existence. You get bonus points if this is done on a new moon, which is a great time to set intentions for new growth. After this, a mixture of belief and action makes manifestation happen. Search for the job you desire, tell people about your plans so that they can help you along the way, and design and build your own website. Next, begin offering free coaching sessions to build up your practice, gather testimonials, and start building a clientele! Before Pisces knows it, they've landed a great new job that allows them the time and freedom to start building the business they want. Asking is key here—if you don't ask, the universe can't deliver. Another big part of this is engaging the community and letting friends and new connections know about the dream. The beautiful thing about Pisces is that the people around them truly want to help them succeed! Letting their community know about their dreams allows the universe to connect them with people who can facilitate quicker growth. Because of their ability to manifest, Pisces will typically never go without enough money, as they can usually find ways to make ends meet. This isn't to say it won't be difficult at certain points in life, but Pisces is so mutable and adaptable that they can usually discover new and creative methods of earning the money they need.

CONCLUSION

As you can see, Pisces is a highly complex sign! Their complexities can be found in their elusive, mystical natures, and their simplicities can be reduced to a few statements about the power of universal love and compassion. Although this chapter has offered some generalizations about the sign, the aim has also been to highlight some of the universal qualities of Pisces's energy. Everyone has preconceived notions about the traits of their particular sun sign, but those always come with layers of biases and assumptions based on the life of the individual. There is, however, an underlying commonality to each sign, and mysterious Pisces is no exception to this rule.

Not every Pisces is shy, introverted, empathetic, or creative. Not all Pisces make music, hug trees, or become involved in toxic relationships. Not every Pisces wants to be an artist or a healer. However, every Pisces does carry a particular sort of sensitivity within them. Every Pisces does yearn for a deeper connection to something larger than themselves, whether it's everlasting love, a higher power, or a lost past. Every Pisces needs adequate rest and retreat from the world around them so that they don't become anxious and overwhelmed by life's struggles. It's safe to say that most Pisces have an affinity to water.

In order to dive into the deeper layers of the sign, one can look to the tarot and the particular cards associated with Pisces and its energy. Tarot's addition to any astrology reading or discussion is helpful because it provides additional context through visualization. The images on any tarot card evoke something in whoever is bearing witness, and that resonance is deeply meaningful. The card associated with Pisces is the Moon. This might throw some for a loop, as the moon is usually associated with the sign Cancer, but the tarot's associations with

The card associated with Pisces is the Moon.

astrology don't always fit into a neat box! In most decks, but particularly in the Waite-Smith deck, the Moon card features a large, full moon presiding over a body of water, presumably an ocean. The moon's glow is reflected in the shimmering water beneath it. Emerging from the water, almost framing the moon above, are two stone pillars jutting out toward the sky. In the foreground of the image are two dogs seemingly howling at the full moon above. A crayfish

Pisces are gifted with the ability to surrender to the discomfort of not knowing what comes next, like in the Hanged One card.

can also be seen moving to the water's surface, apparently attracted to the moonlight. This card takes us to a rather scary place—a deep, dark oceanic void. The Moon card presents a scene that is dark and wet. One might have a sense of drowning in an ocean of chaos. In the middle of the ocean, there's nothing to hold on to. Instead of thrashing around or attempting to tread water, one can lean into surrender. This card invites us to dive deep into the void, to have the courage to confront our shadows, and to hang out there while we gather a sense of centeredness. The Moon card represents the experience of stepping, or sometimes falling, into a void where it can be difficult to know which way is up or down. This card allows us to explore the depths of our being. The deeper we go, the more we're able to relax into the unknown. The more time we spend in the space, the better we're able to cultivate trust in our inner knowing and find our center in the darkness. Often referred to as "the dark night of the soul," the Moon card draws us deeply inward, into a space where boundaries don't exist. While here, we must learn to trust ourselves and our intuitions and navigate through a space devoid of linear direction. This seems to be part of Pisces's major life lesson—to lean into the void and release the fears of unknowing. Faith and intuition are what ultimately lead them back to their center.

Another card connected to Piscean energy is the Hanged Man, which is ruled by the planet Neptune. Pisces and Neptune share similar significations, and this card correlates well to the Piscean experience. The Hanged Man, sometimes referred to by the gender-neutral "The Hanged One," depicts a person hanging upside down from a tree branch. They are tied to the branch by one ankle, while the other ankle is bent ninety degrees, similar to the tree pose in yoga. This person's face appears calm and serene, and a glowing halo surrounds their head, symbolizing a state of enlightenment. This card illustrates the powerful act of total and complete surrender. We see the figure on the card in an extremely uncomfortable position, yet they've managed to move past their physical discomfort, surrender to their situation, and achieve enlightenment in the process. This card comes before the Death card in the tarot, marking it as a gateway to transformation.

> **This card represents a person or a quality within a person deeply connected to their intuition.**

In the tarot, Death is rarely a symbol of physical death, but rather a symbolic ending leading to a profound transformation. The Hanged One prepares the soul for this transformation. The meditative state depicted in this card encourages acceptance of the letting go that's to come. Again, the relation to Piscean energy is stark, as Pisces often find themselves in this state of surrender as they move through life's major thresholds. Pisces are gifted with the ability to dive deep into their psyches, like in the Moon card, and surrender to the discomfort of not knowing what comes next, like in the Hanged One card.

Finally, a discussion of tarot cards related to Pisces wouldn't be complete without discussing the Queen of Cups. This card represents a person or a quality within a person deeply connected to their intuition. The Queens in the tarot are all sensual and nurturing beings who have done the work of discovering their inner magic, which they radiate outward to all who are fortunate enough to bear witness. The Queen of Cups represents a state of highly psychic, nonverbal communication and deep knowing. They are able to dive deep into their psyches, drawing on their keen intuition to receive information from other realms. They are deeply nurturing and mysterious, and can hold sacred space. This card represents a mature Pisces who has fully developed their deeply creative and intuitive gifts. When such a state is achieved, Pisces is able to help others from a place of knowing and centeredness.

Pisces everywhere should know and honor their abilities to create magic wherever they go, help others to see the magic in themselves, and show the world what true compassion and service look like. As long as they learn to take care of themselves first and foremost and navigate through this mysterious world with empathy and trust, they'll be able to make their dreams a reality.

IMAGE CREDITS

Courtesy of Beinecke Rare Book and Manuscript Library at Yale University: v

Cai and Jo Limited: cover, 30, 54, 78, 106, 134, 164, 186, 212, 238, 268, 294

ClipArt ETC: 313

Creative Market: Mio Buono: 25, 26, 28, 110, 169, 317, 318, 319 (top)

Deutsche Fotothek: 119

Getty Images: *DigitalVision Vectors:* clu: 261; duncan1890: 320; ilbusca: 198, 217; powerofforever: 123; ZU-09: 194; *iStock/Getty Images Plus:* NSA Digital Archives: 175

Courtesy of Rawpixel: ii, iii

Shutterstock.com: Artur Balytskyi: 280; Patrick Guenette: 58; Morphart Creation: 205, 231; TALVA: 74, 150, 208, 302; Vlada Young: 179, 301

courtesy of Wellcome Collection: 140

courtesy of Wikimedia Commons: viii, 7, 159, 168; Metropolitan Museum of Art: 176; Midnight Believer: 137; Pearson Scott Foresman: vi, vii, 24, 44, 77, 105, 131, 161, 167, 181, 210, 237, 267, 281, 293, 319 (bottom); Peter Presslein: x; Wellcome Collection: 206

ABOUT THE AUTHORS

ARIES

JEFF HINSHAW is a writer, author, teacher, and astrologer. His experience is deeply rooted in ritual immersion, embodied health, somatic studies, and personal myth making. He is the founder and facilitator of the Brooklyn Fools Tarot Journey and is the host of the astrology podcast *Cosmic Cousins: Soul-Centered Astrology*. Jeffrey works in both one-on-one and group settings with students around the world. His personal studies include "Psychology of the Chakra System" and "Chakra Therapy" with teacher Anodea Judith, author of *Eastern Body, Western Mind*. He has completed over five hundred hours of yoga teacher training and has studied yoga under teachers Leigh Evans, Julianna Takacs, and Kristin Cooper. In addition, he holds a BFA in creative writing and a BA in psychology from the University of North Carolina Wilmington. Jeff's mission is to upgrade the vocabulary of esoteric practices to reflect an all-inclusive accessible lens.

TAURUS

COURTNEY O'REILLY is a Taurus and a New York City–based astrologer and founder of Vibrant Soul Astrology. Her mentors include Rebecca Gordon of Rebecca Gordon Astrology and the world-renowned astrologer and founder of AstrologyZone.com, Susan Miller. Courtney has been featured in such publications as *Women's Health*, *The Dispatch*, and *Well+Good* and has worked with partners that include Planned Parenthood, Capsule, and Garmentory. She offers in-depth one-on-one personal readings and fun mini-reading events and is available for private event booking. Please say hi; Courtney would love to hear from you. Keep in touch by emailing her at courtney@vibrantsoulastrology.com and following her at vibrantsoulastrology.com. You can also follow her on Instagram and Facebook at @vibrantsoulastrology for all the latest astrology news.

GEMINI

COLIN BEDELL is an artist who uses astrology as his primary medium to explore identity and relationships. As the cofounder of QueerCosmos, a comparative astrological resource for LGBTQIA+ individuals and their allies, Colin's work blends spirituality and scholarship with accessible, integrative content. *Well+Good* magazine recognized Colin as one of the most influential people in the wellness industry. Colin is also the weekly horoscope writer for Cosmopolitan.com and has authored three bestselling books on astrology. He appeared as an astrologer on the Discovery+ show *Written in the Stars* and has been featured on *Good Morning America*, *New York* magazine, MTV, and *The Sunday Times*. Colin is committed to teaching and practicing astrology as an art form, using symbolic language, humor, visuals, science, and dance to provide meaningful insights, vitality, and a sense of belonging to his students.

CANCER

ALICE SPARKLY KAT is a queer astrologer of color with five years of experience in individual consultation, lectures, workshops, and writing. After astrology helped them through a bad breakup, they began to do readings for loved ones before beginning to charge for their services. Since their initial interest, astrology has become a way to excavate their family history through colonialism in a new language. As a practitioner, Alice uses astrology to speculate on the ways that culture inhabits biology.

Their work has inhabited the Museum of Modern Art and Hauser & Wirth gallery in New York, and the Philadelphia Museum of Art. Their book *Astrology and Storytelling* enables readers to write a work of fiction based on what the sky looked like at the time and place of their birth. Their book *Planetary Alignment for Mental BLISS* frames mental health issues as social issues. Both are for sale on alicesparklykat.com, along with astrological lessons, articles, worksheets, and other resources. You can follow Sparkly Kat on Instagram at @alicesparklykat for memes and other ephemeral content.

LEO & VIRGO

BESS MATASSA is a New York–based astrologer and tarot reader with a fresh-and-ready Aries Sun, a furry little Leo Moon, and aspiring Virgo status courtesy of a witchy sixth house stellium. Bess fell hard for mysticism as a mini bite, where she spent her middle school days pouring over the glossy pages of *Parkers' Astrology* in search of epic symbols to enhance the mundane and flipping tarot cards at the family poker table. After a Saturn Return breakdown nearly poofed her from the planet, astrology quite literally brought Bess back to life. From astrological walking tours to zodiac perfume-making classes and tarot dance parties, her cosmic craftings are built on the belief that the worlds within us and the worlds around us are always longing to come closer. She's the author of six astrology and tarot books and decks, and has been a celestial consultant for platforms and institutions including *Teen Vogue*, Almay cosmetics, Ace Hotel, and the Rubin Museum of Art. She also serves as a "midwitch" for other mystical makers, and offers creative coaching for authors in the modern spirituality space. Her books include *The Tarot Almanac, NYC Tarot, The Numinous Cosmic Year: Your Astrological Almanac, Zodiac Signs: Leo, Zodiac Signs: Virgo,* and *The Numinous Astro Deck.*

LIBRA

GABRIELLE MORITZ is an astrologer, artist, and writer from the Pacific Northwest, who has been studying the stars since late 2009. She authored the book *Zodiac Signs: Libra* for Sterling Ethos in 2019. Blending traditional and modern astrology, her style is compassionate, intuitive, and practical. Gabrielle is most interested in utilizing astrology to illuminate and uncover our true nature and to improve our ability to meaningfully understand and collaborate with time. She also creates spellbinding imagery rooted in the esoteric at Good Spell Studio, and was a contributing artist to the CHANI App. To follow more of her work or to get in touch, you can head to her website at goodspell.studio.

SCORPIO

DANNY LARKIN is the President of the Association for Young Astrologers. He has studied Hellenistic Astrology with Demetra George and Chris Brenna\19, he toured ancient ruins in Greece with Demetra George. He studied modern and psychological astrology with Liz Greene and the Faculty of Astrology Studies in the UK. Stateside, he studied with Meira Epstein, Rob Hand, John Marchesella, and Annabel Gat. He is certified as the first level by the National Council for Geocosmic Research and is pursuing more advanced certifications.

In 2007, he graduated Magna Cum Laude from Fordham University, earning a bachelor's with special honors in art history. He studied broadly, including courses on Ancient Greek art, temple architecture, and pagan religion.

Danny lives and works in New York City. He meets with clients as an astrologer, writes art criticism professionally, and shakes a mean cocktail at his home bar.

SAGITTARIUS

THE REV. NATHANIEL CRADDOCK (a.k.a. Nate Ryan Caradog), MDiv, is a classical astrologer, priest, United Church of Christ minister, podcaster, queer liberationist, and corgi enthusiast. Nate employs astrology as a spiritual care modality in interdisciplinary, interfaith care settings. He studied Western horary with Wade Caves and Deborah Houlding, and practiced for several years in that tradition before pivoting toward the astrology of India. Nate is a graduate of Freedom Cole's Science of Light Course and is an authorized practitioner in the Srī Acyutānanda lineage of Vedic astrology. He currently studies under Pandit Sanjay Rath and serves as a teaching aide for Science of Light. Nate serves a progressive faith community in southwest Michigan, and maintains an active astrology and spiritual direction practice through Soul Friend Consulting. He previously served on the steering committee of the Association for Astrological Networking (AFAN) and founded the Bluegrass Astrology Circle in Lexington, Kentucky. He now lives in Battle Creek, Michigan, with his husband, Michael, and their corgi. Connect with Nate online at soulfriendastrology.com and on Twitter: @RyanCaradog.

CAPRICORN

KELSEY WILPONE, MPH, is a multifaceted author, astrologer, teacher, and facilitator based in Portland, Oregon. Trained as a health disparities researcher and community health worker, Kelsey believes complexity and nuance are critically important when striving for personal and collective liberation. As a queer disabled disruptor, Kelsey is most interested in connecting with other humans and utilizing astrology to offer support and validation to those of us who are intentionally excluded and pushed to the margins. Kelsey has been a professional consulting astrologer for over a decade. In 2015 she founded Deep Sea Astrology, where she offers collaborative astrology services, including readings, workshops, mentorship, and astrologically-aligned plant medicine. Kelsey opened the fourth Queer Astrology Conference in 2018 with their keynote speech on Generational Uranus and Queer Revolution. In 2022, Kelsey completed a three-part, 120-hour certification in advanced Hellenistic astrology techniques with teacher Demetra George and uses Hellenistic principles to guide their work. To find out more about Kelsey and her astrological practice, visit deepseaastrology.com.

AQUARIUS

TAYLOR MOON is a mom of three, professional astrologer, and deep transformational life coach based in Atlanta, Georgia. She is the author of *Zodiac Signs: Aquarius* and has been the featured astrologer and horoscope writer for several media publications, including Tarot.com, Astrology.com, Youtube, and *Parade* magazine. Taylor's passion lies in guiding people through their healing and self-discovery process with astrology readings, group workshops, and transformational life-coaching sessions. You can get in touch with Taylor Moon by connecting with her on social media via @astrotaylormoon or by visiting her website astrotaylormoon.com.

PISCES

Astrology has always held a place in **SHAKIRAH TABOURN**'s heart. At a young age, her father, a fellow Scorpio, began quizzing her on the planets and their order from the sun. By the age of eight, she already had the names of the celestial bodies in her vocabulary. For as long as she can remember, she has found birthdays to be particularly special. She took great pride in knowing the birthdays of her friends, classmates, and family members. Even back then, she took note of the time of her birth, believing that this information would one day be important. In high school, she would buy birthday books to bring in and show her classmates, who nodded along as their minds were blown by the accuracy the books displayed. Whenever she's asked about learning astrology, she describes it as a remembering, as if this knowledge were information she had known previously, perhaps in other lifetimes. Sparks went off the first time she saw her birth chart in 2012, and she immediately knew she had found something special. She describes her first time seeing her birth chart as being "witnessed by the universe," a divine and cosmic experience. She was hooked instantly, and she didn't sleep that night, as she was too busy relearning this cosmic science. Astrology quickly became the lens through which she views the world, and she hasn't looked back since!

Through the years, she's poured herself into the subject, aiming to learn as much as she can in order to fulfil her passion of sharing this information with others. In her opinion, astrology is an invaluable tool available to people of all backgrounds. Shakirah currently lives in New York and takes clients online. She is the founder and editor in chief of *NFLUX Magazine*, an independent astrology and culture publication that features interviews, horoscopes, embodiment sections, and so much more. In addition, she hosts a monthly meetup for local astrology enthusiasts of all levels called Deep Seekers. She also organizes monthly dinners for New York–area astrologers to connect. She teaches workshops, hosts lunar circles, and writes horoscopes. You can find more information about Shakirah and her offerings at thestrology.com, or on social media: @thestrology.